Growing Up Digital

Other Books by Don Tapscott

Paradigm Shift: The New Promise of Information Technology,
cowritten with Art Caston

The Digital Economy:
Promise and Peril in the Age of Networked Intelligence

Who Knows: Safeguarding Your Privacy in a Networked World,
cowritten with Ann Cavoukian, Ph.D.

Growing Up Digital

The Rise of the Net Generation

Don Tapscott

MCGRAW-HILL

New York   San Francisco   Washington, D.C.   Auckland   Bogotá
Caracas   Lisbon   London   Madrid   Mexico City   Milan
Montreal   New Delhi   San Juan   Singapore
Sydney   Tokyo   Toronto

McGraw-Hill
A Division of The McGraw·Hill Companies

1 2 3 4 5 6 7 8 9 0 DOC/DOC 9 0 2 1 0 9 8 7

ISBN 0-07-063361-4

McGraw-Hill books are available at special quantity discounts to use as premiums
and sales promotions, or for use in corporate training programs. For more information, please write to the Director of Special Sales, McGraw-Hill, 11 West 19th
Street, New York, NY 10011. Or contact your local bookstore.

For Niki, Alex, and Ana.

Contents

Visit us at www.growingupdigital.com

www.growingupdigital.com is a Web site dedicated to the Net Generation. It provides in-depth information and links on the topics raised in this book and also a wide range of discussion groups, activities and projects for kids, parents, researchers, business leaders, policy makers, and educators.

How this book was written

Growing Up Digital was written on the Internet. The research team collaborated with several hundred children and adults located on six continents. The analysis, drafting and editing was conducted by a core team in five locations using a shared digital work space, electronic mail, and computer conferencing. The main reference source was the Web. It would not have been possible to write this book without using these tools.

Acknowledgments

A S MY FAMILY AND I PREPARED TO RETURN HOME AFTER A GREAT ONE-WEEK TRIP TO St. Lucia in early 1992, I overheard a conversation between my daughter Nicole (then 9 years old) and her new-found friend Lauren. The girls were sad that the vacation was over and that they had to part. To my amazement, the girls were discussing what technology they might use to be pen pals. "Do you have a fax machine?" says Lauren. "No," says Niki, peering over at me as if I were some sort of techno-peasant. "Maybe we could communicate through computers," she suggests.

The discussion, which predated the Web and the explosion of e-mail, precipitated a series of events which resulted in this book. Niki requested a fax machine for her birthday and lobbied me about this one day when a TV crew was at our house. The organizers of a conference saw this on TV and invited her to be on a panel of children (consumers of the future) at their next conference. My wife Ana and I started listening carefully to what Niki and our son Alex had to say about computers and found their views fresh and startling. I began to integrate the insights of other children into my writings, consulting, and speaking and came to the conclusion that there is a new generation emerging that will change the world as never before.

The main source of ideas for this book came from N-Geners—the *Growing Up Digital* Kids. A research team led by Kate Baggott (herself 24) held discussions on the Net with about 300 youngsters between the ages of 4 and 20 over a one-year period. Without Kate, I don't think this book would have been written—she is one of the most creative people I have worked with, and throughout was scrupulous to ensure that the experience was a very positive one for the kids and that their rights were respected. Without these kids, I surely would have come to many false conclusions and likely a pretty dry book. They have been an inspiration to all of us working on the project.

Kate also managed the creation of "www.growingupdigital.com". The Web site, a companion to this book, is intended to be the ultimate resource for research and discussion around N-Gen issues. Built by a KIDSNRG (pronounced Kids' Energy) team of five enthusiastic graphic artists (Tsipora Mankovsky and Thanh Phu), writers (Bojan Pavlovic and Javeed Sukhera) and a programmer (Michael Furdyk). The team members are all between the ages of 14 and 19 and they have built a site that is truly a testament to N-Gen skill, talent, and initiative.

Ron Owston of York University (Toronto) hosted a forum over several weeks for students training to be teachers. Our partners at FreeZone—cyber-home to 30,000 N-Geners—were key to the research, especially FreeZone staffer Allison Ellis who worked with us hosting forums, conducting online surveys, and sharing her vast experiences working with these kids. Consultant Gerald Bramm creatively headed up the market research and demographic work and we benefited considerably by census, attitudinal. . . . and survey research conducted by TRU (Teenage Research

Unlimited) and Roper Starch. Jim Hake of the Global Information Infrastructure Awards and philanthropist/entrepreneur Mario Marino were instrumental in helping me find significant and insightful case studies. My sincere thanks to all of them.

The idea of the Net Generation, the initial structure and title for the book came out of a series of discussions with my business partner, long-time collaborator and friend David Ticoll, who is president of The Alliance for Converging Technologies. David, thank you.

David was also one of several of my most respected colleagues—including my wife Ana Lopes, Chuck Martin (author of *The Digital Estate*), Tim Fiala (Burson-Marsteller), Monica Strak (Gridwork), and Joan Grusec (University of Toronto)—who reviewed the draft manuscript. Each of these very busy people invested many hours challenging, enhancing, developing, and scrutinizing the research and my arguments. I am very grateful for their contribution. Alliance colleague Bill Gillies spent several seven-day weeks with me reworking formulations and challenging my thinking. Bill's insistence on clarity, accessibility, and readability had a huge impact on the book. I look forward to our next project together.

An investigation of this scope was very challenging because of the vast range of disciplines covered—ranging through demographics, developmental psychology, economics, marketing, sociology, pedagogy, technology, parenting, and business strategy—to name a few. Throughout the book you will read the insights of many leading (adult) thinkers on these topics. Their views were shared during dozens of interviews conducted over an eight-month period—a quotation without a footnote indicates one of these interviews or discussions.

The manuscript was edited by Jody Stevens of New Paradigm Learning (Toronto) and Mari Florence of Backbone Books (Los Angeles), with Betsy Brown of McGraw-Hill (New York). In addition, Jody managed the overall technical infrastructure of the project, the technical implementation of "www.growingupdigital. com", and supervised the production of the spectacular multimedia presentations which are based on the research and the book. Thanks to McGraw-Hill publisher Philip Ruppel for suggesting several years ago that I work with my kids on a book. My assistant Antoinette Schatz held the fort and research assistant Lenni Jabour always came through.

Authors usually thank their families for providing support through the process of creating a book. My gratitude to my family goes far beyond such support. Many of the big ideas in the book came out of experiences and discussions with my children, Nicole (14) and Alexander (11), and discussions with my wife Ana—as the two of us work to be good parents to a couple of children of this wonderful new generation. Thank you so much Niki, Alex, and Ana.

—*Don Tapscott*

The Louder Echo

The Net Generation has arrived! The baby boom has an echo and it's even louder than the original. Eighty million strong, the youngest of these kids are still in diapers and the eldest are just turning twenty.

What makes this generation different from all others before it? It is the first to grow up surrounded by digital media. Computers can be found in the home, school, factory, and office and digital technologies such as cameras, video games, and CD-ROMs are commonplace. Increasingly, these new media are connected by the Internet, an expanding web of networks which is attracting a million new users monthly. Today's kids are so bathed in bits that they think it's all part of the natural landscape. To them, the digital technology is no more intimidating than a VCR or toaster.

For the first time in history, children are more comfortable, knowledgeable, and literate than their parents about an innovation central to society. And it is through the use of the digital media that the N-Generation will develop and superimpose its culture on the rest of society. Boomers stand back. Already these kids are learning, playing, communicating, working, and creating communities very differently than their parents. They are a force for social transformation.

Moms and dads are reeling from the challenges of raising confident, plugged-in, and digital-savvy children who know more about technology than they do. Few parents even know what their children are doing in cyberspace. School officials are grappling with the reality of students often being far smarter on cyber-issues and new ways of learning than the teachers. Corporations are wondering what these kids will be like as employees since they are accustomed to very different ways of working, collaborating, and creating, and they reject many basic assumptions of today's companies. Governments are lagging behind in thinking about the implications of this new generation on policies ranging from cyberporn and the delivery of social services to the implications of the N-Gen on the nature of governance and democracy. Marketers have little comprehension of how this wave will shop and influence purchases of goods and services.

There is no issue more important to parents, teachers, policymakers, marketers, business leaders, and social activists than understanding what this younger generation intends to do with its digital expertise. This book is based on the belief that we can learn much about a whole generation—which is in the process of embracing the new media—from the children who are most advanced in their adoption of this technology.

The Children of a Digital Age

A communications revolution is shaping a generation and its world, a phenomenon we've seen before. When the baby boomers were teenagers, it was television's turn to establish itself as the most powerful information technology in history. TV's impact on society in general and the boomers in particular was profound. We may remember early television only as *I Love Lucy* or rigged quiz shows, but when the American civil rights movement began to find a voice, it was television that served as the messenger and the mobilizer. When the boomers marched on the streets to protest the Vietnam War, television chronicled and amplified their presence. Just as television redefined the American political process, it has transformed marketing, commerce, education, leisure, and culture.

But to today's media-literate kids, television's current methods are old-fashioned and clumsy. It is unidirectional, with the choice of programming and content resting in the hands of few, and its product often dumbed-down to the lowest common denominator. To digital-savvy N-Geners, television should be interactive. It should do what the consumer asks. It should enable a dialogue and allow for citizens to speak with one another.

This shift from broadcast to interactive is the cornerstone of the N-Generation. They want to be users—not just viewers or listeners. The result is that time on the computer and Net is time taken away from television. Today's kids watch less television than five years ago and much less than their parents did at the same age. The trend will continue as the new media penetrates households, becomes easier to use, and grows in speed, services, and content.

But don't mourn television's passing just yet. The digital media is swallowing TV and in doing so will transform it. Television will be reborn as another facet of the Net. N-Geners will vote and ask questions on talk shows from their homes; play that rock video on MTV a second time; send a video clip of their favorite sitcom to a friend; drill into an advertisement for jeans and try on a pair—using an animation of their bodies on the screen.

Their parents chose between comic books, baseball cards, bikes, basketballs, and episodes of the TV show *Spin and Marty*. Children today have the same joys (*Spin and Marty* being replaced by *The Simpsons*), but from their fingertips they can traverse the world. They have new powerful tools for inquiry, analysis, self-expression, influence, and play. They have unprecedented mobility. They are shrinking the planet in ways their parents could never imagine. Unlike television which was done *to* them, they are the actors in the digital world.

The Net is beginning to affect all of us—the way we create wealth, the enterprise, the nature of commerce and marketing, the delivery system for entertainment, the role and dynamics of learning in the economy, the nature of government and governance, our culture, and arguably the role of the nation-state in the body politic. It should not surprise us that the generation which first grows up with this new medium can be defined by its relationship to it.

The term *Net Generation* refers to the generation of children who, in 1999, will be between the ages of two and twenty-two, not just those who are active on the Internet. Most of these children do not yet have access to the Net, but most have some degree of fluency with the digital media. The vast majority of adolescents report they know how to use a computer. Nearly everyone has experience with video games. The Net is coming into households as fast as television did in the 1950s.

Two-thirds of kids use a personal computer, usually either at home or school.[1] The vast majority of children use video games. Increasingly, all digital technologies are evolving toward the Net. As Fig. 1.1 shows, between 1995 and the year 2000, home access to the Net will have grown from 10 to 46 percent.

According to Teenage Research Unlimited (TRU), the percentage of teens who say that it is "in" to be online has jumped from 50 percent in 1994 to 74 percent in 1996 to 88 percent in 1997. It's now on par with dating and partying![2]

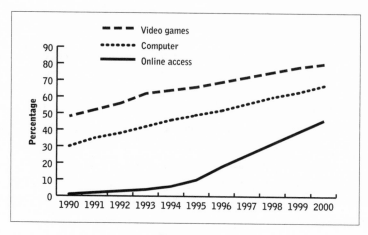

Figure 1.1
Percentage of households with children
who have video games/computers/online access.
Data: Alliance for Converging Technologies.

All this is occurring while the Net is in its infancy and, as such, is painfully slow, primitive, limited in capabilities, lacking complete security, reliability, ubiquity, and is subject to both hyperbole and ridicule. Nevertheless, children and many adults love it and keep coming back after each frustrating experience. They believe it has great potential.

What Do Kids Do with Computers?

Almost everything!

"I use [my computer] to do just about everything except playing games," says 17-year-old Andy Putschoegl of Oakdale, Minnesota. "I run my own business and I create a lot of form letters and whatnot to be sent out to clients. I do a little graphic design—mostly for school Web pages since I don't have too much for my own pages. I even got published in the June issue of *MacWorld* magazine for the graphical tip I sent in." Eleven-year-old Laura Shulak of Montreal, Quebec, says, "Neither of my parents knew how to make a home page, so I did it by myself and then I taught my sister." For 14-year-old Eric Mandela of Rahway, New Jersey, "I sit on the board of a local computer user group and run their BBS." Running a business, publishing a Web page, and belonging to an Internet community are not atypical.

N-Geners are using digital media for *entertainment*. Computer games and video-game cartridges and systems represent a $10 billion industry,[3] $5.6 billion in the United States alone[4]—more than the Hollywood movie industry. Kids report to us that they love computers and the Net primarily because they are fun! My daughter loves checking out Leonardo DiCaprio activities and my son shows his friends video clips from everything from *The Simpsons* to the movie he just saw.

N-Geners are using digital media for *learning*. The computers which populate 60 percent of American households with children are used for learning how dolphins give birth and for composing essays on "my summer vacation." N-Geners surf the Net in teams or alone to do projects or to look up the stats of Wayne Gretzky. Computers have been creeping into classrooms for a decade and teachers are starting to change the way learning occurs, rather than using computers as fancy texts or testing devices.

N-Geners are using digital media for *communicating*. They see digital media as a valuable tool to contact other N-Geners and form relationships. In a 1997 survey conducted by Teenage Research Unlimited, a whopping two-thirds of American children say they have used the Internet from home, school, or somewhere else.[5] By the end of 1997, more than 15 million North American N-Geners will have access to the Internet at home through their own accounts or those of their parents. Chat groups and computer conferences are bursting out all over, populated by young people hungry for expression, discovery, and their own self-development. At certain stages they love to meet people and talk about anything. Over time they mature and their communications center around topics and themes. "E-mail me" has become the parting expression of a generation.

N-Geners are also using digital media for *shopping*. While still in its early stages, increasingly they see the Net as a way to acquire goods and services and to investigate things they would like to buy or enjoy. Not only are they beginning to browse, check prices, and even execute transactions on the Net, but through their cyber investigations they are also beginning to shape the purchasing behaviors of their parents in ways previously unimagined.

They manage their personal finances; organize protest movements; check facts to prove a teacher wrong; discuss zits; check the scores of their favorite team and chat online with its superstars; organize to save the rain forest; make C-friends (cyber friends) or get a C-boyfriend; cast votes; learn more about the illness of their little sister; go to a virtual birthday party; get video clips from a soon-to-be-released movie.

Growing Up Digital was written in collaboration with over 300 N-Geners who provided their opinions, experiences, and insights over a one-year period through a series of online *Growing Up Digital* forums. These forums were hosted by New Paradigm Learning Corporation, York University, and the FreeZone network—cyber home to some 30,000 N-Geners. The research included interviews with a wide range of parents, business leaders, cyber gurus, policymakers, educators, and marketing experts to get their perspectives on the broad range of topics covered in this book. As well, extensive demographic work and market research was conducted by the Alliance for Converging Technologies—a think tank which I chair.

We also strived to make this group representative, selecting young people from different geographies, gender, age, socioeconomic and cultural backgrounds. Our research took us from affluent families and private schools to the tough neighborhoods of East Palo Alto, California. The views and experiences of our *Growing Up Digital* kids are rich with insight. I believe they are a bellwether for the Net-Generation.

What Is Happening to Our Children?

Based on many media reports, we should be very worried about this new generation. They are often portrayed as self-centered, lacking social values, and concerned only about making money when they grow up. They are sometimes described as cynical, angry, violent, and self-absorbed by their loveless culture of rap music, drugs, anger, graffiti, and even pornography.

When it comes to youth using technology, the unease is often stronger than the enthusiasm. The questions often outweigh the answers. Are kids really benefitting from their use of the digital media? Can this technology truly improve the process of learning or is it dumbing kids and misfocusing our educational efforts? What about Net addiction? Is it positive for children to spend time in online chat rooms, and what are they doing there? Are some becoming glued to the screen? What about cyber dating and cyber sex? Aren't video games leading to a violent generation? Is technology stressing kids out—as it seems to be doing to adults? Is the Net a virtual world—drawing children away from parental authority and responsible adult influence—where untold new problems and dangers lie? What is the real risk of online predators and can children be effectively protected? How can we protect kids from the sleaze and porn that is said to be running down the gutters of the information highway? As these children come of age, will they lack the social skills for effective participation in the workforce? These questions are just a sampling of the widespread concerns raised not just by cynics, moralists, and technophobes, but by reasonable and well-meaning people.

In addition to these, you may be wondering about the implications of the new generation for you. Perhaps you are an educator wondering how to fully exploit the Net for your students' benefit. You could be a sales manager trying to resolve the most effective means of marketing to this group, or as a government official you are wondering how scarce public dollars could be best spent. As a business executive, you may wonder what the new generation means to business strategy, management philosophy, or your personal use of new technology. Or you may be trying to be a good parent. The upshot is that you're interested in today's youth and want to understand them. You know that the new technology is important for children but you worry about the dark side. You see the promise but you read all the horror stories and you wonder what is true. This is something very new, very unprecedented. We worry about our children.

Television had a number of unintended consequences. There are legitimate concerns about the unforeseen results of this new revolution. As Alan Kay, now a Disney Fellow, said several years ago: "Much care has to be taken . . . in order for this change to be positive. We don't have natural defenses against fat, sugar, salt, alcohol, alkaloids—or media. Television should be the last mass-communications medium to be naively designed and put into the world without a surgeon general's warning!"[6]

Are the fears about the new generation warranted? What is happening to our children?

While there is much to be learned and many real dangers which warrant good management on the part of business people, educators, parents, and lawmakers, our investigation indicates that the cynics, technophobes, and moralists are dead wrong.

Everybody relax. The kids are all right. They are learning, developing, and thriving in the digital world. They need better tools, better access, more services, and more freedom to explore, not the opposite. Rather than hostility and mistrust on the part of adults, we need a change in thinking and in behavior on the part of parents, educators, lawmakers, and business leaders alike.

Child Development in an Interactive World

Kids use computers for activities that seem to go hand-in-hand with our understanding of what constitutes a traditional childhood. They use the technology to play, learn, communicate, and form relationships as children have always done. On the other hand, the digital media is creating an environment where such activities of childhood are changing dramatically and may, for better or for worse, accelerate child development. Child development is concerned with the evolution of motor skills, language skills, and social skills. It also involves the development of cognition, intelligence, reasoning, personality, and, through adolescence, the creation of autonomy, a sense of the self and values. As you will read, all these are enhanced in an interactive world. When children control their media, rather than passively observe, they develop faster.

There are issues which require management by children and adults. Children can become enthralled with their new worlds and tools, at the expense of other healthy or important activities—like homework. Most children correct such imbalances in their lives themselves, but parents need to be vigilant. Children may have multiple selves in cyberspace—something probably positive but warranting further research. What we know for certain is that children without access to the new media will be developmentally disadvantaged.

Playing Digital

The fact that N-Geners seem to develop faster than previous generations does not mean the end of childhood as some have bemoaned. Rather, they have a new world for play.

The television robbed children of hours of play each day. The digital media is restoring this precious time. When asked why they like computers and the Net, their first response is that "it's fun." However, while they're having fun—playing—they are also developing. Time spent on the Net is not passive time, it's active time. It's reading time. It's investigation time. It's skill development and problem-solving time. It's time analyzing, evaluating. It's composing your thoughts time. It's writing time.

The Net also invites kids to try on the world for size, to put their experiences into practice. Play is productive time in other ways. In games of make-believe, children imitate the roles they have seen adults play; they discard one and adopt another with the ease of changing a hat. Nowhere are more roles available to explore than in cyberspace, and because there is such a variety of exposure, the definition of the roles themselves expand and change.

The digital media is a partial antidote to the confines of limited play space and the tight schedules of today's over-programmed children. The Internet cannot replace the open green spaces, free neighborhoods, and unsupervised play time that previous generations took for granted, but the Internet can partially replicate and supplement what's left of that experience. For children, in particular, this freedom is essential. Many experts have remarked that children love computers because they have absolute control over the machine. Internet connections give kids control not just of their computers, but of their social communication, and their attempts to master situations they will have to face as adults. By necessity, cyberspace has become an N-Gen playground and hangout. It is a place where they play and have fun. It is a place where kids can be kids.

Problems in Paradise

This is not to say that these children are little angels. The digital schoolyard or cyber playground can be tough. Life in some online worlds is sometimes hard for *newbies* (Net neophytes). Kids who are rude or who do inappropriate things can be *flamed* (toasted with nasty messages from all over). There is considerable deception—N-Geners often inflate their age, and college football stars and models seem overly populous in kids' chat rooms. Kids conduct pranks and sometimes kids can be cruel—just like in the physical world. Some youth have participated in cyber sex or taken their parents' credit cards without permission to make purchases. Although frequently overblown by the media, there is some danger of exposure to inappropriate material, unpleasant experiences, or predators.

However, we were continually struck by the overall frankness, sophistication, and maturity with which N-Geners discuss and handle these issues. All of these are manageable, and in the absence of informed and active teachers, parents, and other adults, the kids are doing most of the managing themselves.

N-Gen Values

Few technologies are value free. Television contained strong messages which helped shape the world view of a generation. As the boomers came to power, they took over the media and perpetuated their own ideology. The new media, because of its distributed, interactive, and many-to-many nature, has a greater neutrality. A new set of values is arising as children begin to communicate, play, learn, work, and think with the new media. More than ever before, a generation is beginning to learn. Call it *generational learning.*

Many pundits describe youth today as materialistic, self absorbed, cynical, and demanding of immediate gratification. From our experience, these pundits are wrong. While this generation contains many differing classes, races, religions, and social perspectives, there are some themes emerging.

They are the young navigators. They doubt that traditional institutions can provide them with the good life and take personal responsibility for their lives. They do value material goods but they are not self-absorbed. They are more knowledgeable than any previous generation and they care deeply about social issues. They believe strongly in individual rights such as privacy and rights to information. But they have no ethos of individualism, thriving, rather, from close interpersonal networks and displaying a strong sense of social responsibility.

They appear very determined and even optimistic about the future, but are unsettled about difficulties facing them including AIDS and obstacles to a rewarding adult life. They are quite alienated from formal politics and, depending on age, there are growing discussions about the need for fundamental social change. Those who believe that these youth will be passive supporters of the status quo are in for a surprise.

A Force for Transformation in Business

Imagine the impact of millions of fresh-thinking, energized youth, armed with the most powerful tools in history, hitting the workforce. This wave has just begun. The N-Gen will transform the nature of the enterprise and how wealth is created, as its culture becomes the new culture of work. N-Geners have a different set of assumptions about work than their parents have. They thrive on collaboration, and many find the notion of a boss somewhat bizarre. Their first point of reference is the Net. They are driven to innovate and have a mindset of immediacy requiring fast results. They love hard work because working, learning, and playing are the same thing to them. They are creative in ways their parents could only imagine. The N-Generation has been told that it will be hard to find good jobs, so they have developed great determination. A bigger proportion than any other generation will seek to be entrepreneurs. Corporations who hire them should be prepared to have their windows and walls shaken. The N-Gen will cause a rethinking of management's attitude toward its people. Senior management will have to treat people as if they are the enterprises' most valuable resource, because increasingly in a knowledge economy, they are.

We spent time with N-Geners who were designing the "Workscape of the Future." N-Gen employees will demand fully networked computing environments as more important than a desk. They will consider poor digital tools as cruel and unusual punishment and unacceptable. They cannot be supervised in the traditional sense. Rather they must be given the environment and tools to create and succeed. Management in its current form will no longer be effective.

This wave is entering the workforce at a time when the corporation needs to reinvent itself through the new technology. Those fluent with the new media and comfortable with nonhierarchical ways of working will be critical for corporate success. The writing is on the wall for the technophobic, old-style-thinking boomers. Unless they throw out years of conditioning, they will be washed away by the N-Gen tsunami. Call it *generational displacement* in the workforce.

As consumers, N-Geners already have greater disposable income than previous generations of youth. More important, they influence family purchasing like never before. They have greater power in households because of their command of the new media, and they typically have better access to comparative product information on the Net. As they enter the workforce as a massive wave—the largest ever— they will affect consumption, marketing, and corporate strategy even more profoundly than their boomer parents did. Consequently, their importance as consumers is soaring.

Marketers will increasingly find themselves selling to parents by marketing to their children, especially for new media-related products and services. This will raise far-reaching ethical issues for businesses, parents, and lawmakers because, on the Net, the boundaries between ads and content melt like the cheese on a Whopper.

Because N-Geners are used to highly flexible, custom environments which they can influence, they want highly customized services and products. They are as used to having options as they are to breathing oxygen. As the song says, they want to "change their minds a thousand times." They want to try everything out free, meaning that companies will have to give products and services away and find new models for retrieving revenue. They will also want to purchase any commodity, such as grocery staples, online. The new formula will be N-Gen + the Net = electronic commerce. The Net is becoming a new medium for sales, support, and service of virtually anything, as tens of millions of Net-savvy purchasers come of age.

All this spells trouble for the brand as N-Geners send their smart software agents onto the Net to select everything from cookies to cars. The experience with the N-Gen to date indicates that advertising may be turned on its head as well. This should change our thinking regarding what it means to be a retail company, as every company can directly reach N-Gen customers through their media.

If we listen to the N-Gen, we can learn what products and services will be successful in the future—from financial services to real estate.

Growing Up Not Digital

In *The Digital Economy*, I discussed the issue of a digital divide. If left purely to market forces, the digital economy could foster a two-tiered society, creating a major gulf between information haves and have-nots—those who can communicate with the world and those who can't. As information technology becomes more important for economic success and societal well-being, the possibility of "information apartheid" becomes increasingly real. Such a "digital divide" may mean that for many children *N-Gen* means *Not-Generation*.

For example, in the United States there is a direct relationship between family income and access to computers and the Net. This correlation also exists between the higher- and lower-income schools. Some observers argue that this is just a temporary problem, but our research shows that the digital divide is actually widening, not disappearing. As the new technology trickles into poorer neighborhoods and schools, the better-off children are leapfrogging others—getting not only better access, but a wider range of services, faster access, the best technology, and, most importantly, increasing motivation, skills, and knowledge. This not only exacerbates the fluency gap but also the gap in different economic classes' capacity to learn and to have successful lives. Have-nots become know-nots and do-nots.

The widening digital divide also correlates with a growing wealth gap in the United States. Recent trends show a severe bipolarization of wealth in which the top 20 percent of households—those worth $180,000 or more—have 80 percent of the country's wealth. The top 20 percent of households command a 49 percent share of total income earned in the United States. Their income has grown by 20 percent in the past 10 years versus a 1 percent growth among all households. This skewing of income and wealth is happening faster in the United States—the leading new economy country—than anywhere else and faster than ever before. Child poverty is also growing. In 1974, 10.2 million American children lived below the poverty line—a number that rose more than 50 percent by 1994. In 1996, one-quarter of children under six lived in poverty, making the U.S. child-poverty rate one of the highest in the developed world.

Is there an emerging "revolt of the elites"[7] who will use the new infrastructure to further cocoon themselves—children in private schools, paying for their own social services, surrounded by high perimeter fences in gated communities, shopping for groceries on the Net, identifying closer with friends and business associates in cyberspace, losing any sense of responsibility to others in their physical communities or country?

Globally, most children of the new generation are not growing up digital. In fact many of them will not grow up at all. One billion people were born over the last decade—the biggest increase in human history. However, 97 percent of them were born in developing countries that often lack the ability to feed, house, and educate them.[8] More than half of the 1.2 billion children in the world aged six to eleven have never placed a phone call.[9]

There is also a growing gap between have and have-not nations. Most Net users are in the United States. Europe (excepting Scandinavia) and Japan are far behind. But the real gap comes between the developed and developing world. Most people in the latter don't have telephones, let alone the digital media. When the network becomes the basis for commerce, wealth creation, jobs, learning, health care, and social development, such countries are severely disadvantaged. These poorer countries then become information-poor. Conversely, because they are technology have-nots, they become have-nots in general. Left unchecked, this process will spiral, further polarizing the world into wealthy and poor nations, as the rich and communication-rich nations leap ahead.

A Coming Generational Explosion?

In the final chapter, I outline several scenarios for the future relationship between the boomers and the N-Gen. Sadly, the most likely is one of considerable strife. Unless the boomers have a change of heart about youth, their culture, and their media, the two biggest generations in history may be on a collision course—a battle of the generational titans. An older generation, mistrustful and threatened by new ideas and new tools, will be pitted against a new generation increasingly resentful at attempts to curtail its growth and rights.

Fear, especially when based on lack of knowledge, can get in the way of effective parenting, appropriate government policy, and sound business decisions. We must become unafraid so that we can understand. We must understand so that we may lose our fear.

The digital media is increasingly a reflection of our world—every view, every discipline, every commercial interest, every repository of knowledge. Because it is distributed, interactive, malleable, and lacking central control, it is a vehicle for revolutionary change in every discipline, attitude, and social structure. Never has there been a time of greater promise or peril. The challenge of achieving that promise, and in so doing save our fragile planet, will rest with the Net Generation. Our responsibilities are to them—to give them the tools and opportunity to fulfill their destinies.

We also have an unparalleled opportunity to learn from them for personal and business success and for social development. The people, companies, and nations which succeed in the new economy will be those who listen to their children. We can listen to their views on the world. We can learn from their effortless mastery and application of new tools. By listening and responding to their frustrations of being denied adequate tools and support, we can envision and enact the new partnerships required for a new age.

Read on.

The Net Generation

CHARLIE

BABY furniture

©1996 Tribune Media Services, Inc.
All Rights Reserved.

12-20

The baby boom was the biggest population wave ever—until it was eclipsed by the Net Generation. The N-Generation now represents 30 percent of the population, compared to the boomers' 29 percent. For the first time, there is another generation large enough to rival the cultural hegemony of the ubiquitous boomers. But what makes N-Geners unique is not just their large numbers, but that they are growing up during the dawn of a completely new interactive medium of communication. Just as the much more limited medium of television influenced the values and culture of the baby boomers, a new force is helping shape the N-Gen wave. They are spending their formative years in a context and environment fundamentally different from their parents.

Combining Demographics and Technology

Demographics, the study of human populations, is key to understanding much about the economy, business, and society. It helps us to predict school enrollments, real estate prices, demands on government services from child care to social security, electricity use, and markets for everything from Christmas tree lights to tennis memberships.

The thoughtful demographer David Foot has done much to popularize demographics as an analytical tool, and he has brought fresh thinking to a number of current phenomena. Foot, for example, revisited Faith Popcorn's concept of cocooning—people spending more time at home, curtains drawn, with their families, which was a big change from the 1970s disco scene. Because of the stress of work, crime, and the pressures of life in the 1980s, the disco crowd chose to cozy up in their living rooms. The evidence for this was the booming sales of VCRs, take-out food, and microwave popcorn and a significant rise in pregnancies and the birth rate. But for Foot, Popcorn got it all wrong—confusing cause and effect. He points out that people didn't decide to stay home and therefore had more children. The opposite is true. The baby boom moved into child-rearing years, had kids and, out of necessity, stayed home more. (If you have children, how's your social life?)

However, demographic analysis on its own may lead to some false conclusions. For today's full picture, one must include the impact of new technology and media. Consider how some demographers view office space and the commercial real estate market. One would think that the demand for office space, which has been dormant due to the post-baby boom lack of new office workers, would pick up as the wave of N-Geners hits the labor market early in the next century.

This view overlooks the impact of the digital media on work and the workspace of the future. Increasingly, the large corporation as we know it is giving way to what I described in *The Digital Economy* as new *Internetworked Enterprise structures.* Firms are starting to collaborate together on networks to conduct research, manufacture goods, and deliver services. In this new economy, graduates, and even dropouts, from colleges and universities see opportunities for rewarding professions with smaller companies or even starting their own businesses. Further, because of the Net and the digital media overall, there is new flexibility in location of work. N-Geners entering the workforce will be able to work at their customers' locations, from their car, in a restaurant using a personal digital assistant, from their homes or their vacation properties. Add the impact of today's media to the demographic wave hitting the workforce and it makes sense to shelve those plans for office towers once again.

The major events in the world today cannot be explained without reference to the impact of new technology and media. Consider the fall of the bipolar world and the end of the Cold War. The Communist bureaucracies were overthrown not because people were treated badly, but because they fell far short of their citizens' expectations—expectations fueled by information made available through media and new technologies.

Dissidents in the Soviet underground were able to publish their *samizdat* by getting behind the closed doors which housed photocopiers. Suddenly, faxes started appearing from Tienammen Square. Satellite broadcast networks transmitted *Hill St. Blues* and *LA Law* behind the Iron Curtain, and today in China countless millions have access to everything from election results and CNN to *Baywatch* and *Seinfeld*. E-mail began to creep into the universities and people were emboldened to use the ever increasing telephone networks. Global data communications networks energized the metabolism of commerce and, as economic walls began to fall, so did political boundaries.

There is a fundamental change taking place in the role of technology in business and society. This profoundly affects virtually everything—the economy, business, families, and social existence. By coupling this information with demographic analysis we can develop significant insights for the future.

The Baby Boom (1946 to 1964)

Anyone born between 1946 and 1964 is considered a baby boomer, and the boom was heard loudest in the United States, Canada, and Australia. It occurred for several reasons. First, families postponed having children until after the war. Many young men were serving overseas and not available for fathering. When the war was over, the men came back into the workforce and the pictures of "Rosie the Riveter" in *Life* magazine were replaced with photos of cheery women with baby prams or women working in their shiny kitchens waiting for hubby to come home.

Second, the economy was very strong after the war, giving families the confidence to have lots of kids. It is hard to imagine, but by 1957 American families contained 3.7 children.[1] The 1950s was a time of great hope and optimism. There was peace and the Allies had won the war. The United States was seen as the land of promise, attracting many young adult immigrants, particularly from Europe. These immigrants contributed to the population boom, either by bringing children with them or starting families soon after their arrival. And, as they matured, these great numbers of children grew into a powerful cultural, social, and political force. (See Fig. 2.1.)

The Baby Boom Became the TV Generation

The boomers could be called the *Cold War generation* or the *postwar prosperity generation* or the *growth economy generation* or named according to some other development in society that affected them. However, it was really the impact of a communi-

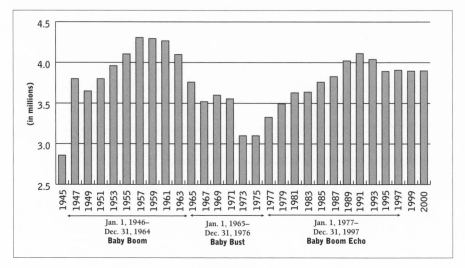

Figure 2.1
Number of births per year.
Data: U.S. Census Bureau, Alliance for Converging Technologies projections.

cations revolution—the rise of television—which shaped this generation and their world more than anything else. It is both a cliché and an understatement that television transformed the world around the boomers.

Imagine—or think back if you can—to the world before television. My own family used to gather around the rather large piece of furniture that was a radio, to listen to news programs and Lux Radio Theater. Our own imaginations conjured up images of the announcers, actors, and their environments. My mother remembers that when TVs became popular, our family just had to get one. "This was the innovation of the century," she says. "It was so exciting to think that you could not only hear people but actually see them."

In early 1953, when the set arrived in our living room, the chairs and sofa were moved from the radio and clustered around the TV. I have vivid memories of Queen Elizabeth II's coronation on June 2, 1953 (the day after my birthday), and of my mother explaining to us that the tears on Her Majesty's face were due to the emotional pressure and also the physical strain of a heavy crown and the rigor of the procession and events. I saw my parents and other adult relatives react in horror as rumors spread that Elvis would shake his pelvis on the *Ed Sullivan Show* and then it didn't happen. I remember my uncle, a music teacher, howling at Kate Smith, saying that she couldn't carry a tune if her life depended on it. I remember Don Larson of the New York Yankees pitching a no-hitter in Game Five of the 1956 World Series. I remember Kruschev thumping his fist on the table at the United Nations and watching in real time the shooting of Lee Harvey Oswald. And I remember falling in love with Annette Funicello of the *Mickey Mouse Club*. The television created a real-time world. It also began to consume a significant part of the day for most people.

This force of a generation introduced to its medium grew with a momentum that swept up the Chicago Seven with *Bonanza,* Bob Dylan, JFK, *Harold and Maude,* marijuana, the Vietnam War, the Beatles, Abby Hoffman. In 1950, only 12 percent of households had a TV. By 1958, the number had soared to 83 percent.[2] The medium had quickly become the most powerful communication technology available. When the American civil rights movement made its demands known, it was television that served as the messenger and the mobilizer. When the boomers marched on the streets to end the Vietnam War, television chronicled and amplified their presence. Television was there to record and broadcast the movements of a massive generation. Right in front of the baby boomers' eyes, television turned youth itself into an event.

In the words of demographer Brad Edmonson, "A generation exists mostly in the minds of the people who belong to it."[3] Generations are forged through common experience. The baby boom generation was shaped by pivotal events such as the war in Vietnam, Woodstock, the Moon landing—all of which were brought to youth by the new glowing device in the living room.

The Baby Bust (1965 to 1976)

Demographers call the period between 1965 and 1976 the baby bust, largely because there were 15 percent fewer babies born in the 10 years following the end of the boom. As the boomers reached the age of majority between 1963 and 1982, the total number of families with children at home fell from 57 percent to 51 percent, and on average there were fewer children per family. New immigrants belonged to demographic groups matching the age of the boomers and their parents. For a decade there seemed to be a relative dearth of young people. (See Fig. 2.2.)

This period is often erroneously referred to by the popular press as

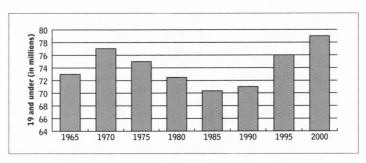

Figure 2.2
Number of individuals 19 years of age and under.
Data: U.S. Census Bureau.

Generation X, from the title of a novel by Canadian author Douglas Coupland. But the characters in Coupland's book are actually a subset of the tail end of the baby boom. These thirty-somethings entered the labor force only to find that their older brothers and sisters had filled all the positions, eXcluding them from meaningful participation in society.

Baby busters are the best-educated group in history. But as teens they looked ahead to an economy rife with some of the highest rates of American unemployment, peaking at 10.8 percent in late 1982. They also saw some of the lowest relative starting salaries of any group since those entering the workforce during the 1930s Depression era.

The baby busters, now adults between the ages of 21 and 33, are aggressive communicators who are extremely media-centered. They are the oldest segment of the population whose computer and Internet habits resemble those of N-Geners and provide the closest adult experience from which we can begin to predict how N-Geners will master the digital universe. Like N-Geners, the baby busters view radio, TV, film, and the Internet as nonspecialist media, available for everyone's use to package information and put forward their perspective.

Baby Boom Echo (1977 to 1997)

The boomers started having children in greater numbers after 1978. By 1997 there were almost as many five- to nine-year-olds (19,854,000) as there were thirty- to thirty-four-year-olds (20,775,000).[4] (See Fig. 2.3.)

One of the key reasons why the echo has lasted so long is the number of baby boom women who have put off having children until their 30s and 40s.

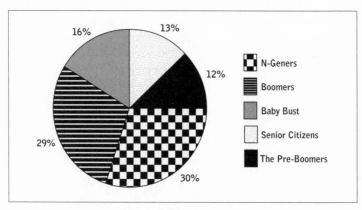

Figure 2.3
Demographic breakdown of the U.S. population as of 1998.
Data: U.S. Census Bureau.

Boom, Bust, and Echo (U.S.)

Boom   January 1946 to December 1964—19 years producing 77.2 million children or 29 percent of the current population. (268.9 million by the end of 1997)

Bust   January 1965 to December 1976—12 years producing 44.9 million children or 16 percent of the current population.

Echo   January 1977 to December 1997—21 years producing approximately 81.1 million children or 30 percent of the current population.

The echo of the baby boom plateaued in 1990 with 4,158,000 births. Between 1990 and 1994, there was a slow decline in the annual number of births, leveling off at 3,900,000 in 1997. Some commentators say the echo generation ended in 1994, since that year births dipped below 4 million (3,953,000). My perspective is that the echo is still happening and may well continue to the end of the 1990s. Certainly it is fading very slowly—less than 1 percent annually after the peak year of 1990.

Relatively few boomers became parents in their early twenties, the typical age for beginning the process of marriage and child rearing. Society has seen other periods of delayed parenting during periods of economic depression, war, and famine, but these weren't the case with boomers. Indeed, at the age of 30, the oldest of the boomers were earning a full 30 percent more than their fathers did at the same age.[5]

There was another force at work when many boomers—specifically middle- and upper-class young people—delayed parenthood. They were prolonging youth. Personally, I was evidence of this. I spent most of the first decade after university organizing various social movements, pursuing postgraduate studies, learning about computing, writing music, researching various issues, and overall trying to understand and change the world. Planning for a family and my career was the last thing on my mind. I knew that when it was time to think about such issues that I would be just fine. Self-confidence grew from economic times and social background.

There was little reason for boomers who were not from working-class or poor backgrounds to grow up. Being young was to be part of something big. In 1955, kids were everywhere. Almost 57 percent of families contained children under the age of 18 and, unlike now, there was a greater likelihood of there being more than one child under each roof.[6]

The Echo Becomes the Net Generation

This wave of youth coincides with the digital revolution which is transforming all facets of our society. Together these two factors are producing a generation which is not just a demographic bulge but a wave of social transformation.

In 1983, only 7 percent of households owned computers.[7] By 1997, the number had grown to 44 percent and a whopping 60 percent of households with children. In 1996, only 15 percent of all households in the United States had access to the Internet and World Wide Web, but during the same period, one in ten Internet users worldwide was reported to be under 16 years of age. And most children use their parents' accounts. (See Fig. 2.4.)

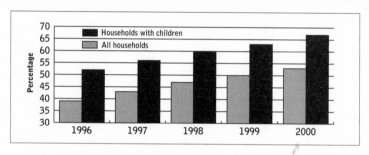

Figure 2.4
Projected U.S. household computer penetration vs.
computer penetration in U.S. households with children.
1996–2000
Data: Nielsen Home Technology Report, Jupiter Communications,
Alliance for Converging Technologies, FIND/SVP.

The penetration of digital media has always been greatest among households with children and it isn't difficult to understand why. According to one family-school research firm, close to 80 percent of parents say they believe computers help children to do better in school.[8] Increasingly, parents need computers and the Net at home for work. And just as when TVs were "the new thing," most families want to own computers. (See Fig. 2.5.)

In 1997, according to a *Wall Street Journal* study, computer sales will constitute over 1.3 percent of total consumer spending, or about 12 times the percentage spent seven years ago. The study also noted that, while seven years ago consumers were obsessed with acquiring the biggest RAM on the block, now they're more concerned with using their PCs as tools to access the Net.[9]

The Net is permeating U.S. households almost as fast as television did in the 1950s. Starting from virtually nothing in 1995, over 40 percent of American households will be connected by the year 2000. Add to this the digitization of TV, and the vast majority of households will have become wired within a 10-year period.

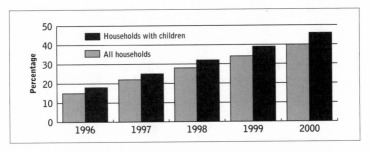

Figure 2.5
Projected household online access penetration in the U.S.
1996–2000

Data: Nielsen Home Technology Report, Jupiter Communications,
Alliance for Converging Technologies.

The growth of the Net has brought instant predominance to a new product category—the Web browser. Jim Clarke, cofounder of Netscape, told me in the summer of 1996 that Netscape had 40 million users. This from a company that was launched only two years earlier—not only the fastest growth of any technology product ever, but the fastest growth of *any* product, and the fastest proliferation of a brand ever. The Alliance for Converging Technologies estimates that there will be over a billion users connected to the Net by the year 2005. Children and teenagers are a significant portion of these pioneers. According to surveys conducted by the Graphic Visualization and Usability Center at Georgia Tech University, as many as 11 percent of the world's Internet users are under the age of 15, and 30 percent of commercial online service subscribers have children at home.[10]

Another barometer of Net impact is the explosion of e-mail, which began in earnest in 1994. It grew from 35 million users in 1995 to 80 million users in 1997.[11] The use of e-mail continues to grow every year by the millions as kids go to college and receive accounts. Their parents also get wired so they can capitalize on this fast, convenient and low-cost way of keeping in touch with their kids. Ditto for grandparents. My kids used to communicate with their grandparents once every month or so. Now that everyone is on e-mail, there are weekly and daily interchanges taking place. Remember the pastel-colored candy hearts kids passed around in school on Valentine's Day? They had little sayings on them like, "Be Mine" and "Call Me." For the benefit of cyber kids, they now come with the saying, "E-mail Me."

In the most recent wave of TRU (Teenage Research Unlimited) interviews, teenagers were asked: Which of the following computer online services have you used at home, at school, or someplace else? 36 percent say they have used an online service at home, 49 percent have used one at school, and 66 percent (two-thirds of all teens) have used one elsewhere.[12]

Interactive technology is also beginning to pour into the schools. After years of technological impoverishment, things are beginning to change. As shown in Fig. 2.6, the percentage of students who have used a computer in school has grown from 29 percent in 1984 to 72 percent in 1997. When students who have used computers in the home only is added to this, we see that a whopping 82 percent of children have used a computer.

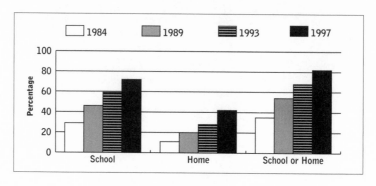

Figure 2.6
Student use of computers, grades 1 through 12.
Data: U.S. Census Bureau, Alliance for Converging Technologies.

The Net and Other Interactive Technologies

In a panel discussion at a conference in Davos, Switzerland, I found myself in a debate with the now-famous financial information media baron Michael Bloomberg. He rejected my view that the Net is becoming central to commerce and the economy. "The Internet is just one of many technologies which are changing things." Let's not get hung up on the Net, he said, but consider how many other technologies are affecting our lives. As an example, he pointed out that in the year 2000, "General Motors will ship more computer power than IBM."

Bloomberg missed the point. The Internet is a network of networks. It embraces a wide range of computing, telecommunications, entertainment, publishing, and other technologies. It spans digitized text, sounds, images, and video and is rapidly enveloping other information forms including *kinesthetic feedback* (where systems give tactile feedback you can feel) and even olfactory information (get ready for click and sniff). As devices from automobiles to hockey pucks become smart communicating objects, they form part of the Net. So-called cyberspace expands every time someone else logs on.

As computers from your desktop to the collar of your shirt become networked, nothing less than a new medium of human communications is emerging, one that may prove to surpass all previous revolutions—the printing press, the telephone, television, the computer—in its impact on our economic and social lives. This is, in fact, a "paradigm shift."[13]

As for Bloomberg's protest about the automobile, it too is becoming a Net appliance. The entire auto industry is getting ready for something called ITS— Intelligent Transportation Systems. This is the convergence of the highways with the Net. My car already has voice recognition for the phone system ("call home") and can log on to the Net. Some cars already have global positioning systems which tell you which turn to take. Toll booths scan your information and ensure collection of tolls at 70 miles per hour. And most N-Geners will travel in vehicles which sense the road, traffic, and other conditions, and drive themselves. This is not science fiction—it is already in prototyping and development.

Related to and quickly becoming part of the Net is an array of other interactive technologies which have become integral to the N-Gen world. The stand-alone computer is an interactive machine. It has a user rather than a viewer. The same is true for new product categories such as digital cameras which, for just a few hundred dollars, deliver 1.2 million pixels of information (or 1280 by 960 dots on the screen). Such cameras cost over $10,000 just a half-decade ago.

Digital cameras use a photosensitive chip called a charged-coupled device that converts an image into pixels that can be transferred to a computer and transmitted over the Internet. Ditto for video games, especially the sophisticated, multi-user, and increasingly networked games used by today's children. New digital, interactive, and networked appliances are emerging everywhere. In each case, the child is firmly in the driver's seat.

The Net—The Antithesis of TV

Many people think the new media and television are analogous because they both involve screens. For example, the term *screenagers* has been used to describe today's youth. TV viewers and Net surfers alike have been called *couch potatoes*. Social critic Neil Postman has said that through the information highway, information is becoming a new form of garbage—and with computers and televisions we will all be "amusing ourselves to death," the title of his 1994 book.

Those who say that the Net is all about a bigger crop of couch potatoes not only have a cynical view of humanity, but they ignore the budding experience with interactive technologies. Unfortunately for these commentators and fortunately for kids, the similarities between the two technologies end with the screen. In fact, the shift is more like from couch potato to Nintendo jockey.

TV is controlled by adults. Kids are passive observers. In contrast, children control much of their world on the Net. It is something they do themselves; they are users, and they are active. They do not just observe, they participate. They inquire, discuss, argue, play, shop, critique, investigate, ridicule, fantasize, seek, and inform. This makes the Internet fundamentally different from previous communications innovations, such as the development of the printing press or the introduction of radio and television broadcasting. These latter technologies are unidirectional and controlled by adults. They are very hierarchical, inflexible, and centralized. Not surprisingly, they reflect the values of their adult owners. By contrast, the new media is interactive, malleable, and distributed in control. As such it cherishes a much greater neutrality. The new media will do what we command of them. And at this moment, tens of millions of N-Geners around the world are taking over the steering wheel.

This distinction is at the heart of the new generation. For the first time ever, children are taking control of critical elements of a communications revolution.

On the Net, children must search for, rather than simply look at, information. This forces them to develop thinking and investigative skills, and much more. They must become critics. Which Web sites are good? How can I tell what is real and what is fictitious—whether it's a data source or the alleged teenage movie star in a chat session?

Further, children begin to question assumptions previously unchallenged. On the Net, there is great diversity of opinion regarding all things and constant opportunities to present your views. This is leading to a generation which increasingly questions the implicit values contained in information. Information becomes knowledge through the application of human judgment. As children interact with each other and the exploding information resources on the Net, they are forced to exercise not only their critical thinking but their judgment. This process is contributing to the relentless breakdown of the notion of authority and experience-driven hierarchies. Increasingly, young people are the masters of the interactive environment and of their own fate in it.

Because the Net is the antithesis of TV, the N-Generation is in many ways the antithesis of the TV generation.

The Web That Ate TV

There are, of course, aspects to TV which have been positive. Not all content is vacuous: TV is a distribution channel for good movies, documentaries, sports events, music, comedy, interviews, and news. It's simple to use. Most of us have programs which we know and usually enjoy. The quality of TV in terms of production values is usually high, especially when compared to most current Web sites. TV and radio have also acquired a level of interactivity with talk shows and phone-in programs such as *Larry King Live.* TV is also somewhat a communal experience as you sit with others in front of the electronic hearth.

There is also a role for passivity. As Frank Biondi, former president and CEO of Viacom, says, "TV is, at bottom, a passive experience, which is its beauty." In other words, the great thing about television is that you can come home after a long day at school or work and veg out in front of the TV.

True, there is some couch potato in all of us, including kids. On Saturday night, your son and his girlfriend may want to sit on the couch and be entertained rather than to construct some elaborate Net experience. Sometimes we want the content to rule rather than ourselves. Indeed, opportunities for "veging" in the digital economy will be even greater than today.

In 1997, it became very fashionable to talk about so-called *push technology* or *Web-casting*. Simply put, content is pushed to your screen rather than you seeking it. Instead of surfing the Net for information, content providers send you new information from categories you have previously requested—such as sports scores for your favorite teams, stocks you care about, the weather, and eventually anything. The *Wall Street Journal* proclaimed that the Net had finally found a viable business model—television.[14] *BusinessWeek* announced that Web-casting would cut through the clutter of the Net "using the same principle as broadcasting."[15] Screen saver software using push technology to bring customized news and information to the screen when your computer is idle—took off.

In reality, push technology is not a return to broadcasting but simply another thread in the richly developing tapestry of the Net. Over time, such Web-casting, including the casting of live TV programs, will be assimilated into the Net.

But television is not dead, just television as we know it—a rigid, one-way medium delivered by networks that schedule programming according to their estimates of likely viewership. Those who view the Net as another TV channel have got it backward. Sometime early in the next century, television programs will become accessible through the Net. Rather than talking about TV versus the Net, we will talk about stored access of content versus real-time access. In *stored* (asynchronous) access, the user picks up previously stored content (information, music video, a drama, sitcom, news program) when convenient. In *real-time* (synchronous) use, people access content (a sports game, election reporting) as it is occurring.

Your favorite TV shows will become a Web incident or site. First viewings of a sitcom, soap, or events like a football game or presidential address will be watched simultaneously by many. Such real-time simultaneous transmissions simply become part of the interactive world. TV schedules will be subordinated to the schedules that really count—those of our own lives and families and organizations. Interactivity enables us to program our lives better and to integrate the content we desire according to schedules that are important, not those arbitrarily determined by a TV network.

Rather than the Web becoming a push medium, TV is moving into the world of pull. If you want to sit back and watch the news, *Casablanca*, or an *I Love Lucy* rerun, go ahead and veg out. The difference is that prime time becomes any time. And if you would rather explore Mayan ruins, visit with your daughter at university, participate in a discussion about college basketball, analyze your personal finances, or find out why you have chest pains, you can do that, too. Ultimately, NBC television will become another Web site and the schedule will exist only for first-time viewings.

So, a new narrative emerges, one that includes push and pull:

- Your 10-year-old is doing a project with another student on Mesopotamia. In particular, they are interested in the development of Cuneiform writing and its impact on the creation of money, trade, and commerce. He sends his agent (a software program) onto the Net to find trustworthy information sources appropriate for a grade 5 student. One of these is a 22-minute documentary entitled "The Cradle of Civilization" produced by the BBC. In the morning, his computer screen and those of the other kid on his project flash advising them both of the documentary and suggesting they get together to watch it after school. The students watch the program at your house, taking video clips from it for their final report which is to be submitted on the Net.

- The screen saver on computers in the medical library advises students that an experimental surgical procedure will be performed at 4 P.M. tomorrow, and will be available through the medical faculty's Web site. Students may ask questions by text or voice to the physicians performing the surgery. During the procedure, which lasts three hours, a medical student records her observations; checks her e-mail, agreeing to a date with that pesky-yet-intriguing history major; and goes for a virtual stroll around the Fort Lauderdale hotel she and a friend are considering staying at during the spring break. The hotel looks good but she is not sure if she wants to spend a week partying in Florida.

- Having found an amazing fare sale on the Net, she is Europe-bound for the March break. Cycling through an unfamiliar part of Provence, France, she consults the PDA (personal digital assistant) mounted on her crossbar for guidance. A "best wishes" video card is sent from Mom in Pittsburgh, including the offer of some extra cash if she needs it, and a television news report about students cycling in France. This gives her renewed energy to speed up, especially after a local weather report forecasting thundershowers in the region comes onto the screen.

Families at home are becoming connected to the Net in a way similar to how the previous generation was connected to the TV—the device is left on all day, in the background. Computers in various rooms at my house are connected at high speed to the Net through a router and hub which give all of us access to my company's file servers and Internet server.

As TV becomes absorbed by the Net, family-room politics will undoubtedly become a new theater of conflict and negotiation. Group channel surfing is satisfying typically only for the person with the remote. Visits to 20 new locations in a 60-second commercial have already been banned in my household by mutual consent of all.

However, most government, private, and TV network research reports project only minor decreases in the amount of television watched by American viewers into the next millennium. One private research company conservatively projects the total decline by the year 2001 will be about 12 hours a year less per person. Both cable and network television can take comfort in these conservative estimates, but there may be something wrong with calculations of media consumption.

What's wrong? To begin with, many of the real projections made by the broadcasters themselves are not made public. Our researchers came across several situations where a broadcaster or association confided in us that it couldn't release its data about the impact of the Net on television because it was potentially harmful to itself.

The data also fail to take into account not only the growing influence of the digital media, but how that influence is greater over young people. For example, the same company that reported only a 12-hour decline by the year 2001 also reported that the fastest growing group on the Internet are 18- to 24-year-olds. These young adults watch less television than any other age group.

Research suggests that the decline in television viewing will be concentrated among the younger audience. Between 1991 and 1996, Nielsen Media Research recorded a drop in viewing time of slightly over two hours per week among the 2- to 17-year-old population. Extending this decline to the year 2000, American children will be watching approximately 100 hours less television a year than they do now. If you factor into the equation the impact of the Net on children of wired families, the numbers are even more dramatic. (See Fig. 2.7.)

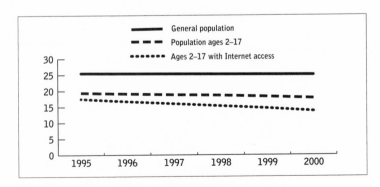

Figure 2.7
Projected decline in television viewing.
1995–2000
Data: Nielsen Media Research, Alliance for Converging Technologies.

Average America Online (AOL) homes spend almost 15 percent less time watching television than the U.S. average. This amounts to an hour less television every day when compared to the U.S. average or just over seven hours less per week.[16] More than 40 percent of respondents in a recent survey conducted by Jupiter Communications and the KidsCom Company said that they watch less television because of their Internet use. When asked what was more fun—television or the Internet—92 percent chose the Internet.[17] In a study conducted by Odyssey, respondents were asked, "What activities are you typically taking time from to go online?" The number 1 answer at 30 percent was television.[18]

Why is this decline concentrated among young people? Children, like the rest of us, are bound by the constraints of a 24-hour day. While the amount of leisure time contemporary children actually have is cause for debate, they do have more options competing for a share of that leisure time. The four to six hours a week 6- to 12-year-olds spend playing video games comes from other activities, as do the 20 minutes to 2 hours a week teenagers will spend reading, writing, and responding to e-mail messages and participating in online forums. The average chat room visit for an 8- to 14-year-old is 16 minutes, but as children and teens have told us, those daily minutes can add into hours.

The reinvention of TV, of course, spells trouble for the TV networks who become a speck in a vast media landscape. Same for traditional TV advertising. As control shifts to the user, it is as easy to brush off a traditional ad as to shoo a fly on a hot summer's day. Advertising will need to be transformed to survive, as we shall see later.

Bob Dylan said, "You don't need a weatherman to know which way the wind blows." Ask any N-Gener who has access to the Net whether he or she prefers TV. Many view TV as the ultimate in passivity. "Kids are bored to death with television. I am, anyways," says 18-year-old Ted McCoy. "The Net is stimulating and interactive. That's something that TV cannot accomplish."

"My friends that aren't connected to the Internet can barely believe that days go by and I never even turn on my television set once," says 16-year-old Kim Devereaux. "I suppose it's because the television is static. You can't really do anything with it. On the Internet you're deciding what qualifies as entertainment on your own. The Internet is interactive. Television is not."

"When watching TV you're allowing yourself to become brain dead," says 15-year-old Sarah Vandervoort of North York, Ontario. "Don't get me wrong, I do watch TV, but I spend more of my free time on the Net. You need to be mentally awake to surf the Net. You can't have conversations with people if you aren't with it. The Net is a communication link between you and the world whereas TV is only a source of communication between you and the media."

"I spend most of my time on my computer but I don't consider it time wasted because I am doing useful things. Where if I was watching TV, I would consider it a waste," says 13-year-old Mike Uttech. "When I go to bed at night, I know I actually did something and didn't just watch TV the whole day. I also think that the leisure time is decreasing as I get older. With more homework and many more things I have to do, not all Net-related but most computer-related, I really don't have time to just sit around."

Just how strong is the N-Gen preference for the digital media over television? Very. Carla Bastida is a 9-year-old who lives in Barcelona, Spain. Last Christmas she was confronted with a choice: the family could replace its broken VCR or buy a color printer. She says that "there was no choice, really. I wanted the printer."

Hollywood and broadcasting executives should take note that she chose the printer because it was "more important" for her and the computer was "more fun" than watching TV and videos. Says Dad, "Carla gets bored just watching TV."

If you contrast N-Geners with their parents, it isn't difficult to see how this rejection of television came about. Baby boomers have witnessed the computer revolution, but they have viewed it through a couch potato mentality. That doesn't mean all baby boomers are getting fat, but that we've become accustomed to the broadcast delivery of information. Keeping current is not widely seen as an interactive activity. To many boomers, keeping current means turning on the six o'clock news (although even that is declining in popularity).

In the midst of the massive social changes and the era of short-sighted but widely practiced corporate downsizing, boomers have embraced computer and information technology but they have done so under duress. Baby boomers are constantly being reminded that computer-facilitated networks are a personal and economic survival tool that will revolutionize everything—whether they are prepared for it or not. N-Geners, on the other hand, view it as a natural extension of themselves. It is, in fact, the specific medium that will follow and perpetuate the force of their youth, just as television has traced the lives of the boomers.

Cyber Drownings and the End of Surfing

Push technology became popular because companies saw it as a way to reach people on the Net with their advertising messages. You could push valued content onto the screen along with advertising. Advertising could be pushed onto your watch as you walked along the street along with stock updates. You won't mind a message pushed onto the heads-up display on your windshield if the information (which comes free) helps you get where you want to go. And if flying toasters on your screen carry a commercial message along with the results of the Dodgers game, more power to them.

But Web-casting also attempts to address another problem—surfing through constellations of millions of data points is a problem for the user. It takes time and there is a lot of junk. The trouble with Net surfing is that there are a lot of cyber drownings. Or, as management lecturer Tom Peters recently said: "I'm concerned that this global economy will in fact be garbage at the speed of light."

Raw data are indeed disorganized, empirical facts. When organized and defined in some intelligible fashion, then data becomes information. Information that has been interpreted and synthesized, reflecting certain implicit values, becomes knowledge. And knowledge that carries profound, transhistorical insights might become wisdom.[19] The new technology enables us to move up the wisdom food chain, if we want to.

Today children access the Web primarily through browsers. The responsibility is on the child to find information—to manually search for content which is trustworthy, appropriate, desired, fun.

Anyone who has surfed the Net knows that this is not a viable model—especially as the sources of information grow every year. In January 1993, when the first browser, Mosaic, was introduced, there were 50 known Web servers. By October 1993, there were more than 500. By the end of 1994, there were 5000 growing to more than 100,000 the next year. By the end of 1997, there were 1.5 million. By March of 1997, content on the Web had grown to accommodate 833,139 different sites or home pages.[20] (Every company I am involved in has one, as does my daughter.)

Manual searches, however, are giving way to active software agents which will do much of the searching for you. The agent (softbot, knowbot, or bot) learns about you over time as you use the Net. And you instruct your agent—in a sense educate it—about what you like or are looking for. You come to trust it, sort of like you trust yourself. It is not passive but it proactively seeks information on your behalf, advising you of important developments within the parameters you specify.

So, after school your daughter's agent, "Cyber-Niki," comes on to her screen or talks to her through the speaker on her PDA (personal digital assistant) as she rides the bus home:

Niki, some very interesting developments today. Leonardo DiCaprio is going to participate in a chat session tonight on the DiCaprio fan club home page—8 P.M. The new album by No Doubt will be out next month, but previews are available on their site. You had a big rush on your home page today, 420 hits, probably because the discussion about censorship on the Net is heating up. You have 18 e-mails and your presence is requested in the Shakespeare forum—Romeo and Juliet. As you probably know, Vanessa was sick and missed school today. She downloaded her homework from the Class Web page but doesn't understand the mathematics assignment. Can you give her a call? And I found that music score for the Billie Holiday song you requested.

Another breakthrough underway in preventing cyberdrownings is the rise of information about information. These are rating systems which evaluate information. Organizations from governments, banks, and school boards, to the Boy Scouts will develop ratings to help children, parents, and anyone else to select trustworthy and appropriate information.

Tim Berners-Lee, who invented the World Wide Web, believes that the creation of information about information is "the beginning of the new enlightenment."[21] This may not be hyperbole. Imagine the power of a system that evaluated all the sites, articles, videos, documentaries, scholarly papers, and speeches on a topic of importance to, say, your business. Over time, or quickly, you may come to trust this pattern and rely on it to keep you up-to-date with any important developments or insights in the field. And yes, so-called push technology can help. But you decide what is pushed to you.

Why Not Generation "Y"?

Some have suggested we describe today's youth as *Generation Y.* I am not convinced this is the best term to use and I think it is important to get it right; terms acquire meaning and they shape our thinking. No one is clear what Generation Y really is. Most of those who have raised the term use it to refer to the youth of today, those who were born at the end of the 1970s when the birth rate began to increase after the baby bust years, but beyond that the notion is fuzzy. More important, Generation Y also builds on the confusion sown about Generation X, which isn't a generation at all but the last few years of the boom.

I also believe that *N-Generation* is a better term in that it codifies in a unified term the power of demographics with the power of new media analysis. It provides additional information about the defining characteristic of members of the echo generation—they are growing up with the digital media. And it is a break from the cynicism which has surrounded the discussion of Generation X. They were viewed as a bitter, disenfranchised, and negative group. The N-Gen is defined by something positive. They are breaking free from the one-way, centralized media of the past and are beginning to shape their own destiny. And evidence is mounting that the world will be a better place as a result.

The Generation Lap

ADAM

AWESOME!! YOU SAW THE WHOLE "STAR WARS" TRILOGY WHEN IT FIRST CAME OUT?!?

YUP. I WAS IN COLLEGE WHEN STAR WARS WAS MADE.

WHOA!...

DAD WAS ALIVE BACK BEFORE THEY HAD DIGITAL ENHANCEMENT!

© Universal Press Syndicate*

I love troubleshooting computer problems for teachers, and it's quite unfortunate that some of them see me as a negative. Outside of school I help out my mom with computer-related projects. I think I am a little less patient with her than with my teachers (it's a normal family thing I guess). My mom used to ask me why I was always on the Internet or playing with the computer, then I started to involve her and show her what I had been doing and she got interested. Now she has a computer on her desk at school (she's a teacher) and uses it all the time. She even sent me a "Virtual Bouquet" this past Christmas!

—ANDY PUTSCHOEGL, 17, Oakdale, Minnesota

When it comes to understanding and using the new media and technology, many parents are falling woefully behind their children. We've shifted from a generation gap to a *generation lap*—kids outpacing and overtaking adults on the technology track, *lapping* them in many areas of daily life. Austin Locke, 15, sums it up perfectly: "For once in our civilization, children are educating older people. Children are more adept at using computers. Parents, teachers, and other adults are looking to children for information and help with computers and other computer-related stuff."

Society has never before experienced this phenomenon of the knowledge hierarchy being so effectively flipped on its head. But it is definitely happening and the situation is magnified with each new technology. University students in their twenties share childhood memories of having to explain to their parents what a mouse or CD player was. The challenge in these episodes was not only how to explain the new technology, but how to convince their parents they needed something they'd never even heard of.

Children—Authorities for the First Time

Most kids love the new technology. In a 1995 study on home computing conducted by Carnegie Mellon University, researchers introduced computers and the Internet into 48 demographically diverse families. In 41 of the 48 families, the heaviest user was a child. They concluded, "Teenagers are central to Internet use at home. They often provide the motivation for parents to invest in a computer, . . . become sources of expertise within the household, and catalyze Internet use by other family members."[1]

Stories about six-year-olds programming new VCRs after their parents' unsuccessful efforts are now cliché. A newer version is the 14-year-old girl whose parents recently asked her to install Net Nanny software on the family computer to keep Internet pornography out of the house. Of course, her parents are oblivious to the fact that if she sets up the system, she then controls it.

Two-thirds of the kids in the *Growing Up Digital* survey on FreeZone said they were more proficient at the computer than their parents.

"This is a unique period in history in that the role of the child in the home is changing," states John Seely Brown, chief scientist at Xerox PARC. He explains that in the past the parents were the authority figures in terms of anything of particular value. The notion of the child being able to do anything new, novel, or really useful for the parent was bogus. Parents traditionally have known more than children in virtually every conceivable domain—with the one exception of immigrant children learning a new culture and language more quickly and acting as translators for their parents.

"So, for the first time there are things that parents want to be able to know about and do, where the kids are, in fact, the authority," he says. "This means that

My Mom doesn't let me e-mail, so I'm busy contemplating a scheme.

PUTTPUTT, 10, f

now you have a different conversation happening around the dinner table." On certain subjects, the parents are the authority, and on other subjects of value, the kids are the authority.

The implications are huge. Family members begin to respect each other for what their authorities actually are. This creates more of a peer dynamic within families and if managed well by the parents can create a more open, consensual, and effective family unit. (More of that in Chap. 11, "N-Gen and the Family.")

This insight can be extended to other social institutions, as well. For example, imagine the changing relationship between students and teachers in Finland. The government has chosen 5000 N-Geners to train the country's teachers on how to use computers. For the first time ever, in one domain, the students will be the teachers and the teachers will be the students. The power dynamic between students and teachers will be forever altered.

The same is true as N-Geners enter universities and the workforce. Managers around the world still make very limited personal use of the new technology. In the developed world, this is especially true in Europe (lesser so in Scandinavia) and Japan. Imagine the impact of this wave of technologically fluent youth, each one commanding power and respect through his or her knowledge of something crucial to the companies' success. Further, being an authority in at least one domain (in their families, schools, and other settings), will N-Geners be satisfied with the old hierarchical model of the enterprise?

Successful companies will be those recognizing that networked structures work more effectively. As Seely Brown puts it: "What you find in leading organizations today is that each one of us is, in some way, an authority in some domains and a student in other domains. We must be prepared to learn major things from our subordinates and vice versa." Peer interaction in homes and schools is setting the stage for the kind of experiences that prepare us to move into the postmodern world.

I think that technology has changed the way adults treat me. They seem to take my opinions more seriously because they realize I just may know something they don't.

KIM DEVEREAUX, 16
Alberta

Seventeen-year-old Andy Putschoegl speaks wistfully of the Apple IIgs of his early childhood, much like his grandparents probably spoke of their favorite stuffed toys. Andy experiences the generation lap every day in his high school classes where he lends a hand to his fellow students and rescues his teachers. During one episode last year, this so-called rescuing entailed hacking the school's computer system. "I suppose you might call it hacking," Andy explained. "What I did was start up the computer from an alternate disk and bypass a lot of the security features. And that was because the media personnel hadn't told the teachers what their passwords were and the teachers couldn't use their computers—not just the Internet—but the regular computers."

Barbara Harr, who runs the Lakeforest Library Connection (LLC) in a Rockville, Maryland, shopping mall, has firsthand experience with the generation lap. One day a child and his mother came to the library to do a homework assignment that required use of an encyclopedia. The child headed for the computer equipped with a CD-ROM encyclopedia and the mother went to the reference shelf. The mother insisted that they use the book since it seemed to have the appropriate information and was easily photocopied. The child couldn't persuade his mom that the computer version was at least as good, if not better. He said, "Mom, it's the same thing. It's right here. Don't you get it?"

Harr notes that parents who are not threatened by the lap can benefit. "Kids are totally surrounded by a multimedia environment, virtually from the day they are born. It is a totally different experience, and there is a comfort level that is established early on. Parents today with young children probably have an advantage compared to other adults because they can learn this new technology with their kids."

Needless to say, some adults have difficulty accepting the generation lap and seeing the potential for growth. Mike Uttech, 13, of Paris, Texas, describes this well: "I have some teachers who won't accept the fact that a student knows more about something than they do. Some of my teachers love me to help out with tasks—whether it is saving files to disks, printing, or other tasks. But other teachers think I'm being rude knowing more than they do. I also find it funny when a teacher won't let me help and then gets the computer specialist at the school to do it. I think that the teachers and adults should listen to us more and maybe even learn something from us."

Technology Is "Like the Air"

In *The Digital Economy,* I described how computer visionary Alan Kay made the now-famous statement that technology is "technology only for people who are born before it was invented." According to the pioneer of learning and technology Seymour Papert, "That's why we don't argue about whether the piano is corrupting music with technology."[2]

Psychologists often talk about the opacity and transparency of computers. *Opaque* computers or interfaces mask the inner workings of the machine. A Mac is considered opaque because the user needs to know very little about the workings of the software to use the computer. *Transparent* interfaces reveal the computer's processes—the underlying software and programming that makes something like a game or

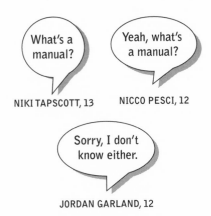

What's a manual?

NIKI TAPSCOTT, 13

Yeah, what's a manual?

NICCO PESCI, 12

Sorry, I don't know either.

JORDAN GARLAND, 12

All in response to my question, "Do kids use manuals?" posed to the "Kids Panel" held in front of 2000 managers at the BOMA conference in June 1996. When I explained the concept of an instruction manual, they recognized the term and told the audience why kids never use manuals. "Why would you?" said Nicco.

program or Web hot link work. Ultimate transparency takes one down to the 1s and 0s of machine language programming or even the underlying workings of the hardware or chips. Leading thinkers point out that many children seek transparency—they want to know how computers and software work and to be able to change and modify these things.[3]

However, as the new media grows in connectivity, content, applications, and user populations, a new kind of transparency is emerging. Increasingly, N-Geners don't see the technology at all. They see the people, information, games, applications, services, friends, and protagonists at the other end. They don't see a computer screen, they see their friends' messages, their 'zines, their fan clubs, their chat groups, Crash Bandicoot, the Sistine Chapel, the Mayan ruins, and Our Lady Peace. This new transparency is really opacity come 180 degrees. A child in a chat group is much less interested in how the IRC technology works than if CYBER-CHICK will be her C-cousin or how MOOSELIPS will respond to her idea.

In this sense, the technology is completely transparent to them. "It doesn't exist. It's like the air," says Coco Conn, cofounder of the Web-based Cityspace project. MIT's Dr. Idit Harel agrees: "For the kids, it's like using a pencil. Parents don't talk about pencils, they talk about writing. And kids don't talk about technology—they talk about playing, building a Web site, writing a friend, about the rain forest."

Tech stuff is natural for me, it takes me a minute to set up a computer. It takes my parents an hour.

WWIII, 14, m

Kids look at computers the same way boomers look at TV. We don't marvel at the technology or wonder how television transfers video and audio through thin air, we simply watch the screen. TV is a fact of life. So it is with kids and computers.

A personal experience made this clear for me. In early 1996, I spent an hour surfing the Web on the Canadian television program *Pamela Wallin Live*. The point was to illustrate to the viewers the wealth of material available on the Net.

When I returned home, my wife Ana (my most trusted critic) told me she thought the show was good, but that our kids found the whole idea of the program hilarious, embarrassing, and dumb. They wouldn't watch it. As my son Alex put it, "Doesn't everyone know how to surf the Net? And if they don't, you don't have to *teach* them."

The next day over breakfast my son explained that, "Dad, no offense, but you adults are obsessed with technology. Imagine a TV show where people watch you surf television! Wow! Let's see if my Dad can find a football game on television! And for the grand finale, we're going to see if he can find a movie!"

At this point, his 13-year-old sister, Niki, came to his support (a rare thing), embellishing a point from a previous conversation. "Yeah, Dad, how about the refrigerator. Remember, it's technology, too. Why don't we have a TV show where we can all watch you surf the fridge!"

Consultant and author Chuck Martin describes the attitude of his eight-year-old son Ryan. "Using the computer is simply something that occurs in the course of his day. He doesn't think about it as using the computer, just like he doesn't think of playing football as using a football."

How things work—from footballs to multimedia machines—is strikingly intuitive for N-Geners. Ryan once came into his dad's home office and asked to use his new IBM Thinkpad—to check out what games came on it. "Without stopping, he quickly figured that the red button in the middle of the keyboard was the mouse, and navigated right through Windows 95 to the Accessories, drilled down to games and within forty-five seconds of picking up the computer was playing a game."

Why It's Easier for Kids

If parents think that their kids are catching on to the new technologies much faster than adults, they're right. It's easier for kids. Because N-Gen children are born with technology, they assimilate it. Adults must accommodate—a different and much more difficult learning process. With assimilation, kids view technology as just another part of their environment, and they soak it up along with everything else. For many kids, using the new technology is as natural as breathing. "I was born using an Apple computer," says Andy Putschoegl, emphatically.

Adults, needless to say, are much more established in their ways. Learning something completely new is hard work, and their established thinking must be changed to accommodate the new technology. The experience of U.S. Secretary of State Madeleine Albright was evidence of this at an Internet demonstration at the American Library in Moscow. Secretary Albright experienced technical difficulties while high school students from 48 countries waited to talk to her online. "I do know how to type," she told reporters. "But I am not good at the mouse. People of a certain age do not have very good eye-hand coordination."[4]

I saw this difference comparing my children's assimilation of computing compared to my wife Ana's adaptation. Initially, she had considerable trouble learning a word processor, for example. Having cognitive structures built up around the use of a typewriter, she would attempt to underline a word by backspacing through each letter and then hitting the underscore key. The correct procedure is, of course, to highlight the word and select the underline option. "Nothing works the way I expect it to work," she said. For children, everything works the way it works. Learning is a discovery, not an accommodation to existing structures.

Documenting the problems adults have in learning to use computers has become a mini industry.[5] There are so many bizarre stories that one begins to think that many of them are part of the Net culture of creating hoaxes. You may have heard a few yourself. The help desk that reported that someone thought the mouse was a foot pedal and couldn't get it to work. The secretary who was asked to copy a disk and came back with a photocopy. The man, confronted with the computer message "Press any key to continue," couldn't find the "any" key on the keyboard. Another "hit" the keyboard so hard he broke it. When asked by a support line if she had Windows, one woman apparently replied, "No, we have air conditioning." One person was said to be found deleting files on a disk using white-out. Another, when instructed to "insert the disk and close the door," inserted the disk and then closed her office door. There are hundreds of stories.

They seem too bizarre to be true. However, the wife of a friend of mine swears to me that the first time her husband used a mouse he actually pointed at the screen with it like it was a TV remote. What can we learn from this? Are adults just stupid?

> I can't remember not using the computer. We had a lot of computers in the house and everybody played with them all the time.
>
> CLAIRE COWSERT-HINRICHES, 8
> Texas

While laughable, the actions of these adults make sense. Boomers are familiar with TV remotes, foot pedals, photocopiers, windows, white-out, and doors. Each of these artifacts has decades of meaning and behaviors associated with them. N-Geners, the younger the better, have a cleaner slate. Absorbing the digital media is easy compared to the other challenges in their lives.

The computer and the Internet have become such strong elements of youth culture that sometimes the generation lap is evident even among children who haven't been raised around computers. Recently 13-year-old Andrew Walker and his younger brother Craig spent the $1200 they'd saved from the proceeds of their paper routes on their family's first computer, but they were already shrewd consumers when they walked their dad and his share of the purchase price into the showroom. "My dad asked about the prices, but I kind of hinted around about what kind of capability it had," Andrew said of the sales negotiations. "Most companies will also try to rip you off by telling you Windows is preloaded and stuff like that, but they won't actually give you the disks. I wanted to make sure about that in case it ever crashes."

Even though Andrew's only previous experience with computers had come from working on his school's "old, crappy PCs," he was more than prepared to participate in the sales negotiations. What is perhaps most impressive about Andrew's role is the importance of the issue he addressed. Although he did not know the terminology, Andrew protected his family from what is known as *soft-lifting*—a fraudulent practice by some computer dealers who install unlicensed software on units they sell directly to the public. Often consumers have no idea they are using an unlicensed copy of the software until they require technical support from the software manufacturer or discover a virus on their brand-new systems.

Cooling the Computer

The different ways of experiencing various media can be explained in what Marshall McLuhan, in his 1964 book *Understanding Media: The Extensions of Man,* termed "the reversal of the overheated media."[6] In McLuhan's analysis, all forms of media can be classified as either hot or cool. A *hot* medium is defined as being mechanical, uniform, repetitive, and specialist. A *cool* medium, on the other hand, is interactive (the word *participation* was used in McLuhan's era), personal, original, and nonspecialist. One of the things we are seeing in the generation lap between baby boomers and N-Gen is a change in the technological temperature: the transformation from broadcast to interactive mentality.

Most parents of N-Geners view computer technology as a hot medium—it is a device that symbolizes productivity in a work environment. Many adults have learned computer skills under duress to perform repetitive tasks such as word processing. Often they are at the mercy of media personnel or a computer expert at the office when they face technical difficulties, and let's not even mention the anxiety faced when one has to learn a new software program.

> I am making my dad's business' home page. He knows zippola about HTML. He knows how to go places (on the Net) but that is not hard.
>
> BURN, 14-year-old FreeZoner

Their N-Gen children, however, have cooled the computer down. They personalize their computers in the same way they personalize their bedrooms. This personalization can take the form of replacing sound effects with voice samples that welcome individual users as they log on or in the creation of screen savers composed of photographs of family or friends that have been digitized with a scanner.

According to the HomeNet study on family Internet usage, conducted by the

Human Computer Interaction Institute at Carnegie Mellon University, personalization of the computer put parents off:

> Many [teens] reported that mastering the techniques necessary to personalize their computers was satisfying in its own right. Most of the adults whom we interviewed considered mastering these techniques to be a waste of time and an obstacle to their use of the computer.[7]

"It has its advantages," 16-year-old Frank Caratozzolo of New Jersey said of the generation lap. "I modify a lot of the stuff on the computer like installing cool screen savers, or playing games on the network, and the teachers don't suspect a thing." N-Geners also realize that their proficiency with computers and the Internet is not appreciated by all adults. "The teachers don't trust me," Frank said. "They think that I am going to break the computer or install a virus onto the system."

N-Gen's use of the Internet gives a whole new meaning to an old Bob Dylan line, "Your sons and daughters are beyond your command."

What About the Generation Gap?

Since time immemorial, youth have been criticized by their elders as being lazy or mischievous, but in the 1960s, the tone of this generational chiding got much tougher. A seemingly unbridgeable cultural chasm opened between baby boomers and their parents. No one over 30 could be trusted and the hippies and hippie-wannabees decried the establishment's greed and materialism. All this was new; before the baby boom, *generation gaps* didn't exist. Kids entered the workforce after a brief childhood. One hundred years ago, only 11 percent of high-school age Americans were in school. Today, 90 percent are. But the postwar boomers grew up during relatively prosperous times and attended school for more years than their parents. They had time to develop and propagate their own youth culture. Rock 'n roll, long hair, mind-altering substances, Woodstock, protest movements, wacky clothes, and new sexual attitudes and lifestyles gave parents high anxiety. And, of course, the ubiquitous boomers also had a new medium communicating their culture—television. Date the birth of the original generation gap to that infamous moment when Elvis' swinging pelvis was blocked out of the *Ed Sullivan Show* by the TV censors.

We don't hear much about a generation gap today; for the most part kids think their parents are pretty cool. "Nearly half of children think their parents are 'up to date' on the music they like," reports market research firm American Demographics. "The children surveyed also say their parents' opinions matter most to them when it comes to drinking, spending money, and questions about sex and

AIDS. They even listen more to their parents than their friends about which snack foods to eat."[8] Further, there are a lot of adults that care about young people and work closely with schools and other voluntary organizations to make sure childhood is as happy and educational as possible. Unlike the 1960s, however, when parents merely thought their kids had gone nuts, many parents, while uncomfortable or nervous about their kids' endeavors, are supportive. It's almost as though the boomers, who often became estranged from their parents, are refusing to let this happen in their households.

But just because today's dad and son can admire each other's ponytail doesn't mean we're in some era of transgenerational bliss. There is a definite get-tough-on-kids mood growing in America. Consider last year's Presidential election where politicians of all parties often cast kids in a negative light, trying to capture adult votes by threatening to take the nation's youth out to the woodshed. Such nastiness was noted by many mass-media journalists. "Curfews, V-chips, harsher penalties for juvenile crime, school uniforms, drug tests to get a driver's license—the candidates were, like, really on their case," wrote Ann Hulbert in *USA Today.*[9]

Some politicians, typified by California Republican Assemblyman Mickey Conroy, called for the return of corporal punishment to elementary schools. Conroy calls the three decades of research that does not support corporal punishment "intellectual psycho babble from the ivory tower" and believes that paddling and knuckle-rapping serve as adequate means of punishing minor offenses. "Let's get back to basics," Conroy has often been quoted as saying. "If you break the law or misbehave in class, you will be punished. Corporal punishment works." There is now open discussion about the death penalty for children, not just among fringe groups, but leading politicians such as California Governor Pete Wilson who has suggested that the minimum age for the death penalty be reduced to 14. Clearly there is something going on beyond fear of youth crime—which has been on the decline in America for four years.

Part of the unease by adults about kids is rooted in their concern about kids and technology. The fast growth of the Internet and the even faster spread of the World Wide Web are frightening many parents, teachers, and other adults. They are uneasy about these powerful new tools being in the hands of children, particularly since many of these adults feel they don't really understand the new technology themselves. Exacerbating these anxieties is a lot of negative media coverage, often focusing on the 0.5 percent of online material that is violent, racist, or sexual in nature. "My biggest fear is some student wandering where they shouldn't go," says one elementary school teacher, reflecting a common concern.

This concern is valid, and sensible steps can be taken to minimize the likelihood of a child encountering inappropriate material. But rather than calling for a reasoned discussion about safe online practices, critics often insist that children should be denied use of the Net, period, and that adult material that is perfectly legal to disseminate through other media, such as magazines or satellite television, be made illegal on the Net. The Net is seen as a particularly dangerous medium that warrants its own special laws.

The result is that kids and the new technology are often unfavorably portrayed publicly:

- Author Theodore Roszak, in an article entitled, "Internet as teacher makes students stupid"[10] writes, "Used as a teaching device, the Web is an expensive way to distract attention and clutter the mind." He argues that the main information kids find on the Web is advertising, saying, "The World Wide Web is primarily an advertising medium." Children who use CD-ROMs are damaging themselves. "CD-ROM materials do more to fragment the attention span than to teach anything. The CD-ROM was invented by clever hackers to display razzle-dazzle . . . capabilities of the technology—point, click, zip, wham, wow!" His main conclusion? Keep technology away from children.

- In a recent nationally syndicated column, Cokie Roberts and her husband Stephen write, "Cyber seduction, cult by computer, kids caught in an indecent web! The headlines have been scary of late as we learn more about the dangers of the brave new world of the Internet." The Net is "yet another influence in . . . children's lives over which [parents] have no control." Or, "the horrible thought that, in the privacy of your own home, your child could be the target of some sick predator was frightening enough."

- In the months after the Oklahoma City bombing, numerous television reports condemn the availability of information about bomb-making on the Internet. Even after arrests are made, television news continues to report on this issue focusing, in particular, on how easy it is for kids to get this information. During this coverage, television news reports reveal that a combination of ammonium nitrate, fuel oil, and blasting caps would create a bomb. When two New Jersey teenagers are injured in their attempts to make a pipe bomb, they tell reporters that they learned they could access the construction instructions via the Internet from watching television news. Many people call for a zero tolerance policy.

- A *Baltimore Sun* columnist tells parents: "If you have a teenage boy and you are on the Internet, he is downloading pictures of naked women. So are his friends. So are the teenage sons of your friends. If you are thinking, 'Oh no, not my boy,' give it up because he is counting on that."[11]

- An 18-year-old student asks a software company why its Internet filtering program blocks such sites as the National Organization for Women and the Jewish Bulletin of Southern California. The software company refuses to answer until, concerned that its software codes have been broken and its list of blocked sites would be published over the Internet, the company threatens the student with a lawsuit. A flame war erupts between the student and the president of the software company. The president sends the student an e-mail message telling him to "get a life and go hang out at the mall with the other kids."

- When 39 members of the Heaven's Gate cult commit suicide near San Diego in March 1997, television newscasts report that most of the dead were young geeks aged 18 to 24. The group is called an "Internet cult." Many point to this as evidence of the danger of youth on the Internet, calling for censorship of the Net. It turns out that most members (average age 38) had joined the cult before the Internet was born and, although some worked to support the group by developing Web pages, the main vehicle for communicating their ideas was actually videotape. Their mass suicide replicated the death of the last of the Catharian monks who, in 1244, ran down a hill into gigantic bonfires—as journalist and media critic Jack Kapica points out—without the help of the Internet.[12]

When so much media coverage is this negative, it is small wonder that the research company Roper Starch has charted a major upswing in adults being worried about kids. In 1991, 11 percent of the population said that their *top concern* was "the way young people think and act." This grew to 21 percent in 1993 and by 1997 had tripled to 34 percent. The main fear of over one-third of adults is youth—and growing!

Recently an army of theorists, moralists, and analysts have waded in to explain the link between the rise of technology and the so-called decline of youth. Typical is Robert Bly who, in the 1996 book *The Sibling Society,* views most of societal woes as rooted in youth, technology, and the decline of adult authority. Children, according to Bly, "have been put into power." Most high schools are "run by their own students." He cynically says, "In many ways we are now living in a culture run by half adults." Everywhere people are rejecting authority and hierarchy, in doing so killing the "vertical gaze" which is so important to civil society. "Like sullen teenagers we live in our peer group glancing side to side, rather than upward for direction." Youth culture has gone to hell. "The Beatles' affectionate lyrics are replaced by gangsta rap." Many youth are "Internet heads." He says today's young "Internet fanatic is no longer figuring out how to remain warm in this climate; he is not curious about mound-building ants or how past cultures did things. He is curious about his own curiosity."

Do you have a Lava Lamp?
Smiley Face stuff?
Peace signs?
Ying Yangs?
Do you think this stuff is cool?
Well . . . It's coming back into style, people! Many stores EVERYWHERE
are selling the things I mentioned above. Thirty years ago, this stuff was more
than popular; everyone wore it! So you think we dress funky?
Take a look into the past. Clothing like bell-bottoms were as popular then as now,
but they didn't wear them in denim, but instead in funky cloth.
Were your parents hippies? You should check out FreeZone's article
about hippie parents to find out
(http://www.freezone.com/kclub/hippies/index.html).
Get into the craze!
I don't know what's causing it, do you?

ERICIO, 10, FreeZoner

(My 11-year-old son Alex would disagree on this latter point. His main activity on the Net to date has been precisely to learn about how past cultures did things.) To Bly, we live in a fantasy world. ". . . video games will provide fantasy death, and the Internet will provide fantasy friendships or fantasy sex." Bly's fear is that youth are taking over everything. "As in television, movies, the music business, advertising is run by the young for the young and almost no older mentors are left."

According to Bly, who are the main culprits? My reading of him says youth, technology, and youth culture. "We are all human beings, now standing in the rubble of a destroyed literate society, looking at the ruins of education, family, and child protection. Technology has destroyed interrelations in the human community that have taken centuries to develop. . . . We are drowning in uncontrollable floods of information. We are living among dispirited and agonized teenagers who can't find any hope."[13] This is not coming from some quack; Robert Bly is a mainstream, well-known, best-selling author and social commentator. While there are some interesting ideas in the book, his reactive hostility is so over the top it should cause us all to listen up.

But if today's youth wave is an echo of the postwar baby boom, are the frequent attacks on today's kids simply echoes of the 1960s and 1970s generation gap? I don't think so. Today's campaign has a much nastier, more personal tone, and may be rooted in boomers' fear of obsolescence. Increasingly, it is said that video games, computers, and now, the Net are to blame for society's ills, but doesn't this sound more like sour grapes than sound reasoning?

47

Four Themes of the New Generation Gap

There appear to be four key factors which open up a new generational abyss which is very different from that of the 1960s.

1. The older generations are uneasy about the new technology— which kids are embracing.

Many adults are coming to view digital technology as more of a detractor than contributor to their quality of life. After all, computers were introduced into the corporate world initially as a means of cutting costs by replacing people with machines. For many of those lucky enough to remain on the payroll, digital devices are making today's work life increasingly hectic. Fax machines, pagers, cellular phones, e-mail, local and wide area computer networks, the Internet—all these technologies are used by some companies to pump up the workplace pace and pressure. Recently, there has been a flurry of books and articles saying that people are nostalgic for the slower—and therefore saner—pace of yesterday.

> My father hates having to get me to show him how to do things on the computer now, but he does ask because he has to.
>
> LAUREN VERITY, 16
> Victoria, Australia

(*Caveat:* Of course, not all adult users of the new technology feel this way. For example, some e-mail and voice-mail users are reveling in new-found freedom, since they can now go about normal lives while on call instead of sitting by a telephone or playing telephone tag.)

For the kids, the new technology is great. They are glomming on to the digital devices as quickly as they come to market. Video games and computer games are multibillion dollar businesses, and as we have seen, the biggest computer user in a family is likely to be a teenager. Adults who are uneasy about the technology will transfer this anxiety to the technologies' most enthusiastic users, giving rise to adults criticizing kids for Net addiction or being constantly glued to the screen.

2. Older generations tend to be uneasy about new media— which are coming into the heart of youth culture.

A bit of history helps keep all this in perspective. The high anxiety that is being expressed about the Net is typical of the social phenomenon Danish media studies professor Kirsten Drotner describes as a *media panic*. "From the advent of mass-circulation fiction and magazines to film and television, comics and cartoons, the introduction of a new medium causes strong public reactions whose repetitiveness is as predictable as the fervor with which they are brought forward."[14]

My mother can't even enter Windows without step-by-step instructions.

DECTIRE, 12, f
New Zealand

As we've seen, Robert Bly represents a school of thought that feels threatened by rap music and music videos. In previous years, Bly-like attacks have been leveled against the habit of reading novels, attending plays, seeing a movie, or watching television. The first English novels were written for the leisure classes and reading them was considered a sinful waste of time, and it was said that comic books would deaden the ability of youth to think. Newspapers published dire warnings after the arrival of the telegraph and telephone, saying that these devices would make women more susceptible to seduction. The allegations we hear today about video games causing kids to become violent were also made of the Three Stooges. When rock 'n roll arrived, it was damned for rotting the minds of its listeners. Senator Joseph Lieberman's assertion that "people who play video games will have a tendency to be more violent in real life,"[15] doesn't seem too different from the attacks senators of the time leveled against the introduction of comic strips in newspapers. "According to these people, newspaper comic strips were going to turn children into hooligans. And these same arguments are popping up now," says popular culture expert and MIT media studies professor Henry Jenkins.[16] If anything, our history of media panics shows us that any fear of media content is accompanied by a discomfort with our children's need to become autonomous and define their own tastes in media.

(*Caveat:* Many adults like the new youth culture, finding it vibrant and refreshing. A lot of boomers, for example, will turn their car radios to alternative rock FM stations.)

3. Old media are uneasy about new media.

The gap is highlighted by the fact that media panics over new forms of media are spread by old forms of media. That broadcast and print coverage of the Internet in newspapers and on television has often been so negative can also be explained through Drotner's historical analysis of media panics. "Those who have invested most in gaining an accepted cultural capital," Drotner writes, "are also the principal victims if this capital loses its currency."[17] Since the Internet has been the primary means of displacing time formerly spent watching television and has provided yet another option for information gathering in place of newspapers, Drotner's words have a special emphasis in our current media panic. Parents are worried about losing control of their children while newspapers and television broadcasters are worried about losing their audiences and so each anxiety comes to fuel the other.

This should not surprise us. People become hostile and defensive when threatened by something new and which they don't understand. Historic innovations and shifts in thinking are often received with coolness, even mockery. Vested interests fight change. Just as the leaders of Newtonian physics argued against Einstein's General Theory of Relativity, so the leaders of traditional media are typically skeptical, at best, toward the new. Both film and print media showed considerable unease with television.

(*Caveat:* While the newspaper and magazine publishers wonder if they will still be in business a decade from now, the growth of new technology has been exhaustively covered by the old media. This is helped by the huge amounts of advertising generated by Silicon Valley. For example, more than half of the advertising revenue of *BusinessWeek* magazine comes from computer firms.)

4. The digital revolution, unlike previous ones, is not controlled by only adults.

At the heart of the digital revolution lies the Internet, which will soon be the means for almost all digital devices to communicate with each other. But although the birth of the Internet was an orderly affair, with government working closely with academic institutions, the Net's massive growth during recent years has been a complete free-for-all. No one is in control of how fast the Net will expand; it is completely a creature of market forces.

People can put whatever they want on the Web. Practically speaking, right now the Web is best suited for text and still graphics. But soon the Net will easily carry audio and full-motion, full-color video. Anyone, and this includes teenagers and younger kids, with a video camera and PC will soon be able to broadcast to the world. Compare this development to the heavily regulated manner in which television licenses were first issued. The television frequencies were viewed as a scarce resource that had to be carefully husbanded.

On the Net, effectively, there is no scarcity. You can do whatever you want to do. The power of the media is being democratized to all age groups.

(*Caveat:* While content is controlled by no one, adults still retain effective control over the guts of the Net. The high-speed, high-bandwidth major arteries of the Net belong to large corporations, and adults still produce most of the software and tools that are used by the new media.)

What we can see from the four themes is that the Net is a challenge to the existing order on many fronts. An old generation that is comfortable with its old communications media is being made uneasy by a new generation and a new communications media that is controlled by no one. For the first time, the new generation understands the new media much better and is embracing it much faster. This challenge to the existing order is a formula for confusion, insecurity, and some nasty books, articles, and TV shows about youth and their culture and media.

I discuss some scenarios regarding the outcome of these conflicts in Chap. 12, but first we need to learn more about the Net Generation.

Means of Reconciliation

If we accept the generation lap, we can take steps to closing the generation gap. Children are authorities—let's live with it and learn from them. When Shoreline District School near Seattle, Washington, expanded its use of computers in education it recognized the generation lap and responded by holding evening workshops to demystify the computer in the eyes of parents.[18] In many places, from the Issaquah School District in the state of Washington to Finland, thousands of students are training their teachers to use computers. Everybody benefits from children's expertise and generational gaps are bridged.

In some schools, the addition of more advanced technologies have only led to increased fears about students' access to inappropriate material. While the fear is inherent in any media panic, teachers and parents can overcome it for their own comfort by defining exactly what is and what isn't acceptable usage of the Internet and creating what is known as an Acceptable Usage Agreement. Parents and students are required to sign a statement agreeing to these terms of acceptable usage, a strategy that challenges cognitive thought by emphasizing Internet use as a privilege and by holding the student accountable for his or her actions.

Kids teaching adults works at home, too. Lisa Weatherford is an single mom who has two kids, Kristen, 14, and Paul, 16. Ten years ago, during her separation, Lisa was working full time and going to journalism school. She decided to buy a computer, both for her own productivity and because she thought her kids might be interested in using the machine as well. She bought a used PC for several hundred dollars and the kids picked it up immediately.

"Although the kids were only in kindergarten and second grade, they would sit on my lap and watch me type my hundreds of homework articles," Lisa remembers. "After I graduated in 1988 and went to work, a friend of a friend sold me an IBM PS/2, one of the first PCs. It had no hard drive so every time we used it we had to load DOS and whatever software we were using. It was, however, surprisingly useful and the kids did their homework and made pictures and played games on it for several years. . . . Anything that I couldn't figure out, they

> I can solve a lot of computer problems with ease, but it tends to tick people off when I give them an exact description of the problem at hand. Most of the answers they give me I have already tried and when I tell them this, they act as if I shouldn't know as much as I know. It seems to me that a lot of people on tech-support lines have not as much experience as I'd like them to have.
>
> RUFO SANCHEZ, 11
> Rochester, New York

would figure it out right away and explain it to me." Lisa didn't fight the lap, she embraced it.

Further, while it is true that one cannot go back and become a child again, one *can* learn to experience new media in much the same way children do. "They," meaning adults, says Andy from Minnesota, "need to sit down with that computer for a few hours and play with it so that they have some idea. . . . Then they'll be hooked too."

A Granddaughter Helps a Grandmother Get Wired

A case in point of embracing the lap to bridge the gap occurred in my extended family. My siblings and I bought our parents a PC for Christmas. It was shipped and installed in their winter home in Florida. Our mother, Mary, is 75 and father, Don, is 78—both retired teachers. Dad recently lost most of his eyesight so it was up to Mom to learn how to use this strange contraption and then share the results with him. She spent a few days getting used to the mouse and keyboard, but hadn't ventured into applications or onto the Net. We decided she needed some professional training and sent our 13-year-old daughter Niki to Florida for a visit. Niki is no geek, but she has been using a Mac since she was very young. The following are excerpts from a grandmother's diary of five days with an N-Gener.

Saturday, March 8.
My first time! Wow! What an experience!

When computers began to be common in my working world, I was at the point of retirement and so it seemed that my contact with them, in a very personal way, would be nil. As time passed I really did begin to feel "out of it"—sort of like the only person at a party that doesn't know how to do the Macarena.

When my children told me that they were going to bring us into the computer world I felt rather overwhelmed by the whole idea. I felt so uninformed and computer illiterate that I really feared I would be a big disappointment to everyone and maybe even a complete failure. However, after the computer was set up and I had a chance to get used to the mouse (that took a few days), I thought that maybe this would be OK—even fun.

I was thrilled to learn that Niki was coming for a visit because it was too late to enroll in the computer course at the local seniors' cultural center and I knew that if anybody could help me she could. Children these days just seem to be fluent with technology.

I was surprised that she could work the computer because it is a PC using the Windows software and she is used to a Mac, which I understand is different. But it didn't take her long to figure it out. She even got my printer working, which apparently hadn't been "installed."

The first thing she showed me was how to paint a picture on the screen. I think that Picasso's reputation is safe; however, I may start a new school called primitive computer art. We had a lot of good laughs! This is really fun! Afterwards she showed me how to send it to the whole family as an attachment on e-mail. At first we omitted the letter "c" in com and it didn't go through. But now I know you have to get it right with e-mail. We also answered the e-mail that has been collecting in my in-box. I loved that. What a great way to communicate. It's so easy! But I have decided to keep Niki right here so she can keep right on helping me.

Sunday, March 9.

Today Niki showed me how to get on Netscape. She asked me who was my favorite movie star from my teenage days and soon I had found Tyrone Power on the Internet! It was a nice picture of him and I could see why I had thought that he was really handsome.

Niki is a good teacher. She doesn't just tell me what to do, but asks me what I think we should do next to get the desired results. That helps a lot. I said I wanted to draw another picture—"My Second Drawing"—a very imaginative title, and we sent that one off to the family as well. Niki said it was a big improvement over the first one. It was lots of fun to produce it and I learned more about the various drawing tools at my disposal.

We printed the picture and now it is posted on my fridge. I used to post my grandchildren's artwork on my fridge. Now my granddaughter is posting mine! Isn't life interesting?

Monday, March 10.

Today we checked our mail and answered it. Niki helped me put the picture on the monitor as the "background." Now I'm going to see it daily, but it's actually quite pretty and suits the purpose, sort of like a tablecloth. I don't know how she knows how to do things like this given that she is not used to PCs.

After that we went on the Internet and searched for information on various subjects. I learned that the underlined words with blue type are links that I could click on for more information. We clicked on the Blue Jays since we had been to a ball game that afternoon against the Texas Rangers in which we lost 6-1! Niki has been really inquisitive about alligators in Florida, so we researched that too.

I also found out how to get into the games part of the computer and played a few hands of bridge. My partner was pretty good because we won! Niki also showed me her "home page" that she is working on. It will take people into topics when they click on little drawings like a treble clef (for music), popcorn (for movies), theater masks, and a computer. Her friends will be able to go there and discuss things and she can give her ideas on various things. Sounds like a terrific idea.

Tuesday, March 11.

Today Auntie Anne (a visiting relative) felt sick and since she was sleeping in the room with the computer, our activities were curtailed until evening when she decided to go to the weekly bridge game. We did our e-mail and then we searched the Net for other things. We looked for baby names since both Kathy (my daughter) and Laura (my daughter-in-law) are pregnant. We decided to e-mail information on good names—like their history and meaning, and people with those names—to the respective parties. Niki showed me how to cut and paste this information from the Internet into an e-mail message. Before closing off we checked the Web site of my paper from back home . . . very nice to get information from home instantly into our house down here. Niki also wanted to check up on Leonardo DiCaprio! I guess that's OK. It seems innocent and safe enough, but I wonder what trouble she might get into on the Internet. I've read so much about all the horrible things, but we haven't seen any evidence of that.

Wednesday, March 12.

Today the usual, checking mail and news. I thought it would be interesting to search on our family names. There are lots of Tapscott references (hundreds on Don alone) and we honed in on a Horace Tapscott who is a musician. It turns out that he is black. I wondered how that came about, because I think all Tapscotts are related. We also listened to him talking about himself on the computer. Amazing! I think he must be a very interesting person.

After I played some more bridge—which is really great because on a computer you can have a game even if you haven't rounded up four players as you have to do when not on a computer. Niki looks interested in bridge. Maybe I will teach her when she's really interested and ready! I'd like to return the favor of being a teacher. Niki also signed into the chat group at FreeZone. There are thousands of kids who know each other only from communicating with computers.

Niki goes home tomorrow. I feel more confident that I can figure some things out for myself. I really want to get good at this. It's fun and it's a challenge. I'm so excited that at my age it has been possible for me to experience what these things can do. If I have trouble I know I can always send Niki an e-mail.

The Culture
of Interaction

A new youth culture is emerging, one which involves much more than just the pop culture of music, MTV, and the movies. This is a new culture in the broadest sense, defined as the socially transmitted and shared patterns of behavior, customs, attitudes, and tacit codes, beliefs and values, arts, knowledge, and social forms.[1] This new culture is rooted in the experience of being young and also in being part of the biggest generation ever. But most importantly, it is a culture that is stemming from the N-Gen use of interactive digital media. We should pay attention because the culture which flows from their experiences in cyberspace foreshadows the culture they will create as the leaders of tomorrow in the workplace and society.

N-Gen Communities

With the advent of the Web, millions of children around the world are routinely gathering online to chat, sometimes to discuss a common interest, such as sports or the guitar, but often with no specific purpose to the conversation other than to be with, and interact with, kids their own age. Instead of hanging out at the playground or variety store, or going home to watch TV, more and more kids are logging on to their computer and chatting with their buddies from as far away as the other side of the world and as close as next door.

Virtual communities, according to Howard Rheingold, the inventor of the term, are "social aggregations that emerge from the Net when enough people carry on public discussions enough, with sufficient human feeling, to form webs of personal relationships in cyberspace."[2] In many ways, N-Geners are forming various kinds of communities on the Net. These may involve friends they know from school and their physical world, but increasingly they extend out to others.

Our research indicates that interest in Net-based communications usually starts around age 11 for girls and 13 for boys—basically during adolescence. At these ages, children seek autonomy and the creation of an identity. The Net seems to provide a vehicle to explore the self and for children to establish themselves as independent, self-governing individuals.

Interaction helps kids grow, requiring them to develop values, to exercise judgment, to analyze, to evaluate, to criticize or to come to the aid of another. Interaction encourages self-reliance, although they often call on their cyber friends for emotional support. Girls in particular seem to seek and benefit from the peer support in cyberspace.

Discussions on the Net can be synchronous or asynchronous. *Synchronous* discussions happen in *chat rooms* which are like giant telephone conference calls— whoever is on the line can jump in whenever they want with their views. Instead of speaking, they simply type. They can also just sit back and listen. The interaction is live and immediate, with the conversation going for hours and hours, and people constantly joining and leaving. Some chat rooms have a specific topic and others do not.

Just how prevalent is chatting among N-Geners? Of the 28 percent of American children who had potential Net access at the end of 1997, between 6.7 and 7 million individual N-Geners are characterized as *active users,* or those who participate in Net activities independently. Eighty-five to ninety percent of this population, about 5.9 million N-Geners, were participating in live chat on a regular basis. These industry estimates were reinforced by results of both *Growing Up Digital* forums. And 76.4 percent of respondents to our FreeZone survey responded that their favorite activity on the Net is chatting. However, 100 percent of these kids are regular chatters on the FreeZone site.

Chat is one of the most readily accessible activities for all age groups of N-Geners. In addition to FreeZone, there are dozens of other N-Gen communities online ranging from chat sites operated by individual children's Web pages, to the 18 different chat areas offered to young subscribers on America Online. Two of the best known Web-based sites are the Milwaukee-based KidsCom and Seattle's Headbone Derby. Headbone is a site with a classroom focus where both text features and several online games can be found. Chat opportunities are embedded in the narrative of some games. Headbone estimates it has just under 100,000 registered users.

KidsCom, which has a home-based focus, has over 150,000 active, registered users between the ages of four and fifteen. "The KidsCom Graffiti Walls, where kids can chat live with other children from around the world, are among the most popular areas of our site and have been since we launched in February 1995," says KidsCom Company President Jorian Clarke. "For us so far, chat ranks higher in popularity than even online games and electronic pen pals."

Asynchronous discussion groups are called *bulletin boards* or *forums*. These are more like community bulletin boards. People can post notes that others can read at any time. The participant can post a response to material that's there or start a new discussion on a different topic. Participants can check back whenever it suits them to see what new material has been added.

Toward the end of adolescence, talking just for the sake of talking loses its appeal, and kids gravitate to online forums organized around a topic such as guitar music, chess, basketball, or political issues. This is probably not a developmental issue, but rather something that all users go through, including adults.

Coco Conn, the cofounder of Cityspace, recalls, "When I first got on [chatting] in '92, I was on a pretty funky server [chat group], and I would rush home from work to see who was there and follow the conversation, and talk with people and hang out." She says it was really exciting at first, but eventually, "I found it pretty ungratifying to have random conversations with strangers." She describes it as going down main street every day to see who you meet. Walking into an art gallery and participating in a discussion about an artist who interests you—that is, around a topic—would be different.

The FreeZone Story

The model we chose to explore the issues typical of N-Gen communities is FreeZone, a virtual community of 30,000 N-Geners between the ages of eight and fourteen that is about 55 percent female. Based in Seattle, Washington, FreeZone is a monitored Web site that provides information exchange, chats, and real-time events. FreeZone was started in April 1995 by part-owner Free Range Media, a company that offers Web services for client sites and whose president had an interest in children's education. The site was affiliated with various software products and online services, but when the contracts expired, the site was redesigned.

"We decided to open up FreeZone and renewed the things that were most popular with kids: the chats, the e-pals, the bulletin boards, but we redesigned it so it was less a magazine and more an interactive community," editor Allison Ellis explains. "The chats, e-pals, and bulletin boards are all monitored and screened. In many cases, staff members will host a chat or get a discussion going on the bulletin board—so we're involved that way, but really it's up to the kids to talk about whatever they want."

Virtual communities built by and for N-Geners differ on how much adult monitoring goes on, what kinds of age restrictions are put in place, and what rules are enforced—called Netiquette. The sites are designed to offer parents and teachers reassurance that their N-Geners are participating in a monitored "children's only" site with content controls, such as those offered by America Online, rather than a chat where all age groups are present. Not surprisingly, most of the teenage N-Geners we talked to preferred chat sites where there is no monitoring and no content control.

One day I participated in a live FreeZone chat for an hour and a half with 29 N-Geners, representing at least five different American states and three Canadian provinces. By the end of the session, my head was spinning. It was a challenge to keep up with the children, and as I asked them questions they kept reversing the process to quiz me. This was not to be rude or intentionally disorderly. Rather they were curious about everything to do with the book and my company and the project and my home page and my kids. In doing so, they were inadvertently keeping the exchange mutually beneficial—and as it turns out the forum got top marks from those who participated. In subsequent chats many of them told other kids that they had missed a really interesting experience.

One 14-year-old girl using the handle MELANIEB14 asked: "Don, how would a teen become an author? Did you have to do courses in a college?" BURN asked me: "Is *Growing Up Digital* just gonna be about kids on the Internet, or just basic advanced technology stuff that we deal with?" The community assumption that we were all partners in the information exchange was apparent in how they treated me, not as some distant authority, but like another FreeZoner, an exchange that, on the surface at least, showed healthy skepticism for the traditional adult-child relationship:

VIPER2:	Dude, Don, I didn't know Cyber-Families even existed!
Allison@FreeZone:	VIPER2, please don't call Mr. Tapscott "dude" OK? Let's be polite here.
Don Tapscott:	Allison, my kids call me Dude, so actually I don't mind. (Perhaps Mr. Dude would be better.)

Not all community events on FreeZone are about exchanging information or anonymous socialization. In fact, some events, like the celebration of COOKIE MONSTER's birthday party, transcribed as follows, are collective descriptions of a completely imaginary physical event that is created as it doesn't happen. Amazingly, the following transcription contains many elements of slapstick—physical comedy without the physical. The following is part of COOKIE MONSTER's birthday celebrations.

DAFFODIL:	wHAT EVER GAME WE ARE PLAYING i WILL PLAY
PHEONIX:	OW!!!!!WHO PINNED A DONKEY TAIL ON MY BUTT?
DIONNE:	Here is a cake in your face CM!!!
COOLJ:	hey i made the party!!!! :-) congrats CM
MR.:	I have to go my dog is getting clobbered by my cat *poof!*
COMET-THE-DJ:	*COMET is blindfolded and handed a tail with a VERY sharp pin. She wanders around aimlessly for awhile before coming into contact with something . . . Its MOOSELIPS! COMET has pinned the tail on MOOSELIPS!*
Peter@FreeZone:	This cake is so good!
COURTNEY:	DIGITAL talk to me!!!!!!!!!!!!!!!!!!!!!!!!!!
COOKIE MONSTER:	EVERYONE READ MY 4:44!!!
PHEONIX:	Ew! What's all this moose droppings doing on me? *Washing body*
COOKIE MONSTER:	whoops sorry dioone, that wiould have been me!!
PIRANHA:	*gets the donky right on the butt*
Peter@FreeZone:	MOOSELIPS are you okay?
COMET-THE-DJ:	Hi Pete! You missed an awesome foodfight!
COURTNEY:	My mail DIGITAL are you still here?
KITTEN:	HI COOLJ!!!!!
JOSH:	HEY! MOOSELIPS! Watch Out!
Dena@FreeZone:	PHEONIX, be careful!
COOKIE MONSTER:	PIRANHA is the winner!!do you want the prizi behind dor 1 2 or 3?

DAFFODIL:	i GOT SOME MAIL BUT THE PERSON DID NOT LEAVE THEIRNAME.
Peter@FreeZone:	So I hear, happy birthday CM!!!!
PHEONIX:	Coz, now MOOSELIPS has two tails!
PHEONIX:	*Throwing cake at COOLJ*
KITTEN:	JOSH . . . READ MY 4:43 MESSAGE!!!!
COMET-THE-DJ:	Hi COOLJ!
COMET-THE-DJ:	Whoops! Sorry MOOSELIPS. Hey CM, do I still get a prize? Moose, Donkey, theres not much of a difference!
MOOSELIPS:	Actually that wasn't mine that was yours PHEONIX, you shouldn't do that to yourself, OK, Here are the Food fight rules; (ducking a piece of cake)

1) Throw the cake as hard as you can

   (MOOSELIPS gets one right in the eye)

2) You must stay at least two feet away from the next person, PHEONIX (in other words, nothing too disgusting)

   (MOOSELIPS shoots cake out his nose at COMET)

3) Make sure no one leaves this party until they REEK like PICKLE CAKE!!!

POW!!

(MOOSE gets it right in the lips!)

The beauty (and curse) of the Internet is that you can try, if you want, to be anything or anyone that you please. Step one in this process is creating a nickname or Net handle, which for safety reasons is particularly important for kids. Gender and social stereotypes are often challenged by nicknames. "Our own prejudices come in and we think automatically that someone who's got the FreeZone name of MACHINEHEAD is a guy. Actually, MACHINEHEAD is a girl. CYBERCHICK is also a girl. We have to say sometimes, 'Give me your stats again so I don't call you he instead of she,'" Ellis explains. "They'll come on and say: 'Does anybody want to chat with me?' And then another person will respond and say 'Yes, what are your stats?' They want to know age, gender, a brief description, where you live, what you look like—but it's not always that important. I've never seen race mentioned much. I don't know whether that means all of our kids are white and they assume all the other kids are, or if it doesn't really matter—which is what I'd like to think."

Cyber Families and Friends

There is no community-building without relationship-building. N-Geners build friendships online without regard for physical proximity. "They don't consider themselves strangers after they see each other a couple of times in the chat rooms. Nor would they consider the staff to be strangers," says Ellis. "Little kids have asked me to be their cyber-sister," says Ellis. "When I asked them what that meant, they said: 'Nothing. It just means you have to say 'hi' to me next time we're in the chat room.'"

KEROPPILOVER: I have a couple of cyber-sisters and a cyber-boyfriend. In my eyes, cyber-families last for a long time, because you don't just tell someone, 'I don't like you, so you're not my cyber-sister any more!'

BURN: You start a cyber-family by asking an Internet friend to be, like, in your family. And they last for a long time if you are good friends.

Cyber dating is a light introduction to romantic relationships in N-Gen communities. "You'll see someone say 'Are you a girl? If you're a girl, would you be my C-girl? Are you C-single?' C stands for 'cyber' so as to separate the real-life girlfriend from the cyber girlfriend. It's possible to have several different relationships," explains Ellis. "Cyber dating is fun, you can be as outgoing and crazy as you want, and everyone knows it's just a big joke," FreeZoner KEROPPILOVER says. "Even though you actually do care for each other in a weird kind of way!"

What the FreeZone cyber dating transcripts reveal are not the lurid invitations to engage in cyber sex that adults fear. Instead the transcripts show us that N-Geners are openly playing with the idea of romantic relationships and the idea of themselves as romantic beings. Discussed further in the chapter on play, this experimentation has more to do with adolescence itself than it does with the Internet.

Chat rooms, like other communities, are not free from assertions of power or hierarchy—every exchange presents a drama in group relations: alliances, attacks, acts of diplomacy, and bullying. While children-only sites, such as FreeZone, continually have new entries and graduations, that is, children just get too old for the site,

GREENGOBLIN:	Would anyone like to be the c-girl to a 12/m/green eyed/ brown haired/great sense of humor/goblin guy?
ASZA:	If any one wants to chat, type 34.
CHOW:	WWf-I'll chat with ya?F\12\blue eyes\
GARNET:	Does anyone want to be my c-boy? Please. I'm 13/f.

some unmonitored sites preferred by teenage N-Geners become closed communities. *Closed communities* are formed when a group of regular chatters, through their familiarity with each other, form a family or a clique that new chatters may find impenetrable. This clique simply ignores the new arrival.

Gender Differences in Virtual Communities

Even though traditionally "pink-collar" jobs have been computerized at a greater rate than traditionally blue-collar jobs, computers and the Internet are perceived to be largely male bastions. However, the situation is improving for both girls and women. Between the fall of 1995 and spring of 1997, the male majority on the Internet fell from 66 percent to 58 percent.[3] Among N-Geners the gap may be even narrower. The population of FreeZone is actually 55 percent female, as is coincidentally the population sample of our *Growing Up Digital* forum. We initially approached an equal number of boys and girls, but more girls said yes to our interview requests and the girls were less likely to drop out of the forum as the months went by.

The Internet has made computers much more interesting for girls. Girls' group play is dominated by the pattern of building villages. A computer that can't communicate with other computers lacks the necessary tools for building community, and therefore isn't really seen as a toy or means of having fun.

N-Gen Language

In his well-known book, *Amusing Ourselves to Death,* Neil Postman decries the shift from the text-based communication of Guttenberg's revolution to the visual imagery and oral medium of television. He laments the decline of the "Age of Typography" and the ascendancy of the "Age of Television" as "the most significant American cultural fact of the twentieth century." He, I believe correctly, argues that this change dramatically shifted the content and meaning of public discourse. "As the influence of print wanes," he says, "the content of politics, religion, education, and anything else that comprises public business must change and be recast in terms that are most suitable for television." Postman acknowledges that this view is consistent with Marshall McLuhan's aphorism, "the medium is the message," that is, the best way to understand a culture is to examine its tools for conversation.[4]

The development of human language enabled culture. Recorded symbols introduced a new form of conversation and the codification of history. The alphabet led to many cultural breakthroughs including an enhanced sense of posterity, the emergence of science, and the extension of commerce beyond the village. Plato described how the recording of ideas and views was the beginning of philosophy— requiring not just debate but the scrutiny of ideas. For Postman, "Writing freezes speech and in doing so gives birth to the grammarian, the logician, the rhetorician, the historian, the scientist—all those who must hold language before them so they can see what it means, where it errs and where it is leading."[5]

However, Postman did not anticipate the rise of the digital media in which communication is primarily text-based. He cannot be fairly criticized for this failing in 1985, although many of us at that time were writing, with limited recognition, about the interactive, many-to-many, text-oriented nature of digital communications.[6] But today, his critique, while poignant, is incomplete and badly dated when he laments that humanity is undergoing a "vast and trembling shift from the magic of writing to the magic of electronics."

Rather, humanity is turning back to written language. We are undergoing yet another vast and trembling shift from the magic of television to the magic of the interactive digital media. As with typography, and unlike the broadcast media, communications are recorded—based on the written word. Only this time such communications are many-to-many (unlike the press and TV which are one-to-many). Digital communications are both real time (chat), and nonsimultaneous (e-mail, voice mail, computer conferences, bulletin boards, Web sites); and they extend beyond the eyes and ears to embrace (eventually) all the senses. While N-Geners do have all the world's information at their fingertips, it isn't accessed simply by pointing the mouse over the right link and clicking. It is accessed by choosing the right link to click on from a menu of items in the thousands. Never before has it been more necessary that children learn how to read, write, and think critically. It's not just point and click. It's point, read, think, click. The introduction of multiple media into this environment will not change the importance of the written word as the primary form of discourse—because text offers so many benefits, as previously described. This is certainly the case for the foreseeable future; in the much longer term, as science fiction writer Neal Stephensen describes in the novel *Snow Crash,* there may be text-free cyberspace communities.[7]

> Everyone in FreeZone including me, is always trying to seem smarter than they are.
>
> SPICY97, 12, f
> Christchurch, New Zealand

But the budding N-Gen typist faces a challenge. Highly personal and interactive text-oriented communication lacks all the subtle cues of face-to-face communications or even voice intonation on the telephone. Lacking facial expression, body language, tone of voice, clothing, physical surroundings, and other contextual information, the N-Gen has had to innovate within the limitations of the ASCII keyboard. As a result of this, a new script is emerging with new combinations of characters, new abbreviations, new acronyms, and neologisms to add contextual information, subtleties, and emotion to communications.

In *The Future of the Book,* Italian author, semiotics professor, and critic Umberto Eco said: "I think that in the coming years, passionate love messages will be sent in the form of brief, computer language commands that will be as meaningful as 'I love you' and 'I cannot live without you.'"[8] The task of creating the commands that Eco describes has fallen to N-Geners who seek to have greater control over the connotations their words invoke. They do this by coloring brief, definitive messages with text symbols and abbreviations that refer back to the physical or emotional responses of an unseen writer. In effect, these text symbols act as connotative road signs reducing the number of interpretations a reader can make. Another dimension is added to the relationship between definition and connotation, upon which our understanding of language depends.

Megan's Cyber Smileys

Eleven-year-old Megan Strouse (a.k.a. Bow Wow) is an active FreeZone user. She has developed an interest in collecting *Smileys*—the combinations of ASCII characters that children, and many adults, use to communicate nonverbal information. Smiley development has also become both a dialect and a bit of an art form as Smileys are used as tongue-in-cheek short forms to depict everything from a pointy nose to Marge Simpson. We asked Megan to put together her top Smileys from her collection. To view, rotate the page clockwise 90 degrees.

:-)	Smiling
:-D	Laughing
:-}	Grin
:-(	Sad
:-&	Tongue-tied
:-||	Angry
:-@	Screaming
:-P	Sticking tongue out
;-()	Flirt
:-0	Astonished

8-)	Wide-eyed or glasses
:-I	Apathy
:-o	Shocked or amazed
:-]	Happy sarcasm or smirk
:-[	Sad sarcasm
;-(	Feel like crying
:'-(	Crying
%-)	Happy and confused
%-(	Sad and confused
I==I:I	Abe Lincoln
}:)	Mischievous
:-\	Undecided
:-*	Kiss
:-#	My lips are sealed
}:(	Mad
:\	Nervous
;-)	Wink
8o|>	Guy with goatee or mad dog
>: |o	Eating and dropping crumbs
:>|	Pointy nose
}}}}}} :-)	Big hair
X:)	Little boy with funny 'do'
":o)	Cowlick
d:-D	Baseball hat on
*<{:O})	Santa Claus
(:o{|)	Grandpa or bald man
@@@:)	Marge Simpson
:-#	Face with braces
&: (	Bad hair day
:o[+]	Nice teeth or huge grin
&;o{)	Pretty woman
S87)	Cool dude
&: (~	Drool
# : *	Tasting something sour
d:-D-\-<	Waving bye!
*<S:-D	Party time!

Megan also explains that "there are a lot more Smiley faces than what I've found, so start exploring yourself. Or you can just make up your own, use you imagination! Whatever you do, just have fun! (I sure did.)"

An N-Gen Glossary of Abbreviations

In addition to Smileys, new words, other abbreviations and spellings are emerging.

kewl	cool
*	denotes physical response/action taking place in real space, for example, *wink* *smile* *blush*
jc	just curious
bmf	biting my fingernails
brb	be right back
bbl	be back later
btw	by the way
imho	in my humble opinion
lol	laughing out loud
lmao	laughing my ass off
rotflmao	rolling on the floor laughing my ass off

Netiquette

The most obvious codes of a given culture are its systems of etiquette. These codes are not so much about which fork to eat your salad with as they are codes about how people show respect for one another. On the Internet, a system of tacit codes popularly known as *Netiquette* has evolved. There is a considerable debate about how deeply these rules of Netiquette have penetrated the Internet community since, as many have noted, the medium is impossible to control. However, on the Net, as in society, cultural codes are maintained not through control, but through contract. Members of a culture agree to uphold certain behaviors to maintain their rights. The Internet has come under fire and has been threatened with censorship so often of late that these codes have been embraced faster than they might have without this attention.

In Netiquette, as in etiquette, respect for others translates into respect for other's rights. "This is your site. By logging on to your site I expect to follow the rules you have set. Just like I don't expect to walk into someone's house or a business cursing or causing a disturbance," says 14-year-old Eric Mandela of Rahway, New Jersey. "I feel that your Internet server is like your house or business, or any other place where kids hang out, and it should be run by your rules. You should be allowed to censor anything you want, and if people don't want to follow those rules, they can go somewhere else. If someone is causing a disturbance, you should have the right to ban them. Also, they should have the right to put anything legal they want on their site."

The rights Eric is talking about also come with a sense of responsibility. David Esmay, 10, of Buffalo, New York, wants to be a famous hockey player when he grows up, but if that doesn't work out he says he'll be a Webmaster just like his mom. David is planning to build his own Web page "with lots of sound effects and my stories" as soon as he and his mom get time to sit down and design it. David likes to write ghost stories, but says he will post fairy tales on his Web site. "Little kids might read them and get nightmares," David says of his decision. "That's something I don't want to happen."

N-Geners take Netiquette seriously. At FreeZone, Allison Ellis has noticed that kids are likely to be ostracized by others in the chat group if they are rude. One reason for this emphasis on Netiquette is that N-Geners have an almost hyperawareness of legislation, software, and adult interference that they fear will limit the rights of kids on the Net. The worry that a few bad kids will ruin the Net for everyone is a source of frustration for many N-Geners. "I have encountered MANY kids on [Internet chat] and e-mail that love to destroy everything instead of using it proper-

---

**Participant Rights and Rules for
the *Growing Up Digital* Interactive Forum**

You know the rules of Netiquette or else you wouldn't be here. It all comes down to the golden rule: "Treat other people as you would yourself be treated."
You are entitled to express your opinions.
You are entitled to an audience.
You are expected to learn.
You are expected to teach.
You have a right to disagree.
You have a right to respond.
It is your privilege to change your mind.
It is your privilege to remain silent.

ly," says 13-year-old Mike Uttech of Maple Grove, Minnesota. "When some kids get mad at someone they either ICMP Bomb them, flood them off IRC, or cause many more problems. There should be some way to get these abusive kids off the Net totally. If people do what some of these kids do in real life they will get in trouble with the law. So why should it be any different on the Net?"

The 10 Themes of N-Gen Culture

1. Fierce Independence.

Typical N-Geners have a strong sense of independence and autonomy. This trait is derived largely from the active role they play as information seekers rather than the passive role of information recipients. N-Gen's unprecedented access to information also gives them the power to acquire the knowledge necessary to confront information they feel may not be correct.

The practice they get in constructing their own identities and roles in virtual communities also helps them to assert their personalities when communicating in other social settings. "It takes a really independent person to be able to go against what everyone believes and stand by what they say," says 18-year-old Courtney Angerer of Oakdale, Minnesota. "I think kids being able to express themselves more openly comes from the realization that it's okay not to be a popular airhead."

Independence from institutions and creative autonomy are also reinforced in N-Geners who participate in the creation of this information. After writing for *Spank!*, a popular e-zine based in Calgary, Alberta, 14-year-old Neasa Coll has no interest in working on the newspaper at her high school. "It has everything in it that you'd never get a chance to write about or talk about in a student newspaper," says Coll. "I consider student papers to be quite bland. But definitely not *Spank!*"

2. Emotional and Intellectual Openness.

When N-Geners go online they expose themselves. They will maintain online journals and post their innermost thoughts on a Web page or in a chat room, but then they will warn each other about the dangers of sharing personal information like addresses and telephone numbers with others on the Net. Professor Christine Ward Gailey, a social anthropologist at Northeastern University who has been studying girls and computers for the past 10 years, observes that there is also a paradox rooted in the emotional openness of the Net that enables it to exist. She says, "They want to spill their guts, but they don't want to deal with the repercussions, whether it's meant in terms of the judgments they might face or damage to their reputations." Sometimes such problems are avoided through the anonymity of the Net.

Self-expression is a priority for those who have the means of production.

Home pages contain a mix of links, software downloads, biographical information, artwork, and creative writing, content that blurs the distinction between public and private lives. Not only do N-Geners show their work to a wide audience, but the communication loop makes that work, their lives, and their online identities open to criticism. Fifteen-year-old Reanna Alder found her Web-page guestbook filled with responses from individuals who continually visited and revisited her page to attack her ideas. "I have had people flame me on the Net, and spam my guestbook, and even create a page just to mock me because of things I said on my page (I think mostly they just wanted to pick on someone), and it was hurtful," says Reanna. "It was kinda shocking to be picked on like that, for no real reason (they picked on the fact that I am a feminist, but there are zillions of feminists on the Net!). I exchanged a few e-mails with them and their ISP's, I got rid of my guestbook, and it just stopped."

Even in light of her experiences, Reanna doesn't think Internet communications should be any less personal. "The Internet would be a REALLY boring place if no one revealed any of their personality, or their life," she concludes. "That's what true communication is. It involves vulnerability."

3. Inclusion.

N-Geners are moving toward greater social inclusion with technology, not exclusion. Their art and the international populations of their virtual communities show a global orientation in their search for information, activity, and communication. Thirteen-year-old Lauren Bane of New Zealand says: "I definitely believe that it is a wonderful opportunity to meet new people and sample different cultures." While virtual communities with a global reach are considered important and interesting, N-Geners are quick to point out that it doesn't exclude physical communities. "I love to chat with kids from all over the world," says 13-year-old Leslie Vanbavinckhove of Oostende, Belgium, "but they can't replace my friends from school."

The Internet is encouraging kids to move from a national to a global orientation. "To me, the Internet is a completely different multicultural world where almost everybody gets along," says 17-year-old Michelle Andrews from Victoria, Australia. "We are so far away from other cultures, but I don't feel that way anymore. The Internet has already linked us closely with England, Canada, and the U.S. and we're slowly getting closer to our Asian Neighbors." While N-Geners appreciate the global capabilities of the Internet, they harbor no illusions about universality. They realize that Internet access is a privilege. "Things are different here," says 13-year-old Jade Winsley of the Isle of Man. "Not many children here have computers of their own and especially since telephone charges are so much higher, parents won't let them spend much time online."

Many N-Geners believe that their global awareness will lead to a population that is more tolerant. "When a user joins a chat session, they are not judged based on their looks or skin color, but on their personality. The Internet provides an alternative, a place not of racial issues or prejudice," says 15-year-old Deanna Perry of Florida. "If someone were to make a prejudiced comment in a chat session, several people would probably have a problem with it."

Though it is capable of helping you make new friends all over the world, the Internet can even help build bridges within a family. Fourteen-year-old Emily Smith of Brainerd, Minnesota, is deaf and the Internet has enabled her to communicate with family members who do not know sign language. It has also allowed her to connect with other members of the deaf community who share a common culture based on behaviors created by their deafness and sign language.

4. Free Expression and Strong Views.

The N-Geners we met claim that the Internet has exposed them to a much greater range of ideas, opinions, and arguments than they would have experienced without the Net. Not surprisingly, N-Geners insist this diversity is to their benefit and is a key element of the Internet's appeal and usefulness. They want it to stay that way.

"I know that I am entitled to full access to Internet culture, which includes controversial sites," says Reanna Alder, 15. "If my parents or anyone tried to censor me, I would find a way around it. This is because of the way my parents have raised me. It's already been deeply rooted into my being that I have the freedom and responsibility to educate myself. No one has the right to hide information from me or invade my privacy."

Almost all of the adults we encountered who work with N-Geners commented on how articulate they are as a group, and that the youngsters had views on subjects that seemed advanced for their age. While this is to be expected from the Net-savvy elite demographic group, we can expect that the interactive environment will strengthen verbal ability and the expression of ideas in every group. There is an element of surprise in discovering that the reasoned, adult thoughts you've been reading in a national issues forum, for example, sprang from the mind of a 15-year-old. N-Geners, by and large, don't make assumptions about levels of communication and age. They consider access to information and the expression of opinion to be fundamental rights.

5. Innovation.

N-Geners live and breathe innovation, constantly looking for ways to do things better. According to Howard Rheingold the offline world does not offer opportunities to build your own world, it's already been built for you. "The online world is like an empty canvas," he says.

Currently, software and Web content companies develop children's versions of their products only after they've discovered children are using the original grown-up version. For example, before the development of real-time chat rooms specifically for kids and teens, N-Geners were figuring out how to use bulletin boards, supposedly in a time-delayed format, to conduct chats amongst themselves. It was N-Geners who started key-pal registries located on personal Web pages and administered by the site's owner. It was N-Geners who formed clubs based around the discussion of video game codes and serial storybooks such as *Goosebumps* and *The Babysitter's Club*—long before companies realized the Net was a viable marketing tool.

The N-Gen culture of innovation is often one step ahead of children's Web content producers and software developers. This catch-up includes new commercial investment in the production of electronic magazines, or e-zines, and the design of avatars, digital rooms to house chat and key-pal clubs which, when under adult control, have a tendency to become sponsor-driven. N-Gen is so at ease with the new media and the technology that supports it, it is certain that N-Geners will be the first to accept and participate in these enhanced versions of their own cultural creations. But their ease also ensures that they are moving on to the next activity, independent of whatever tools developers are currently working on.

6. Preoccupation with Maturity.

When children insist upon a certain degree of independence and autonomy, adults have to reevaluate exactly what it means to be a child when that child has been growing up digital. The changing nature of childhood makes itself most obvious when N-Geners are contrasted with the baby boomers who, as a generation, have spent their lives obsessed with being youthful. N-Geners insist that they are more mature than adults expect.

Overall, N-Geners resent the fact that their ideas and activities are often suspect for the sole reason that they are children. This resentment plays a factor in N-Gen's preference for the Net over broadcast technologies. "Since I have connected to the Net I have been watching a lot less television," says Eric Mandela of Rahway, New Jersey. "I also don't like to talk on the phone that much. Whenever I call adults they do not take me seriously. When I am using the computer, no one knows that I'm not an adult. Once I make first impressions, then I can tell them that I am fourteen. I get much more respect."

In return, adults do seem willing to acknowledge that kids who use computers are more mature than those who don't. "Before I started to use the Net, I was the person everyone thought was a ditz," FreeZoner CAFFEINE says. "I started using the Net and learning about computers, and everyone thinks I'm smart now." The

N-Gen emphasis on adhering to the Netiquette codes is the contract among them as a community, to reinforce this belief that N-Geners do not consider themselves mere children.

One child we learned about goes online with a dictionary. She doesn't lie about her age but she knows that spelling errors are a giveaway that you're a kid. Howard Rheingold points out that there isn't a nefarious purpose behind actions like this. "Kids want to be treated as adults by adults and they're not."

7. Investigation.

In N-Gen culture you look under the hood—you investigate.

When it comes to using technology, N-Geners' initial focus is not how it works, but rather how to work it—how to post a message, use a simulation program, query a database. If just being able to use technology satisfied their curiosity, we would have cause for concern. Technology is not value-free. It is important for children to understand the assumptions inherent in software and to feel empowered to change those assumptions. As explained in the last chapter, we've changed our view on the transparency of things. To children, computers are like the air. As adults, we often judge children to be computer-literate because they know how to use computers. This justifiably troubles Sherry Turkle, who, to my knowledge, was the first to explain transparency and opacity as related to computers.

She tells the story of Marsha, who is described by her teachers as computer-literate. Marsha uses a program called SimCity to construct virtual cities and has developed her own personal top 10 list of how things work in cities. One of the rules that she has derived from using the program is that raising taxes leads to riots.

Turkle raises the question, "Is Marsha computer literate or illiterate?" Marsha knows how to use the program but not how the program works. Because Marsha has never programmed a computer or constructed a simulation, she has no conception of "how one might write the program so that increased taxes leads to increased productivity and social harmony." Turkle says: "When you and I were growing up, transparent meant that you could open something up and see inside." If it was transparent you "knew how to act on it and how to change it. Now, transparency means the opposite." Turkle wonders if Marsha is being challenged to think about the underlying assumptions or even political ideas contained in this powerful simulation program.

Turkle is right. We must be vigilant to ensure that we do not change our thinking regarding what it means to understand something. Understanding does not simply mean being able to work it. Surely understanding means more than this—to place something in context; to be able to fathom the values of its creators; to know why it works this way, not just how.

However, the evidence is strong that N-Gen culture contains a strong ethos of curiosity, investigation, and the empowerment to change things. For them, it is not enough to be able to use hot links (linking you to different Web sites), they want to be able to create their own. My son and most of his friends do not accept the assumption inherent in video games that you must pass one level to get on to the next. None of these children are geeks but they all seem to know how to hack (reprogram) games to go to any level they like. The procedures for such hacking are shared among them on the Net, by word of mouth, and in their video game magazines. As SimCity becomes a networked game, Marsha will be sharing her top 10 list and its assumptions with other children who no doubt will challenge it in the spirit of free expression, contrariness, and investigation which seems to be prevalent in N-Gen culture. The likelihood of Marsha accepting the view that raising taxes causes riots and therefore should be avoided in the real world is much less today than previously when her parents may have heard this view from a teacher or on television. Interactivity and person-to-person communication encourages investigation among youth.

8. Immediacy.

I remember as a kid writing a letter to the Mousketeers and waiting for many weeks before I heard back. Interactivity, to the extent that there was any in the broadcast world, occurred at a seemingly glacial pace. In N-Gen culture, for example, when chatting online with their favorite sports or film star, responses are instant.

Compare the trip to the library with an online search. In school libraries and libraries in small municipalities, it may take days or weeks for a book to arrive. Compare the time lapses of a photo sent in an envelope to a pen pal in another country with photos sent by e-mail. Compare the process of searching through various information sources for a college course in the 1960s with hotlinking through readings listed in the online notes prepared by today's professor.

Boomers lived in a slow-motion world compared to the Net Generation. While there are legitimate concerns about the implications on quality of life and stress (discussed later in Chap. 5, "The N-Gen Mind"), the N-Gen world is a real-time world.

For the first few decades of computing, most computer systems were *batch*— taking input in the form of cards, tapes, or terminals and then processing the information to be output on printers or screens. The gap between input and output could be hours—often occurring overnight. The term *real-time* is used to describe computer systems which have instant movement of information from input to output. The human autonomic nervous system is real-time—when you touch a hot stove (input) there is an instant reaction (output). The same is true for the systems which auto-pilot an aircraft.

Movies and television were like batch systems. Today, video games and many other software programs use real-time animation. These may look like video, but rather than being a series of frames which are stored in advance and displayed in rapid sequence, the content is software-controlled and rendered or created on the fly. With real-time animation, a child can fully interact with the moving environment— for example, turning the car to the left or turning to the right to walk up the stairs (all on a screen). Real-time animation enables genuine interactivity, 3D navigation, and photorealism. Similarly we could consider a chat room as a real-time system. Each participant's comments can be immediately posted for everyone to see.

As systems become real-time, and as information moves at light speed, the metabolism of youth culture is accelerating. This does not mean the rise of a generation that seeks immediate gratification as some have charged. As you will read later, this is a cynical view which cannot be justified. Rather, it means that more events occur in an N-Gen minute. The children of the digital age expect things to happen fast, because in their world things *do* happen fast.

9. Sensitivity to Corporate Interest.

The shift from the broadcast to interactive mentality has been one that has involved turning away from media monopolies. N-Geners feel that too many perspectives are being left out of the broadcast images and they believe corporate agendas play a role in this shortfall. However, on the Internet, there has been such a flurry of creation involving so many people working in a home-grown cottage industry, there is an even more intense sensitivity to corporate interests. One of the reasons Microsoft's *Slate* had to delay its plans to charge for access is that people were wary of getting their information from a source where the corporate relationship—in this case, between *Slate* and Microsoft—was not only well known, but so well known it reminded people of the broadcast monopolies.

Now that N-Geners can do what previous generations left to so-called experts, they hold no awe for media technologies or the personalities behind them. What this has translated into is a suspicion of corporate media outlets. "Ninety percent of television, like ninety percent of Microsoft, is evil," one N-Gener told us he believes. "Nobody loves the company owned by the richest man in America."

For many, the problem is not corporations in general, but specific corporate actions on the Net. Howard Rheingold, who developed the concept of the virtual community, believes the sensitivity is really to companies wasting their time or exploiting them. "Heavy-handed promotion is hated. *Spamming* (unsolicited broadcast messages) is extremely hated. People will only give you their attention if you give them value." If you attempt to sell ketchup in a discussion group you'll be "bozo-filtered" (software which cuts you out of the conversation). Having an authentic reason to participate— usually hard to achieve by marketers—is also important. Says Rheingold, "Nobody gets online sincerely to talk about how much they love ACME ketchup. They're obviously bullshitting. People who are obvious shills are not authentic."

10. Authentication and Trust.

Rheingold's comments lead to another theme of N-Gen culture. Because of the anonymity, accessibility, diversity, and ubiquity of the Net, children must continually authenticate what they see or hear on the Web. Many sites provide inaccurate, invalid, or even deceptive information. Fraudulent businesses seek the gullible. Anonymous participants in discussion groups make untrue statements with fewer perceived consequences. Pranksters spread false rumors. Who can the child trust? What sources of information are valid? Authentication of everything is required to establish trust.

The power of rumor is only as strong as the desire for easy answers. Immediately after writing the line you have just read, I had a momentary case of writer's block. So, I checked my e-mail and waiting for me was this message:

> Little Jessica Mydek is seven years old and is suffering from an acute and very rare case of cerebral carcinoma. Her condition causes severe malignant brain tumors and is a terminal illness. The doctors have given her six months to live. As part of her dying wish, she wanted to start a chain letter to inform people of this condition and to send people the message to live life to the fullest and enjoy every moment, a chance she will never have. Furthermore, the American Cancer Society and several corporate sponsors have agreed to donate three cents toward continuing cancer research for every new person that gets forwarded this message. Please give Jessica and all cancer victims a chance. If there are any questions, send them to the American Cancer Society at ACS@AOL.COM.

It was the third time since I started studying N-Geners in their natural habitat that I had received this particular chain-letter hoax. When the awe of just how much can be accomplished by the pushing of buttons is still fresh, it shouldn't come as any surprise that newbies (those who are new to the Internet) believe major fund-raising drives could be achieved by sending e-mail around the world.

"If you meet someone in a chat room, I think it's almost impossible to decide if what you're reading about someone is true," says 14-year-old Neasa Coll. "After all, how many of us haven't lied to others on the Internet? I don't think there's ever a way to tell for sure whether someone you know only over the Internet is lying or not. However, after years of a relationship, there should be a certain trust built up between each person, and lies should not be needed." And, on the Internet, there is always a

Say someone e-mails you saying a virus is on the Net. E-mail them, ask them if there's any Web pages, newsgroups, etc., you can go to to find out more. Contact your ISP, see if they know anything about it. Basically do all you can to look into its background.

KELLY RICHARDS, 15
Alberta

way to verify the facts, even if it takes deception. "There's really no way you can be sure, but just studying how they talk to you, and others, maybe observe them on different occasions," says 16-year-old Darla Crewe, "is revealing. Maybe even come in using a different alias yourself."

Some chat room veterans insist that after a while the truth is the easy way out. "It's so hard to remember what you've told one person and what you've told another," says 17-year-old Lauren Verity. "Besides, most of the people I chat with have home pages with their photos on them, so everyone's going to find out what you look like eventually."

Pretending to be someone you're not is easy on the Internet, and there is a huge range in the types of incidents that can occur when your N-Gener adopts other persona. Many adolescents exaggerate their age when they are in chat rooms. Some of them do it only occasionally when they are using a secondary alias, some of them do it all the time. One 11-year-old boy in our forum said: "With everybody sharing information, it's not easy to tell who's who! If you're 14, and you're having a conversation with another Doom fan, or you know, you could be talking to a 50-year-old who likes those kinds of games! Or, a 10-year-old might say the right things to make a 40-year-old have a crush on him! This last one actually happened to me! I was in a chat room and a 40-year-old seemingly liked me! She sent electronic kisses to a person who she thought was someone her own age! I, to this day, have not told her my true identity!"

If you are using the Net as a research tool for a class assignment, then in your bibliography you include the URL and other info about the site and the teacher can look it up if they don't believe you. I have had this happen to me before and I asked to go to the media center and showed them my Internet pass (we need one to be able to use the Net for anything at school), and printed out the page and then showed it to the teacher. It works most of the time.

MIKE UTTECH, 13

"My kids and I talk about the legitimacy of sources all the time," says teacher Kathy Yamashita. "They know that information about paintings from the Louvre is more legitimate than, say, The Personal Picasso Page from someone we know only as Frank from Florida." Vinton Cerf, one of the pioneers of the Internet, agrees that as traditional sources of information come online in greater numbers, authenticity is easier to gauge. "In fact," Cerf says, "we've already seen many mainstream media outlets migrate to the Web and take the credibility they earned there with them."

Consider the source is already almost a mantra among N-Geners who get much of their learning materials from the Web. Among the things they look at are writing styles and production values. "I usually can tell by the way they put things or say things," says 10-year-old Colleen Kirchharr. "I also check the URL, since quite often there may be a directory labeled 'rumors' or some other," says 11-year-old Rufo Sanchez. "Then, if that doesn't work, I'll always turn to one of the search engines. If there's something out there that I need to know about, well, they'll usually turn it up for me."

Authentication leads to trust—the *sine qua non* of N-Gen culture. Trust is an indispensable condition for virtual communities. It is established when a child has a persistent identity online and participates in regular interaction. Trust is not the same as liking someone. BREEZY may not like CYBERCHICK but he trusts her because she has established an identity over a period of time. He has come to believe in her—that she is a person with an identity and who accepts the rules of N-Gen culture. He may grow to like her, enjoy her virtual company, and have fun talking with her and seeking her advice. They may share common beliefs and co-organize a boycott, create some software, or arrange through their parents to meet each other and fall in love.

Similarly, the child that authenticates and uses a service or information source over time grows to trust it. The e-mail system is trusted because it works, is reliable, and delivers value. A search engine is trusted because it is authenticated through personal use and word of mouth among other kids. An environment like FreeZone is trusted because it is safe, moderated, persistent, and fun.

Awareness of the needs for authentication and skills for verifying and establishing trusting relationships and trustworthy sources will serve N-Geners well in later life. Much of their learning and work will be online. More important, in an increasingly complex and uncertain world, these abilities will be valuable as the culture of interaction becomes the dominant culture.

From the *Growing Up Digital* Forum

AP2:   Is the Internet changing the nature of childhood or are children changing the nature of the Internet? I think both. I grew up with the computer. I've used the computer ever since I was three. I knew DOS at four or five. When we got a modem, I got CompuServe. I've grown up with the Net and I definitely wouldn't be the person I am without the Net. I also change the Net: I have my own Web page. (Adam Peretz, 11)

AL2: I think that it is a bit of both. Kids are one of the driving forces of the Internet, because of our incredible abilities to adapt. If the Internet had come along 20 years down the road, I don't think that I would adapt to it as quickly as I did. Also, the Internet is changing kids in many ways. Penpals are written to through e-mail. Homework assignments are passed around through file attachments. The telephone is growing old because it requires synchronous communication (both people have to be on the line at the same time), whereas e-mail is asynchronous. (Austin Locke, 15)

NC1: This revolution doesn't go one way. The Internet is changing the nature of childhood, but children are also changing the nature of the Internet. As much as us kids like to take credit for great feats, we did not design and create the Internet. However, we do affect it. Look at all the "green-light" "red-light" search engines which censor us from unacceptable material. There are so many great sites out there that are geared toward kids, we have had a huge impact on the Internet. The Internet is also impacting kids, however. Hardly anyone goes to the library anymore for school research—you can get much more up-to-date information on the Internet, so why pass the chance up? Kids today are growing up with the Internet, and the Internet is growing up with kids. (Neasa Coll, 14)

JP: I think that the Internet has a major influence on the kids of the world. The Internet and the kids of today are the future so the kids need to know what they are doing for their future. The Internet will be an important part of our future so we need to understand the Net. (John Perry-Pool, 12)

The Media Defines the Culture

At the heart of N-Gen culture is interactivity. Children today increasingly are participants not viewers. They are incited to discourse.

What do you do during TV commercials? Do you watch the commercial; jump to another channel; hit the mute button; or leave the room? Researchers have found that everyone from preschoolers to adults show decreased attention to station breaks.[9] It explains why commercials are now broadcast at much higher volume than the programs.

As noted earlier, television audiences are becoming smaller and more discriminating. Today's young television audiences are more than just uppity—one might go so far as to say that N-Geners are refusing to be reduced to spectator status. It is not television, specifically, that is coming under attack, but rather, the nature of broadcast culture itself.

Broadcast technology, like television, is hierarchical. It depends upon a top-down distribution system. Someone somewhere decides what will be broadcast and our role in this is limited to what we choose or do not choose to watch. There is no direct feedback from the viewer to the broadcaster. Nor is there any direct interaction between viewers unless they are sitting on a couch in the same living room. In TV culture, viewers have no real power, except to channel surf.

Where N-Geners do find power is on the Internet because it depends upon a distributed, or shared, delivery system rather than a hierarchical one. This distributed, or shared, power is at the heart of the culture of interaction.

The late French post-modernist Michel Foucault developed a model for the diffusion of ideas that he called the "Web of Power." Foucault believed that the "incitement to discourse," or the start of discussion about a particular subject, leads to increased knowledge on that subject, which leads to increased power. Power comes from any given person who starts a discussion. The discussion forms a web outward to the discussion group, weaves its way out from there through other conversations, and sometimes even returns along the same or new paths to where it started. The lines of the web branch out in every direction, but they also branch inward. Communication is possible in every direction. Though Foucault died before the World Wide Web was born, his Web of Power model elegantly captures the N-Gen culture of interaction. Users of the Internet, participants in the culture of interaction, gain knowledge and power through their interaction with other users. The interactive culture of the Internet is nonhierarchical and is not distributed; it is a real "Web of Power." All participants can have their own home pages, their own e-mail addresses, their own

> I think it's [TV] too predictable to make time for. The shows change but the situations stay the same. They're fake. I like the Internet more because it's a form of communication, a way to socialize and make new friends all over the world. It's a way to educate yourself about the things that interest you.
>
> DARLA CREWE, 16
> Nova Scotia

interactive identity or identities. On the Internet, everyone is a producer of culture, everyone is a participant. The purpose of the Internet is communication. The feedback loop from user to user is continuous. It is initiated and maintained not by the support technology, but by people. The communication of information is contextualized by relationships between individuals, the communities these individuals create, and, ultimately, the culture they sustain. N-Gen activities suggest that they are creating and sustaining an Internet culture based on the principle of interaction.

Means of Transmission and Social Transmission

All forms of communication technologies including letter writing, the printing press, the telegraph, telephone, radio, television, and the mainframe computer are concerned with transmission of information. In many ways, the Internet is the first interactive means of social transmission since the village storyteller in that both the storyteller and the story (i.e., both the information and its source) are present to all members of the tribe and subject to collective scrutiny.

Narrative interaction is epitomized by the figure of the traditional storyteller. Still prominent in many Native North American and Southern African cultures, the storyteller is a member of a circle. The history of interaction in narrative media is one of distance between storyteller and audience: a break in the circle. Troupes of players and musicians moved from performances in the village square on market day to fully enclosed theaters that were to become more and more elaborate, until performers found other homes in studios and on sound stages.

It isn't just performance arts that have seen the space between their stories and their audiences widen. Distance also came to have a symbolic function. The Celtic Druid performed his rituals in the fields; the Roman Catholic priest performs his on a raised platform behind an altar. The politician, a representative of the people, stood on a soapbox to rise above those who would cast their votes. The curtain was drawn over members of midway freak shows and drawn aside only for those who paid to gawk. Interaction in media has come full circle with the advent of the Internet. As spatial distance becomes more irrelevant through advances in communication technologies, the impact of symbolic distance is weakened.

Of course, old media (letter writing, the telegraph, and the telephone) can be considered interactive, but these are closed dialogue systems. In a telephone conversation or in an exchange of letters, participation is defined by the relationship between the individuals at each end—the information is not meant to be shared outside that exchange. In other words, these are means of private, rather than social, communication. In many ways, this history explains the personal nature of so much Internet content such as individual home pages and online journals. They are written with the intimacy of one-to-one in a medium that is many-to-many.

As broadcast technologies, television, cinema, and radio communicate information through dictation, not dialogue. Unlike closed dialogue systems, broadcast technologies are open or public systems; but what they are open to is reception rather than interaction. Viewers and listeners have a relationship, not with each other, but with the information itself. When the broadcast technologies became the common way of delivering public information, broadcast became the primary means of social transmission.

In the case of television, the values it transmits are those of the postwar period of its infancy. Television's program formulae depend upon an audience of people who believe that they are members of a growing middle-class who will gain greater and greater prosperity through a combination of technological progress, increased levels of educational attainment, and hard work. Needless to say, the monocultural behaviors reproduced and transmitted by the broadcast media became inconsistent with the outcomes of the existing cultural, economic, religious, and social systems. Increasingly, throughout the 1980s, poverty, race, health, and gender played a role in the dissatisfaction with the broadcast formulae. Culturally, our sense of what were known and unknown outcomes was thrown into question, partly by the rise of the digital media.

These rising elements that either support or challenge the established media formulae are known as *paradigms*.

This does not mean that TV is a completely passive activity. Social psychologist Sherry Turkle says we may have underestimated the active, cognitive, emotional activity going on during television watching. "There is a lot more going on in people's heads as they are manipulating that material than we have traditionally given them credit for," she says. "People are interactive [watching TV] in that they are constructing or deconstructing narratives in their minds." She adds that "there is a lot more passivity in the way kids are learning from computer interaction. Just because they are interacting with a computer doesn't mean they are building and making something of their own."

Nevertheless, there is significant dissatisfaction with the broadcast paradigm—and this is concentrated among young people. The cultural products N-Geners are producing for distribution over the Net are part of an evolutionary process. This process has gradually evolved toward a model of increased interactivity in producing the means of social transmission that speaks to all society. In other words, N-Geners think broadcast TV leaves too much unsaid.

All of this is changing as television becomes part of the digital media. The equivalent of millions of TV channels will create wide cultural variety, changing the monocultural orientation of TV. The addition of interactivity to TV will enable viewers to become users—for example, during a talk show, being able to ask questions, vote, give opinions, ask for background information, or dig deeper on a topic.

Zines, Video Zines, and E-zines

I agree with Brian Goldfarb, the curator of education at New York's New Museum of Contemporary Art, when he says that, "no other generation has been more thoroughly schooled in media culture and the use of media technology as a means of expression than today's youth."[10] Young people are employing everything from photocopiers, video cameras, computers, and the Internet to further their media creations.

The best-known of these youth media creations is the *zine*—self-published labors of love containing journalistic and creative writing, band profiles, comics, and manifestos, often in the form of parodies. Zines provide a hint of what you would read in school newspapers if there were no staff advisor. Zines are distributed by mail and through mini trade shows where the independent producers gather to trade, sell, and network their publications. Increasingly, zines are also distributed over the Net with aficionados offering reviews, descriptions, and buyer contact information on their personal home pages.

Video zines are also becoming increasingly widespread as camcorders and editing software become more available to individuals and as the Internet becomes an accessible channel for commercial distribution. Video zines, unlike zines, are not the sole property of young people, but the medium was first developed by students working with equipment available in schools and community organizations.

"What a fantastic time to be alive with the means of production," says Nix Picasso, 43, former VJ for the British pop-video show *Riverside*. "It just means that you can go out with your camera without going through the hassle of getting a commission and shoot a wonderful program with zero budget." Picasso has done exactly that with the production of *D-Program,* a video magazine "devoted to giving a platform to people with dangerous and very sane ideas that are threatening the status quo."

The first video zine to have widespread distribution in North America and Europe is often reported to be Channel Zero, a media outlet in Toronto originally run by a group of people in their 20s. The goal of Channel Zero was to not only confront the exclusive nature of broadcast programming, but to take back ownership of the medium and make inclusive TV for the global village.

The premier issue, *Planet Street,* featured profiles of two Parisian gigolos, a shoe-shine technician-philosopher from Belize (who also happened to be a crack addict), and a schoolboy named Hope living in the new South Africa. The goal in presenting these news stories was to put the human back in human interest. In other words, the subjects talk about their lives rather than their issues. In response to the question "Do you have different races at your school?" Hope replied, "Yes, running races, swimming races, all kinds of races."

According to Channel Zero founder Stephen Marshall, 28, "Vid mags represent a new form of television . . . one that is free of commercial interference." Channel Zero launched a Web site that it hoped would be more than just a promotional tool to sell the channel's videos. "Baby boomers sell each other stuff," Marshall says. "We're trying to sell ideology."

"What I'm saying is that broadcast news is totally finished. You have to go play by play," says Marshall. "If you can't take me through an event that happens in that day, and put it in the context of history, the context of the day and the context of the future of the day—the future of our history, then you won't have hit me. That's what news has to do and CNN isn't doing it."

Video zines are distributed via videocassette, since the Internet currently lacks the physical capacity to bring full-color, full-motion video to every user. It's coming— perhaps not tomorrow, but soon. In the interim, the most effective use of the Internet is for *e-zines,* or electronic magazines. The Net allows the zine to be interactive; real-time chat forums and bulletin-board sites accompany articles and youth readers can discuss the issues raised in the articles or raise topics independent of posted content.

The first youth culture online magazine by and for young people is *Spank!* Robin Thompson is the cofounder and publisher of *Spank!,* and she sold her car to fund the venture that now boasts readers and writers from five continents. After only eight issues, the magazine was drawing 80,000 readers (from over 250,000 hits) a month. Those are modest numbers when one considers that traditional teen print magazine *Seventeen* has a circulation of over 2 million worldwide, but e-zines like *Spank!* have overhead costs of less than $1000 per monthly issue. Initial costs to create the site can be considerable but the overhead costs at *Spank!* will not rise appreciably with increases in readership.

Each issue of *Spank!* generates hundreds of reader responses in the form of formal e-mail messages which are posted like letters to the editor on the site. These "Random Taggings" are like instantaneous responses on a bulletin board that others can read immediately after they are sent. In addition, *Spank!* received 2400 inquiries and submissions from would-be contributors in its first eight months. These contributors are paid one cent per word. Most contributors are between the ages of 13 and 20, members of the same age group the zine is targeting. The type of content is different, too. "I think most teen magazines aren't giving teens the credit for being as intelligent as they are," says Thompson. "There's no point in us doing that typical stuff because other people are doing it and they're doing a good job. I personally think it's moronic, but you know they're aimed at white, middle-class American girls and we're trying to reach a broader audience than that."

There is no novelty surrounding *Spank!* because it is online rather than in print. N-Gen's see no mystique shrouding computers and, in their view, no expertise is required for Internet access. "*Spank!* readers aren't computer weenies," Thompson states. "Computer weenies are completely thrilled with the Internet itself. It's a big, complicated toy to them. Most of our readers are more concerned with using the Internet as a tool to talk to other people, it's not a huge toy thing to them."

The introduction of youth zines to the Internet is a quantum leap forward in the democratization of the media for kids. There have always been some media that looked at the world through youthful eyes, such as campus newspapers and student radio, but in the overall media scheme these were insignificant. Their audiences were minuscule and the people who worked on the papers and radio stations were young adults, not adolescents.

Spank! represents another league altogether. Its distribution is worldwide. Its production costs are virtually zero, meaning that very soon there will be thousands of other *Spank!*alikes, as more and more kids catch on to how accessible the Internet medium really is. The costs of production will be so low that many of these zines will simply be labors of love. The producers won't care whether they have advertisers. These *Spank!*alikes will soon include audio and then full-color, full-motion video as the capacity of the Net grows.

The study of various forms of zines helps illustrate a continuum in the development of the interactive arts that can be applied to the study of other cultural universals. The formula that is refined through the development from zine to video zine to e-zine is one that expands the initial concern of media information delivery until it includes activity on the part of the consumer and provides the opportunity for communication. All the artistic endeavors involve breaking down the mystique of expertise in terms of creation, technical execution, and distribution of the product; breaking down professional hierarchies; and increasing the number of people active in cultural creation. Zines challenge the one-to-many dictates of conventional print media by parodying the relationship between editorial and advertising content. Video zines challenge the influence of broadcast monopolies by applying a demographically specific aesthetic and providing a context for replay on the Internet. The electronic zine provides information through articles, accepts feedback and original submissions that turn readers into authors, and provides the communicative opportunity that strengthens the feedback loop.

Overall, they provide a portrait of the culture of interaction—the antithesis of broadcast culture. This N-Gen culture foreshadows the new culture of work, consumption, and social life and it is leading to a change in the psychology of young people—the topic of the next two chapters.

The N-Gen Mind
Part I

Do N-Gen children think differently? Do their experiences with the interactive media affect their minds—their personality, their self-esteem, concept of self, intelligence, and the way they process information—for the better? Many pundits say no. Robert Bly, author of *The Sibling Society,* asserts that "we are lying to ourselves about the renaissance the computer will bring. It will bring nothing. What it means is that the neocortex is finally eating itself."

Bly's views do not coincide with our experiences. The N-Geners with whom we had ongoing contact while researching this book gave us no indication that their thinking was impaired. To the contrary.

Overall, these kids seem to be different from the TV generation in a number of ways. And the trends emerging are good news for children and for society. They are alert, aware, focused, and certainly in control. What most working parents wouldn't give to embody these contemporary virtues seldom seen in the daily whirlwind of unpaid overtime, sleep deprivation, and never-ending household chores. The irony of the situation is that the kids of stressed-out parents sit in front of a PC and become the perfect portrait of these four virtues and it suits them as much as *The Thinker's* pose suits the Rodin sculpture.

Of course, it is impossible to know to what extent the psychological characteristics of this generation are affected by their experience in the interactive world. There are many other variables beyond the depth of their exposure to the new technology. For example, a large proportion of the baby boom has devoted considerable attention to effective child rearing and their children's education. For many other children there has been little parental involvement. As with any generation there is also wide variation within it because of the differences which distinguish us all, such as ethnicity, attitudes, personality, intelligence, knowledge, socioeconomic strata, and age.

However, by examining the behavior and views of a cross section of children who are advanced users of the Internet, some directions begin to emerge. We met a wide variety of kids from many different backgrounds who together covered all these variables. We communicated with kids from community computing centers in the inner city through to private schools in affluent neighborhoods. From these children, the contours of how the new media may be affecting the N-Gen mind are emerging with clarity.

Three Impressions of N-Gen Personality

From working with these children, several initial impressions emerge.

1. Acceptance of diversity.

N-Geners appear extraordinarily tolerant in many areas. Yes, as the now famous *New Yorker* cartoon noted: "On the Internet, nobody knows you're a dog." It may also be that nobody knows if you're black or white, tall or short, rich or poor, able or disabled, attractive or a geek—and, in some cases, whether you're real or a bot (a computer program with humanoid characteristics). Children regularly take on the personas of others or avatars. You may be someone else or something else like a cartoon character or an inanimate object. The fact that you're communicating with a toaster is not important—it's what the toaster has to say. Antiappliance prejudices are about as prevalent in kids' online forums as are antiblack prejudices—that is, virtually nonexistent.

2. A curious generation.

Every generation shows curiosity. Childhood is all about exploration, discovery, and investigation. Many TV generation kids have turned over a rock looking for bugs, run through a rain shower to see what it would feel like; or climbed over the fence into a forbidden backyard to see if the evil grinch really lived there. But there is something about the shift in control from the broadcast world to the interactive world that elicits intensely heightened curiosity. Basically, children have a new world to explore. This virtual world contains much of the world's knowledge, millions of their peers, countless virtual places to discover, and thrilling, enchanting, and bizarre new experiences unimaginable when the TV generation was growing up. As virtual reality and artificial intelligence mature, this new world will continue to beckon with more allure.

3. Assertiveness and self-reliance.

Access to the media enables children to assert themselves more than any previous generation. FreeZone moderator Allison Ellis describes it as "a generation that is always sticking up for themselves—taking what is theirs." Even though the FreeZone site is monitored, the children view it as their site and they are adamant that it should not "be taken over by adults." In one instance, a girl was opposed to cyber dating—and she thought the FreeZone moderator was encouraging it. The girl was worried that this would destroy the FreeZone world. To organize against the moderator and to gain support for her point of view, she created a home page and advertised it to others. This was the digital equivalent of the 1960s petition (other kids were asked to sign it), protest leaflet (explaining the issue and the evidence citing the moderator as the promoter of cyber dating), demonstration (a show of popular support), and a 1960s "be-in" (where others discussed the issue and expressed their militancy in the chat room itself). The moderator was forced to come forward and explain her position—that she wasn't promoting cyber dating, trying to wreck the FreeZone world, or take over the kids' world.

According to *Growing Up Digital* researcher Kate Baggott, "They begin to develop self-reliance at an early age: they can find what they want and what they need quickly, easily, and honestly. Many express that they don't feel they need protection on the Net from anyone or anything." There is evidence from chat rooms that they prefer to discuss problems among themselves rather than with their parents, but will find support—not advice—among their peers on the Net. There may be cause for concern here. Developmental psychologist Joan Grusec believes that "society already has enough problems caused by reduced parental influence, lack of reasonable respect for authority, competing values from peers, the community, and TV." For her, the independence encouraged by the Net has a dark side.

It is not clear the extent to which independence means rejection of parental influence. Because of a high degree of confidence and a new openness encouraged by some parents, educators, youth workers, and even religious leaders, N-Geners are more likely to raise controversial subjects with their parents and other adults. Kids bring home condoms given to them at junior high school. My family has frequent discussions about issues that would have been unthinkable when I was growing up. This phenomenon can be better understood by looking at other aspects of the N-Gen mind.

A Contrarian Generation

Other aspects of the N-Gen mind are clearer to understand and explain. To begin, this is a contrarian generation.

Because they have the tools to question, challenge, and disagree, these kids are becoming a generation of critical thinkers. I can think of nothing more singularly important to the future of humanity.

They accept little at face value, probably because there is a medium to challenge things. Unlike the TV generation which had no viable means to interact with media content, the N-Generation has the tools to challenge ideas, people, statements—anything. These youth love to argue and debate. They can instantly comment on any information they find with the click of a mouse (blast off a message to the Webmaster on any site). And they are constantly required to make a case for something. They must then rely on their point of view, test it, and alter it if appropriate.

As the schools transform themselves for relevance, they are also learning to think critically there as well. (More on this in Chap. 7, "N-Gen Learning.")

How different from my memories of the 1950s and early 1960s. If kids' hero Captain Kangaroo said it, it must be true—and there was certainly no way to ask Mr. Green Jeans a question. If you didn't like Topo Gigio on *Ed Sullivan,* that was tough luck. Challenge something at school and we got the strap or stood in a corner. Even in the height of the youth radicalization of the 1960s, options for critique were limited. You could march in the autumn antiwar demonstration. You could write a letter to the editor or occupy the president's office at the university. But one overriding fact persisted: the main communications media of the time were unidirectional—the print and broadcast media. Communications came from the top down. Communicating through the media was something, in large part, done *to* you not *by* you.

This new media provides a platform for millions of youth to argue, worldwide and in real-time, on chat lines or at different times through online forums or bulletin boards.

"They never asked what we thought about censorship, but we're going to tell them anyway." That's the rallying cry of Peacefire, an Internet-based anticensorship organization founded by and for youth. To gain full membership in Peacefire you must be under 21 years old, although really old people—those 22 and over—can be associate members. Peacefire was founded in August 1996 to "represent students' interests in the debate over freedom of speech on the Internet." Translation: "There were very few people in mid-1996 speaking out against installing Cybersitter-type software on every school terminal in America." Setting aside for a moment the legitimate concerns of parents and educators about children accessing inappropriate information on the Net, Peacefire is evidence of the contrary character of the N-Gen. The organization operates the *Cyber Rights and Digital Libraries Encyclopedia* (CRADLE); designs Web pages in exchange for a $10 per hour donation to the legal fund for the lawsuit against New York State and the Communications Decency Act; provides information about blocking software; and runs newsgroups for the discussion of issues related to under-18s and their cyber rights. (Incidentally, children whose computers have the Internet-blocking software Cybersitter installed cannot access Peacefire's Web site.)

Solid Oak software, makers of Cybersitter, found out just how contrarian this generation can be. Bennett Haselton, an 18-year-old Vanderbilt University student and cofounder of Peacefire, installed Cybersitter on his home computer and kept track of which sites it blocked. Many blocking software producers do not list the sites their systems block access to, and Haselton was surprised that sites for the National Organization for Women and the Jewish Bulletin of Southern California were among those which Cybersitter censored. Acting out of the conviction that free speech "is not harmful to those under 18," Haselton contacted the company and asked why the sites were blocked. The company did not respond until Haselton took his questions to the media. Soon afterward, the student found himself threatened with a lawsuit by Solid Oak.

"Their main concern was that they thought I had broken their codes to find out what sites were blocked, which I didn't, and [Solid Oak] thought that was illegal," Haselton says. "They were also worried that I would take their site list and post it on the Internet because I had broken the code on their whole file."

The resulting media attention has affected Solid Oak and it has proven that companies run by mature adults can be as contrary as N-Geners. "Get a life! Go hang out at the mall with the other kids or something," it e-mailed Peacefire. The company recently posted an employee-of-the-month spoof on its Web site featuring a photograph of a monkey called Bennie Weasleton. "Bennie is a young intern in our PR department," the site reads. "His tireless efforts over the past few months have resulted in a significant increase in sales revenue."

How much of an effect can 400 contrarian teenagers have on the sales revenues of a software company? At least one of Cybersitter's competitors is very interested in this answer and is watching the controversy closely. Recently, Haselton was surprised to find the name of the president of NetNanny added to Peacefire's associate membership list.

The Cybersitter controversy is not the issue foremost in Haselton's mind. "Certainly it's true that if they hadn't done this, there would be a lot fewer visitors to our site. But as an organization that's trying to gain credibility for action," Haselton says, "we can't exist forever as the people who became famous because some big company tried to push them around."

Haselton and Peacefire's 400 teen members have a lot of work yet to do. There are Web pages to design and legal bills to pay. Peacefire is named among the 15 plaintiffs in the suit brought against the state of New York and its implementation of the Communications Decency Act.

The new media also provides an environment where millions can check facts, recall previous statements, and investigate implications. At their fingertips, children have access to the historical repository of human knowledge and increasingly the tools (agents, bots) to find what they need.

This contrariness has huge implications for everyone. For example, business will need to rethink how to conduct public relations to an interactive world of N-Geners. Public relations experts James Barr and Theodore Barr describe the new realities of cyberspace marketing in which information is shared and sifted by thousands of knowledgeable people. They note that time is collapsed, facts are quickly checked, loss of credibility can be instantaneous, second chances are rare and harder to obtain, grandstand plays better be perfect, and the playing of one audience against another is far easier to detect.[1] The old approaches of broadcasting messages and publishing press releases will be inadequate. More on this in Chap. 9, "N-Gen As Consumers."

Self-Esteem

A 7-year-old girl is in a public hospital room because she has a rare skin disorder that causes her to have scabs all over her body. The first time she logs on to Ability On-Line on her computer, she posts a message that expresses some of her interests and an admission that she has only one real friend because other kids are scared of her. Within seconds a response tells her that she has just made a lot more friends.

Since September 1991, Arlette LeFevre—"Dr. Froggy" as her patients call the French-accented head of psychiatry at Toronto's Hospital for Sick Children—has been connecting children to Ability On-Line. Members telnet to Ability On-Line from across Canada and around the world. There are now over 7500 young people with disabilities or chronic illnesses communicating with one another and adult mentors through over 300 online conferences held on the BBS (bulletin board service). Adults who have "been there and done that" encourage children who, because of the physical and social barriers they face, often feel isolated from their peers at school that their futures are limited and that their lives are less meaningful because of their disabilities.

Fourteen-year-old Sarah Evans doesn't feel that way. For the past four years she has been using Ability On-Line. As host of the service's cerebral palsy conference, she has come to know just what digital media means to kids who have disabilities. While in the hospital four years ago, Sarah, who has cerebral palsy, was given a

Commodore 64, which even then was considered a fossil from the early age of home computing. If anything, Sarah's story proves that technology doesn't have to be cutting edge in order to serve a purpose. Sarah says her first computer didn't give her confidence, but it gave her the opportunity to express her confidence.

The Commodore 64 opened the door to both increased communication and independence. First, it connected her to Ability On-Line and a virtual community of people who understood exactly what social and physical barriers she encountered at school and elsewhere because of her CP. "It helps kids get to know people," Sarah says. "Sometimes people don't want to take the time to get to know you. I still have that problem, but not online. I have many friends on the BBS who I've never met in person. I don't know what they look like and I don't need to know. It just doesn't matter."

Sarah says it is physically easier for her to communicate through keyboarding and easier for others to understand than her speech because "people just don't usually want to take the time to try to understand."

"It's even more important for kids with disabilities to have computers to help them get their work done," Sarah says. "Even if there's someone to write it down for them, it's still not really their work. A computer helps me make sure my work is mine." Sarah used the old Commodore 64 to write her first book at the age of 10!

In the 1930s, sociologist G. H. Mead described "the self" as a blend of how we think different important people in our lives view us—what they think of us.[2] He called this the "generalized other." The self develops when children can imagine what others are thinking about them and realize the meaning of actions taken by others toward them. If a child imagines that others view him or her in disregard, low self-esteem can result. When a disabled girl sees others acting as if she were a freak, or worse, calling her a freak, her self-esteem is lowered. Conversely, when she is online and she imagines that others think she is interesting, her self-esteem is strengthened.

Psychologists refer to different types of self-esteem in child development. *Social self-esteem* refers to the child's relationship with parents, siblings, and peers. *Academic self-esteem* becomes a factor on entering school and the child receives feedback about him- or herself in relation to other classmates. *Physical self-esteem* refers to physical appearance and abilities. In cases of physical disabilities, social self-esteem and physical self-esteem can become so low as to paralyze the child and even inhibit the development of academic self-esteem. By reducing the effect of the disability on the construction of the self, programs such as Ability On-Line can have an enormous effect.

There is evidence that the self-esteem-enhancing function of the interactive media is not limited to children with visible disabilities. "The first time I went into KidsCom everyone was so nice," said 11-year-old Victoria. "They're much nicer than in class. People don't judge you based on what you look like."

Chat moderators, teachers, parents, and community workers who spend time with N-Geners invariably told us that they think this is a confident generation who think highly of themselves. It is not completely clear why this is the case, but here are a few thoughts.

One factor has to do with the interactive nature of the media itself. The influential developmental psychologist Jean Piaget explained that the construction of the self occurs as the child acts on its environment—as the child takes actions to understand what he or she can do.[3] This may explain why television is such an unproductive medium for self-esteem development—the child does not take actions but rather is acted upon. Even educational programs cannot change this nature of TV. Barney, the purple dinosaur, and his chorus invite children to sing along with their program, but the characters' actions are unaffected if a child wants to change the lyrics or speed up the tempo or simply feels that today is not a day to sing along. It may also explain why the interactive media appears to contribute to self-esteem. There is always someone on the Net who will listen to the reason why you do not feel like singing.

Children take actions continuously upon their world. But this is different from taking actions on Lego pieces (also a wonderful experience for child development, not to mention being fun). There is an important distinction between acting on the physical and acting on the social world. TV allows neither. Lego allows one. The Net allows both. The actions taken on the Net involve reading, assessing, imagining, composing sentences, searching for information, discovering new places, and interacting with others. Even with video games, which are becoming very sophisticated and multiuser, the child takes actions—leaping, stick handling, hitting (everything from cyborgs to baseballs), steering, and shifting into warp drive. The child begins to understand new things she can do.

Self-esteem also seems to be enhanced in chat groups because kids can always have another chance—they can adopt another self. In the real world, children can be labeled or isolated early in life and take years to shake it off. You may remember someone in your class who was characterized as a nerd, nose-picker, fatty, or creep—or you may have been that person. A nasty nickname can take years to shake. In cyberspace, if the child doesn't like how he has been characterized, he can adopt a new identity. The other children forget about the old creep and you've got a new self. Allison Ellis of FreeZone has 30,000 registered users but she knows the actual number of children is smaller because some of them have more than one identity. "If you came into the chat room as one kind of kid and made some other kids angry by being rude," she says, "you can change your identity and come back as a different or better person." On the Net, you get a second chance. There may be more opportunities to get things right. Kids get an opportunity to test the waters on the Net before experimenting with elements of their persona in real life.

> I am young, but not a child any more.
> I'm a hard worker, but enjoy free time. I am
> older inside than out, and I have lived, but have just begun.
> I am a friend to some, an enemy to others, but to most just another face.
> I am lost, but I cannot be, because I'm right here. All I know is that
> I am someone who has a long way to go in life. Sometimes I act
> like I know it all, like I have experienced so much more
> than others, but I really haven't.

KELLY RICHARDS, 15
Alberta

Is it possible that through the Net, children, in particular adolescents, have a new tool and a new environment for the construction of their identities?

In response to the question on the *Growing Up Digital* forum, "In fifty words or less please describe Who Are You?" 14-year old Neasa Coll replied, "I am a disconcerted soul, unsure of what lies ahead. I am not insecure, in fact I am quite confident in myself, with goals and dreams that I strive to reach, but at this turning point in my life, I can't help but wonder what the future holds for me. While trying to revel in the joys of adolescence, I find myself surrounded by messages describing adulthood as the magical time when a person can really enjoy life. I hope that when I do reach this age I will not lose my sense of child, it will merely be displayed in a taller, stronger body." Fourteen-year-old Matt Kessler replied: "I'd have to say I'm very shy unless I know a person very well. This doesn't happen though in cyberspace. On the Net, I am one of the most outgoing people I know. Probably why I spend so much time there. If I'm with friends, I am very comical and have a good sense of humor. But when I'm alone, or with strangers, I am very serious and keep to myself. Other aspects: I enjoy sports, both watching and playing them. I have a strong sense for writing, and also read every day. I'm thinking all the time."

These statements are examples of the quest for identity first explained by psychoanalyst Erik Erikson as the most important personality achievement of adolescence and a critical step in becoming a productive, fulfilled, and happy adult.[4] Young adults' identities define who they are, what they value, their views, what they hope to pursue in life. Erikson described how it is not till adolescence that children become absorbed by the task of forming an identity. In complex societies, teenagers experience a period of confusion as they experiment with the alternatives before settling on a set of values, goals, and directions. Adolescents during this period question important assumptions that defined them in childhood. They question, rethink, analyze, explore, and eventually create a foundation that provides a sense of sameness as they shift through different roles in life.[5]

> I consider myself to be somewhat cynical, and extremely principled, and yes, a little angry. I usually resent being told to do things which I feel are a waste of time. My basic philosophy toward life is: do whatever makes you happy. As Denis Leary said, "Happiness comes in small doses," so you should go after those short moments whenever you can.

DAN ATKINS, 17
Malibu, California

What are the implications of children having vast new avenues of exploration at their fingertips? Compare the passive adolescent watching television to the active N-Gener involved in various Net-based discussions, interacting with various services, taking action in games, e-mailing friends for advice, searching for sources of information. One would think that this process of adolescent exploration would be richer for the N-Gener. Surely, you would think that the child as active rather than passive recipient would have a greater sense of empowerment to make informed choices.

There is much work to be done to understand the new media and the self. For example, the presentation of the self in everyday life has been a topic of much interest to psychologists and sociologists since the publication of an important book in 1959 by Erving Goffman entitled *The Presentation of Self in Everyday Life*. In the book, Goffman views interaction as a "performance" shaped by environment and audience to give others "impressions" that are desired by the actor. To establish an identity, individuals create a "front" which allows others to understand who they are. The front creates an appearance, personality traits, context, and attitudes which unite with the individual's behavior.

In cyberspace, the elements of the front need to be constructed almost completely by the child. In text-based chat rooms (the norm today), the child's age, size, clothing, hair length, facial features, physical demeanor, overall appearance, geographical location, social context—all the elements of the front—are unknown. The front must be constructed online. Such cyber fronts may be names or more complicated avatars and eventually become whole personalities. This provides infinitely greater possibilities for the child to create a self, or selves, which works for him or her. If it's true, as the previously noted cartoon says, "On the Internet, no one knows you're a dog," it is also true that on the Internet, everybody is a cat—with at least nine lives.

The research also showed that higher self-esteem and confidence seem a somewhat fragile phenomenon for some children. A kid's confidence can be crushed quickly online in a flaming or if the child is ignored or criticized. Allison Ellis says there are a few kids in particular that she worries about when she goes home at night. They may say online, "I hate myself," or "I'm ugly, nobody likes me, why would I want to be your C-Girl?" (cyber girl). When this happens in FreeZone, a moderator intervenes saying something like, "Stop being so hard on yourself—you're great and we all love you." Usually a child will receive support from others in FreeZone as well. In other online environments, depending on who happens to be involved, the reaction can range from support to indifference to hostility. Feelings can also be hurt if nobody chats with you. Sometimes there can be 50 children in the room—and they all have their own conversations going on. A lonely soul may say, "Talk to me, talk to me." The monitors may respond with something like, "Why don't you be assertive and ask someone a question rather than waiting for someone to talk to you."

> I guess most people would see me as a caring, helping, smart person who knows her limits. I have learned to be patient with people who are rude or do not understand me or my busy family. And I have learned to help people who I don't exactly like.
>
> COSSANNA PRESTON, 12
> Saskatchewan

In several extreme cases, there have been suicide threats. As with such threats in the real world, they need to be taken seriously although they may be a call for help or just attention. The FreeZone staff has taken suicide training to help them intervene in such situations.

Multiple Selves

As previously mentioned, the Net permits children to experiment with morphing their own identities. This can be both positive and negative. At any time, a 13-year-old may have, say, five windows open. In one she is herself sending an electronic mail message to her grandmother. In another, she is Kramer from *Seinfeld* behaving like him in the T2 chat room and having conversations with a stop sign, a happy face, and a Pamela Anderson from *Baywatch*. In another, she can be TROJANFAN identifying herself with her favorite football team on ESPN's Sportszone and attracting discussion about college football. In another, she can be someone she knows flirting with someone who has her own name. In a final window, she is the proverbial fly on the virtual wall watching the goings on in a MUD.

This is very different from the child who is a student during the day, an athlete after school, a daughter over dinner, and a musician at her evening piano lesson. Here she is playing different roles at different moments in time and in different locations. As MIT psychologist and professor Sherry Turkle points out, "Windows have become a powerful metaphor for thinking of the self as a multiple distributed system."[6]

Turkle explains how in traditional settings of the physical world, one steps in and out of character. In virtual spaces one has parallel identities which, if extended, can become parallel selves and lives. For one of Turkle's subjects, real life (called RL) "is just one more window."

This can be positive, as explained earlier, in that children can enhance and create images of themselves and their worlds that are more satisfying than the real life images. They can also develop the confidence and knowledge to prepare for better realities. "I'm not afraid of anybody or anything [online]," says FreeZoner BUFFMAN, 15. "In real life I'm a little hundred-pound shrimp. But online I can be anybody."

> Right now I am talking to 3 of you in emo, one in a kind of chat site, and I am looking up something on abortion for a friend . . . but I have a window open in T2 and one in Petes . . . another chat site . . . *smile* if I had powwow working I would be there too . . . *smile* so what are you doing at the moment? Besides writing to me? *smile*

LOZ, 16, online with Kate Baggott,
Growing Up Digital Researcher

Sometimes kids adopt a new identity for practical reasons, but they really want to reassert their old identity. A kid who is banned for inappropriate behaviors from a supervised chat session such as FreeZone may adopt a new identity to get back in. But if CYBERDUDE gets banned for swearing, he may come back as CYBERDUDE2. He could have changed his name to NETGUY, but he wants to keep CYBERDUDE because that's his dominant identity—as a bad boy who hacks (disrupts) chats.

> I change my "character" every time that I am chatting, the thing that I cannot do with my friends.

SPICEGRLS, 11, f
Hertliya, Israel

What are the implications of a child being able to construct multiple fronts and thereby create multiple selves? Allison Ellis describes a striking situation: "I know there are some kids that have five different names that they use on a regular basis. One of them may come in as SAILOR MOON and CYBERSWEETIE, and they'll have two different browsers open and they'll be chatting with each other, like their imaginary friend, which is really weird. It could be a popularity thing—like 'Hey, someone's talking to me!!!' But we don't know if it's an actual conversation, or just the same person talking to themselves."

Is there a dark side to multiple selves which is not fully understood? If children generalize this behavior to real life, will they be more reckless because they have learned on the Net that it matters less what you do? On the Net the child may have nine lives, but not in her physical world—fail that test and you've failed the test. Insult a friend and you may have lost a friend. This may be true, but there are consequences of abandoning a Net-based self as well. A child can lose a friend on the Net. When he comes back as someone else, he has lost his old relationships. As Turkle says,

"Continuity is important for relationships." Children, therefore, are forced to think about the consequences of their actions online, that is, to manage the self.

Worse, is there a danger that children might lose control over the process of self selection and become schizoid, perhaps with multiple personalities in real life?

> The Web is the only place where you can insult someone and not have to worry about them pulling a gun on you.
>
> JEDI5, 10, m

Turkle says that this is a false concern. She explains that multiple personality disorder results from a severe trauma where a child creates different personalities as an extreme defense mechanism to wall off the traumatic experience. "When you have trauma that's repeated, [that] you have to live with, like perhaps a father who abuses you at night, but then pours the Cheerios for you in the morning and takes you to school—you have to be able to put the abuse in a box and continue to have the Cheerios poured for you because you still need the father." A child creates a piece of him- or herself— a persona or an alternate person which is split off. "The rest of your self doesn't even know that person who holds the dangerous secret."

For Turkle, multiple personality is about self-disintegration—the opposite of what's happening when children create multiple selves on the Net. In cyberspace, children are having fun and are fully conscious of what they are doing. They are not creating walls but breaking down walls. "They develop better relationships and more communication with different aspects of their self." To her, "the Net is not about splitting off, it's about acceptance and greater harmony."

This is leading to some important new thinking regarding the self away from a view that stresses oneness, or as Turkle critiques, "a personality for all seasons." Rather, through the Net, the N-Gen may be the first generation to accept and effectively manage the many selves that flourish within us.

Intelligence

The publication of Richard J. Herrnstein and Charles Murray's 1994 book, *The Bell Curve*, sparked a new round of debate about the meaning of intelligence test scores and the nature of intelligence. The authors concluded that, among other things, racial differences in intelligence tests were due to underlying differences between races rather than environmental factors. The American Psychological Association convened an authoritative task force to explain this issue and shed light on the debate.

The report noted that individuals differ from one another in their ability to understand complex ideas, to adapt effectively to the environment, to learn from experience, to engage in various forms of reasoning, and to overcome obstacles by thinking. Although these individual differences can be substantial, they are never entirely consistent because someone's intellectual performance will vary on different occasions, in different environments, as judged by different criteria. Concepts of *intelligence* are attempts to clarify and organize this complex set of phenomena. "Although considerable clarity has been achieved in some areas, no such conceptualization has yet answered all the important questions and none commands universal assent."[7] In fact, the report noted that when two dozen prominent theorists were recently asked to define intelligence, they gave two dozen somewhat different definitions.[8]

> I don't believe one should be measured by smartness. Everyone has the mind and skills to accomplish anything. It's just a matter of taking the time to do it and having initiative. Having access to the Internet does not make anyone smarter. It just increases their learning skills if they take the time to utilize the information that is available.
>
> DEANNA PERRY, 15
> Florida

At the center of the controversy is the measurement of individual differences in intelligence testing. This is a complex issue. (Although it should be noted that the task force rejected Herrnstein and Murray's theory.)

There is a growing appreciation that there are various forms of intelligence and that a single IQ score may be misleading at best. The "theory of multiple intelligences" developed by Howard Gardner includes musical, bodily kinesthetic, and various forms of personal intelligence as well as more familiar spatial, linguistic, and logical mathematical abilities. He argues that psychometric tests, such as IQ tests, address only linguistic and logical skills plus some aspects of spatial intelligence; other forms have been entirely ignored.[9]

For example, the 13-year-old student who gets average grades in most subjects but who scores 40 points a game in basketball or who performs with a national ballet troupe shows very high kinesthetic intelligence. Other students may be gifted musically. We can now speak of emotional and social intelligence which, incidentally, may be critical attributes in the emerging economy and organizations which emphasize teamwork and cooperation.

The key issue for us here is not individual differences, but the development of intelligence. The best-known approach is that of Swiss psychologist Jean Piaget.[10] He argues that intelligence develops in all children through the continually shifting balance between the assimilation of new information into existing cognitive structures and the changing accommodation of those structures themselves to incorporate the new information.

Notwithstanding problems with the schools, drop-out rates, and many alienated sectors of the youth population, the evidence is strong that children who are growing up digital are more savvy, and even smarter than boomers were at similar stages of growth. They also have a significant advantage over members of their cohort who are growing up unplugged. Overall, 47 percent of the U.S. population demonstrates low or no levels of literacy. The N-Geners are soaring over these people, as well as their youthful counterparts who are not wired. In one study, after following two groups of students for three years—one in a high-income area with low access to technology, and one in a lower-income area with high access to technology—researchers found that access to computers alone could displace other factors, such as household income, in improving children's writing skills.

> I think the Internet has made me smarter, because it has given me a broader knowledge of things. . . . I asked my mother whether it has made any difference in the way I communicate and she thinks I talk more now.
>
> **JOELDINE HAYTER, 15**
> New Zealand

"We purposely chose a comparison school that people have higher expectations of because of parent income and established neighborhood," says York University education professor Ron Owston, one of the researchers on the project. The high-technology-access school was in a working-class neighborhood near the Ford Motor factory. "At first these kids were behind in their writing competency compared to the comparison school and then by second year, they matched them. By the third year, they surpassed them largely."

According to research conducted by psychologist Patricia Marks Greenfield at the University of California at Los Angeles, children are registering average raw intelligence scores that are 15 points higher than those reported on tests 50 years ago. (Average IQ, of course, is still 100 as it is a measure of intelligence normed to be 100.) Greenfield suggests this improvement in intellectual performance is largely due to the fact that current IQ testing formats have not developed at the same rate as the visual skills kids have developed to play video games and use computers.[11] Further, because the Net is a text-based communications medium, kids are constantly being challenged to compose ideas into text, increasing their visual/verbal skills.

There has been ample evidence regarding the impact of television on intelligence. The broadcast medium itself, and more important, the content which is broadcast (how shall I put this kindly) has an intellectually numbing effect. In a review of this material, psychologist Laura E. Berk explains how, overall, television inhibits social learning. At early ages, children cannot judge the reality of TV material. For example, it is not until age seven that they understand that TV fiction is not real—that there are actors and scripts. Because of this, children tend to imitate what they see on the screen. Television viewing is linked strongly to aggressive behaviors, ethnic and gender stereotypes, and consumerism. It is true that educational programs such as *Sesame Street* can work well as a teacher. Children who watch *Sesame Street* have been found to score better on tests designed to measure the program's learning goals; and *Sesame Street* viewing is positively related to vocabulary development. However, the rapid-paced format of the program has been criticized as discouraging the development of imagination. A bigger problem is that most television is not like *Sesame Street*. TV does not support intellectual and cognitive development because it is not designed to take into account children's developmental needs. Other researchers have argued that passive viewing of such complete sensory information leads to reduced mental effort and shallow information processing.[12]

The many hours spent watching television might otherwise be spent on activities which require verbalization, sustained thinking, imagination, creative thinking, and interactivity with other children and adults. As put by psychologists Valkenburg and van der Voort: "There is evidence that TV may adversely affect a number of conditions that are important for creative imagination, that is, the ability to disassociate oneself from existing information, a reflexive style of thinking, sustained effort, and the peace and quiet necessary to give a matter careful thought. . . . It is also possible that TV suppresses creative imagination via its role as a time-consuming activity. TV viewing occurs at the expense of time spent with verbal media, such as radio and books, which could stimulate imaginations more than TV viewing does."[13]

Compare TV watching to the digital media where children are active. They must seek out. They are always reading. They must compose their thoughts. And they must evaluate. For example, on the Net they must evaluate what is real. "One of the problems of the Net," says 14-year-old Caleb Murphy of rural New York State, "is that you never know what's real, and who's telling the truth." Children must constantly analyze, weigh, probe, and take stock of everything they find. Coco Conn describes this well. She points out that when we grew up, we never felt that we could look at a picture and feel that it was a fake. We grew up very innocently—adults would tell us reality and we accepted that. A fact was a fact. "Children today have the luxury of understanding that everything they see or hear is not necessarily true," she says. "They see a photograph and know it could be totally fabricated. Kids today are developing a higher level of self-confidence—an ability to look critically at what their parents would simply accept as a given."

It doesn't take much imagination to see how such an active, self-directed cognitive activity would help in the construction of complex brain structures and intellectual capabilities. Especially when compared to watching a cartoon on television.

Computers in the school can have a positive impact on learning and thereby intellectual development. Computers are more effective teaching devices because processing computer operations mirrors the operations of the human cognitive system as information travels from sensory memory to short-term memory to long-term memory. They also enable self-paced and student-oriented learning as opposed to "one-size-fits-all learning." New technologies are increasing not only intellect but the amount we can teach our children, and also how much they retain. This issue is investigated further in the chapter on N-Gen learning.

Having said this, the first three years of life are the most important in terms of the development of intelligence, and the digital media is currently used very little by this age group. As the technology matures, we can expect that even very young children may begin to benefit.

Spatial Orientation

Children develop a number of *spatial operations* at different stages of development. These deal with distance, directions, and the relationships between objects in their world. How is this process affected when the children participate in a virtual world?

When psychologists discuss *spatial orientation,* they are referring to operations on the immediate environment. There is no evidence that this is different for N-Geners. While N-Geners understand the basic operation of spatial distances, as did previous generations, they appear to lack appreciation of global distances. They may be the first generation with a truly global perspective. The world to them is (to use a term of Nicholas Negroponte) "the size of the head of a pin."[14] My daughter happily chats with people from anywhere on the planet as if they were next door, oblivious to the question of where they are.

Someone who has been very close to these kids over many years is Coco Conn, director of the project Cityspace. Coco has been working with N-Geners to help them create virtual cities. Cityspace confronts children with the task of cooperatively building environments—creating virtual streets, buildings, rooms, even furniture. To do this, they must negotiate with other children from multiple locations. They must collaborate regarding the ownership and use of material that they can't hold or touch. In the non-cyberworld, whoever is holding the doll or baseball largely controls how that object is used. But the virtual objects of the cyberworld require kids to develop more sophisticated negotiation skills and a clearer understanding of the concept of ownership. As children begin to work in such environments, their concept of space and distance change, to name a few.

"The United States is insular, and children know very little about the cultures of other countries. The Net will change this," says Coco. "It will allow the kids to navigate to other countries and spend time with non-American kids. It will create a different matrix in their minds of the world." She describes how adults picture the world as a big ball with other countries being far away, and to get to another country you have to get on a plane and fly there. Adults write-off large parts of the world because we can't imagine ourselves actually ever going there. In this generation's mind, the grid will be much different, with them understanding that decisions they make at home will have implications for people living beyond their immediate neighborhood and country. "Today's kids are far more aware of the global context. They know they are a small piece of the whole. They are much smarter in understanding that the world is a tiny place and they are much more globally conscious."

A good example of this global orientation occurred when the FreeZone staff staged a mock election during the 1996 U.S. presidential campaign (most of FreeZone's 30,000 accounts are American children). MOOSELIPS decided to run for president. His candidacy was greeted with some consternation from others making comments like: "Is this a U.S. election? There are other countries in the world you know." Children from other countries made statements like, "What about us in Malaysia?" The kids agreed that it was inappropriate to have a U.S. election campaign only. As a compromise, they continued with MOOSELIPS' campaign but launched a separate election for the position of president of FreeZone. So, through this exercise, thousands of American children were confronted with the global and international character of the world.

N-Gen Thinking

Is this a generation of children who are beginning to process information and reason differently than the rest of us?

Psychologists have found the computer analogy to human information processing very helpful. The best-known approach views information as being stored in a very short-term "sensory registry," then active working memory, and then, as deeper cognitive structures are developed, long-term memory. As information flows through these different levels of hardware, it can be operated on by software—called *control processes* and *mental strategies*.[15] As Laura E. Burk explains, using computer-like diagrams and flowcharts, researchers can "map the exact series of steps children . . . execute when faced with a task or a problem." Computer simulations of mental operations can be developed and used to understand and predict outputs of information processing.[16]

It will be a long time, if ever, before computers can simulate human brain functioning, but the information-processing model is useful in helping us study how the new media may affect thinking. This research is in its infancy, but let me give an example of the change.

The typical boomer wrote an essay in school by conducting research, developing an outline, and composing the essay from beginning to end. The tool for construction of the written word was the pen and paper or, perhaps, the typewriter. The input of information and the output was typically done in a serial fashion. Similarly, boomer children watched the *Ed Sullivan Show* beginning to end and then tuned in to the next program.

The N-Gen child takes in and outputs information in a somewhat different manner when working with the digital media. Information is input from multiple sources and occurs in a less sequential manner. Using software, the child can organize information into complex structures containing links to other information. It is quite likely that this is beginning to change what occurs between input and output, that is, processing—cognition and reasoning.

The idea that computers could free humans from linear thinking was first practically explained and demonstrated by visionary Douglas Englebart. In an important 1962 paper, he explained how the computer could augment human intellect. "One of the tools which shows the greatest immediate promise is the computer, when it can be harnessed for direct, online assistance, integrated with new concepts and methods . . . every person who does thinking with symbolized concepts (whether in the form of English language, pictographs, formal logic, or mathematics) should be able to benefit significantly."[17]

By 1967, he had implemented an "augmented knowledge research workshop" at Stanford Research Institute in which people used something called *hypertext* to compose ideas in a systematic, nonsequential way. The workstations used by knowledge workers were computer terminals which contained a few innovations themselves. Foregoing the urge to invent a better mousetrap, he just invented the mouse—a radical new device to control the cursor on the screen. Unlike the mouse (which roared), a four-key, pianolike key set never caught on.

I have vivid memories of the day in 1978 when I first met Englebart. This unassuming man spent several hours showing me around the workshop and I took a test drive on a workstation. I had been using a word processor for several years, but this was something totally different. For example, ideas could be composed conceptually, rather than from beginning to end—that is, you build a high-level structure of the document, then a second-level structure and so on. Text contained within it *links* to other text in the document or to other documents which could be stored on other computers. This idea was really the precursor to the World Wide Web, in which documents contain *hot links* to other documents. Today, when I receive an e-mail message from a teenager full of hot links to the youth's Web site and other locations, we are both beneficiaries of Englebart's genius. In many ways, Englebart is the father of the digital media, although few recognize this.

Englebart remembers a young software developer named Jeff Rulifson who, in 1967, had recently graduated with a computer science degree. Initially, Rulifson resisted using the hypertext document creation tools, complaining to Engelbart, "I don't think that way." Today, Rulifson is not only an active user of the new media but a leading designer working for Sun Microsystems.

Another of the active users of the workshop in the 1960s was 16-year-old Dean Meyer. It was Dean who convinced me to meet Engelbart. Dean, along with

Doug's daughter, Christine, were the youngest-ever users of hypertext as a thinking tool. Doug referred to them at the time as "the first of a new generation."

Meyer believes using the technology changed the way he thinks. Whenever he composes text he is forced to think conceptually—that is, he must create a high-level structure for, say, an article and use the hypertext tools to build successively more detailed structures. "I just think in terms of structures and I see conceptual structures very quickly." He believes this has had a tremendous impact on his personal thinking style. "It has allowed me to be able to put my thoughts in an appropriate sequence as I write, as I speak, or negotiate."

Meyer is convinced that hypertext tools can help develop clear thinking. An underlying software structure for text forces the author to define the salient points. His description is illustrative. "You must know how thoughts fit together: the flow of them and the structure. Pointing out what is important and what's not. Being able to put your outpost in order. Knowing the relative importance that is given not only in the flow but in knowing what is subsidiary to what. What is the down level vs. what are the main level points. It means that if you go on a tangent, how to pop the stack and pick up where you left off. At a level of prose, it's getting your grammar right, to balance the weightings and make the flow clear, the words attractive and demonstrative of the concept."

On the other hand, while Meyer says he would score high on a scale of systematic thinking, he would probably be low on the scale of intuitive thinking. He wonders if he is so focused on what he knows that he may be less open to considering new directions. "Perhaps my creativity to consider radical departures from my current cognitive structures is lower." He also wonders about the implications of such tools on long-term memory. Because the links and structures are contained in software within the text, he doesn't need to remember them. "Perhaps I don't practice my memory as much," he notes.

It is important to note that Meyer is not talking about the current Web, but rather the use of sophisticated hypertext tools for composing documents. While more investigation is needed, it appears that new tools may change our thinking process.

Overall, while there is much more to be learned, it appears that the doom-sayer's view regarding how the Net is affecting child psychology is wrong. Rather than the "neocortex eating itself," children appear to be developing their cognition, intellects, and abilities better. From our research, the children of the digital age appear to be smart, accepting of diversity, curious, assertive, self-reliant, high in self-esteem, and global in orientation. Evidence suggests they process information differently than their predecessors; they have new tools for self-development and making their way through adolescence. All of these will serve them well later in life.

But what about the development of their social skills? This is the topic of the next chapter.

The N-Gen Mind
Part II

SALLY FORTH

© North America Syndicate*

If growing up digital appears to be helpful in developing thinking and intellect, what about the impact on social skills and behavior? Through our research, we heard tales and theories regarding how children were becoming glued to the screen; losing their attention span; becoming "Net-addicted" and becoming stressed out, vain, and even cruel through Net interaction. Again, while there is much to be learned and important problems to be managed, overall it would seem that conventional wisdom is wrong.

Glued to the Screen: Are Kids Losing Social Skills?

"Kids today have no friends, and they have the social skills of a tack." "I think kids are becoming withdrawn and isolated because of the Internet." "Don't you think there is something about programming a computer that turns you into a geek?" (Comments to me in recent interviews or discussions.)

I recently received a short handwritten letter forwarded to me by my publisher in New York. It was from a woman whose full name I'll keep confidential.

> Dear Mr. Tapscott,
>
> Read your book *The Digital Economy*. . . . I suspect the only promise "it" holds is an increase in social isolation and lunacy. An increase in hypertension and personality disorders are already being reported. Spending one's life in front of a CRT Video Screen doesn't seem like a life to me. By the time the world goes fully computerized, I probably won't be here . . . but I feel sorry for my children and my grandchildren.
>
> Mrs. R. K.

I wish I had a dollar for every time I've heard that computers are isolating our children. What's the truth? The kids we worked with don't think the computer isolates them but rather the opposite. "Yes, I spend less time doing other activities than I used to (not that there's anything to do in Delaware!), but not too much less. I've made more friends actually because I can talk to other Web people at school," says Daniel Castillo, 14.

The reason they feel this way is that the Net is a communications medium. Unbeknownst to the critics, the computer has changed from a tool for information management to a communications tool. Today, it is primarily text-oriented. Tomorrow, text will be enhanced by audio and video. But even in its somewhat restricted text format, children love to communicate. This begins around the age of eight when children begin to take their newly acquired reading and writing skills for a spin. "I think that the ages of 8 to 14 is a very social group—they love to talk," says Allison Ellis of FreeZone. "It's great if they get a discussion or a heated debate going. Once they get into name calling, we draw in the reins. And there's no swearing. But, aside from that, pretty much anything goes." Having participated in a *Growing Up Digital* chat session on FreeZone, I can say that "love to talk" is an apt descriptor.

In fact, the whole discussion of social skills is quite ironic. As explained earlier, the

> I do think my favorite thing about the Internet is making friends. You can see the world through other views if the people you know can only tell you how they feel and not show you or explain out loud.
>
> **MICHELLE BALDWIN, 13**
> Oregon

main victim of time spent on the Net, computer, and playing video games is television. Children have begun to replace passive, nonsocial, isolated viewing of TV with active use of the digital media.

Further, such use is increasingly a social activity. The new games from Nintendo, Sony, and Sega as well as computer-based games are often designed for multiple users. Observing my own children, one of the first things that occurs when a friend drops over is the Sony Playstation gets cranked up and the kids head out into space. The same kinds of conversations occur while traveling through the galaxies as happen over the Lego set or the model train.

> Of course, the Internet is a shallow and unreliable electronic repository of dirty pictures, inaccurate rumors, bad spelling, and worse grammar, inhabited largely by people with no demonstrable social skills.

Tongue-in-cheek commentary by students at the American University's Washington College of Law in a recent mock trial of the Communications Decency Act.

Much interaction with video games, computers, and the Net involve face-to-face communications as friends work on a project or show each other cool Web sites, or as parents and children share the digital experience together. Gene Giordano, from Rochester, New York, has three children ages 15, 13, and 9. He says that the Net increases interaction with his kids, not decreases it. Says Gene: "I spend a lot more time showing my kids stuff on the Net, and them showing me stuff too, than we do watching TV. You're not just sitting there watching something, you're learning from each other."

There is also a new generation of games emerging which are Net-based. No one watches the *Jeopardy*-style Net show *You Don't Know Jack*—everyone is a contestant. The game is played on the Net and everybody competes, and all the winners are rewarded.

Rather than losing social skills, N-Geners are actually developing these skills at an earlier age than their parents' generation. It's not just a new toy in the home to share with friends and siblings, but the N-Generation children have a new medium to reach out beyond their immediate world, to experience and to engage in play, learning, and overall social intercourse.

Digital kids are learning precisely the social skills which will be required for effective interaction in the digital economy. They are learning about peer relationships, about teamwork, about being critical, about how to have fun online, about friendships across geographies, about standing up for what they think, and about how to effectively communicate their ideas. When they challenge another child about having the C-name KKK, ask a newbie about her hobbies, float an inquiry regarding "kewl" sites about Leonardo DiCaprio, team up with kids from many countries to construct a virtual city, ask a C-friend to initiate the parental process of arranging a face-to-face meeting (such as 12-year-old Nicco Pesci's Utah ski trip with his 13-year-old C-girlfriend), learn how to deal with a flame, chair a video conference, learn from a digital mentor, or help a grandmother learn how to use the Net, they are enhancing the social development which occurs offline in day-to-day life. It is not the N-Gen children who are being robbed of social development, it is those adults who, through fear or ignorance, deny themselves the experience of participating in the great revolution of our times.

Jordan Garland, 14, is an active user of the new media. He uses the Internet for school research, looking up everything from whales to mythology. Like other kids, he uses word processing to create essays and graphics tools for illustrations and title pages. Sometimes he works alone and other times with other kids. Jordan plays both acoustic and electric guitar, locating sheet music in guitar archives online. He also frequents chat rooms such as a music room where people talk about "stuff like what bands you like, and what instruments you play," he says. "It's a good way to meet people from all over the world, and get their opinions. Besides, it's fun." According to his mother Karen, he's on the computer at least an hour per day, depending on the weather. If it's nice out, he's out skiing, doing track and field, or playing with his band.

I met Jordan at a conference of Building Owners and Managers. He had been recruited to a "children's panel" I was chairing, discussing information technology in front of an audience of 2000. He struck me as a bright and thoughtful boy and contributed well to the panel. He also appeared a bit shy and, given his extensive use of computers, he might be unfairly stereotyped as the kind of boy who is "glued to the screen" and for whom the technology is not a positive force.

His mother believes the opposite to be true. "His shyness is a natural occurrence for adolescents. The computer provides him with a vehicle for social expression, an outlet to explore relationships, to talk to people and get new ideas." She says: "I don't view the computer as a negative force for these kids. It's what's happening in their world. If you reject that, you're rejecting what's important to adolescents today. It's their future."

The "Attention Span of a Gnat"?

Conventional wisdom says that because children are multitasking—jumping from one computer-based activity to another—their attention span is being reduced. "Most kids have the attention span of a gnat," complains one observer.[1]

The research does not support this view. It is ironic that it is often the same people who charge that today's kids are becoming glued to the screen that also say they have lost their attention span.

A more thoughtful view comes from demographer Eric Miller. "Kids hate to be bored. This is no joke; it is a real issue. They have shorter attention spans, are used to a diet of highly stimulating visual information. From an early age they are gratified instantly and so have less patience for delay of any kind."[2] True, they are used to a stimulating environment. True also, kids hate to be bored. This is not surprising, given that they are more knowledgeable, likely smarter and more active than their boomer parents. Interaction with the digital media is many things but it is not boring—perhaps explaining why so many of the *Growing Up Digital* kids said TV was boring by comparison. But, as for instant gratification and short attention spans—at best, loaded terms—the evidence isn't there.

"I don't buy that these kids have short attention spans," says Dr. Idit Harel, author of the book *Children Designers* and founder of MaMaMedia. "They think in different ways than adults. Sometimes they are multitasking. Other times they can get into something and spend many hours on it if it makes sense to them."

All young children are easily distracted and focus on problems for short periods of time, but attention improves with age. Teachers are often told to plan classroom activities and lessons according to the age-plus-five-minutes formula. That is to say a typical six-year-old first-grader can be expected to stay on one task for about eleven minutes.

At the root of concerns about attention span is the fear that our children will not be able to focus on something and therefore not learn. This concern is consistent with the view that students need to be able to absorb a specific curriculum as the primary challenge of learning. However, it is not new thinking that the content of a particular lesson is one of the least important elements in education. What is more important is learning how to learn. John Dewey said this well many years ago when he wrote, "Perhaps the greatest fallacy is the notion that a person learns only what he is studying at the time. Collateral learning . . . may be, and often is, more important than the spelling lesson or lesson in geography or history."[3]

Moreover, it appears that by using the digital media, children become more able to ignore inappropriate sources of information and concentrate on the information which is essential for doing something, such as completing a task. Central to attention is adaptability—the ability to adapt their attention to the particular requirements of the situation. Another is planfulness—the ability to allocate attention according to a goal and sequence acts ahead of time.[4] Rather than killing attention, it makes more sense to view experience with multiple information sources, as it occurs on the Net, as helpful in developing this capability. For example, in researching a project on pollution, the child must take multiple steps: evaluate information along the way; organize findings through cutting from digital documents or creating bookmarks; postpone action in favor of an alternative; coordinate many different activities; segue out to a chat line to check on friends and then cycle back to the project; allocate time; remember a previous experience or site: overall control, adaptation, and planfulness—the key elements in the development of attention.[5]

The preceding example involves working on a school project, but the same can be said for the free-time entertainment activities of children on the Net which all involve similar actions and attentiveness. Compare this type of activity to the child watching television. The child's attention span may appear good as he sits in front of the TV for an hour. But is this really developing the skills necessary for attention development? Overall, the evidence is that the digital media is not a problem to be concerned with, but instead a boon to children's development.

Sometimes Kids Are Cruel

Kids face substantial problems at any school—rural, urban, or suburban, private or public. If there isn't a real threat of drugs, sexual abuse, and/or violence, the fear of these things is transferred from adults and the fear itself becomes a threat. K–12 students also have concerns that are completely separate from the concerns of adults. "By the time children reach school age," a typical child psychology text notes, "they have mastered two essential concepts: that human beings are alike in being both agents of external events and experiencers of internal events, and that human beings are different in their experience of events. One's own internal state may not accurately predict those another person would experience in the same situation."[6] What this means is that kids at this stage notice similarity and difference, and it also means that they can respond to their perceptions with compassion, cruelty, or indifference.

Regardless of how individual kids respond, the social picture is not a pretty one. In the United States, it is estimated that as many as 3 million children are bullied each year and every day over 100,000 kids stay home from school because they are afraid of one of their peers.[7] Countless other children experience merciless teasing because of their height, weight, skin color, fashion sense, or hair style. Sometimes kids are cruel to each other and it is the responsibility of adults not to forget that it is neither fair nor easy for kids to deal with.

If face-to-face interaction is not always a positive experience for this generation, do children behave differently on the Net? Initial experience would suggest that while there are many new sources of support and encouragement, chat-line interaction can sometimes be tough.

"Tons of people get bullied on the Net," observes Reanna Alder, 15. "It's not true that just because you don't HAVE to reveal anything about yourself, you won't get picked on. If you get noticed in a positive way you will also, most likely at some point, get picked on in a negative way. And besides, most people want to reveal things about themselves, and if you don't, you get ignored. If you make everything up, you

There is a kid in my school who used to beat me up.
He was really popular. All the other popular kids thought it was
funny. It might be funny for them, but it is NOT fun for me.
This kid would do everything from throwing snowballs at me from inside the
room, to throwing me up against the wall. Luckily, I don't get this treatment
anymore because they think it's boring. All that happens now is they mouth
off to me. Don't be mean. Be nice and earn friends by being nice.
Don't earn friends by beating up people. Don't be the bully.
Be the peacemaker.

DET, 12, m, FreeZoner

can still be picked on." Some children, however, reveal little of themselves, instead constructing their ideal self. Ted McCoy, 18, of Calgary, Alberta, says on the Net kids create "masks" which make it hard for them to bully each other, "because nobody would ever reveal the points that make them vulnerable."

While the digital media is a vehicle for these kids to change the world, it is also a reflection of the world the way it is. Fifteen-year-old Kelly Richards explains: "I think that there's a certain amount of freedom from violence, but not completely. You can always delete messages with violence, or completely ignore them, but they're still there. There is no escape from violence anywhere, even on the Net."

The kids all note that such violence is not physical. Says Colin Cowsert-Hinrichs, 11, of Houston, Texas, "I think that in a way, it isn't as bad on the Net because in real life (not that the Net isn't real) you can receive physical and mental harm. Chances are someone is going to stick up for you. It's just not the same psychological thing as in real life!" Darla Crewe, 16, agrees: "You can't always just walk away from harm in the real world . . . but on the Net . . . you can only receive mental harm. And besides that . . . you can just go somewhere else . . . or ignore them completely. Or if you get really mad you can just hit that nice power button that is SO effective! :)"

In the school yard or streets, racism, sexism, discrimination based on socio-economic status, and the cult of beauty have historically been a physical basis for identifying those to be ostracized or brutalized. Does the Net eliminate this, leading to a new era of cooperation among children? Fifteen-year-old Deanna Perry of Florida says: "In chat sessions, people are judged not on looks or skin color, but by their personality. The Internet provides an alternative, a place without racism or prejudice. It's not as easy to make prejudiced comments about someone online when you cannot physically see them."

The Internet definitely gives kids a break from the cruelties of reality. You can meet people on the Internet who have never seen you—they don't have the chance to judge you by your looks. You can plan your first impression, and you can finally get fair treatment. Treatment that is not based on the way you look, the way you act, or the way you dress. People on the Internet judge you by your thoughts and opinions. Sure, not everyone's got to be like you, but at least you've had the chance to let people know who you really are. The Internet shows a person's personality, and not the shell that we see in real life.

NEASA COLL, 14, Alberta

Most of Lauren Verity's friends are gothics. Victoria, Australia, is not the most friendly place for gothics, and even though 16-year-old Lauren is not one, she gets painted with the gothic brush. Gothics, Goths, aka Vamps and Zombies, are Shelley/Byron wannabes carried over from the punk movement. They wear mostly black, violet, and scarlet Victorian-looking clothes (lace and velvet) and wear white makeup. They tend to listen to The Cure, Marilyn Manson, and other ethereal kinds of bands. They hold both physical and online gaming events, such as Dungeons and Dragons, but with a vampire twist. They are big into shock value.

Lauren compares life at school versus life on the Net, for someone with Goth friends:

I always get hassled a lot at school because my friends are gothics. . . . I'm not, but that doesn't seem to matter. . . . It sucks and it's really cruel. . . . We have people hiss at us, and call us devil worshippers and stuff. . . . I think they [the teasers] are the most pathetic people on earth . . . what matters is "who" people are, not "what" they are . . . that's why I like the Net coz it makes people judge you for you, not what you look like, or what race, or religion, or color you are. . . . I'm starting at a new school tomorrow . . . so *fingers crossed*, but I don't expect to escape it . . . sure I won't get the stuff I used to, because my friends won't be around . . . but I'm sure the kids'll find something else . . . but that's just the way that people are, right? . . . that's society for ya. . . .

Unfortunately, while the physical basis for picking on someone is absent on the Net, some children will find other bases. Reanna Alder, 15, explains: "It's very easy to make nasty comments about people, even when you can't see someone. As soon as they reveal something about themselves, you can insult them. Sure, you can't use racial or gender slurs if you don't know what they are, but there are plenty of other names to call people."

The *Growing Up Digital* kids were unanimous, however, that in cyberspace it is harder for one child to isolate another. Deanna Perry explains that "if someone were to say a prejudiced comment in a chat session, several people would probably have a problem with it." Darla Crewe adds: "On the Net people don't seem as shy to speak up for one another . . . so if you're in a chat room and someone is making fun of you or whatever . . . chances are someone is going to stick up for you."

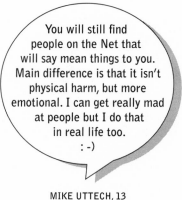

You will still find people on the Net that will say mean things to you. Main difference is that it isn't physical harm, but more emotional. I can get really mad at people but I do that in real life too.
: -)

MIKE UTTECH, 13

Vanity?

Lots of kids create their own home pages. This has led some observers to conclude that these children are vain.

There are as many kinds of kids' pages as there are kids. They create home pages to organize around some issue, to support their favorite singer, to solicit information on a topic, or for a school project. One category is the generic kid page—a place where the child can showcase his or her work, views, and meet with friends. Children are using the Net as a new publishing medium and a new meeting place. Their personal pages become places to say, "Here's who I am. Here's what I'm interested in. Have a visit and sign my guest book." This is something completely new. Children could show their art to the rest of the world by making snowmen in their front yards, or by posting their drawings in the corridor at school. A handful would see what they had done. Even fewer might get back to them with comments. With the Net, they have something very different at their disposal.

There are important safety issues here. A child should never post a photo of themselves or give out their address, phone number, or other identifiers. Furthermore, parents need to be aware of what the child is doing. Setting aside these issues, which are discussed in the chapter on parenting, we estimate there are now many thousands of children with such sites.

Allison Ellis does not view this trend as vanity, but rather as something positive: "When I was that age, I had extremely low self-esteem. If I had a vehicle like this for getting credit for things that I did, for expressing my personality, and being around like-minded people, it would have really helped me." Building self-esteem is important for every child. Not false esteem where the child is praised gratuitously for any action, but real self-esteem where the child is appreciated for his or her accomplishments. Says Allison, "I think everyone deserves a chance to express themselves and be important—it doesn't have to be at the expense of anyone else."

Stressed-Out or Stress-Relieved?

In one very significant way, members of N-Gen are just like their parents. Kids today have to be too many things to too many people. Everyone is stressed-out and stretched thin.

When it comes to stress, the children report that the Net is a double-edged sword. It adds another time-consuming activity to the already hectic day of homework, extracurricular activities, family responsibilities, and physical friendships. Says 16-year-old Kim Devereaux, "The Internet eats up a lot of my leisure time. When I have a free night with homework, I find that I'll spend much of it on the computer. Sometimes, it makes me feel as though I haven't relaxed at all."

The Net is also changing our perception of children—from being ignorant to competent. Surely this shift places additional pressures on them. Add to this what psychologist David Elkind describes as the growing demands on contemporary children for maturity—"participating in competitive sports, for early academic achievement, and for protecting themselves against adults who might do them harm. While children might be able to cope with any one of those demands taken singly, taken together they often exceed children's adaptive capacity."[8]

Yet overall, they report that activity on the Net is enjoyable and even stress-reducing.

"I disagree with anyone who thinks that the Internet stresses people out

> I have a lot of friends as it is . . . and being on the Internet is like multiplying it by two . . . and widening the age/location/variety of friends I have. . . . I think it's half pleasure and half pressure because when I log on . . . I always have at least 100 new messages all to me and besides that I usually have at least another 50 mailing lists I'm on . . . so it's a pressure to find time to read it all, it's also a pleasure because it's from friends . . . also . . . a lot of my family is on the Internet . . . and without it I probably wouldn't hear from them hardly at all . . . it's a big pressure to find time to write back . . . and read all the mail . . . and keep your quota down . . . and and and and . . . but everything has its pleasures and pressures . . . up sides and down sides . . . don't they??!!! :)

DARLA CREWE, 16
Nova Scotia

more," says Nicole Padua, 13, of Northville, Massachusetts. "It helps me to relax when I'm stressed-out over school or anything else that has gone wrong. Sometimes when you have a problem you can go in an IRC and ask for help. I've seen people ask for others' opinions on personal problems because they can trust them not to go gossiping to another friend."

Fourteen-year-old Neasa Coll says that being connected to the Internet, "makes the world smaller," which she enjoys. "My closest relatives live in Boston. The rest of them live in Europe, so guess how long it used to take mail to reach them! E-mail has allowed me to 'talk' to them several times a day, and it's fun. I don't necessarily think the Net gives us more leisure time (it actually uses it up), but it is definitely another of life's pleasures."

When asked if the Net relieves or increases stress, Kelly Richards, 13, describes both sides of the coin. "Keeping track of Internet friends, foes, and clubs can get to be stressful, but when you're actually dealing with them it's fun! The friends you meet can be the best you've ever had, and you know them so well it's hard to believe that you live miles apart. It's a fun release of energy sometimes if you need to relax, or just have some fun. Going on the Internet can keep you from doing something like trashing someone's house or something. So basically it's a lot of pleasure, but it can be stressful until you learn to—what's the word?—deal with it."

Net Addiction

"Our children are becoming addicted to the Internet." "A generation of addicts." If you believe the mass media, we're facing a big problem.

Various tongue-in-cheek addiction checklists circulate on the Net. You are addicted if, "You wake up at 3 A.M. to go to the bathroom and stop to check your e-mail on the way back to bed. You turn off your modem and get this awful empty feeling, like you just pulled the plug on a loved one. You ask Santa to bring you an ISDN line. You start using smileys in your snail mail. You get a tattoo that reads, 'This body best viewed with Netscape Navigator 1.1 or higher.'"

Broadly defined, *addiction* is persistent, compulsive, and harmful use of a substance resulting in withdrawal symptoms when use is terminated. The term has been extended, sometimes semi-seriously, beyond substances. Robert Palmer's now-classic tune says he's addicted to love. People talk about being addicted to cheesecake or chocolate. But somehow when we discuss children's *Net addiction,* the term is extended in a very serious way.

It's true, children who are wired will say that they love the Net. Lauren Verity is a good example: "I luv the Net . . . chat sites means talking things through with your friends . . .because that's the only reason why they're there, is to talk . . . so you can find people who will listen . . . I hardly ever watch TV anymore, because I spend so much time on the computer . . . but I luv it all, and I would-n't give it up for anything . . . the emos can get hard though . . . I'm not good at replying to them . . . but still I luv it . . . plus it's really interesting to find out what your friends are doing halfway around the world from you . . .".

Me, I'm a chataholic.

LOOPS, 11, f

But to use the term addiction, we would have to show both compulsive use, serious withdrawal symptoms, and knowledge on the part of the user that use of the Net is harmful.

"I think the media has created a bad rap," says Allison Ellis. "People that have truly gotten addicted, have addictive personalities." Working with thousands of N-Geners, she's convinced that the kids keep coming back because they enjoy something, which overall is beneficial to them.

Dr. Idit Harel has the same view. She argues it is senseless to talk about being addicted to technology—you have to examine the function. "Holding power is not because of the technology," she says. "It's because the media enables them to do things which they care about—which are attractive and enjoyable. Kids with a Nintendo joy pad are not addicted to technology, they are racing a car. They are having fun, and playing with other kids." Kids on the Net are not using technology. Rather they may be "trying to solve a mathematical problem, designing or building something, or solving a puzzle—trying to figure something out."

Curiously, if you ask children online if they are addicted, they will invariably say yes. On the other hand, they don't seem too concerned about it because they don't believe that it's harmful to them.

My sister and I both find chatting on the Internet very addictive. I'm trying to balance my time on it.

JOELDINE HAYTER, 15
New Zealand

When it comes to the term *Net addiction,* Sherry Turkle, MIT psychologist and professor of the sociology of science, says, "I hate it." To her, "the whole addiction thing is making us sound stupider than we need to sound about the complexities of this phenomenon. It is blinding us." She says the term addiction has a very specific and important meaning and by using it in this context, we close ourselves down to a lot of interesting dialogue about the Net and its implications.

Turkle says that if your child is addicted to a substance, you have one job and one job only—get him or her unaddicted. Unlike the Net, there is nothing positive that can be said about dependency. Turkle gives the example of heroin, something to which one is addicted. Unlike the digital media, no one can be said to use heroin to learn and work through problems and to explore different aspects of their self. "The drug takes away your ability to work through issues. It does not empower you to confront, learn, and deal with your issues in a constructive way."

While parents need to be concerned about any compulsive behavior of their children, there is clearly some antitechnology bias built into the hyperbole about Net addiction. You don't hear people talking about "book addiction," for example. Rather, we use the positive term "voracious reader." Or a child who "loves to read." Adults are concerned about addiction to video games, computers, the Net—in particular, chat lines—anything their children do that parents don't completely understand, or govern.

The issue is one of balance. If a child becomes involved for a prolonged period of time in something which is causing disequilibrium in his life, we should be concerned. If she is giving up her sports team, homework is suffering, friends are being neglected—then there may be cause for concern. However, experience shows that compulsive use of the new media is fairly rare and that when it occurs it is usually a temporary problem. It is also hard to argue that this is an activity—such as drug abuse or smoking—which is harmful. Further, N-Gen children show a remarkable ability to self-correct. Which brings us the striking story of Caleb Murphy.

Net Addiction: Caleb Murphy's Net Abstinence Diary

The topic of Net addiction is raised frequently by kids in chat rooms. One of them, 14-year-old Caleb Murphy, who goes online after helping his parents milk the cows on their dairy farm in central New York state, announced that he was planning to go offline completely for a while because he was worried that he too was addicted to the Internet and spending too much time in chat rooms. Caleb wanted to see whether he could break the habit. Researcher Kate Baggott, fast on her feet, sent a note to Caleb asking if he would be interested in keeping a diary of this thoughts over 14 days to share with readers of this book. "Could it be a diary of one week of abstinence?" Caleb asked. "I don't know if I could do two weeks without talking to my Net friends." After several more e-mail exchanges, Caleb agreed to go without the Net for two whole weeks. Below are excerpts from his diary.

December 2, 1996.
Hi, I'm Caleb Murphy and I'm a Netaholic. That used to be a joke on the chat line I frequented. As people's grades in school began to slip, and the relationships with real-life friends disintegrated, people started to realize it wasn't a joke. That is probably why I decided to go on a two-week Net abstinence, to see if I could raise my grades and do things with my friends, whom I feel I've ignored lately.

I spent an hour on the Net earlier today, sending e-mail to my best Net friends and updating my home page with a message announcing my decision. When a few of my friends heard about my upcoming abstinence, they decided to try it too. It became a challenge to us, and I know I at least was looking forward to it, kind of.

I'm looking forward to the chance to get out more, and to do some things I didn't used to have time for, but am frightened by the thought of being away from my "home away from home" for two weeks. It scares me. I had a knot in my stomach as I disconnected for the last time for a long while. It was rather awkward when I left, I had been hoping to meet some of my friends on our chat line, but only one was there, and so I e-mailed the rest. I almost feel like I'll never see some of them again, but I'm sure I will. Who knows, though.

Two weeks may not seem like a long time to people who have never been on the Net, or were lucky enough not to get addicted. But for someone like me, two weeks seems like an eternity. I spend sometimes more than two hours a day surfing, many more on weekends and nonschool days. If I decide my life is a lot better without it I may hardly ever go on even after my abstinence is over.

December 3, 1996.

Today being my first full day of abstinence, I didn't have too much problem staying away from the Net. It'll be a couple more days before I really start to feel isolated. I do miss talking to my Net friends, but I can deal with that. I'll probably call one or two of them soon. I did my homework early today, got it out of the way. After work, I spent the evening reading, listening to music, and relaxing. It felt rather good to stay away from T2, the chat line I frequent. There had been too much fighting and arguing there for me to stand lately. That's another reason I left. Net people were starting to get on my nerves.

Maybe there's something about the Net that makes people on it irritated. Actually, I'm sure there is. It can get very frustrating when it's slow, or when you run into someone you don't like, like someone with the handle CYBERNAZI, or KKK, or someone posting offensive pictures, etc. It sometimes makes me want to punch the thing, and put a hole right in the monitor. I've heard stories on the Net of people who have done things like that.

Maybe it's also the frustration of meeting a great person, someone you would love to know in real life and talk to without a computer or a phone between you, and never being able to really meet them because they live on the other side of the world. The Net brings us all together, but it also reminds you of how far apart we are.

December 4, 1996.

The need for the Net that I was expecting hasn't come yet. It's possible it won't, but I haven't been away from it for very long. T2 is such an easy place to miss. I first went to a chat line, one called Talker, on Memorial Day of 1996. I came in as a newbie, with absolutely no idea of what was going on. I started to make friends, communicating with them through e-mail and meeting on the chat line. I also started to learn a little about the Net, and how to use it. I frequented Talker until late August, when

I logged on only to find it not there. None of the addresses I had for it worked. I found out soon after that it had been shut down, for reasons I'm not sure of. At this time I had just finished my home page, and was rather proud of it, although it wasn't much to be proud of. After the shutdown of Talker, there was a massive e-mail campaign to those who shut it down, expressing our anger. Finally they created a new Talker, which was scorned by all the Talker veterans because of its differences to the original. Right after the original's shutdown, T2 was made, and I heard about it through a Net friend. A relatively small group from the original Talker started frequenting T2, and it became a replacement for Talker.

But many of my Talker friends never came to T2, and I was forced to meet new people and make almost entirely new friends. Since the amount of people in T2 was small, there were often only two people there at a time, so it was easy to meet everyone.

December 5, 1996.

Life without the Net has certainly been different, and I'm not sure if it's good or not. I constantly wonder what's happening in the chat line, if anyone else announced their pregnancy or the birth of their sister's child, etc. etc. A lot was happening when I left. Tomorrow night I'm gonna call a Net friend, one of the ones who's doing the two-week abstinence too.

I've already broken a couple of habits I had when writing on the Web. I always used . . . on the Web . . . like this . . . because commas and periods were too picky . . . and this was easier. . . I've stopped now to write this.

There are so many things I can't wait to do when I get back on. I've already written a list of things to do, so I won't forget over time. I guess the "withdrawal" is starting to set in.

I saw an article my parents were reading today in a newspaper about Net addiction. I'm gonna try to find it, and maybe critique it, see what's right and what they are wrong about.

I've been listening to music a lot, and calling a lot of people. I guess I'm finally getting back to normal life, like it was for me eight months ago, before I had the Net.

Looking back over this entry, I guess the withdrawal has come finally, just not strong yet. I've abstained from going anywhere near the Net for three and a half days now. If only I could keep it up for another week and a half. I'm sure I can. I think I can . . . I think I can . . . I think I can . . .

December 6, 1996.

Today I woke up to snow everywhere outside, and my prediction from the night before came true. School was closed today. I spent the day watching a movie, playing computer games, and calling people. All in all, a slightly boring day. It would have been better if I'd had the Net. One of the best things about it is it gives you something to do when you have nothing to do.

I found that newspaper article about Net addiction. I read it twice, and then read the list of things that may show you're addicted to the Internet. I decided I was not fully addicted, because I didn't fit all the descriptions that were provided. For instance, I don't involuntarily make typing motions with my hands. At least I hope I don't.

The article gives a statistic that less than 5 percent of Americans who go online are actually addicted. Considering that almost everyone I know online claims to be, either the statistic is wrong or my friends don't know how deep a true addiction is. Some of the stories in here (and stories I've heard) are frightening . . . it's hard to believe people get that into it. I can understand having trouble tearing yourself away from it, and a little further than that, like taking all meals to the computer, but comparing it to cigarettes and alcohol . . . wow . . .

Reading what I wrote last night, I now know I can . . . if I go on like this, I can make ten more days. I'm going out tomorrow night, and around noon. I'm gonna try to keep myself busy. If I get through this weekend, I can get through all of it. Just as long as I don't start air typing.

December 9, 1996.

I had an almost irresistible urge to log on today. I abstained. When I got home from jazz band this afternoon, I walked into the computer room, sat down, and moved the mouse to Netscape. Luckily I stopped myself before I clicked. I played computer games to avoid the urge. I must either have a strong will or my addiction isn't very deep.

I just realized how much I have that I got through the Net. I'm listening to midi files I downloaded a couple of weeks ago, a lot of my guitar music I downloaded off the Net, a lot of the things I have in my room I printed or copied off the Net. I used the online phone books all the time for phone numbers, and now I need someone's number and I have to use Directory Assistance (ugh . . . how primitive . . .) to get it. If I'd never gotten the Net there would be a lot I would have to do without.

I was thinking today about the differences between my online friends and my other friends. I live in the boonies, way out in Central New York, and a lot of my friends are farmers or have some connection to a farm. But I have never met a farmer on the Net, except one person, who happened to also be an offline friend of mine. My online friends also always seem more lonely and willing to talk than offline.

Another thing is my online friends all seem to have great stories to tell, of amazing things that have happened to them and great (or terrible) things that are happening to them. I often wonder how much of it is true. At first I didn't always tell the truth online. I figured none of them would ever meet me, so why not lie, try to sound more interesting. After a bad experience with a lie I told, I never told another serious one on the Net. Everything I say there is true, except for maybe just a little exaggeration now and then. But I've caught some online people lying to me, by asking them in-depth questions on things they said they knew about, and really didn't. And I've been told things I know aren't true, just because they are so unlikely. That's the problem with the Net. It's hard to tell when someone's lying.

December 11, 1996.
I called an Internet friend tonight. She told me about things I'm missing in the chat room, new people that have come, and old people that have left. Now I'm more anxious than ever to get back. I miss it so much. This is hard. I don't think I realized how long two weeks would seem to me. And with a lot of new things to look forward to online, I can't wait till this is over.

To open this writing program, I clicked on the wrong icon, I clicked on Netscape, my browser, simply because it had become a habit for me . . .

sit down at the computer--->click on Netscape--->log on.

I was so used to it after doing it for eight months, I click on it just about every time I sit down. It's very habit-forming.

I've discovered lately a lot of friends of mine who go online that I didn't know about. Some of them have AOL so I never see them, some go on at their neighbor's house, and most just go around looking at things on the Web, never getting involved.

This week I've certainly done a lot more than I would have without the Net. I've gone places, called people, done things I've never done before and I did it all without the Net! I'm so proud!

But I am really starting to miss my Net friends, and these midi files are getting boring, I need some new ones. And some new games. I need to work on my home page. I need to go to the chat line. All these "I needs". . . it's scary. What would I do if I knew I could never get back online? Die? Or something close. A long depression, anger, general mood swings, who knows?

December 12, 1996.
I discovered positive and negative aspects of the Net today. I had a project due in school on the 13th, and since I wasn't allowed online I was able to have a lot of time to do it. When I am allowed on I spend too much time on and not enough time doing homework, something that will change after these two weeks. But to complete my project I needed a couple of pictures, which I knew I could get online. My parents had to go on and find what I needed in order for me to get the project done. When I

got it I still took another hour to get it done, and I could have gone faster if it had been me going online to get the map.

I've really missed the Net today. Even though it would have kept me from working hard on my project, I would have had it easier and of course I miss T2.

December 13, 1996.

This makes it tough. I just heard from a Net friend that I called that the old Talker is back! Remember I mentioned it about a week ago? Well, it was brought back. This means my old friends might come back. Oh man, I am so excited. This is really gonna make it tough for three days, especially a weekend. I can make it.

I'm really feeling the boredom setting over me. When I have nothing to do, I wish I could go on, talk to my friends. I am also often pressured by hearing of a home page for a company, or a friend of mine's, or a new chat line—but I only have to wait three more days.

I was wondering today what the future of the Net will be like. A lot of people speculate that there will be a crash of the Net sometime, that could seriously screw up the world for awhile. I think it's very likely that that could happen. A good hacker could screw up the system for a while, or seriously disrupt something, like air traffic, subways, etc. There are certainly people with the know-how and the guts.

But I think and hope that someday the Internet will be as common as TV, e-mail will replace snail mail, and computers will be a more useful thing than they now are. It's the typical sci-fi future, but I believe it.

December 14, 1996.

I suppose since I only have three days left (if you count this one) I should start going over what I've learned, what I've decided to do from here, what I've decided NOT to do from here. I guess tonight I'll figure out what I'm not gonna do.

I'm not gonna let the Internet come before my homework. My homework grades went up these two weeks, and I'd like to keep them up. And my homework might come along a little better once I get access the Net again, cause I'll have access to more resources.

I'm not gonna spend really long periods of time online. I'm gonna cut down on how long I spend chatting, updating my page, and just doing surfing. It's pointless, often boring and it makes my eyes hurt, not to mention it annoys my parents.

I'm not gonna put the Net in front of doing things with my friends. I have been quite good about it in the past, but I found out that how much time I spent on the Net was annoying a couple of friends, so that's gonna end.

Those are really most of the changes I'm planning to make. Even a lot of what I was GONNA do got in there. Oh well.

I found out that one of my friends who also went on abstinence lasted for awhile. I suppose she's still offline, although she's checking her mail, which I heard when I called an online friend. The friend I called also tried for two weeks, and lasted almost one week. She also told me about my one other friend who tried. She lasted two days. That's addiction. Although I only would have lasted three or four, maybe five days without the incentive I had.

I guess the Net really is quite addictive. I could stay away from the TV easy, or at least a lot easier than I can the Net. Eventually we'll start hearing about people suing AOL or Netscape because they were divorced or lost their job because they spent too long online (sounds ridiculous, but it's not unheard of).

December 16, 1996.
Wow, two weeks already? It's about time. It seems like it's just dragged on and it also seems it's sped by. When I wanted to go online, and I missed it, it was the slowest two weeks of my life. But when I was doing things with my friends and getting out more it went quick. So I guess it was both positive and negative.

I really learned a lot about the Net, and the lack of, these couple weeks. I learned that the Net has become part of my life now, almost as much as school, and I can't go without it. I'm addicted, no doubt about it, and I don't care. It's worth it.

I learned how much I depend on the Net for communication, education, and just fun in general. It gives me something to do when I'm bored, and even when I'm not, it provides a good escape from the life of a high school student.

I learned that I should never, ever, spend two weeks offline again. It was worth it this once, but if I ever did it again, I might die.

I learned how hard it can be to have to write a certain number of words, every day. Luckily it was on a broad topic. I learned a lot about diary writing (a relatively new experience for me) and a lot of discipline as far as writing every day and not being able to log on. It taught me better self control, something I can sometimes use.

I learned that I should put homework in front of the Internet (or try at least). Bad homework grades are not worth the time I spend surfing.

I also gained a little insight into what it might be like to be addicted to a substance. Trying to stay off what you're addicted to is a lot harder than I or most people imagine. It takes a lot of self control and effort.

gone

Six months after he completed his Net abstinence, we followed up with Caleb to see if he was able to adhere to his Internet resolutions.

"I have been involved in a lot of extracurricular activities like musicals and sports," Caleb reported. "I have been spending more time with my friends. In terms of grades, well, they're down, but I don't think that has anything to do with the

Internet. It's a grade 9 slump that I think everyone at my school goes through. Grade 9 is a lot harder than what I had to do previously."

In hindsight, Caleb has become suspicious about the term *Internet addiction*. He now thinks his earlier usage was just an enthusiastic phase and that Internet addiction was just the most readily available term to describe it. "I am definitely not addicted to the Internet anymore and I really don't know if I ever was," Caleb says. "It's something I control both in how long I use it for and what I use it to do."

If Caleb was a Net-aholic, the world needs more of them. Here is a boy who thoughtfully acknowledges that he has a possible disequilibrium in his life. He is concerned about how the Net may be negatively affecting his schoolwork and relationship with real life friends. He takes steps to investigate this through a two-week period of reflection. To help muster the courage to cut himself off, he spends the first few days thinking about the negatives—for example, he remembers being bugged about people with C-names like CYBERNAZI and KKK. He reflects on the issues which have come up on the Net—topics like censorship, addiction, the viability of the Net infrastructure, privacy. He thinks about friendship. He tries to understand how he feels about being away from his Net friends and lacking access to the Web. He ponders what is real in cyberspace. In doing so he reveals that he is articulate for his age. He reveals that he actually has a full life—he is a conscientious student in the school jazz band, with strong real-world friendships, and he is fulfilling his responsibilities to his family around the farm.

He conducts a thoughtful review of the benefits he receives from the Net and concludes these are considerable. He finds that his need for the Net is actually a need for Net products like midi files, new guitar music, a sense of community when he is away from his offline friends, and communication. He adjusts his life to find balance—real-world friends and homework will come first. In forming these improved work habits, he has examined not just his Net usage but his tendency to procrastinate as well. He will take steps to better ensure his privacy on the Net by reflecting before providing personal information. Through a comparison with a newspaper definition and his own understanding of Net addiction, he challenges his initial assumption that he is indeed an addict, and in doing so he draws conclusions about the dangers of substance abuse and the importance of self-discipline.

The most striking observation is that while Caleb appears to be an extraordinary 14-year-old, he is actually quite typical of the children with whom we have worked. In his story we see the contours of an N-Gen child—smart, fluent, social, analytical, self-reliant, curious, contrarian, creative, articulate, media-savvy, bored with television—a child that interacts with his world, and creates and achieves balance.

N-Gen Learning

FISHER

MIZZ HARPER?

IF WE'RE ABLE TO FIND ALL KINDS OF INFORMATION ABOUT SCIENCE AND MATH AND HISTORY AND NEWS AND STUFF ON THE INTERNET...

...WHY DO WE NEED YOU?

CAN I GET BACK TO YOU ON THAT?

2-12

Like millions of girls her age, 11-year-old Esra Korukcu of Avanos, Turkey, loves to skip rope and ride a bicycle. During the winter her understanding parents allow Esra and her sisters to roller skate in the living room, "but we have to take care not to break anything."

Esra's life is absolutely unremarkable, yet kids in thousands of American classrooms have read on the World Wide Web a detailed account of how Esra spends her day. They know her hobbies, what her school is like, what her parents do for a living, and that she has a scar on her knee from falling off her bike. This information is available on the Web because Esra has volunteered her story to GlobaLearn, an inspired company of young adults who travel the world and chronicle their journey through the eyes of children.

In 1997, the company organized a five-month trek across Asia, following the same route as Marco Polo, and later in the year another expedition traveled through Brazil. In each community, the expedition spent a day with a young boy or girl, such as Esra, who are called *hosts*. A profile of the host is prepared, sharing the youngster's thoughts on subjects such as family, school, hobbies, local community, and life in general.

"On school days," Esra tells us, "my morning begins at 7:30 A.M. when I get up. I wash my face, get dressed, and then join my family for breakfast. I love milk and always have it for breakfast, along with bread, *pikmas* (Turkish jam), *sucuk* (soo-jook—a Turkish sausage), and cheese. If I am lucky, my mom lets me have chocolate spread on my bread."

The youngsters that GlobaLearn meets with are asked whether they have any special wishes for the thousands of kids who will be reading their stories. Fifteen-year-old Ufuk Sahin from Istanbul, Turkey, replied: "If I had to give a message to kids all over the world, I would have to say 'make peace and stay cool.' I do not like to give advice though, probably because I do not like being given advice."

GlobaLearn is one of the earliest and most elegant examples of how the Internet can bring the world into the classrooms of the nation. The company was founded by Murat Armbruster in 1993 with a mission "to prepare children for global citizenship and develop in them the skills, awareness, and determination to become responsible stewards of the earth."

To tell their story to the world, GlobaLearn's expedition team travels with state-of-the-art electronic equipment, including portable computers, digital photo and video recorders, high-speed modems, and a mobile satellite transmitter. The data is sent via satellite to GlobaLearn's New Haven, Connecticut headquarters, where it is edited and formatted for presentation on GlobaLearn's Web site—a process that takes about an hour each day. GlobaLearn also provides curriculum materials, including lesson plans and reproducible worksheets, on its Web site.

At noon each day the team takes a photo of what it is doing and puts this on the Net. Each of the five team members also submits a daily journal, often investigating some aspect of the local culture or economy, such as a visit to a cheese or pottery factory. The idea is to stimulate kids in the classrooms to conduct similar research into their own communities—making them active participants rather than just passive observers. Students use the field teams as extensions of themselves to investigate the historical, cultural, and physical features of the earth's environment. This supplements the data from the students' explorations of their own communities. Students are then able to make "dynamic comparisons between their experiences and the experiences of others in different countries."

Kids in the classrooms are encouraged to submit questions to GlobaLearn's New Haven headquarters and each week 10 questions are randomly picked and relayed to the expedition. Questions range from "do you get carsick?" to "how do the clothes in Turkey differ from the United States?"

There is also an area on GlobaLearn's Web site where kids and teachers from different classrooms can discuss issues among themselves or comment on the expedition. The feedback is very positive. One Oakland, California teacher concluded: "My students are most interested in the host profiles, but some of the investigations have also held their interest. They like hearing about different foods, too. Someone else said there is so much stuff, it's overwhelming, which is almost so, but it's good to be able to choose from the wealth. Thanks."

GlobaLearn promises that future expeditions will continue to focus on children while maintaining a commitment to its initial concept: "That learning must be engaging and exciting; that the world is the greatest resource for learning; and that technology has given education an invaluable medium by which to access the world and participate in it."

Learning in a Knowledge-Based Economy

The Net Generation children using GlobaLearn are beginning to process information and learn differently than the boomers before them. New media tools offer great promise for a new model of learning—one based on discovery and participation. This combination of a new generation and new digital tools will cause a rethinking of the nature of education—in both content and delivery. As the N-Gen enters the work force, it will also place profound demands on its employers to create new environments for lifelong learning.

Growing up is about learning. However, the economy and society these kids are growing into is very different than that of the boomers. The destination is different and so is the route the kids must take.

An economy is a system for the creation and distribution of wealth. As I explained in *The Digital Economy,* the new economy is based on human capital and networks. In this economy, knowledge permeates through everything important: people, products, organizations.

In the new economy, wealth is increasingly created by knowledge work—brain rather than brawn. There have always been people who have worked with their minds rather than their hands. In the new economy, they are the majority of the work force. Already, almost 60 percent of American workers are knowledge workers and 8 of 10 new jobs are in information-intensive sectors of the economy. In the past 25 years, the number of Americans with college degrees has tripled from 12 to 37 million. The percentage of adults who are college graduates has doubled from 11 to 22 percent.[1] The factory of today is as different from the industrial factory of the old economy as the latter was from the craft shop of the earlier agrarian economy. A typical AlliedSignal plant is full of robots and brimming with microprocessors, and many of the plant workers have engineering degrees. Some Nortel plants have a work force averaging a community college degree. The N-Gen is destined for a world of knowledge work.

Increasingly, key assets are human. Consider Netscape as a new-economy company. When evaluating the assets of a new-economy company like Netscape, you don't ask old-economy questions like "How much land does the company own?" or "What is the value of Netscape's manufacturing facilities—its plants?" Rather, the only meaningful assets are contained in the minds of the managers and employees of the company.

The dominant form of capital in the emerging economy can currently be examined in the computer room of your local school's library. More than any other generation, these children need—and want—to construct solutions to the growing problems that threaten this small and increasingly fragile planet. If this is true, there is no more critical challenge facing business and government than to understand how that capital can be nourished—for the betterment of the individual and for all.

More important, the N-Generation will not only become the means of production, it will become the dominant social force, shaping not only economic activity but our social structures, the environment, and human existence. What kind of education will equip the N-Generation for this task? How will it acquire the values, the critical thinking, the collaborative skills, the mastery of communication required to protect and advance society?

If we intend to answer these questions through our educational systems, we have to look at the kinds of students who are in our schools or will be entering them soon. One example of an N-Gen preschooler is four-year-old Ryan McNealy, whose parents decided to get him a computer because they felt that he was watching too much television. They bought Ryan several children's educational programs, which he installed on his Mac and taught himself how to use. He particularly liked *Reader Rabbit,* which reads stories while the text is on the screen. Says his father Brian, "It was like a video game to him, but we soon learned that he was actually not just playing, he was learning."

After a few months, Ryan asked his father to come to the computer to see something. He pulled up a digital story and proceeded to read it off the screen. His father thought he had simply memorized the story, but Ryan insisted that he was reading. His father handed Ryan a children's book and he read that too. Ryan, still four, now conducts science experiments which he learns from his computer. Recently he was in the fridge getting ice cubes and headed out the door. Dad was puzzled and followed him. Ryan placed the cubes on white and black construction paper in the sunlight. He was investigating the impact of color on heat absorption.

Now, imagine being Ryan's kindergarten teacher.

Broadcast Learning

Historically, the field of education has been oriented toward models of learning which focus on instruction—what we can call *broadcast learning*. The term *teacher* implies approaches to learning where an expert who has information transmits or broadcasts it to students. Those students who are "tuned in" take the information they are "taught"—i.e., which is transmitted to them—into active working memory. The field of educational psychology is rich with research, theories, and lessons regarding what impedes such information from being received and stored for subsequent replay. It has long been thought that through repetition, rehearsal, and practice, facts and information can be stored in longer-term memory, which can be integrated to form larger knowledge structures. The product of this is certain outcomes and behaviors—which, in turn, can be measured during testing.

The lecture, textbook, homework assignment, and school are all analogies for the broadcast media—one-way, centralized, and with an emphasis on predefined structures that will work best for the mass audience.

This approach has been the foundation of authoritarian, top-down, teacher-centered approaches to education which go back centuries. At the extreme, reinforcement and punishment were said to enhance learning. I remember my father describing how he was hit with a ruler for giving the wrong answer to a question. More recently, a school of psychology called behaviorism, popular in the 1960s and 1970s (and still in vogue in some circles), emphasized the importance of reinforcement in learning. Positive reinforcement is said to result in certain outcomes. Similarly, negative reinforcement, or the lack of positive reinforcement, leads to the extinguishing of certain behaviors. So when a rat exhibits desired behaviors in a cage (called a Skinner box, after the founder of behaviorism B. F. Skinner), the animal is reinforced through receiving a food pellet. The rat has been taught the relationship between doing something and being reinforced. Behaviorism extrapolated from the experience with rats to humans and was an important influence in education for many years.

At home you can do what you want with your computer. If you wanna go surf the Net, you can do that. If you wanna write a letter, you can do that. At school you can't simply "do" something, you have to be "educated" how to do something. And you certainly can't decide what you wanna do.

TIARK ROMPF, 14
Germany

Today, teaching methods and even many computer-based instruction programs are largely based on this broadcast view of learning. The teacher is primarily a transmitter. Curricula are designed by experts who presumably know the best

> My parents home school my brother and me, so my mom has found a lot of things we use in our daily lives on the Internet. My family has downloaded some educational software and we used information from the NASA sites for a report we wrote last spring. We are also in the Science-By-Mail program and we use e-mail to keep in touch with our project scientist. The Internet seems to be a great resource for our family.

MICHELLE BALDWIN, 13
Oregon

sequencing of material and how children can best learn math, acquire a new language, or understand Mesopotamia. Programs are not customized to each student, but rather designed to meet the needs of a grade—one-size-fits-all, like a broadcast.

Of course, many teachers have worked hard to be more than just transmitters of information, measurers of retention, and judges of performance. Dating back to Sidney Poitier in *To Sir With Love,* Hollywood and the television networks have made a mini-industry of great teachers. Most of us can recall at least one teacher who inspired us to be our best; who jolted us into thinking differently; who enabled us to process and integrate information from different fields; who helped us acquire knowledge and values. I remember listening to my high-school music teacher take us through a vivid and passionate tale of Tchaikovsky's life. As a class, we imagined the anguish Tchaikovsky must have felt as we listened, enchanted, to the Symphony *Pathetique.* Not one of us stirred. We were enthralled and inspired to work hard on developing our musical abilities.

But, notwithstanding the noble and sometimes heroic efforts of teachers, working with large class sizes and limited resources, the delivery system of education is still very much designed around the broadcast model. This is especially true today, in a time of cutbacks in educational spending in many countries. When you have a class with 38 students and no technological tools for a different approach, broadcast not only makes sense, it is the only option.

The Crisis in Education

It has become cliché to say that the educational system in the United States and other developed countries is in crisis. True enough, some schools look more like war zones. Test results are not encouraging. Parents are not happy. There are cutbacks in funding in many advanced countries. And, overall, there is a feeling that, given all the improvements in technology and epistemology, we could be doing much better.

Further, the echo wave is crashing into a school system which is designed for fewer kids. (See Fig. 7.1.) United States school enrollments will continue to increase at least until the year 2006, with 54.6 million school-age children. The previous peak was set by the boomers in 1971, with 51.3 million attending American schools. And, unlike the previous boom in student population, this one is a "long, slow, rising wave and we see no immediate falloff," according to a U.S. Department of Education study entitled, *A Back to School Special Report: The Baby Boom Echo.* Between 1996 and 2006, public high school enrollment is expected to increase by 15 percent, the number of high school graduates will increase by 17 percent and college enrollment is projected to rise by 14 percent. The ethnic composition of the schools will continue to change as well, with Latino-Americans and Asian-Americans the fastest growing segments of the student population.[2]

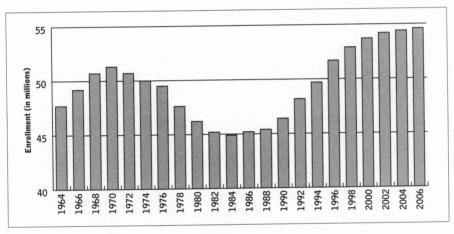

Figure 7.1
Enrollment in public elementary and secondary schools (in millions).
1964–2006
Data: U.S. Department of Education, National Center for Education Statistics.

The implications of student growth are jarring. Assuming the current broadcast teaching model (as the Department of Education report does), 190,000 new teachers will be required. Add to this the 175,000 teachers who retire or change professions each year and need to be replaced. The report calculates that 6000 new schools will be needed, not including the replacement of older, badly out-of-date schools and facilities. There will be approximately $15 billion in additional annual operating expenditures. A myriad of concerned parents and well-intentioned educators are working to address the problem. There is growing appreciation that the old approach is ill-suited to the intellectual, social, motivational, and emotional needs of the new generation.

Six Truisms and Corresponding False Conclusions

In our research we have been impressed and sometimes amazed by how the digital media enable a new view of education and, more broadly, learning. Yet we also heard every conceivable argument against using the digital media to transform the model of learning. Many of these arguments start off with a true statement and then draw a conclusion which is unwarranted.

Truism 1: *"The problems with the school system go far beyond the schools."* True enough. By the time kids get to the schools, many have already been significantly damaged. The most critical period of brain development is the first three years of life. Because of the breakdown of the traditional family, many children are lacking good parental attention during this formative period. The number of single-parent families has grown from 10 percent in 1965 to 28 percent in 1996. Most children come from families where there is no stay-at-home parent. (See Fig. 7.2.) The percentage of families with both parents working has risen from 37 percent in 1975 to 62 percent in 1996. In most families, both parents must work to get by. This is a big change. Combine this with working single parents and we've got a whopping 64 percent of families where all parents are working. Overall, parents spend 40 percent less time with children than they did at the peak of boom families, and many of these hours are spent watching TV, where opportunities for meaningful interaction are reduced.[3]

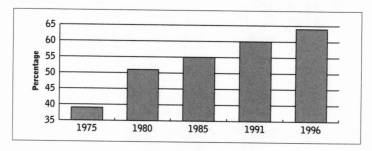

Figure 7.2
Percentage of single- and dual-parent families
with no stay-at-home parent.
Data: U.S. Bureau of Labor Statistics.

When children come to school hungry or from dysfunctional family situations, lacking motivation and seeing no hope to better their lot in life, then the schools will be troubled places. It is true that to really fix the schools we must fix much of what ails us as a society.

False conclusion: *"We should not take dramatic steps to transform the schools."* Of course the problem of the schools cannot be addressed in isolation, but this is not to say that we shouldn't take steps now to rethink the education system—both what is done at schools and how it is done. There are numerous examples of teachers, administrators, and parents who work together to create a school of the future. In so doing they change the context. A good example is the River Oaks School in Oakville, Ontario, which I described in *The Digital Economy*. Most students have a desktop computer, used for interactive, self-paced learning. The curriculum has been changed significantly, as has the role

> Most teenagers are failing because of drugs and possibly because they do not care about school. I am having problems because I hate school, find it boring and some classes are difficult for me because I just moved to a totally different territory where all the curriculum is different from where I used to live.

AMY MOYER, 15
Yukon Territory

of the teacher—all for the better according to everyone involved, including parents. The result was improved student learning and higher student motivation. The River Oaks project didn't solve the problems of the community, but it has helped change the community by improving community involvement in the welfare of children. It not only changed the children, but the attitudes of parents and local businesses, for the better.

The old saw "everything is connected to everything else" cuts both ways. Schools are a product of economic, social, and values structures. But, conversely, change a school and you change the world.

Truism 2: *"We need to understand the purpose of the schools—the ends of education, not just the means."* The most articulate spokesman of this view is social critic and technology skeptic Neil Postman. "Should we privatize our schools? Should we have national standards of assessment? How should we use computers? How shall we teach reading? And so on. . . . These questions evade the issue of what the schools are for. It is as if we are a nation of technicians, consumed by our expertise of how something should be done, afraid and incapable of thinking about why."[4]

Postman argues that the schools should serve several purposes: to help students understand that we are all stewards of the Earth, relying on each other and protecting our small planet; to cure the itch for absolute knowledge and certainty; to encourage critical thinking and the ability to disagree and argue; to encourage diversity while understanding that this does not negate standards; and to develop and use language, which is the basis of making us human, and which enables us to transform the world and in doing so to transform ourselves ("when we form a sentence we are creating a world").

False conclusion: "*We should table any discussion of means until we have agreement on the ends.*" Let us accept Postman's aspirations for education. While Postman's discussion of the ends of education may be laudable, he misses an important point: the means have become the ends. The broadcast approach to learning (which Postman does not appear to support) is becoming antithetical to the ends he espouses. The schools are not producing the language-rich critics, arguers, collaborators, and stewards he seeks—in part because the broadcast model of learning is an obstacle to such development.

Conversely, in adopting the new interactive model of learning, N-Geners are already assimilating the learning goals Postman espouses. They aren't just discussing such goals—they're achieving them. They rely on each other for learning. They debate everything online. They are critics. They are tolerant of diversity in their collaborations. And they communicate by forming sentences—they are creating their worlds. Through a new communications medium, N-Geners are already becoming what Postman aspires for them. McLuhan's words are ringing true through the N-Generation: Their medium has become the message. It's not a case of ends before means. The means are beginning to create new learning results. Postman's hostility toward technology is misdirected as he tilts at the windmills of the broadcast media.

What about the critics who say that e-mail and chatting are not improving communication skills because the spelling, punctuation and style are not proper? My observations tell me the critics are wrong. Time spent using these services is time spent reading. Time spent thinking about your response is time spent analyzing. And time spent composing a response is time spent writing. Such intense communications activity can be either very immediate with tight time pressures, such as on a chat line, or reflective, such as on a bulletin board or e-mail. Writing is like a muscle; it requires

> At 15 I'd say I'm already very competitive at school. I've managed to stay at the top of my class throughout my first two years of high school and the competition has really helped me stay there. No, I don't agree with adults when they say that technology is being introduced to children too early. I feel that it is never too early for an introduction to technology. It stimulates young children and gives them a boost in learning. It allows younger children to fully reach their potential and it can really help in reports and projects.

MELISSA EDWARDS, 15
Memphis, Tennessee

exercise. These kids are developing a powerful muscle that will serve them well in future work environments.

Says Allison Ellis of FreeZone, "The more chances that kids have to read and write, the better." In fact, on FreeZone, if sentence structure, grammar, or spelling inhibits the child's ability to communicate effectively, the FreeZone moderator will correct them by saying, "Hey, I didn't understand your point because you didn't complete your sentence." Moreover, language is something which evolves. The N-Generation is using the characters of the ASCII alphanumeric keyboard to add rich nonverbal elements to written communications. Their creativity in doing so seems infinite.

Truism 3: *"The solution to the problem of education is not technology."* It seems that in every discussion I've had recently about United States government's efforts to get computers into the schools, someone will say that computers aren't the answer. "It won't help to just throw computers at the wall, hoping something will stick." "I've seen lots of computers sitting unused in classrooms. I've even seen them sitting for months in their packing boxes." "Isn't technology a solution in search of a problem?" Or, as David Shenk, author of the book *Data Smog*, says, "Let's be very skeptical when people like the President and Vice President say [computers and the Internet] are going to revolutionize education. I think that is absolute hogwash."[5]

Theodore Roszak, who wrote *The Cult of Information: A Neo-Luddite Treatise on High Tech, Artificial Intelligence and the True Art of Thinking*, said in a recent article, "People who recommend more computers for the schools are like doctors who prescribe more medicine. What medicine? How much medicine? For what reason? The same questions apply to computers."[6]

Of course, unloading millions of computers into school warehouses and classrooms will not cure what ails contemporary education, any more than dumping a random selection of books into schools 200 years ago or prescribing random medicine to a patient would. To rephrase an election slogan, "It's the curriculum, stupid."

False conclusion: *"We should abandon or delay efforts to infuse schools with the digital media."* Rather than "People who recommend more computers for the schools are like doctors who prescribe more medicine," it is more true that "People who oppose computers in the schools are like doctors who oppose the use of modern medicine." Unlike medicine, the use of the new media to transform education will not be determined or sanctioned in some educational equivalent of the FDA. Rather, it will grow from the rich experience of students working with teachers, researchers, business people, and educators to forge, through actual experience, a new model of learning.

This is not to say that children should be guinea pigs. There is plenty of experience already to show that the new media can be a stimulus for change.

The digital media are a necessary but insufficient condition for reinvention of education. Computers and the Net are simply preconditions for moving to a new paradigm in learning. However, every project we investigated that introduced the Net and computer technology to students has been a stimulus for more far-reaching change. Such initiatives raise issues for teachers, parents, educators, and students to address. They encourage curiosity and experimentation. They enable the natural leaders for change to come forward and debunk old stereotypes. They pose questions raised by Roszak—but in real life, not academic debate. What is this new technology about? How can we use it? How might this affect the way we teach and the role of the teacher?

Most importantly, such initiatives provide the children themselves with the tools they need to learn and to catalyze the rethinking of education. Changes to a century-old system will not come about because of some top-down decree from educators. The schools need to become learning organizations themselves. Teachers, administrators, and students need to learn as organizations together. And I have become convinced that the most revolutionary force for change is the students themselves. Give children the tools they need and they will be the single most important source of guidance on how to make the schools relevant and effective.

Truism 4: *"It's dumb to teach children how to use computers instead of teaching them math, science, reading, and writing."* This statement was made to me by Michael Bloomberg in the previously mentioned debate at a recent conference of business leaders in Switzerland. Or, as Julianne Malveaux writes in a *USA Today* column entitled "Make Basics a Higher Priority than Internet," "Computer literacy is no substitute for basic literacy."[7] We can certainly all agree that kids need to learn the basics, and if we must compare, then this is more important than learning the exec function in Windows 95. Furthermore, numerous studies have shown that teachers who approve of computers in the classroom seek, as a primary goal, to "teach computer literacy."[8]

False conclusion: *"We should abandon or delay efforts to get the digital media into the schools."* Bloomberg and those like him have it wrong on three counts. First, use of technology does not inhibit learning about math, science, reading, and writing. The opposite is true. The research to date shows that when appropriately integrated into a curriculum, the new media improve student performance, not to mention motivation, collaboration, and communication skills. Even when it is not part of the curriculum, use of the new technology helps in learning basic abilities. Chat groups involve reading and writing. Compare this to television.

Second, fluency with the new media is required for productive life in the new economy and effective citizenship in the digital age. It is important that children know not only how to keyboard, search the Net, participate in a virtual community, or use important software applications (all learned effortlessly by children), but that they understand the underlying assumptions behind technology. As explained in the previous chapter, children don't need to become geeks, but they do need to know about software and how it works and to feel empowered to change their online world and the rules of the game.

Third, children acquire fluency with the media not just by studying these media but by using them to do other things. Comments like Bloomberg's are ironic in that they paint a picture of a teacher explaining to students how to use computers. The opposite is more likely to be true in many classrooms because of the generation lap. The students teach themselves. While they're at it they can probably teach their teachers as well. This has been the experience to date.

These new-breed teachers know that they are not just teaching children about computers but rather using computers to help children learn. "I teach cyber arts, but I don't teach computer courses. I teach extended media. I teach video production. I teach imaging. I teach photography and a lot of it uses computers. . . . But it is not a computer class," says Kathy Yamashita, cyber arts teacher, Northview Heights Secondary School, North York, Ontario. While Yamashita's comment is insightful, in reality students are also acquiring computer fluency. Says Alliance for Converging Technologies president David Ticoll, commenting on this case, "If she's teaching techniques for image enhancement on a computer, she's teaching a computer skill, just like teaching photography involves camera and lighting skills." Learning about anything in the digital age should enhance fluency with the digital media as a by-product—just like learning in the age of the printing press also enhanced reading and writing skills.

Truism 5: "Learning is social." Most understanding is socially constructed. Through conversation and dialogue, children come to their own understanding of an experience. This is true for adults as well. Learning organization theorist Peter Senge argues forcefully that learning within organizations tends to occur in teams.[9]

False conclusion: "Computers are used individually, therefore they inhibit learning, which is done socially." The computer has shifted from a tool to automate and manage information to something broader—a communications tool. Anyone with experience using the Net, even in its current, relatively primitive form, can grasp this concept. E-mail, chat sessions, bulletin-board-type forums, video conferencing, and shared digital workspaces are all communications tools. This is true for Web sites, which increasingly involve interaction with people. For example, children's personal Web sites are used as a way to share information and opinions with others —interactively.

Furthermore, much Net-based activity in homes and schools involves face-to-face interaction. When children cluster around computers at River Oaks School, you can hear their excitement—literally—by the buzz and laughter in the room. The same was true when my son and I searched the Net for his project on fish. True, to get the photos he needed we had to look at a lot of snapshots taken of fish in personal aquariums around the world, not to mention the products of assorted trout-fishing expeditions. But the experience was a very social one.

Truism 6: *"Teachers are skilled, motivated professionals dedicated to the advancement of their students."* Both my parents were teachers. They cared deeply about their students. They took it personally when a student failed or could not learn. Society has made a huge investment in teachers—there are currently 3,092,000 teachers in the United States. Increasingly, teachers work under very difficult conditions. It would be wrong to place the blame for the crisis in education at the feet of teachers. Further, there are many examples of teachers who enthusiastically support the new view of learning and the role of the digital media.

False conclusion: *"Teachers are not an obstacle."* It shouldn't surprise us that many teachers resist change. When a shift like this occurs, leaders of the old are often the last to embrace the new. Old paradigms, if I may use that word, die hard. Teachers have been schooled in the broadcast mode of pedagogy. As evidence, a 1997 survey of 6000 United States teachers, computer coordinators, and school librarians found that 87 percent believe that Internet usage by students in grades 3 to 12 does not help improve classroom performance.[10] This is an amazing number, perhaps explained by the sad reality that most of these teachers have not attempted to use the Internet to change the way learning is imparted.

"Everything they learn from day one reinforces their role as the sage on the stage," says Michael Dore, director of the Hacienda/La Puente Unified School District in Southern California. "So when they get computers in the classroom they use them for drill and kill—practice and testing. By training, teachers reject the discovery model of learning." Education and technology specialist Bob Beatty is involved in a project to get 40,000 students wired in the city of London. Referring to the role of teachers as maintaining discipline and order, he says, "It's strange, but there are never discipline problems when the kids are using their computers. The only problem is peeling them off the screen."

Teachers have legitimate concerns about their role as the learning model changes to interactive from broadcast. The irony here is that if they don't change and transform their classrooms and themselves to the new model, they face even greater threats to their job security. Society will find other ways to deliver learning and bypass them. The huge rise in the number of home schooled students from 20,000 in the late 1970s to more than 600,000 today in the United States alone, is evidence of this.

From Broadcast Learning to Interactive Learning

Unfortunately, as mentioned above, computers in the schools today are used primarily for teaching basic computer skills, for traditional "drill and kill" instruction, for testing, and for record keeping.[11] The N-Gen experience to date with the digital media points to a new paradigm in learning. The new media enable—and the N-Gen needs for learning demand—a shift from broadcast learning to what I call Interactive Learning.

The Technology of Interactive Learning

In the mid-1970s I was doing graduate work in educational psychology at the University of Alberta and found myself in one of the first classes to take an online course. We learned multivariant analysis (advanced statistical procedures) using a Computer Aided Instruction (CAI) package called Plato. This course was set up by a visionary in computer-mediated education named Dr. Steve Hunka. We sat down in front of a computer terminal which was connected to a computer-controlled slide display, all connected to a minicomputer. (This was before PCs.) The course was fabulous. It took me step-by-step through the material, but, unlike in traditional courses, I could stop and review something I didn't understand or fast-forward through material I felt I had grasped. I could test myself at various points and the system kept a record for me of how I was doing. Eventually, when I was ready, the system gave me a formal test. The final exam was also conducted on the computer. (And yes, I did actually get an A. In fact, I became so interested in this new technology that Professor Hunka became my thesis supervisor.)

However, because of the cost of such systems, the effort required to create the "courseware," the considerable expertise required for implementation, and the

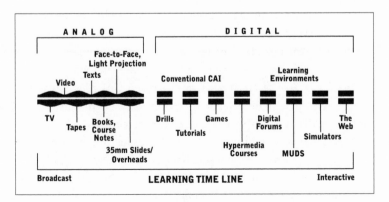

Figure 7.3
The technologies of learning.

huge cultural change in the teaching model, these CAI systems didn't really take off. Today the situation has changed dramatically. There is a wide range of tools and the Net itself, which creates a new paradigm in the delivery of learning. Figure 7.3 shows the continuum in learning technologies from broadcast to interactive learning.

Several of the analog technologies are shown. At one extreme is television, over which the learner has little control. Watch the show when it's played, from beginning to end. An improvement was videotapes, which could be viewed somewhat independently of time and location. For example, the African Virtual University, sponsored by the World Bank, is enabling engineering students to take courses in electrical engineering from a professor at the University of Massachusetts at Amherst. The stateside course is videotaped and transmitted via satellite to participating institutions in Ethiopia, Ghana, Tanzania, Uganda, and Zimbabwe. The professor is available by telephone three times a week to answer questions that the on-site instructor can't answer or for which clarification is needed. Eventually, the Virtual U will be available in more than 40 countries on the African continent.[12]

Books have greater portability and interactivity than television. They can be scanned and, in the case of texts, you can jump ahead or back. Face-to-face lectures may also have a degree of interactivity, as the lecturer can stop, take questions, or even hold a discussion. However, interactivity and discovery are limited because control rests with the presenter and the group rather than the individual learner.

The situation changes profoundly when information becomes bits. Conventional CAI includes *drill programs* where the user is presented with facts and then asked to recall them or to perform some operation based on the facts. *Tutorials* are more elaborate and can cover a broader range of material, as in the case of my statistics course. *Games,* if appropriate, can provide the learner with a more flexible and creative environment for learning many things, from visual-motor skills and rules to the nature of gravity.

CAI programs can improve learning performance by one-third—the student gains one year for every three. This is true even though CAI software programs are still fairly primitive, usually only using text. As the software matures, CAI will become much more interactive and richer, using graphics, audio, and video.

A good example of an interactive text-based CAI program was set up by Ron Owston, professor of education at York University. He designed a hypermedia course for prospective teachers which has two dozen modules.[13] Each module has a topic description and suggested readings with corresponding hot links to the original source. There are also electronic seminars available to each student where the professor participates on more of a peer basis than as the authority who owns all knowledge. Outside experts and facilitators are invited (I was one). There are various assignments which the students submit online, and also research tools to help students conduct in-depth investigations of topics and data. The environment also contains information regarding the process of the course, such as schedules, marking systems, and so on.

Gabriela Parada, 24, one of the 120 students in the course, raves about the system. "Ron has created an online environment which has forced many otherwise online-illiterate students to get online. I have observed a whole campus of students struggle with the initial technophobia of logging in or setting up connections from home and the significant anxiety that produced. Now these same students are in awe of the potential and powers of technology. Since all of Ron's readings for the course are on the Web, students have quickly learned to navigate so as to find the readings. In the online seminar groupings, students must take the knowledge they acquire from the readings on the World Wide Web and then comment and discuss. They are again forced to participate in a virtual community using a messaging system.

"Previous to this course, less than 5 percent of the students at my campus were Internet literate. This course has opened up a window to the world of technology and many are rethinking its role for their future classrooms."

The new media have helped create a culture for learning,[14] where the learner enjoys enhanced interactivity and connections with others. Rather than listening to some professor regurgitating facts and theories, students discuss and learn from each other with the teacher as a participant. They construct narratives that make sense out of their own experiences. Various digital forums, such as the ones we organized to research this book, enable brainstorming, debate, the influencing of each other—in other words, social learning.

Initial research evidence strongly supports this view. For example, in the fall of 1996, 33 students in a social studies course at California State University in Northridge were randomly divided into two groups, one taught in a traditional classroom and the other taught virtually on the Web. The teaching model wasn't changed fundamentally—texts, lectures, and exams were standardized across the two groups. Despite this, the Web-based class scored, on average, 20 percent higher. Students in the Web class had more contact with one another and were more interested in the class work. They also felt that they understood the material better and that they had greater flexibility in how they learned.[15]

An imminent N-Gen foray into multimedia communications environments is the Multi User Domain (MUD). As explained earlier, a MUD is a "place" on the Net where users create their own dramatic adventures in real time. MUDs are evolving into virtual meeting places and learning places—virtual social realities—on the Net. Soon your kids studying science will be able to meet in a troubled bioregion and share data, research, and solutions, or to have a meeting in a space station about the results of an experiment on the impact of gravity on viruses.

When you go for a virtual reality ride through the human cardiovascular system at a multimedia theme park, you are experiencing the next step in the evolution of digital learning environments—virtual reality simulation. This began with flight simulation systems which enabled airplane pilots to gain experience with emergency situations, such as losing engine power, in a safe environment. Virtual reality (VR) today usually involves some kind of clothing such as a glove, goggles, or headset. In special centers, the same effect can be experienced with large screens and hydraulics to move the cabin.

The ultimate interactive learning environment will be the Web and the Net as a whole. It increasingly includes the vast repository of human knowledge, tools to manage this knowledge, access to people, and a growing galaxy of services ranging from sandbox environments for preschoolers to virtual laboratories for medical students studying neural psychiatry. Today's baby will learn about Michaelangelo tomorrow by walking through the Sistine Chapel, watching the artist paint, and perhaps stopping for a conversation. Students will stroll on the moon. Petroleum engineers will penetrate the earth virtually. Doctors will navigate through your cardiovascular system. Researchers will browse through a library. Auto designers will sit in the back seat of a car they are designing to see how it feels and examine the external view.

Eight Shifts of Interactive Learning

By exploiting the digital media, educators and students can shift to a new, more powerful, and more effective learning paradigm. Figure 7.4 outlines these shifts.

1. From linear to hypermedia learning.

Traditional approaches to learning are linear. This dates back to the book, which is usually read from beginning to end, as a learning tool. Stories, novels, and other narratives are linear. Most textbooks are written to be tackled from beginning to end. Television shows and instructional videos are designed to be watched from beginning to end.

But N-Gen access to information is more interactive and nonsequential. Notice how a child channel surfs when watching television? I note that my kids go back and forth between various TV shows and video games when they're in the family room. No doubt this will be extended to surfing the Net as our TV becomes a Net appliance.

When we observed our N-Gen sample surfing the Net, they typically participated in several activities at once. When surfing some new material, they hyperlinked to servers and information sources all over the place. Seven-year-old Robert Huang and his sister Franny, eleven, came to our office to show us how they surf the Net. Robert looked up the movie *Independence Day*, followed links to fans' pages, and returned to the search engine. Interestingly, Robert entered three different searches, but he never went more than two pages away from the *Independence Day* site. If a download took too long or a page disappointed him, he hit the back key to return to the site.

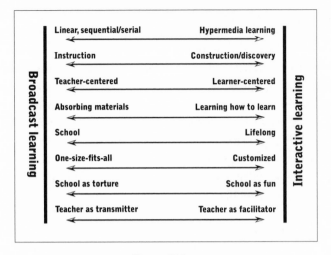

Figure 7.4
The shift from broadcast to interactive learning.

Franny was a little more focused. Her pet hamster Bupsie was pregnant and she wanted to see sites about baby hamsters. After conducting a *Yahooligans* search, she followed several links to other hamster owners' pages. She traced the mouse over the length until she found a link to an online journal which, with text and photographs, traced the development of a baby hamster from its blind and hairless infancy to adulthood—a process that takes only a few weeks. Franny intentionally avoided a guinea pig link on one hamster page because, "I don't like guinea pigs, but some people in South America eat them and even I don't want to see a fried one."

2. From instruction to construction and discovery.

Seymour Papert says, "The scandal of education is that every time you teach something, you deprive a child of the pleasure and benefit of discovery."[16]

At the risk of sounding equally heretical, there is a shift away from pedagogy—the art, science, and profession of teaching—to the creation of learning partnerships and learning cultures. The schools can become a place to learn rather than a place to teach. According to John Seely Brown, head of the Xerox Palo Alto Research Center (PARC), "Pedagogy had to do with optimizing the transmission of the information. What we now find is that kids don't want optimized, predigested information. They want to learn by doing—where they synthesize their own understanding—usually based on trying things out." Learning becomes experiential.

This is not to say that learning environments or even curricula should not be designed. They can, however, be designed in partnership with the learners or by the learners themselves.

This approach is described by educators as the constructivist approach. Rather than assimilating the knowledge broadcast by an instructor, the learner constructs knowledge anew. Constructionism argues that people learn best by *doing* rather than simply being told: constructionism as opposed to instructionism. The evidence for constructionism is persuasive, but it shouldn't be too surprising. The enthusiasm youngsters have for a fact or concept they "discovered" on their own is much more likely to be meaningful and retained than the same fact simply written out on the teacher's blackboard.

Seymour Papert illustrates the difference in his lucid book *The Connected Family.*[17] He explains that an instructionist might make a game to teach the multiplication tables. A constructionist presents students with the challenge of inventing and creating the game.

Computers today are used to teach mathematics using the drill and kill narrative. "How dull that is!" says Coco Conn. "That's why we never learn math, because it's *all* about *math.*" She describes the Cityspace project, where children from multiple locations collaborate to construct virtual cities, right down to the streets, buildings, and rooms in the buildings. "In projects such as this, you're dealing with a lot of math because the kids are sitting there thinking about the scaling of the model, how many polygons they can put in their object—all about thinking spatially and mathematically. They are doing it in a way that's fun and also relevant to something that they are creating." Conn explains that when the project was demonstrated in a four-day workshop, "We had the math teachers tell everyone what the kids were doing with math, and everyone was astounded."

3. From teacher-centered to learner-centered education.

The new media enable centering of the learning experience on the individual rather than on the transmitter. Further, it is clear that learner-centered education improves the child's motivation to learn. Learning and entertainment can then converge.

It is important to realize that shifting from teacher-centered to learner-centered education does not suggest the teacher is suddenly playing a less important role. A teacher is equally critical and valued in the learner-centered context, and is essential for creating and structuring the learning experience. Much of this depends on the subject; no one would suggest, for example, that the best way to learn the piano is the discovery mode.

In the past, education has tended to focus on the teacher, not the student. This is especially true in postsecondary education, where the specific interests and background of the teacher strongly influence the content. Much of the activity in the classroom involves the teacher speaking and the student listening.

Learner-centered education begins with an evaluation of the abilities, learning style, social context, and other important factors of the student that affect learning. It would extensively use software programs which can structure and tailor the learning experience for the child. It would be more active, with students discussing, debating, researching, and collaborating on projects.

4. From absorbing material to learning how to navigate and how to learn.

This includes learning how to synthesize, not just analyze. N-Geners assess and analyze facts—a formidable and ever-present challenge in a data galaxy of easily accessible information sources. But more important, they synthesize. They engage with information sources and other people on the Net and then build or construct higher-level structures and mental images.

> Students are encouraged to think openly and think for themselves, only after memorizing everything they are told by a teacher or made to read in a textbook. By this time, if you think for yourself, question things that don't seem right or question things that don't seem relevant, you go away empty handed, ridiculed for "not paying attention to the teacher."
>
> MATTHEW MACDONALD, 18
> Nova Scotia

"In our generation, we reach for the manuals—if we don't know how to do something, we ask," says Seely Brown. "We don't engage directly with the unknown and then do sense-making afterwards. Kids today engage and synthesize. Our generation is good at the analysis of things, as opposed to the synthesis of things."

Educom is a consortium of universities and colleges dedicated to the transformation of higher education through information technology. Carol Twigg, Educom vice president, notes how the knowledge explosion has an impact on the curriculum in postsecondary education. She notes that the cliché is that by the time a student studying to become an engineer graduates, half of his knowledge is already obsolete: "To use your broadcast metaphor, the professor says 'Here is your curriculum, I will broadcast it at you, you will somehow absorb it and then move on and be prepared for life.' This is literally a joke." She says we can no longer prepare students to live in a world of rapid change by 'shoveling' knowledge at them. "No one has yet come to grips with this whole concept of learning how to learn. No one is doing that in a full curricular sense."

5. From school to lifelong learning.

For the young boomers looking forward to the world of work, life was divided into the period when you *learned* and the period when you *did*. You went to school and maybe university and learned a competency—trade or profession—and for the rest of your life your challenge was simply to keep up with developments in your field. But things changed. Today many boomers can expect to reinvent their knowledge base constantly. Learning has become a continuous, lifelong process. The N-Gen is entering a world of lifelong learning from day one, and, unlike the schools of the boomers, today's educational system can anticipate this.

Richard Soderberg of the National Technological University puts it well: "People mistakenly think that once they've graduated from university they are good for the next decade—when they're really good for the next ten seconds." This is a reflection of the knowledge explosion in which the knowledge base of humanity is now doubling annually.

6. From one-size-fits-all to customized learning.

Mass education was a product of the industrial economy. It came along with mass production, mass marketing, and the mass media. Businesses everywhere are shifting to what I described in *The Digital Economy* as a molecular or individualized approach. We have markets of one, where a soccer club is treated as a market composed of individuals. There are production runs of one—highly customized—from bread to newspapers. We customize products with our own knowledge.

Schooling, says Howard Gardner of the Harvard Graduate School of Education, is a mass-production idea. "You teach the same thing to students in the same way and assess them all in the same way." Pedagogy is based on the questionable idea that "optimal learning experiences," as John Seely Brown describes them, can be constructed for groups of learners at the same age level. In this view, a curriculum is developed based on predigested information and structured for optimal transmission. If the curriculum is well structured and interesting, then large proportions of students at any given grade level will "tune in" and be able to absorb the information.

The digital media enable students to be treated as individuals—to have highly customized learning experiences based on their background, individual talents, age level, cognitive style, interpersonal preferences, and so on.

As Papert puts it: "What I see as the real contribution of digital media to education is a flexibility that could allow every individual to discover their own personal paths to learning. This will make it possible for the dream of every progressive educator to come true: In the learning environment of the future, every learner will be 'special.'"[18]

> To me, "growing up digital" means having fun while you're learning.
>
> CHRISTOPHER HOUSEH, 8
> Illinois

In fact, Papert says of the one-age-classroom-fits-all model "community of learning" shared by students and teachers: "Socialization is not best done by segregating children into classrooms with kids of the same age. The computer is a medium in which what you make lends itself to be modified and shared. When kids get together on a project, there is abundant discussion; they show it to other kids, other kids want to see it, kids learn to share knowledge with other people much more than in the classroom."[19]

7. From learning as torture as learning as fun.

Maybe torture is an exaggeration, but for many kids class is not exactly the highlight of their day. Some educators have decried the fact that a generation schooled on *Sesame Street* expects to be entertained at school—to enjoy the learning experience. These educators argue that the learning and entertainment should be clearly separated. As Neil Postman says, ". . . *Sesame Street* does not encourage children to love school or anything about school. It teaches them to love television."[20]

But doesn't that say more about today's schools—which are not exactly exciting places for many students—than it does about the integration of learning and entertainment? I'm convinced that one of the design goals of the New School should be to make learning fun! Learning math should be an enjoyable, challenging, and, yes, entertaining activity just like learning a video game is. And it can be! Besides, *Sesame Street* let the entertainment horse out of the barn. So did video games, the Web, FreeZone, MaMaMedia, and a thousand others.

> I believe strongly that what I teach has nothing to do with technology. I think it is essential that my students have access to technology. But I say to them, you are learning a way of thinking, problem solving, and planning, 90% of which occurs in your head and in your creativity. You are creating dreams and ways to attain those dreams. That's what we are doing in education.
>
> High School Cyberarts Teacher KATHY YAMASHITA

It is said, however, that if learning is fun it can't be challenging. Wrong! Try getting through the seven levels of Crash Bandicoot or FIFA soccer on your kids' video game if you think entertainment and challenge are opposites. The challenge provides much of the entertainment value and vice versa.

Why shouldn't learning be entertaining? *Webster's Ninth College Dictionary* gives the third and fourth definitions of the verb "to entertain" as "to keep, hold, or maintain in the mind," and "to receive and take into consideration." In other words, entertainment has always been a profound part of the learning process and teachers have, throughout history, been asked to convince their students to entertain ideas.

From this perspective, the best teachers were the entertainers. Using the new media, the teacher becomes the entertainer and in doing so builds enjoyment, motivation, and responsibility for learning.

8. From the teacher as transmitter to the teacher as facilitator.

Learning is becoming a social activity facilitated by a new generation of educators.

The topic is saltwater fish. The teacher divides the grade 6 class into teams, asking each to prepare a presentation on a fish of its choice covering the topics of history, breathing, propulsion, reproduction, diet, predators, and "cool facts." The students have access to the Web and are allowed to use any resources they want. Questions should be addressed to others in their team or to others in the class, not the teacher.

Two weeks later, Melissa's group is up first. The students in the group have created a shark project home page with hot links for each of the topics. The presentation is projected onto a screen at the front of the class as the girls talk. They have video clips of different types of sharks and also a clip of Jacques Cousteau discussing the shark as an endangered species. They then go live to Aquarius—an underwater Web site located off the Florida keys. The class can ask questions of the Aquarius staff, but most inquiries are directed at the project team. One of the big discussions is about the dangers posed to humans by sharks versus the dangers to sharks posed by humans.

The class decides to hold an online forum on this and invite kids from their sister classes in other countries to participate. The team invites the classes to browse through its project at any time, from any location, as the site will be "up" for the rest of the school year. In fact, the team decides to maintain the site, adding new links and fresh information throughout the year. It becomes a living project. Other learners from other countries find the shark home page helpful in their projects and build links to it. The team has to resource the information, tools, and materials it needs.

The teacher acts as a resource and consultant to the teams. He is also a youth worker—as one of the students was having considerable problems at home and was not motivated to participate in a team. Although the teacher can't solve such problems, he takes them into account and also refers the student to the guidance counselor. The teacher also facilitates the learning process, among other things participating as a technical consultant on the new media. He learns much from Melissa's group, which actually knows more about sharks than he does (his background is art and literature, not science). The teacher doesn't compete with Jacques Cousteau, but rather is supported by him.

This scenario is not science fiction. It is currently occurring in advanced schools in several countries. The teacher is not an instructional transmitter. He is a facilitator to social learning whereby learners construct their own knowledge. The students will remember what they learned about sharks as the topic now interests them. More importantly, they have acquired collaborative, research, analytical, presentation, and resourcing skills. With the assistance of a teacher, they are constructing knowledge and their world.

Needless to say, a whole generation of teachers needs to learn new tools, new approaches, and new skills. This will be a challenge—not just because of resistance to change by some teachers, but also because of the current atmosphere of cutbacks, low teacher morale, lack of time due to the pressures of increased workloads, and reduced retraining budgets.

LEAP: Toward a New Approach

Andrea Schorr had an interesting experience when she ran a community computing center in New Haven, Connecticut, called the LEAP Computer Learning Center. The center was open seven days a week and worked with local schools.

For almost all the kids, the only exposure they would have to computers was at the LEAP center. However, one class of third-graders had a computer-savvy teacher who also arranged for a couple of Macs and a phone line in his classroom, and then collaborated with LEAP so that each of the kids had an individual e-mail address. These kids obviously had more exposure to computers than students in other classrooms, and became an ad hoc test group.

Schorr noticed a clear difference as this class became more computer literate than the other youngsters. "They were able to do more things and had more exposure and a higher comfort level than the other children we worked with. E-mail for these kids became a tool of personal expression—rather than having the e-mail use just for specific projects, we allowed the children to use the accounts at will.

"On occasion we invited people who had various jobs in New Haven to come in and talk about their work. The kids started asking the speakers if they had e-mail addresses and began e-mailing them.

"It broke down the power dynamic that exists between a kid and an adult. I can't imagine any of the students picking up the phone and calling the speaker at home—that's just not possible for a child of that age—but what they could do was send a message from school. And they did that. It encouraged the individuals' expression and gave them a communication tool.

"The class with the computers also demonstrated a lot of initiative. They often would come up with ideas for projects and take them in other directions, whereas other classes needed more coaching and a more highly structured project.

"These third-graders progressed much faster than children that didn't have access to these machines. This is a particularly interesting age range, because third- and fourth-graders are beginning to develop their writing skills. They have come out of the phase where they are learning the alphabet and they are just beginning to start as writers. The quality of the writing of the computer-equipped class surpassed that of the other children in their same age range at another school in the New Haven district. It seemed to be enhancing their writing fluency, and definitely there was an attitude change. They saw this as fun.

"The kids were so excited to check their e-mail. This wasn't a video game. I think that goes against what many adults think computers and the Internet are about for kids. They don't think of it as something that can encourage a level of writing and communication."

MaMaMedia: Toward New Learning Products

What do Web pages, sandwiches, houses, and villages have in common? To the category "things that are built," renowned author and educator Dr. Idit Harel would add one more crucial item: knowledge. Harel and her team of designers at MaMaMedia in New York City have developed an educational site based on their belief that children learn by doing—what we've discussed as constructionism. The MaMaMedia team also believes that the Internet offers the raw materials to build with. "Our experience tells us that the computer, and the Web, are full of exciting things to do," Harel says. "Places kids can explore. Draw. Write. Build. And play. Places where children can have fun and be challenged, too."

When children go to the MaMaMedia site, they tend to spend a lot of time there rather than simply checking out a few pages and quickly moving on. Harel is proud of this and believes the site's success is a direct consequence of its constructionist design. There are no instructions on the site, only activities in which children achieve mastery through experimentation, trial, and error. There are two components to each of these exercises: the method and the content. Children have to discover the method of accessing the activities and then categorize the content in order to extract knowledge from it. The first step in learning how to learn is being able to group objects according to similarities and differences.

Most people are comfortable with the notion of hierarchies, and as one moves down a hierarchy the categories can become finer. For example, the five classes of vertebrates are fish, amphibians, reptiles, birds, and mammals, and mammals can in turn be divided into carnivores and omnivores. To make kids comfortable with this idea of layering, the MaMaMedia site invites the kids to build sandwiches, with each layer of the hierarchy being equated to a layer of lettuce or tomato in a sandwich. Kids are invited to build their sandwiches from Web sites that MaMaMedia has already visited and found appropriate for the 4- to 8-year age group.

The kids' sandwiches can include the items that interest them the most, and they are encouraged to share their online discoveries with other MaMaMedia visitors.

In another activity, categories are housed together in different clusters. Using avatars of surf shops, art galleries, and post offices, kids can build and name their own villages for others to visit, each avatar containing a directory of favorite shark sites, or art work, or a link to the village owner's mailbox.

MaMaMedia's goal is to tame the enormous amount of information that is available on the Net and help young children gain mastery of the skills they will need in order to manage such information. The use of metaphors such as sandwiches and villages makes the Web less intimidating and encourages the kids to have fun and experiment. Dr. Harel believes that the implications of constructionist experiences, like MaMaMedia, will have incredible implications for N-Geners. "These aren't kids who only consume media," she says. "But they are constantly learning how to create media as well."

The Future of Schools and Colleges

A recent public broadcasting program discussed corporate influence in the schools. The big issue debated was the potential dangers of Coke machines in the school cafeterias. While we should be concerned about the idea of company-sponsored learning with everything from ads on the blackboard to company-sponsored teachers, the producers created a tempest in a teapot and missed the real issue. For those concerned about corporate influence in education, the issue is not corporations in the schools. Rather, unless there is a big change in direction, the corporation will become the school!

Some schools, colleges, and universities are working hard to reinvent themselves, but progress is slow. This is truest for public institutions, but now both are in peril. Add to this tardiness the fact that N-Geners will perform knowledge work requiring lifelong learning and you have a formula for the privatization of education. This does not mean simply that companies will take over public schools. Rather, the private sector is tending to shoulder a growing burden for learning. Evidence for this is articulated in the little-known but very stimulating book *The Monster Under the Bed* by Stan Davis and Jim Botkin. The book argues that education, once the province of the church, then the government, is increasingly falling to business since it is business that ends up having to train knowledge workers. Say Davis and Botkin, "With the move from an agrarian to an industrial economy, the small rural schoolhouse was supplanted by the big brick urban schoolhouse. Four decades ago we began to move to another economy, but we have yet to develop a new educational paradigm, let alone create the 'schoolhouse' of the future, which may be neither school nor house."[21]

Because the new economy is knowledge-based and learning is part of day-to-day economic activity and life, both companies and individuals have found that they need to take responsibility for learning simply to be effective. The enterprise becomes a school in order to compete. Motorola U now has formal accreditation for courses it provides to employees. Many larger companies such as Xerox, Andersen Worldwide, and IBM have huge university-like campuses.

Davis and Botkin present data to show that in 1992 the growth in formal budgeted employee education grew by 126 million additional hours. This represents the equivalent of almost a quarter of a million additional full-time college students— 13 new Harvards. This is more growth in just one year than the enrollment growth in all the new conventional college campuses built in the United States between 1960 and 1990. "Employee education is not growing 100 percent faster than academia, but 100 times—or 10,000 percent—faster,"[22] say Davis and Botkin.

And for Carol Twigg, this is just the beginning. "Once the business community takes the step to integrate themselves with education, there will be an explosion in learning products. They're all still trying to sell to the higher-education buyers instead of the end consumer. Once they get that piece, then I think we will see a real change."

Another factor is that sales and education are converging. Every spring the telecommunications company GTE has held seminars in over a dozen cities. The program, which is attended by the company's customers, is called "GTE University." The company understands that to sell in the new economy you need to educate your customers. The company cannot market sophisticated telecommunications services unless its customers understand the current innovations in networking and how these can be applied to the competitive success of their firms. The sessions are also strongly attended by local government executives who need to know how the new technologies can help them deliver better, less costly government.

A logical step for GTE would be to expand this program into full courses on various topics. Such courses would be unique—not currently offered by any traditional universities or private training companies. GTE could probably charge for attendance as the demand would be very strong. Further, they could seek formal university accreditation or partner with some institution which can already grant degrees.

All this spells trouble for the schools and colleges that don't transform themselves. Many parents who can afford it are turning to private schools, private tutors, home schooling, and extensive use of CD- and Net-based learning environments as an alternative to public education. There is the obvious danger of a two-tier education system—one public for the lower classes and one private for the upper classes. Similarly, nonproactive schools and public educators will find themselves losing control over curriculum as attractive interactive learning products such as *Bill Nye, the Science Guy* seep into the system. But unfortunately, many politicians seem more concerned with cutting educational budgets than attempting to address the fundamental problems of the education system.

As the N-Geners graduate from high school, we can see big changes coming in the nature of and the delivery system for postsecondary education as well. In *The Digital Economy*, I argued that the universities and colleges were in deep trouble. With tenured professors, teachers threatened by technology, a history of little competition, and teaching traditions dating back centuries—to name a few problems—many educational institutions have become mired in the past. If the universities don't reinvent themselves in terms of their delivery system and relationship with the private sector, many will be doomed. This view was controversial, to say the least.

Educators really took note when none other than Peter Drucker shocked the post-secondary world in the March 10, 1997 issue of *Forbes* magazine. Confirming leading educators' worst nightmare, he stated publicly: "Thirty years from now big university campuses will be relics." Referring to the impact of the digital revolution, Drucker said: "It is as large a change as when we first got the printed book." He continued: "It took more than 200 years for the printed book to create the modern school. It won't nearly take that long for the big change. . . . Already we are beginning to deliver more lectures and classes off campus via satellite or two-way video at a fraction of the cost. The college won't survive as a residential institution. Today's buildings are hopelessly unsuited and totally unneeded."[23]

But isn't there a role for face-to-face communication? What about learning as a social experience? Clearly, the undergraduate residential campus is a transition place for youth in moving from home and high school to the world of knowledge work—not to mention that many still remember the university experience as the greatest time of their life.

But graduate studies may be better handled through integration with companies, private and other research laboratories, field work with government agencies, and other organizations. One thing is guaranteed. The status quo will not survive. The centralized university will give way to more distributed molecular structures, just as the centralized corporation is becoming internetworked. The university as mainframe will be replaced by the university as network.

These ideas are increasingly coming into the mainstream. Carol Twigg notes that when faculty place their courses on the Web, students don't want face-to-face interaction or small groups. "They are organizing peer discussion groups on the Net. They like being able to participate in the middle of the night—you know how kids are," she says. "Even with the primitive technology of today you don't hear kids saying, 'Oh dear, I wish we could get together once a week so we can see and touch each other.'" Children get together for other reasons, primarily social, and have ways to do this beyond the school.

One of the strongest trends is a shift to part-time education. Many students need to work to fund university attendance. Many more in the workforce are registering in university courses as part of the trend in lifelong learning. According to the

National Center for Educational Statistics, part-time students are now the new majority. Nearly half of college and university students attend on a part-time basis—6.6 million in 1993, up from 3 million in 1970. Over the same time period, the number of full-time students grew by only 38 percent. During 1994, 76 million adults (40 percent of the population) participated in one or more adult education activities. Those with more education are more likely to take additional courses. College graduates are nearly twice as likely to sign up for adult education courses, compared to those who have not attended college.[24]

The same trends are occurring at the graduate level—which has historically been primarily residential. According to Twigg, "Every time a company like AT&T hiccups and 40,000 people lose their jobs, thousands go back to school."

The academic calendar will be tossed out as well. The old view was, "Our calendar is based on an academic year with two semesters with courses on alternating days of the week." The new calendar does not belong to the university. It belongs to the student. Anticipate changes regarding faculty as we shift from the autonomous professor to teams which collaborate to create learning environments for students.

The New Teacher

As the digital media enter the schools and are instantly embraced by savvy and fearless N-Gen students, whither the teacher? Given the growing evidence that interactive media can dramatically improve the learning process, clearly teachers will need to change their role. Rather than fact repeaters, they can become motivators and facilitators.

A colleague, Phil Courneyeur, who has spent the last decade as a teacher in the developing world, has a helpful perspective: "In many settings, we need teachers who are youth workers, not transmitters of information. The biggest impediments to learning are social, not informational. Teachers need to have the expertise, the motivation, and the time to address the social and psychological roadblocks to learning. The schools should be right up there with the family as an institution which holds society together and helps us move forward."

As Tony Comper, president of the Bank of Montreal, says: "Kids doing a random walk through all the information in the world is not necessarily the best way for them to learn. Teachers can become navigators providing meta-learning—crucial guidance and support regarding how to go about learning." Professor Owston at York University in Toronto agrees: "We do have to make sure that the engagement with the Internet is stimulating and intelligent. We must remember that it's not the Internet itself that will do that—it's the teacher who mediates the student's engagement with the Internet." However, to do this, teachers need to become at least as fluent in new media as their students.

What is the new teacher like?

Small miracles have been occurring over the last three years at William Lyon Mackenzie Collegiate in North York, Ontario. The Emerging Technologies program mixes grades 10 to 12 to work on projects involving teams and the new media. The students learn by discovery. Through teams they source answers to their questions and resources to conduct their projects—from other students, outside parties, and the Net. The learning model is one of student-centered discovery enabled by emerging technologies.

When the program began, teacher Richard Ford told the students on their first day of class that their first project was for each to design their own Web page and present it to the group by Friday. When he asked how many knew how to design a Web page, 6 of the 32 kids in the class indicated they had some experience. Richard then suggested to the class that they should remember those faces, "because they are your mentors."

The students learn to cooperate, work in teams, solve problems, and take responsibility for their own learning—by doing. If there's something they don't understand, they must ask everyone else in the class before they can ask the teacher. Right after the first class, one girl asks, "What's a Web page?" Richard shrugs and says, "I don't know." Within a few days the kids have gotten the message. "And who's the last person you ask for help?" says Richard. Everyone replies in unison, "You are."

The model is that everyone relies on everyone else, sharing their expertise. Richard told them that if everyone didn't present their Web page on Friday, then everyone would get a zero. On the second day of class some of the kids were going around asking others if they needed help. However, when the learners have exhausted all routes and cannot find a solution to something, they can approach the teacher (called the facilitator). He then will work with them as a team member to find a solution or a resource which can help them.

In this class, there were only 15 computers for 30 kids—so they had to share the technology. The class was also very diverse, with children from Korea, India, Pakistan, Sri Lanka, Switzerland, Ukraine, and Russia. There were 15 different languages spoken in the class, with several of the learners having poor English skills.

Several kids were petrified to give presentations, but they got a lot of support from the class. One boy who spoke almost no English had to be coaxed by the others to stand up in front of the class. He mustered up the courage to approach the front of the room, then, turning, stood there and said "My Web page. . . . First time. . . . Graphics. . . . See link. Thank you." All the other kids applauded. "It was a very emotional moment for everyone," says Richard. "Everyone knew what an accomplishment it was for this boy to speak in front of everyone else in another language, presenting his first Web page." Afterward, outside the classroom, he approached Richard and said to him, smiling broadly, "I am proud."

For Richard, "There is something that happens when you decide for yourself that you're going to learn something and do something. This is much more powerful than when someone else says you have to do this."

"The kids not only learned about the new media and developed language and presentation skills, they learned about how to interact with clients and meet deadlines and most important they learned about how to share expertise and how to source it as well," says project coordinator Vicki Saunders. "The kids work 10 times longer because they are so excited about their projects."

I want to graduate with a résumé, not a report card.

TSIPORA MANKOVSKY, 14

After the first week the learners launched into Web design for real clients. One group built the software for the Canadian Broadcasting Corporation movie Web site. Another did the design for a New York-based artist named Carter Kustera—who came into the class for a week to work with them. IBM hired the group to do a CD-ROM about a conference called "Minds Meeting Media," where 1900 kids came together in Toronto to present their projects to other kids from across the city. Kids from grades 2 to 13 presented their animation and multimedia projects and all this was captured on a CD.

For their midterm "exam," the students had to create a three-page Web site or a three minute video. They were placed in groups of four, selected intentionally to help them overcome their obstacles to development. For example, all the "blockers" were put in one group. The project had to have a purpose. The students also had to discuss their own individual contributions and to assign marks to each other. The kids really had to wake up and work hard. A lot of buttons were pushed.

According to Vicki, "Richard is able to find the hook that turns kids on."

Richard has a radical view of the role of the teacher. "I don't teach. If I teach, who knows what they will learn. Teaching's out. I tell kids that there are no limits. You can create whatever you want to create. If it's impossible, it will just take a bit longer. My main function is to get kids excited, to consider things that they haven't done before. I'm working to create citizens in a global society."

He also deemphasizes his role as a judge. "We're trying to create a stage for them to present their ideas and their work to others. If a student hands something in to a teacher, she doesn't necessarily learn. The intention of the work becomes to satisfy the teacher's vision. We're not expanding the student's vision.

"For example, I whisper to a student who is doing a project on his home country, 'What about if you were to present this project on the Web?' The student realizes people will read it and see it. They might e-mail him back. They might set up a newsgroup. Maybe someone from their home town might join the conference. He may be able to share his ideas with others around the world."

Richard acts as a facilitator to set a hook. "If they grab hold, they're off on a voyage of discovery. We both discover. I learn through each of them—I learn about how people carry each other from village to village when he puts a photo on the Web. I learn about his culture when people begin to communicate with him from the other side of the globe.

"Everything you do affects others. We're asking kids to create their place in this global society. Whatever you want is possible. There are no limits. You create who you are in your space."

Student Aziz Hurzook took Richard literally. Aziz is a real innovator. He learned how to use a music synthesizer for his project and then created an audio CD. For his presentation he told the class to listen to campus radio at midnight. The radio station played the world premier of his music. He later set up a booth advertising Web development services at a conference on the new media. The experience was very positive. People were buzzing all around his booth and he realized there was a big opportunity here. Aziz created a company called "Caught in the Web" and took on his first client. The company had $1.5 million in revenue last year.

Says Richard: "If they can't create their own network, then they'll have to go to an authority figure. But if they stop and think about it, they are the authority! They are in charge of their own learning. Only they can decide to do something. And if they choose to do it, there is nobody on this earth who can stop them. Not only will they do something far more creative than you can imagine, they will probably break new ground while doing so."

N-Gen at Play

Can Jennifer come out and work?

Drawing by Cheney, © 1996*

Having Fun in Cyberspace

Shocking as it may sound, in many ways a computer is a $3000 toy. It's a toy that adults and children can both use to find inspiration, stimulate the imagination, explore the world and meet other human beings, and gain new experiences that can rejuvenate their senses and personalities. This process—as most, but, unfortunately not all, adults will remember—is known as play. Detractors often criticize use of the Internet in schools and libraries for the sole reason that N-Geners think it is fun. I'd recommend that they lighten up!

Play has its own pursuits: amusement, competition, expending excess energy, and companionship—all of which can be fulfilled on the Internet. N-Geners view cyberspace as a fun place. "I just love everything about the Web," says 11-year-old Laura Shulak. "I could barely last the two weeks of my family's vacation without it. It took me so long to catch up with everyone."

Just as in the real world, kids at different ages use the Net for different forms of play. Youngsters like 6-year-old Emma Bowen of Newcastle, England, use their Web sites to collect games and jokes. She sticks pretty close to the home page. An 11-year-old will be more adventurous. "I log on, check my e-mail, check a few of my fave Web sites to see if anything new's happening, bop over to Infoseek and research something, download some strange piece of frivolous, useless software," says 11-year-old Rufo Sanchez of Rahway, New Jersey. "While that's bursting my 28.8 [modem], I hop into an IRC and chat with some of my buddies. When the download's over, I check my USENET groups for new messages. And to top it all off a nice relaxing game of Avara, a 3D networkable game that you can play 'cross the globe. I usually stay up till eleven o'clock, midnight not uncommon."

Play Is Productive

Xerox's John Seely Brown, a researcher whose work depends on creativity, knows that innovation cannot exist when one lives solely within the confines of the work world. "I think that we have underestimated the importance of play in general," Seely Brown says. "This technology and the way children use it may be opening up the kid part in all of us. It may enable us to get back in touch with free-form thinking and playing with ideas, images, relationships with other people, and so on. To be able to engage in more of a playful brainstorming, playful construction of ideas is increasingly important, as is the importance of being able to recognize the multiple forms of intelligence that we all have.

"Any one of us tends to have one kind of intelligence that is more natural to us than other kinds. The new technology begins to honor multiple forms of intelligence, provide a medium for each kid to be able to create and experience things that optimize how his brain is structured at that moment. So I think the playfulness and the multiple forms of intelligence come together and make a very rich tapestry."

Accessing the diverse forms of intelligence and the wisdom that opens the mind to diversity is not easy in an era when the notion of play seems under attack. Certain segments of society are publicly worried that our children are having too much fun. Criticism in an antiamusement vein has drummed up support for "back-to-basics" education, i.e., rote memorization, in place of the more creative teaching methodology that makes learning fun through encouraging students to embrace the notion of self-directed learning through discovery.

According to play theorists Joanne Quinn and Kenneth Rubin, the very concept of play took a beating once before under the influence of the Protestant work

> Many TV cartoons have such bad graphics. Like on the Flintstones they keep using the same background over and over again as Fred is running along. And they aren't even 3D. I guess they made those things before they had computers.
>
> ALEX TAPSCOTT, 11

ethic which "fostered the attitude that play was recreational, trivial, and inconsequential behavior."[1] Play has been a topic of serious study for the past three decades, and psychological, philosophical, and sociological observation supports the position that it is an essential element in human development. Says psychologist Irene Athey: "When the family and school climate is propitious, providing adequate space, materials, and benign supervision for free expression through play, the child develops a healthy attitude toward self and others as well as a zest for life and an openness toward new experiences."[2] Adults may be forgetting to encourage their kids to play because their own lives are increasingly stressful. The pace of business is constantly accelerating, and most adults correctly feel they have little employment security. They know that in the digital economy, competition doesn't come from competitors only—it comes from everywhere. Everyone is working harder with less down time and this obviously affects our behavior toward children.

Henry Jenkins, a professor of Media Studies at MIT who has studied the historical and social implications of play, notes that "for decades, the fantasy was that the advent of new technologies would shorten the workday and produce more leisure time. In fact, there is growing evidence that the workday is lengthening again and that the average American is working longer hours now than several decades ago. The same thing is happening to our children.

"For one thing, parents place their kids in more structured spaces in order to get child care while they work those longer hours. In many other cases the school day—especially in private schools—is starting to lengthen. My own son leaves home every morning at 7 and doesn't get back from school until 5 or 5:30. Some of that is commuting. Some of it is the longer school day. But this means he has very little goof-off time, especially given the fact that the school system requires two to four hours of homework per night or more. This is a constant source of anxiety and conflict for us as a family, even though I understand his needs for time as well as space. I don't want him skipping on homework and I don't want him going to bed too late. I think this is a dilemma in many households."

Kids of middle- and upper-income families are enjoying less and less spare time. Playtime outdoors after school has been replaced with after-school programming, extra lessons, and league sports. In addition, parental mistrust of neighborhood environments and the educational system, a lower birthrate, and the subsequent increase in the financial resources spent per child have created an environment in which children have less time to themselves and are subject to more intense adult supervision than previous generations. And, unlike the boomers themselves, N-Geners growing up in this economy have been subjected to the belief that every moment must be filled with productive activity. The result? A generation of children with less control over their real movements.

As housing density goes up, kids' play space goes down. A century ago, the typical American boy had an average play space of ten square miles of forest or prairie. The space has steadily declined over the decades, so that today the play space available to most children is only as large as one to five rooms. "My son has never had a backyard," says Professor Jenkins. "For him, as for many contemporary urban youngsters, the outdoor play space is the park a few blocks away—visits to which require preparation and supervision."

Boys seem to be more affected by this reduction in play space than girls. "Girls' play has traditionally always taken place under maternal supervision and been directed toward the development of female domestic skills," says Professor Jenkins. These feminine play patterns were in direct opposition to the play of boys. "The diminishing spaces where boys used to play affects the relationship between mothers and sons. A great deal of boys' development as individuals depended upon boys doing things their mothers didn't approve of without their mothers knowing. Now they're playing video games in the living room and their mothers know all about it. And so, because their mothers don't approve of the video games, there's more conflict."

Interactive and Video Game Supremacy

Children play on computers. The main reason they like to use the Net is because "it's fun." Video games are big business. (See Fig. 8.1.) According to one of my son's video game magazines, Nintendo sold 2.3 million of its N64 systems in the first six months of 1997—383,000 systems per month. The Sony Playstation has sold more than 4 million systems. While some parents may be concerned about so-called addiction, most seem to think that computer games and nonviolent video games are probably positive. Engaging the child in an interactive experience, developing hand-eye motor skills, giving the child a sense of accomplishment, keeping the child off the streets, and just encouraging having fun are all judged by many parents to be valuable or, at worst, benign.

My wife Ana recently took our son Alex into the local video game store to exchange a game. She listened to the 20-minute conversation between Alex and the Sony Playstation expert (not the Nintendo 64 expert—that's someone else). She reports that she understood little of the conversation—that it sounded like a cross

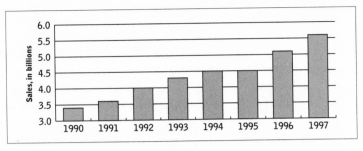

Figure 8.1
Electronic games–wholesale sales in the U.S. (in billions of dollars).
Data: Electronic Industries Association.

between two movie critics discussing esoteric art films and two engineers discussing software design. The way I figure it, Alex is learning and developing himself while he's playing (and he still loves soccer, hockey, baseball, school, the piano, and his friends).

What parents don't approve of is the violence of online and video games. The two main genres of video games have been labeled in England as 'Platformers' and 'Beat-'em-ups.' Platformers, (the more innocent of the two genres) such as Sonic Hedgehog and Super Mario Bros., involve figures jumping from one platform to another, avoiding obstacles and death. Beat-'em-ups, such as Mortal Kombat II and Street Fighters, involve vicious battles between animated characters where one or the other can be eaten alive or blown to smithereens. Some parents feel that video game playing is worse than a violent movie or television show because in the video game the children initiate actions. Parents not only fear that children will become numb to violence, but that they will use aggression and violence as solutions to problems they come up against in their everyday world.

The kids sure don't see it this way. Says Michael Young, age 14, "I don't think violence in video games does anything to people. Why would it? The violence is so fake. I wouldn't pull out a bazooka and shoot anyone. Video games are fun. It's not video games that make people violent. It's more likely the way they've been brought up."

Eleven-year-old Colin Hinrichs of Houston, Texas, has outwitted his video games and doesn't seem as impressed with their violence as he is with mastering the skills needed to solve the puzzle of the games. "I either use passwords that I get off the Net, or I use strategy that I practiced by messing with the controllers," Colin explains. "Sometimes I just press all the buttons at once to see what they do. I've been through every configuration on the control that there is. There's one more thing, I play long into the night after my

[When it comes to video games] play value, which is the same as fun factor, is more important than graphics, sound, or control although kids want everything.

ALEX TAPSCOTT, 11

parents think I've gone to bed. What do they call it? SegaEye. That means you played too much Sega, that my eyes look like road maps of the game."

While violence itself seems secondary to skills, it does work to ensure that the world of interactive gaming on the Net is still very much a little boy's club. "I have yet to see a girl play an interactive 3D game over the Net. I think that is because they are mostly violent, gory games," says 11-year-old Rufo Sanchez. "I know there are plenty of girls out there who like to play games, but I have yet to meet one." The reason for this violence, and boys' attraction to it, is rooted in the traditional play patterns boys have always exhibited. Video and computer games replicate almost exactly the backyard culture of a boy's play space.

"Boys' culture is traditionally violent and aggressive. Children hurt each other or got hurt trying to assert their masculinity," says Professor Jenkins. "Video games displace that violence. Aggression, physical combat, challenges, dares, stunts, etc. have historically been central aspects of how boys bond within our culture. One way to think about it is to recall that predatory animals, as children, play at stalking each other, pouncing on each other, tussling, and wrestling each other. Boys raised in a competitive free-enterprise culture play at competing with each other and mastering each other. It's not surprising, and it may be an important training ground for boys to learn how to be men in a society where the realm of boys is so far split off from the realm of men."

Violence in video games became a widespread concern in the early 1990s, when one in three homes had Nintendo or some other video game. Before that, computer games were seen as a largely positive activity. In the mid-1970s, when microcomputers were entering the private sector, parents encouraged their children to play, thinking that once they were computer literate and had mastered the games, they would use the computer for educational programs. But children did not tire of playing computer games. Parents tired of watching their children playing games and began to worry about their emotional and physical health. Conflicting news coverage and research data about the harmful effects of video game playing on children has also fed parental anxiety.

The National Coalition on Television Violence found that 9 of 12 research studies reported harmful effects on children, identifying "a short-term relationship between playing violent games and increased aggressive behavior in younger children." But the researcher, Dr. Jeanne Funk, suggested that it was probably not a good idea to ban children from playing video games. "Limiting playing time and monitoring game selection according to development level and game content may be as important as similar parental management of television privileges." Another research project suggests that the only negative aspect of playing video games is that some games are "solitary in nature" and that a two-player game provides "a cathartic or

> I have grown up playing games that many consider to be violent, and I turned out fine. The truth of the matter is that, for me, I often feel that these games are a great way to relieve frustration without acting violently toward anyone in the real world. It can be very satisfying after having a bad day to go home, turn on the computer, and play a game like Quake. If I hadn't had Wolfenstein 3D or Doom when I was in junior high, life would have been a hell of a lot harder.

DAN ATKINS, 17
Malibu, California

releasing effect from aggression."[3] Yet other research demonstrates that playing video games has considerable therapeutic and educational value for a diverse range of individuals including adolescents, athletes, the elderly, cancer patients undergoing chemotherapy, stroke victims, and quadriplegics.[4] That video games are fun is clear.

Though it may be discomforting to admit, throughout history children have always played violent games. Early in this century, young boys played "war" with lines of tin soldiers, knocking them down one by one, or in one fell swoop, in a simulated battle. The next generation played cowboys and Indians or cops and robbers, where the youngsters themselves fell down and played dead. When parents stopped buying soldier figures and fake guns, children created their own weapons and continued to play out good guy/bad guy plots. Children are attracted to violence and critical studies of older media forms, including the fairy tale, suggest it is not always in children's best interests to remove from their cultural experience all material that parents deem is too provocative or violent.

This is not a simple issue.

- Clearly much of the concern about violence in video games and other media is misplaced—the main sources of violent behavior lie elsewhere. These include parental violence toward children and violence between nations which portray the use of force in the real world by important institutions—parents and government—as an acceptable way to solve problems or vent anger.

- Nevertheless, the impact of video games, television, film or other media violence (such as the gory details of murders in the print media) probably has a negative impact on violent behavior in society, as does the proliferation of weapons.

- The impact of media violence on an individual child's behavior is probably very specific to the child and his or her social context. There is no evidence, for example, that the use of 'Beat-'em-up' video games leads to violent behavior of well-adjusted youth coming from loving families. The impact is also probably specific to age. Just as it makes sense to restrict a 10-year-old's access to movies with extreme violent content, so it makes sense to restrict age-inappropriate video games. Age ratings on video game packages do appear to be helpful and appropriate.

- Most violent games today are cartoon-like. This will change as games become more realistic and, 3D, and eventually realistic of virtual reality, ensuring that this issue will not disappear.

- It is inappropriate for children of any age to spend significant parts of life using violent video games, or any video games for that matter. Conversely, for most children it makes little sense to deny access to age-appropriate video games simply for fear that these will lead to antisocial behavior. Successful parenting is a question of balance (more on this in Chap. 11, "N-Gen and the Family").

Gender Games: The Difference Between Boys and Girls

Conventional wisdom says that because boys spend more time playing video games than girls, they develop sharper computer skills and are more comfortable working with technology later in life. However, studies conducted since the advent of the home computer, video console, and hand-held Game Boy have noted that girls have been playing as enthusiastically as their male peers. Also cast into doubt is whether boys are indeed better than girls at playing these games. "That's something we don't see in the literature very often," says Professor Christine Ward Gailey, a social anthropologist at Northeastern University who has studied girls and computer games for 10 years. "We just assume they're better and that's not necessarily true."

In the home, girls come together in groups of twos or threes, playing in unison or taking turns. Gailey has found that girls prefer games with rich female protagonists, strong visual imagery, and narrative elements, "but they are willing to compromise on the graphics if the narrative is especially good." The girls in the sample often scoffed at the violent games, like Mortal Kombat, that their brothers preferred ("You kill everyone and then you win . . . duh," one nine-year-old said), but they did admit to playing these games both against their brothers and by themselves. "I play it when I really feel like beating up the boys at school," one 12-year-old said.

Gailey noted that girls often redesign the games in their minds in order to give themselves a more meaningful role. "They weren't interested in being a sleeping princess who gets rescued, so they'd have to create another narrative so that the protagonist, visually represented as a male character, wasn't their savior. They'd say things like, 'well, I'm sleeping, but he works for me and I'm giving him directions through mind control.' There's no reason why there can't be more games where they don't have to do mental gymnastics in order to identify with the characters," says Professor Gailey. "For example, I can't tell you how wonderful it was to see the look on the African American girls' faces when they saw a character who looked like them. They were absolutely delighted."

Even though I don't have quite the same amount of time to play as I did then, I still find myself begging my parents to buy games. I do, for some reason, find myself wishing every now and then for those games I had when I was younger, even though the ones I have now are much better and more realistic. [The objects of Melissa's sentimental longings are Test Drive and the Talking Coloring Book.]

MELISSA EDWARDS, 15
Memphis, Tennessee

Traditional play patterns among girls depends upon interrelationships. In other words, girls build villages. "They want to explore relationships and complex narratives that study the effects of those relationships," says Professor Gailey. "Designers need to come up with games that call on real skills and draw on the girls' desire to understand the interrelations between characters. They also want an outlet for their aggressive tendencies without actually having to kill anyone."

Mattel toys released its *Barbie Interactive* collection on CD-ROM in late 1996, just as Professor Gailey was conducting her research. In the first two months, *Barbie Interactive* sold 500,000 copies, outselling all the other previous blockbusters in the computer game industry. Several of the girls in Gailey's sample received *Barbie Fashion Designer* as Christmas presents. "Oh no," one of the girls in Gailey's study said. "The companies are going to see how well this sold and think they know what we care about and that's all we'll get." A 12-year-old who had been playing with *Kid Pix* since she was 4 said: "If you're good at this game, you get to play Home Shopping Network when you grow up." Another nine-year-old, after playing with her CD-ROM three times, said: "This is a boring game. I can pick out my clothes any old time."

A representative of Mattel responded to Gailey's findings by saying that the sample audience was too old for the games. The prime age for Barbie is between the ages of four and seven, which reinforces Gailey's assertion that *Barbie Interactive* is a bestseller because "she's the only game in town."

"I like to imagine a video game format where Barbie kicks butt," says Professor Jenkins, the expert in boys' culture. "We need to create more opportunities for girls to play in unstructured areas." The girls in Gailey's sample agreed. For them, *Xena, Warrior Princess* would be a better character for N-Gen girls' games. "Xena has friends who are both men and women," one nine-year-old said. "She's Barbie with muscles and attitude." This is especially important for girls who previously had no socially acceptable way of expressing their anger and aggression—something video games provide.

While there are computer games for girls, the graphic interfaces of these games are inferior to those of the Sega and Nintendo games played by boys. The games also fail to provide the essential community-building features that are so essential to girls' play patterns. It appears that it's the Internet, not games, that is providing that.

Gender: Communication + Community = Friendship

Girls' play on the Internet has little to do with the technology itself and a lot to do with the previously mentioned play patterns that have been observed in female culture since the beginning of humanity. "And how did girls start chatting in large groups anyway? Is it some kind of strange instinct from way back when?" asks 14-year-old Matt Kessler of Silverdale, Washington. "Before women had any power and were forced to do the men's bidding, they stayed in large numbers to protect each other. Is this still with us? In school I always see girls sitting around in groups and 'flirting' with each other while us boys like to 'hang out' in two- or threesomes."

"A girl's search for identity is through her connection with others," social theory has to say in answer to Matt's questions, "while boys search for self through distinguishing themselves from others."[5] Nowhere are these "two orientations toward relationships that are gender related, though not gender exclusive"[6] more profoundly obvious than in cyber play. Before the advent of the Internet, many girls were unable to view the computer as a useful toy.

Eleven-year-old Amanda Kidd of Dale City, Virginia is one N-Gen girl who has successfully used the Internet to transform the family computer from a productivity tool into a toy. "My parents bought this computer in 1992 and became computer freaks! I wasn't very interested in computers, I would just get on it to write a report," Amanda remembers. "Then they got a modem and online service and my life changed. I joined a lot of clubs and I was fascinated by all the *cool* clubs. After a while the clubs just fell and left me hanging. I was so depressed. I was going to join more clubs but I didn't want to join more clubs that would fail. So I took one of my interests, reading *Babysitters' Club* books, and created a club. I have lots of e-mail friends. Members in my club are a lot more than just kids who are in my club, they're my friends."

Amanda is not alone. "When I first got on I noticed that there were some clubs on the Net. Most were just for girls, but there were a few for just boys or girls. Since I love to write and I love to be in charge, I decided to make up my own club," says 14-year-old Kristen Sacco of California. "It is *C'est La Vie,* or fondly called CLV by all the members! There are about 175 members and since I feel the club is getting too large, there is a waiting list." Alana Johnson, 13, of Palo Cedro, California, says, "I also have my own online girls club called *Just for You!* which is very successful."

There is one major similarity between the play communities girls build in cyberspace and the communities they build among school and neighborhood friends—"the conversation is, in a sense, the relationship."[7] In cyberspace it is the number of conversations and the number of friendships that becomes infinite.

While there are examples of boys who participate in online social clubs like those described by Amanda, Kristen, and Alana, 11- and 12-year-old boys just don't seem to have the same affinity as girls for building communities in cyberspace. Part of the reason is that boys use language for different reasons in their play. "A boy uses language to assert a dominant position in a hierarchy, to draw and hold an audience, or to compete with another person for the floor, thereby expressing his individual identity within the group. Since the rules are a crucial aspect of many boys' games, dispute resolution is a frequent type of conversation in which wielding power and control—without bullying—is an important skill."[8]

Beyond the Pen Pal

The Internet enables N-Geners to build and maintain friendships around the globe. These "key-pals" or "e-pals" are much different than the pen pals of previous generations. With the Net there is constant communication and instant gratification. N-Geners can create a richer relationship based on shared cultural experiences on the Net by viewing the same Web sites and visiting MUDs or chat rooms at the same time.

"The best thing about the Net is the ease of communication between people from around the world, which is what creates the possibility to make friends from around the world," says 14-year-old Matthew Ginsburg-Jaekle from Boulder, Colorado. "Places that used to seem infinitely far away from me when I was in elementary school now seem much closer. I know people from regions completely opposite from those which I have visited or lived in not because of international travel, but because it takes a matter of seconds for me to visit foreign countries (via the Web, of course) or send and receive mail from a pen pal clear across the world from the United States." Amy Moyer, 15, of Whitehorse, Yukon, agrees. "I am a chronic IRC user and have also met many good friends over the Net. I have friends in Hong Kong, Germany, Norway, even Prince Rupert, British Columbia," says Amy. "We trade music, we have sent letters and pictures. It is all very interesting."

The Net as a virtual playground also provides a social outlet for those who live in isolated communities or whose real experiences take place in situations where there isn't a central focus on peer interaction. "Since I'm home schooled and I live in a small town, I think I have more Net friends than other friends here," says Joeldine

Hayter, 15 of Te Puke, Bay of Plenty, New Zealand. "I did get bored and lonely for friends of my own age before the Net. It's cool to hang out with people my own age, even if it is only on the Net."

International Flirtation

At this stage in adolescent development, when there is such an obvious increase in communication between the sexes, it would be naive to believe N-Geners are using this tremendous communicative opportunity to create global networks for future business deals. N-Gen has taken adolescent flirtation global. "I got online and got a boyfriend the first day," says 12-year-old Alexis. "He's nice, well, he's okay. He's 13, he's got red hair, and he's from Florida. You can talk better online because you have the Net in common. And it's easier to ask them out because if they say no you don't care." Not that Net dates don't have their own risks involved. "On the Net," 12-year-old Charlotte cautions, "when you ask them out, you can't see their eyes so you don't know if they're sincere."

At age 12, Charlotte and Alexis still participate in chat rooms sponsored by children's Web content providers, but in a few years, as teenagers, they will join the N-Gen teenagers who have left those rooms. With these rooms they will also leave behind the well-defined rules of Netiquette, the strictly enforced regulations regarding the use of profanity and the constant monitoring by adults engaged for this purpose by site management. What N-Geners discover when they leave these protected spaces is what adults recognize as the typical feature of adolescent flirtation: all of it is awkward, more than some of it is silly, and a certain percentage is offensive.

Thirteen-year-old REN5 of FreeZone has advice on C-dating and Web relationships. "Before you jump into a relationship, get to know the person really well by spending time chatting with them. See what they are really like." He advises, "If you don't think they are the one for you then tell them you just want to be friends. And remember, don't lead anyone on! Even though you can't see each other—feelings can still get hurt." He is typical of cybersmart kids who, in environments like FreeZone, are savvy about safety: "And don't ever give out any personal information about yourself like your home address, phone number, or school name."9

Falling in Love

Marshall McLuhan said, "In the electronic age we wear all mankind as our skin." When one observes adolescent N-Geners interact in this medium that is beyond television, one realizes that in their intense and emotional play, N-Geners have stripped away the skin of the electronic age, leaving every nerve exposed. Once again, play theorists offer the explanation for this emotional nudity: "Play provides the major opportunities for learning about social relations involving the opposite sex and for developing an awareness of personal feelings associated with matters of love and marriage."[10]

> Some people can lead you on in believing that they really like you, when they really may have 2 or 3 other c-guys or gals on the side!
>
> RENS, 13, m
> FreeZoner

The ways in which play leads to the awareness of those personal feelings start to look different when the Net is the primary toy used in that play. It is an issue of which adolescent N-Geners have an almost hyper-awareness.

Some N-Geners see the potential for love as one of the Internet's great benefits. "One friend, he is 17 and from the USA, who we may meet next year because he's going to college in Australia, has a girlfriend, who he is planning on marrying when they are older, who he met on the Net," 15-year-old Joeldine Hayter of New Zealand said. It isn't the only love story Joeldine knows: "I have a cyberbro in the USA who is 28. He met a girl who lived in the USA, but in a different state. They fell in love, then met and became engaged and were married recently."

Others view love stories with little personal interest. "I mean, sure, there are emotions and I suppose there could be love over the Net and it has a lot to do with what people say," said Andy Putschoegl, 17, of Oakdale, Minnesota. "But I'm more of a face-to-face kind of person, you know what I mean? I like to get to know someone in real life."

Most experiences fall somewhere between a love story and a need for face-to-face contact. "I can't say that I haven't fallen in love over the Net. I haven't gotten into a serious relationship or anything. I think it was just puppy love. I have spoken to many guys on the Net and liked them but I've lost contact with them. I have relationships outside the Net and I like to stick with those," says 17-year-old Michelle Andrews of Victoria, Australia. "I do think the Net is changing the way friendships and relationships are conducted. Outside the Net, people are attracted to looks more than personality. Over the Net you don't know what the other people look like so the only way you can fall in love with them is through their personality. My pen pal is a guy. I spoke to him over the Net and we are very good friends. I didn't know what he looked like but he was a really nice person and he sounded really nice on the phone. A while ago I got a video from him and I have to say he wasn't the best looking guy I've met. That didn't change anything, though. We are still good friends."

Courtney, 17, and Jason, 18, actually met on the Net. "He had his own BBS and a friend of mine gave me the number and I called and chatted with him and things developed from there," Courtney remembers. "And only after a few weeks of talking did I find out he lived just down the street and around the corner from me and that he worked for my dad. . . ."

Sexuality

I would be remiss if I mentioned N-Gen relationship-building without some mention of sexuality. Setting aside the issues of pornography, sexual harassment, and sexual predators (discussed in Chap. 11, "N-Gen and the Family"), there is still considerable unease among adults about the notion of consensual sexual talk on the Net by young people. While there is no cybersex at FreeZone, it is a part of the Internet. How does this translate into the lives of N-Geners?

MIT professor of the sociology of science Sherry Turkle, in her discussion of "Children and Nested,"[11] indicates that starting around age 10 (though most of her subjects were in their teens), online sexuality, from flirting to outright virtual sex, is a normal part of the social lives of kids who have computers. Often their online relationships are extensions of their in-person relationships, only with fewer of the social pressures and insecurities that accompany adolescent experiences at parties or one-on-one. It allows the kids to explore more in-depth conversational and emotional aspects of their relationships rather than focusing on getting physical.

In general, it seems that both girls and boys found online sexual experimentation a safer and less terrifying prospect than the toe-to-toe version. Of course, there is always the possibility that the kids will find themselves on the receiving end of unwanted advances, just like in real life. But as one 12-year-old girl who goes online as 18 indicates, "she feels safe because she can always just 'disconnect.'"[12]

Although this was not an issue specifically addressed in the *Growing Up Digital* forum, it was raised independently by several participants in their ongoing correspondence with my researcher Kate Baggott. Our research also turned up the general feeling that cybersex is much safer than sex in real life. This is the first generation to deal with the complexities of reaching puberty while constantly being reminded that reckless or "casual" sex is not only unwise, but possibly lethal. For youngsters grappling with their own sexuality and often conflicting desires, virtual sex seems to be a welcome proxy for putting one's toe in the water without getting wet. As one 16-year-old Australian girl said, "It really doesn't mean that much, it's just something that's really fun to do, that leaves no mess, no side effects, and it's the best form of contraception you'll ever find . . . sex can be *very* harmful out in the really real world." In her experience, cybersex always seemed more like a romance novel. She writes:

"Okay, well I don't take it serious much, like with X, the guy I went out with for ages, we did it like twice when we first met, but I didn't take it that serious at all, and after that we didn't, like it just seemed silly. But then I'd say stuff like 'ummm, man this is hard (for me to describe), ummm, okay.' Well, with X, I would always say stuff like "*goes to him and takes him into her arms giving him a slow passionate kiss on the lips . . .* so what did you have for dinner?" and stuff like that, like it really didn't mean that much, it's just fun to do . . . ummm, the guys always seem to start it, and they always set the scene, like X would say, '*takes her out onto the lawn and lies down beside her under the stars*' and stuff like that."

In the end she concluded, "I guess it's really just a fantasy. They always say stuff like 'holding your slender body close,' like they make you out to be a perfect person and stuff." Of course, that's a different issue altogether.

A 17-year-old American boy had a similar feeling—that it was something to check out, but nothing to go crazy over. (He also experienced a certain awkwardness or difficulty in talking about cybersex.) He wrote:

"I tried it a few times just to see what it was like (wow, sounds like everyone's excuse for smoking pot), and it didn't appeal to me. I have friends who spend literally hours talking to other kids online and engaging in cybersex. My understanding of the definition of cybersex is when one goes into a chat room of some sort, finds a person to their liking, and begins sexual advances. If the other person likes this, then they will reply. Many pseudosexual acts take place and generally the people on both ends are pleasuring themselves. It's a lot of 'now I'm doing this to you' and 'oh that feels good' kind of stuff. I think some kids use it as a release, and really, it's not hurting anyone as far as I can see. Nobody's getting pregnant and it's safe sex. But the downside is that some kids can get addicted and spend *far* too much time doing this. . . . Wow, that was weird to write. A lot more difficult than I thought."

So the perception that cyberspace is full of dangerous sexual behavior on the part of youth may be somewhat of a myth, especially as far as these teenagers are concerned. They seem more interested in developing both the emotional and the physical side of real relationships, with the Internet as just one more "safe" mode of communication. Any kind of cybersexual behavior is almost always consensual because of the possibility of disconnection. Of course, as Turkle points out, if harassment does occur, or any situation that is confusing or threatening, the best option is to be able to talk to an understanding parent, without fear of reprisal. Just like in real life.

The Drive-In Movie of the Digital Age

The problem with relationships, it seems, is that Net communication never seems to be about just two people. "I have to admit," Courtney says, "that I am a bit leery when he says he was chatting with people for an hour or whatever. It makes me nervous that he is talking to other girls, but I try not to bug him too much about it."

It is parents, not members of N-Gen, who may be concerned by the prevalence of digital relationships. If you read Ann Landers' syndicated advice column regularly, then you will have read tales told by abandoned spouses whose mates have run off with their cyber lovers. Is the Net a high-tech harlot that will lead to the breakup of families? Are romance and this new communications medium a couple bound together by the vows of selection and opportunity? Is this as true for teenagers as it is for adults? Young love is frightening, especially if you're the parent of a teenager.

The Net needn't make that more frightening. In fact, there are actually some comforting advantages when your teenager's social life with the opposite sex is online. For example, the top ten reasons parents should relax about cyber love, according to the *Growing Up Digital* kids, are:

10. Alcohol isn't served in IRCs
9. Time on the Net is time away from the TV
8. No curfew disagreements
7. Meeting someone in a chat room doesn't require new clothes
6. Heavy breathing won't fog up a computer screen
5. The car won't run out of gas
4. Kids have to read and write to chat
3. Your son can't get someone pregnant in a chat room
2. Your daughter can't get pregnant in a chat room
1. No one ever contracted an STD through a modem cable

Playing in the MUD

A MUD is a "place" on the Net where users create their own dramatic adventures in real-time. Other forms of MUDs are MUSEs, MOOs, and MUSHs, depending on the software tools used in constructing the experience. Invented in England in 1980, MUDs, or Multi User Dungeons (also called multi user dimensions), were initially text-based virtual realities. You typed text codes to enter "rooms" such as ballrooms, castles, offices, taverns, warehouses, prisons, or closets—each with its own entrances, objects, and written description. Unlike chat room exchanges, MUDs host intensive, ongoing games in which online characters are constructed over months and adventures are played out over weeks. While the typical chat room visit lasts about 16 minutes, the average MUD session lasts well over an hour.

The first MUDs were elaborately structured games that the participants constructed as they played in the style of Dungeons and Dragons. They allowed people to meet and move around in an imaginary world while killing monsters and sometimes even other players. But according to Xerox PARC chief scientist John Seely Brown, "Talking to other players turned out to be more interesting than killing them, and now MUDs are intended as virtual hangouts—exotic worlds where people can gather and chat without leaving their chairs." MUDs are evolving into virtual meeting places and learning places—virtual social realities—on the Net, but unlike chat rooms, where communication is the only objective, the atmosphere of a MUD requires one to sustain the virtual environment through both action and communication. In other words, in the MUD the environment not only influences the communication, it is the communication. If the MUD you're in is a virtual swimming pool, someone has to get splashed.

While individuals of all ages have been known to play in MUDs, the largest age group and heaviest users of MUDs are people between the ages of 17 and 23. Young adults are especially drawn to the mysterious world of MUDs because these virtual realities often make the transition from childhood to adulthood easier. "For people whose lives are controlled by parents or professors or bosses," Howard Rheingold, author of *The Virtual Community,* says, "there is a certain attraction to a world in which mastery and admiration of peers is available to anyone with imagination and intellectual curiosity."[13]

These oldest N-Geners quickly learn to find the adventure or social MUD that best suits their needs and tastes. One function of MUDs, as Amy Bruckman and Mitchel Resnick point out in *The MediaMoo Project: Constructionism and Professional Community,* is to provide neutral ground or (in Ray Oldenburg's words) "third places"—home and work being first and second—where people of similar interests and values can come to relax and socialize.[14] MUDs are superior in that places in the real world are usually closed for a number of hours each day and only cater to those who are geographically close. MUDs are open round-the-clock and are frequented by people from around the globe.

Courtney Roby, age 18, a freshman studying electrical engineering at the University of Colorado, who in her free time studies dead languages and is building an electric vehicle to be raced this summer, MUDs for six hours a day—usually from 9 at night to 3 in the morning. Such a hectic schedule, Courtney admits, has affected her social life. Eventually, when she grew tired of her friends bugging her about the hours spent at her computer, she agreed to compromise: "We've basically agreed that I won't get pestered about spending so much time MUDing if I spend the weekends with real people. Besides, I pointed out that as recreation it's much more normal than reading ancient Greek."

Although Courtney has only been MUDing since last September, when she discovered MicroMuse accidentally by telnet, she's put so much time and effort into understanding the coding system that she's become a mentor. "It's always nice to learn things quickly. I'm much more tolerant as a mentor than I am in real life . . . there are habits (and people) which annoy me while I'm mentoring but on the whole I'm much more patient than I am when trying to teach people things off MUSE."

When a participant tries Courtney's patience or sexually harasses her, she has learned to use gags or pagelocks to cut them off but has found that "having a reputation for being capable of insulting" is a more effective long-term measure. Although she visits 19 different MUDs, including a world inhabited by half-human, half-animal creatures and known for its sexual happenings, she has only been propositioned twice. Courtney finds online sex "sort of silly" and prefers an easier social interactive environment.

Colin Coller of Saskatoon, Saskatchewan, prefers books to films and MUDs to chat rooms because he likes to give his imagination free rein. He discovered MUDs in the ninth grade—earlier than most teens—and insists he learned more from MUDing than he did in the classroom. "I spent more time online during high school than I did on high school," Colin says. "My marks were terrible, even in computers. I was learning how to patch kernels, program in C, use SQL, set up and secure networks, and write network commands on MUDs. Learning how to program in BASIC (a language I had been fluent in for eight years) . . . just did not keep my interest."

MUDing not only provided Colin with a creative outlet for his imagination but brought him in contact with people of like interests whom he would never have had the opportunity to meet in the isolated community of Saskatoon. At the young age of 18, Colin is a programmer for International Road Dynamics, which he describes as "an intelligent transportation systems company," but plans to enter the University of Saskatchewan's Computer Science program in the fall.

Before he discovered MUDs, Colin was very self-conscious and quiet. "Meeting people on MUDs who liked the personality I never really let show in real life helped my self-confidence a lot." A year ago Colin went to Cleveland, Ohio, for a job interview, met several of the people he had encountered online, and became particularly close to one female. He remained in Cleveland for three months and his relationship with the young woman blossomed. When he returned to Saskatchewan, Colin continued to exchange words and intimacies with his girlfriend online. Such clandestine meetings are common among young people on MUDs. It is not unheard of for two people to meet online, become acquainted, and marry in virtual space or even to carry their relationship into the real world. A problem sometimes occurs, however, when one of two MUD participants is 'playing' with the other and merely wants to have a casual fling or sex online. In particular, female MUDers, still a minority, have on occasion been overwhelmed and driven away by male participants and predators.

Bryon Stanoszek, age 18 and a first-year student at Akron University in Ohio, is another extraordinary individual who created a life for himself from MUDing, but Bryon is rare because, at the age of 13, he gained access to MIT's machine and created his own MUD, WindsMARE. Since 1992 there have been 451,736 log-ins to the game, and Bryon is understandably proud of his achievement. "Of all the people that have ever visited my game, they have told me that it was the best on the Internet for a few individual factors," says Bryon. "The player acts like how they would in real-life situations to play the role of a hero (unknown at the start) in a developing journey of epic proportions." The aspects of role playing and of being able to explore other aspects of their personalities in the safe environment of Byron's MUSE and other MUDs has helped young people find their place in the adult world.

N-Geners Aren't Always Angels

Mischief is also part of play. If so much of our development as individuals is dependent upon our grasp of the activities our parents don't know about, then pushing the limits on behavior norms (no matter how angry it makes adults) has to be considered a normal part of growing up. We've all been children, and because of that experience we know N-Geners get into trouble in cyberspace, but the kids weren't offering up confessions. What they were worried about was defending themselves against media perceptions of N-Gen mischief.

"I don't know how many kids get into mischief," says 14-year-old Nicholas Cofrancesco of Vermont. "I know I have seen some shows on TV that show kids who have abused their rights on the Internet by making bombs and such, but I think most kids use the Internet the right way and not the wrong way." Matthew Ginsberg-Jaeckle of Colorado, 14, agrees that kids on the Net aren't that bad. "The truth is," says Matthew, "that a very small percentage of all kids who use the Internet have ever been, and much less regularly go to any kind of sites such as 'How to Make a Bomb' or pornographic sites. I believe that it is just that the kids who do receive more attention than the kids who use the Internet to learn from, to communicate with, and to use as a valuable educational tool." Nevertheless, N-Geners aren't always angels and they do get into trouble in cyberspace.

If mischief is an assertion of autonomy, then it is also an expression of personal power. Unfortunately, many people feel that they gain power by dominating someone else. The Internet is not immune to these power struggles. In fact, it is the central theme of Internet mischief. Allison Ellis found out that even the youngest N-Geners engage in power struggles when, to passionate protests, Ellis announced that she was going to shut down the FreeZone chat box to go on a dinner break. "I felt bad—they were good, responsible kids and they didn't seem to be causing any trouble. So I tried an experiment," Allison explains. "I told the group to assign a host (monitor) and that I would be back in a few minutes. Lesson learned: Never leave chat unattended without adult supervision!"

DIGITAL: COMET she said I was host first!!!

MYTH: Ok*PUNCH* no problem *PEEING ON WALL* what are the rules??? *BUSTING WINDOW* We need rules. *DRINKING FROM TOILET*

COMET: MYTH, you bad boy! You stand in the corner onone leg til I tell you you can come back!

MYTH: Sure DIGITAL *PEEING ON DIGITAL's LEG*

COMET: MYTH, I want you to think about what you did, you hear me?

DIGITAL: MYTH don't want to kick you out but I will if I have too k!!!

MYTH: Ok.

MYTH: I'm thinking!!!! Boy, sure is lonely over here in the corner. Maybe I'll take a pee *PEEING IN CORNER*

DIGITAL: shutup COMET I'm host got it!!!

DIGITAL: *Crapping on MYTH's foot!!!*

COMET: MYTH, how much water did you drink???

COMET: DIGITAL, hosts aren't supposed to say shut up! I may have to kick you out!

COMET: You guys calm down! MYTH, now what do you have to say for yourself?

COMET: DIGITAL stop it! Allison said she'd be checking in on us!

Did you ever call the smoke shop and ask them if they had Prince Albert in a can? N-Geners never have—call display and last number return telephone technologies have all but made the crank phone call obsolete—except on the Internet, where a voice cannot be used as a means of age identification. "Well, they'd pick up a box of—say macaroni or something—get the address off the box, and then they'd message all the companies and say, like, 'I found a crack in my box of macaroni and it was green,'" says one 14-year-old girl of her friends' prank. "They'd pretend to be adults and stuff, then give their names and addresses, or whatever, and a few weeks later a box of macaroni would show up in the mail for free."

Some pranks can be more worrisome. Recently an angry New England father complained to Connie Stout, the director of the Texas Education Network (TENET), that his 10-year-old daughter had received a sexually explicit message from a TENET account holder. The father understandably wanted some disciplinary action taken against the educator who had sent the message. The author even had the gall to include his home address and phone number.

Stout asked the father how he thought someone in the Texas school system could have come up with his daughter's e-mail address. He said that his daughter had her own Web page, and when Stout

> Only once
> or twice [online]
> I told a fib.

SHELLBERT, 11, f
FreeZoner

looked at the Web site she saw a number of pictures of the girl and her friends in cheerleading uniforms. In addition to the pictures, the daughter gave her full name and a clickable send-to e-mail address. "While we would never distribute personal photographs and our address for all to see in the local newspaper," observes Stout, "the publishing capability of an Internet home page essentially solicits comments from all over the world."

The message's purported author was a high school principal. Stout phoned him and told him about the sexual message he had allegedly sent to a 10-year-old. "Needless to say there was stunned silence on the other end of the phone." Although he had a TENET account, he did not use it, and the principal's office didn't even have a computer. He had given it to a classroom teacher.

Stout easily traced the message's origins to a networked computer in the school, and the time stamp showed that the message had been sent during the lunch hour. The message's real authors were quickly identified as two students. The teacher had lent her TENET account to the students to upload files for a class project. While they were logged on, they went surfing the Web, happened across the young New England girl's site, and decided on a whim to fabricate a message from the principal, with whom they were upset.

> I'm just me online but sometimes I lie about little things.
>
> **FISHGIRL, 12, f**
> FreeZoner

One of the two students was a contract student coming to the school from a neighboring district. His contract was canceled because of the incident and he was no longer allowed to attend the school. The other student was suspended for three days. The teacher who had given out the account had a reprimand placed in her personnel file.

This is an example of the digital frontier. Like the Old West, it's a place of recklessness and unclear norms of behavior. The students saw this as a harmless prank, which it was not. The teacher had given the account to students—unwise. The father had permitted his daughter to place pictures of herself on the Net—again unwise. The 10-year-old girl became the victim of inappropriate actions by all concerned.

Newbies Do a Lot of Flame-Baiting

The most common kind of mischief on the Net is the flame, and the people most likely to receive flames are Newbies. Confused? Here are the N-Gen definitions of these Internet terms: "A flame is like a hate letter, a mail bomb, a bad comment," says 16-year-old Darla Crewe of Halifax, Nova Scotia. "Kids are automatically blamed for flames."

"I think the term [Newbie] goes for anyone who's one to eight months on the Internet, who aren't experienced users," says 17-year-old Andy Putschoegl of Oakdale, Minnesota. "They're the kind of people who you'd expect are sending e-mail that's generally considered flame bait, but they just kind of have to take the hint after the first couple of responses." In other words, if inexperienced Newbies post stupid or silly messages to an otherwise serious newsgroup, or breech chat room Netiquette along the lines of imposing their comments into someone else's conversation, they are likely to find flames in their mail boxes. Talk about a technological trial by fire!

Not all flames are a result of flame-baiting. Many flames, such as leaving a profanity-laden posting on a Web page guest book, or sending an abusive, aggressive, or threatening e-mail message to someone, are nothing more than mean-spirited and are the equivalent of any other act of vandalism or bullying.

Fortunately, Newbie flamers get caught. They get caught because the standard setup of any e-mail program embeds the originating address in the message itself. Like any publisher, Web site owners can, and often do, publish the flames they receive with a link to the senders' e-mail box. What this means is not only can the victim respond to the flamer, but so can the victim's other readers, which is disastrous for the Newbie flamers who share e-mail accounts with their parents.

Problems in Paradise

Dorothy Ellen Wilcox, a teacher in Alaska, wrote her M.Ed. thesis on the effects of the Internet on her elementary school class. Wilcox has done a lot of work on flaming and believes, based on the experiences of her students, that flaming is often intended to intimidate girls and women into silence. In response, women have developed strategies for staying included, such as "passive lurking (becoming invisible by remaining silent), changing their names to androgynous or male aliases, becoming competent flamers themselves, and even beginning their own electronic bulletin boards in an attempt to bring gender equity to the Internet."

Serena, a 14-year-old N-Gener from California, has no interest in being invisible or lurking passively. She has, however, been flamed and has taken a very active stance against those who flame her. Serena is the president of her own Jared Leto fan club. Much of her Web site is devoted to the young actor who is best known for his role as Jordan Catalano on *My So-Called Life,* and visitors can ask to be put on his fan club e-mail list. One visitor did exactly that, but then changed his mind. He asked to be taken off the list which, due to an error, Serena did not do. The visitor says he asked to be removed three or four times; Serena says he asked just once. As a result, the visitor flamed Serena.

Serena decided the best course of action was to reprint the flame on her

Web site and encourage others to send their comments about the note to its author. Here is the preamble from her site that she has given us permission to reproduce: "This mail is not written by me, so any and all cuss words, or anything you have against it is not my fault. It is copyright of the person who wrote it. Don't think that I get a lot of hate mail or anything, it's just that there are some people that seem to really hate Jared, so they decide to bitch to me about it 'cause I'm the president of his Fan Club. Then there are also some people that have never met me but decide they don't like me, and again bitch to me about it. I don't take any of this at all personally or anything—in fact, they crack me. I think they are hilarious, so I decided to post a couple so all of you can get a coupla laughs from them. You can even send them some hate mail too! Oh, and please don't send me any mail bitching at me 'cause you don't like my page or this page or something. If you don't like it, leave, or else your letter will probably end up on here. Anyway, here is some hate mail. Enjoy!"

Here is an excerpt of a flame Serena received: "OK now do u get the fucking point bitch. . . leave us the fuck alone . . . or u can just keep getting these things again again . . . and again and again and again . . . hahahahhahah u fuckin bitch ... fuck off with this ugly asshole jared leto mother fucker . . . by the way . . . who the fuck is that dumb ass that u people r drooling over . . . fuck off . . . oh and show this email at your fuckin meetings . . . bitch . . . i don't give a fuck."

In response to the flamer's invitation, Serena did show the letter at the meeting of the Jared Leto fan club in its entirety. Since the cyberspace meeting place is accessible to everyone all the time, Serena posted the message, including the flamer's e-mail address as it appeared on the original letter, and suggested: "Send some hate mail of your own back to him if you want. Please do. I certainly won't mind."

A lot of people sent messages, and we sent a note asking the author what he had hoped to achieve with his filthy diatribe. It turns out the author shared an e-mail account with his father. The response we got was from the flamer's father, saying his son must have been "up to no good again." Astonishingly, he did not apologize for the note, but repeatedly complained about the "unauthorized use" of his e-mail address on Serena's Web site, even though his son said he didn't care who Serena showed it to. "Do you condone this sort of thing?" he asked.

A few months after this incident, we asked Serena to comment on the episode. "I don't even know why I thought of a hate mail page, it's just that the letters I was receiving were doing the total opposite effect on me than what I suppose the senders had intended," Serena replied. "Instead of getting me all pissed off, I found them hilarious. I decided to just post them for fun, so I did. It turned out to be much more popular than I thought. I think that I might have taken some offense to the letters if I actually knew the person, or if it was a face-to-face kind of thing, but since all they were, were letters sent to me from people I didn't know and most likely never would, I didn't care.

"The reason I posted the e-mail address was never meant to do any harm. First off, I never thought people would even go to that page, let alone send them hate mail, but from all the letters I got from people on the Net telling me what they wrote them, I guess I was wrong. To me, I think that I have the right to post their e-mail address because they were the ones starting it. They shouldn't send someone evil letters if they can't handle the idea of actually receiving some themselves. I feel that it was their fault in the first place, and if I had been asked nicely to remove their e-mail address then I would've, but instead I was threatened. I mean, that doesn't really make *me* want to help *them* out."

Hacker Bravado

"Will a 14-year-old hacker bring my company to its knees?" the old-guard executive asks in the famous IBM print ad. The 1983 film *War Games*, starring Matthew Broderick, about a young hacker who accidentally almost starts World War III, had particular resonance in late 1997, when a British court fined a 19-year-old student £1000 for downloading dozens of secret files from the Griffiths Air Force Base and Lockheed, a missile and aircraft manufacturer, three years earlier.

If the Internet were the Wild West, hackers would be the cowboys. They are depicted in user mythology as the macho men of technological prowess who, depending on your perspective, are heroes as protectors of the right to access information freely or villainous bandits who steal copyrighted material from its creators for their own profit. It is a title many N-Geners aspire to, but in the N-Gen practices behind the mythology of hackers there lies, not so much theft or idealism, but a political power struggle that pits one user's cyber rights against another's.

Many corporations, individuals, and organizations who post materials on the Web have had their pages hacked. Advertisers have reviewed their pages only to find the images manipulated to parody rather than sell the product. Other organizations have found messages and manifestoes posted where information once was. All of these cases reflect the necessity of checking your Internet service provider's security measures. Is there a firewall? Has the provider hired a professional hacker to attempt to break through the security features and close off any trespass routes?

Most N-Geners don't have the knowledge to engage in this kind of hacking, but they can be seen practicing related skills in unmonitored chat rooms. In one example, baby hackers were advising each other how to access the information one has to enter in order to log on to a site. They were then reposting the form data to adopt another chatter's alias or identifying icon. The object of this hack was, literally, to put words into someone else's mouth.

N-Gen Unplugged

In many ways, mischief is only mischief if you get caught. Every Internet exchange leaves an electronic trail, which has negative implications for privacy issues but positive ones for catching the perpetrator of the crime. As we saw in Serena's case, communication on the Net is not one-way and technological expertise isn't always necessary to turn the tables in the power struggle. Serena chose to handle the problem of flaming by making the flames public, which subjected her flamer to flames. Hacking and flaming are not technological pranks, they are attacks on individual rights. When N-Geners are caught threatening others there is a course of action. With the removal of two cables from their wall outlets, baby hackers and child flamers can go from "growing up digital" to "N-Gen unplugged."

N-Gen as Consumers

According to this analysis, Gibbons, last year your department spent forty-five thousand dollars on candy alone.

"**I** do like to buy things over the Net. I can find the best price within 10 minutes and that's checking 25 stores," says 14-year-old Eric Mandela of Rahway, New Jersey. "I also don't need to deal with operators who get your orders wrong or want to talk to your parents. With the Internet, I can buy whatever I need and then pay my parents back when they get the bill."

"I love being able to skip all of the fancy advertising if I'm in a hurry," says 18-year-old Andy Putschoegl of Oakdale, Minnesota. "I don't have to wait for something to load if I just need to click on a link to another page. I don't even pay attention to the ads on search engines because I'm there for a different purpose—to look information up. If only I could skip the commercials on TV."

The Net will change the way goods and services are sold for two reasons.

First, the Net itself will become an increasingly important sales channel, going far beyond how the multibillion-dollar mail-order business already operates. Second, the Net will become a powerful promotional and advertising tool, helping to secure the sale of goods and services sold by other means. These factors will significantly change virtually every aspect of marketing as we know it today.

Old-economy marketers who claim that the Internet is no way to reach consumers are missing out on the opportunity to market to a generation whose voracious appetite for video games has made both Sega and Nintendo bigger than Hollywood, and whose preference for the interactive rather than the passive is turning the kids away from television in droves.

Today's N-Gen already has significant purchasing power. At 88 million strong, this generation's economic clout will grow dramatically during the coming decades as the kids become older and their disposable income climbs. For example, Peter Zollo of Teenage Research Unlimited (TRU) says: "Teen spending is on the rise and few teens are saddled with the debts that stifle adult spending like rent, utilities, and groceries. Teens' considerable income is almost exclusively discretionary."

N-Geners are also becoming important consumers because of their rapidly growing influence on adult consumption. They have strong views regarding what their parents should buy for them and even what parents should buy for themselves. Youth, especially teens, are also trendsetters—truer for the demographically muscular, wired, smart, and media-savvy N-Gen than previous generations. At the Alliance for Converging Technologies we estimate that American preteens and teens spend $130 billion directly and influence the spending of somewhere upward of $500 billion.[1,2] Due in part to the generation lap, marketers of new media-related products and services will increasingly find themselves selling to parents by marketing to their children.

It isn't only computers, video games, and high-tech purchases that children influence. Exercising their digitally nurtured assertiveness, they are starting to influence and direct their parents' dollars toward areas such as everyday grocery and clothing purchases, and they expect to be consulted about major household purchases like cars and appliances.

Several sources estimate that youth influence how 20 cents of every dollar is spent. In the past, kids had little basis on which to exert such influence, but with digital media they now have a way of often becoming more knowledgeable about a given product than their parents. Imagine the power these children wield when they can access data their parents don't even know exists. Think about a 13-year-old girl influencing her parents to buy a Volvo based on safety statistics she has downloaded from the Web.

N-Geners often refuse to let their slower parents take control of family purchases even if they must begrudge them control of the purse strings. And it isn't just parents but sales personnel and company "experts" or "specialists" who are on the receiving end of N-Gen's healthy skepticism. Everything from groceries to computers must be able to withstand the scrutiny of suspicious, knowledgeable teens and pre-teens. It is now often children who take control not only of purchasing decisions, but of sales negotiations.

Not only are old-style marketers largely ignoring the medium and this growing channel, but they are also ignoring the fact that the Net is changing the very nature of the consumer. The consumer of the future is downstairs in the rec room right now. Imagine how the intensity and involvement of N-Gen interaction on the Net will change future transactional services when extended beyond the tacky business of today's home shopping networks.

The 5 Themes of N-Gen as Consumers

1. N-Geners want options.

The availability of choice is a deeply held value in the N-Gen culture. The marketer's mantra as far as N-Gen is concerned should be "give them options to buy their loyalty." Having grown up in a free and interactive world, nothing is more foreign to the members of N-Gen than artificial constraints. There are few product categories where generics are treated as equal. Even with light bulbs, N-Geners want information and choice regarding environmental/energy use, tone, wattage, and brand.

This pattern is initially derived from years of channel surfing on TV and now from Internet habits—navigating in a world of seemingly limitless choice. In one 15-minute surf session, we observed 12-year-old Winnie Cheng launching a Net search for pages about hip hop band, The Fugees, who she'd wanted to hear after seeing their photograph on an entertainment magazine cover. She quickly scanned through 20 of the 68 matches looking for the icons and buttons that would link to audio clips. Finding none, she launched another search on *The Simpsons* and took a routine look through the 3 pages, out of a possible 1906, that she reads regularly. In the two months she has been surfing the Net, Winnie says she has only noticed one advertisement. The ad was for a Hong Kong newspaper and, because she takes Mandarin lessons, she was attracted by the Cantonese characters that were at once familiar and different.

Although they inhabit an atmosphere of choice, N-Geners also feel the occasional need to reground themselves in the familiar. Teenage members of the N-Gen in particular have developed strong attachments to the products of their childhood. They may sit down to e-mail friends on all continents before breakfast, but breakfast is still Count Chocula or Cap'n Crunch.

The choice-as-atmosphere phenomenon can be illustrated by the popularity of the Mövenpick Marche restaurants in Toronto. "You can get anything you want. They have everything," explained eight-year-old Ricky Cheng. The upscale cafeteria-style restaurants serve hundreds of different items. During a lunch break from a focus group examining N-Gen issues, the three children involved all chose the quintessential kid favorite, cheese pizza with pepperoni.

What is different about these N-Geners choice of pizza is that they hesitated to reject anything outright. They chose pizza only after they previewed the Thai noodles, the quiche, and the curried zucchini. On the Web there are always more options than there is time to explore. The first few seconds after a Web site is contacted are crucial. If the introductory graphic is too slow or blocks of text look unexciting, the mouse will move toward the 'back' button and the former list of options. The challenge for advertisers lies in finding the sites the N-Geners actually slow down to read. If the current success stories of various Web sites reveal any solution, it lies not in production but in the information and entertainment value of content. Sites tied into television programs are often the first visited by members of N-Gen. Andrew Walker, 13, started memorizing TV tie-in addresses a year before he and his brother even bought their computer. These sites, however, are only stepping-stone sites that, like many corporate sites, are abandoned once newbie N-Geners have practiced exploring the Web. The attitude on the Web is one of consumer control, but true to the N-Gen faith in tolerance, consumer control is not so much anti-corporate as it is extra-corporate. "Support the Nike conglomerate, buy bottled water, and eat your TV dinner so long as you take action. Support what you believe in, what is important to you," 16-year-old Emily Thompson of Maplewood, Minnesota urges the readers of her Web page.[3]

Marketers must learn to harness the interactivity of the Net if they expect to attract the attention of young people who are reaching higher levels of their intellectual potential earlier in life than ever before.

2. N-Gen customization.

Because they are used to highly flexible, custom environments which they can influence, it appears that N-Geners want highly customized services and products. Customized just to meet their needs? FreeZone's Allison Ellis thinks this is inherent in the medium. "On the Net, there is always a different or better way," she says. "Here is an upgrade, download this, make it faster,

> The Internet has definitely made me much more susceptible to advertising. I'll see a lot of pages on a certain game, for instance, that all say it is great, and I'll think to myself, "Wow! All of these people like it, I've got to get it." This can be a bad thing, though, as it distracts from what the Internet was originally intended for, which is information.
>
> DANIEL CASTILLO, 14
> Newark, Delaware

change this—so the kids have those expectations that things will be done to suit their needs. If they're not, they'll just go somewhere else or they will just do it themselves."

Products also acquire knowledge content by being customized. My daughter and I spent some time setting up our home telephone system so that it has the features and services which are needed by our family and my business. The telephone system is unlike any other family's. It has certain kinds of phones in various places in the house. It has unique voice-mail messages, autodial numbers, privacy features, speed-dial numbers, background music, security codes, conferencing capabilities, and a paging setup that is special for our family. The telephone contains knowledge about our family.

Another is the bread we buy. Dumb products can also grow in knowledge content, as in the case of Stone Mill Bakery near where I live. We can specify the ingredients for our own custom-made bread, order it over a computer network, and have it delivered that afternoon. The bread increases in knowledge content. Our (in this case my daughter's) ideas, culture,

> It's cool when a game lets you customize your own car. It becomes your car rather than somebody else's. It's even better when you can design your own games like Zaros [a system for Sony Playstation].
>
> ALEX TAPSCOTT, 11

knowledge, and tastes about bread become part of the loaf—it knows about her. It even knows when we want bread, and soon she'll press the bread icon on the screen in our kitchen and a message will be sent causing a loaf of her bread to be made. She is not just the consumer of bread; she becomes the producer—or more accurately, what we can call the "prosumer" of bread.

The N-Gen is entering a world of highly customized products and services which will be shaped by them, not just as a market but as individuals. This is causing changes in learning and the relationship between working, learning, and daily life as a consumer. Daily life for N-Geners will increasingly include diffusing their knowledge and personal information into products—everything from bread to in-line skates.

> If we have control over the computer, then I believe that as a consumer it makes us more resistant. We can shut off our computers at any time, or request a server to block out certain IP addresses. I also believe that if computers provide the reward of knowledge, we may find a way to create the program or applications ourselves. Then we might not even need the product being sold to us.
>
> DEANNA PERRY, 15
> Florida

3. They want to change their minds.

Video games and the Net are environments in which mistakes can be immediately corrected and situations can be recreated. When your Sonic Hedgehog or Super Mario Brother runs out of life because of a motor skill mistake, you can just flip the reset button. A link to a Web site, even the wrong Web site, is easily corrected with the click of the button. But not only do N-Geners expect to have the opportunity to correct their mistakes, they expect to be able to change their minds. In the marketplace N-Geners want to be able to, as country singer Shania Twain says, "change my mind a thousand times." Marketers should say, as Twain sings in the same song, "Hey, I like it that way."

4. They try before they buy.

To repeat, N-Geners are not viewers or listeners or readers. They are users. They reject the notion of expertise as they sift through information at the speed of light by themselves, for themselves. It is difficult to convince them that they *must* have anything. Here other industries can learn what the software and video games industry has already adopted—make your product free to use for a limited time. If its use becomes integrated into the N-Gen routine, making activities faster, brighter, and easier, then the product becomes indispensable and the companies can begin to charge. Learn from the pre-N-Gen N-Gener named Gates—go for market share. Give it away if you have to.

5. Technology doesn't dazzle—function counts.

Unlike the baby boomers who witnessed the technological revolution, N-Geners have no awe of the new technology. They have grown up with computers and treat them like any other household appliance. To members of N-Gen it takes no more expertise to go online or install software than it does to open a box of crayons or write in a notebook. Attempting to market something based on its high-tech futuristic qualities may have worked on the children of the '50s, but it won't fly with N-Geners, who are concerned with what they can do immediately, not with what they can do in the future. This is an audience that cares about function, not form; about what the technology will do, not the technology itself. Teenage Research Unlimited does work for Nintendo, which has the top-selling video game system Nintendo 64. Peter Zolla says that when it comes to video games, "Kids could care less that it's 64 bits. They don't even know what a bit is. They care about what it does . . . 'what does this really mean to me?'"

How Big Will N-Gen Cyber-Commerce Be?

Overall, the evidence shows that cyber-commerce is exploding. To begin with, there is the Net economy itself—the growing opportunity for services delivered through the Net. This got a big boost in 1997, when big players such as Disney and Microsoft announced services based on huge investments and big expectations. Disney Online is a subscription-based Web service targeted directly at the 'Internet generation' of children, which Disney Online defines as ages 3 to 12.[4] For $4.95 per month, subscribers get access to news, cartoons, and games.

More importantly, companies are using the Net to sell their goods and services. The question raised by many detractors, "But can you make money on the Net?" is looking pretty myopic at the time of writing this book. The question was always silly, like asking 50 years ago, "How do you make money with electrical power?" Or with roads. Or with the telephone. Increasingly the issue for e-commerce stragglers is how can you make money *without* the Net! It's a new infrastructure for the creation of wealth, as new models of the enterprise emerge. It is also a new medium for sales, support, and service of virtually anything, especially given that tens of millions of Net-savvy purchasers are coming of age.

For example, Chrysler is predicting that by the year 2000 one-quarter of its sales will be online, up from 1.5 percent in 1996, meaning that the local dealer is going to face some stiff competition from dealers across the country as buyers use online resources to comparison shop beyond traditional geographic boundaries.[5]

Security is not a barrier any longer, but rather a manageable issue. The only major barriers left to successful online commerce are those of familiarity and availability. But when 14-year-old Eric says, "With the Internet, I can buy whatever I need and then pay my parents back when they get the bill," it is obvious that there is a growing number of people who are comfortable with online commerce and even prefer it to some types of regular shopping. Evidence shows that once customers buy a product or service online, they are much more likely to do so again.[6] Availability is also growing by leaps and bounds. Ninety-eight percent of corporate America is forecasted to be on the Web in the next two years,[7] and the number of people online is growing by more than 50 percent every year. Internet appliances such as Web TV might boost this number even higher.

The ease with which purchases can be made on the Net will grow substantially with the imminent arrival of digital cash. Currently, the dominant method of paying for goods or services purchased on the Net is a credit card—something most N-Geners don't have. And because of minimum transaction costs, many merchants won't use a credit card for purchases below a certain dollar value. Digital cash will solve both these problems. It is money stored online and spent as easily as cash is today at the local shopping center. This will enable an N-Gener to effortlessly make dozens of micropurchases in the course of one Web session, each costing just pennies. Five cents will buy him a one-time play of his favorite music group's new video. The next step will be the formation of N-Gen consumer clubs as groups of like-minded youth band together to negotiate volume discounts, special services, or unique arrangements with marketers.

Forecasts for Net-based commerce are bright. Predictions for the turn of the century range from Forrester Research's $7.1 billion for consumer retail sales, to the Yankee Group's $10 billion, to IDC's recent $40 billion estimate. The Institute for the Future foresees sales online reaching 2.5 percent of *all* retail sales by 2005.[8] Forrester predicts that business-to-business e-commerce will reach $65 billion in value by 2000, almost 10 times their predicted consumer spending levels, and a hundred-fold increase from 1996's $600 million.[9] This is an astounding rate of growth. As Intranets are driving the success of many Web businesses, so business-to-business commerce will drive the whole Internet commerce field. Standards will be set, e-commerce companies will grow and learn, and workers will become familiar with ordering goods and services online. The synergy between this and consumer e-commerce will boost both areas and as the N-Gen ages and grows in purchasing power and influence, these predictions for e-commerce may turn out to be conservative.

Building Relationships

Cheryl Darlington is an N-Gen consumer of financial services. The Darlington family has had a computer in the house since Cheryl was in elementary school. She went to computer school when she was eight years old, three hours per week in the evenings. "Computers were just something that I always used." She put her personal finances on Quicken when she was a student and used the Net extensively to research various financial issues. Cheryl's father, Lloyd, who is a senior executive at a bank, wasn't really aware what she was up to until one day they were driving together and started to talk about taxes. Cheryl gave him a number of suggestions he hadn't considered. "I was flabbergasted," he says. "She not only knew a lot about technology but through use of computers she had extended this to considerable knowledge about financial services and banking."

Today, Cheryl does all her banking on the Net through Mbanx—a virtual bank. "You can do anything there." She sometimes calls Mbanx up to talk and finds that "they're really happy just to talk to you about finances, even if you're not doing a transaction. You can always talk to the same person—you don't just randomly call into some number. I've actually received calls from them to give me some advice about something. I feel like I have a relationship with them."

As the wave of N-Geners begins to come of age, relationship marketing will take on new significance. For example, old-style marketers in a bank view customers by product or service—customers of a mortgage, a checking account, or an insurance policy. N-Geners don't want to be treated as sales, they want to be treated as individuals—that is, as customers or people. New-economy marketers look at the relationship, not the sale or deal.

Take the hypothetical example of Martin—a 22-year-old N-Gener fresh out of engineering school. He has leased a nice apartment and bought a great car, in part because he feels that he needs these things to meet a great woman. But he's a bit overextended and misses a car payment. Two different scenarios emerge. The old-style bank is advised by the car loan system that a payment has been missed and a customer agent calls Martin, essentially to hassle him into paying up. The new-style bank has a complete financial picture of Martin—they know him as a customer and they know that he will be important to them for the next 50 years. They deliver financial planning services on the Net, help him reorganize his loans, and overall strengthen the relationship rather than killing it.

Relationship marketing in the latter scenario is enabled by the bank's Intranet (which brings together information about Martin's various activities with the bank) and by the Internet (which enables the bank to reach out to Martin on a continuous basis). These networks are the technological precondition for relationship marketing. Martin's generation is the human precondition—a generation of open-minded, independent youth who are fluent with technology and who want relationships with suppliers of goods and services.

Here lies the necessity of investing in what I call *second generation* Web sites. First-generation sites are informational; second generation sites are transactional—enabling the user to actually do something differently. Corporate sites offering brochures and groovy graphics are not enough to attract the attention of the N-Gen. When my son Alex visited the *Toy Story* movie site after seeing the address on a TV commercial, he was profoundly disappointed. He didn't want to look at Mr. Potato Head, he wanted to play with it.

Whither the Brand?

What will happen to the concept of "the brand" as the N-Gen becomes the dominant force in purchasing? Will brands still exist in an interactive world? This is obviously an important issue to companies when you consider that (literally) trillions of dollars have been spent in establishing brands, and brands are central to the strategy, success, and survival of many companies.

A trademark is something owned by a company. A brand is something which exists in the minds and actions of customers in the market. It is really a relationship between a customer and a product or firm. Youth, especially teens, have been very brand-conscious dating back to the boomers. In addition to wanting a good (quality) product, they want cool products, with cool names, used by cool friends and cool celebrities. While the Net provides a powerful new medium for establishing and maintaining relationships, there is considerable evidence that the combination of the new generation with the new media may spell trouble for the brand—at least as we've known it.

Brands were established, in part, as a result of mass communications. Using the one-way broadcast and print media, marketers could convince people through relentless one-way communications to "Just do it!" If you said "Things go better with Coke" enough times, you could establish the Coca-Cola brand in the market. The key phrase here is "in the market." Customers come to trust a certain product, service, or company. They identify themselves with it. They have a sense of belonging to something important when they make a purchase.

It can therefore be argued that in an interactive world with N-Gen customers, the brand will be harder to establish and may evaporate. Consider the impact on the brand of the "N-Gen as consumer" themes discussed below:

- *N-Geners want options.* There are more options today then ever before in product and brand choices. Kids are growing up in an atmosphere of choice, especially in cyberspace. This in itself undermines brand loyalties.

- *N-Geners want customization.* Perhaps you won't be cool because you wear Gap jeans. You'll be cool if you wear jeans I've never heard of. Fourteen-year-old Niki Tapscott says she'll send her agent (she calls her "Cyber-Niki") onto the Net to do her shopping, try on clothes, and check out new products. Cyber-Niki won't know The Gap from Guess, but it'll know what the real Niki likes in jeans—style, materials, fit. With the help of her cyber friend, Niki will custom-manufacture the jeans on the Net. Ditto for chocolate chip cookies, tennis shoes, and bicycles.

- *N-Geners want to change their minds.* The Net is creating a new vehicle for consumers to sift through information, authenticate, check facts, and make comparative evaluations. Unless a brand is based on strong value—i.e., the product is the "best"—it will be harder to maintain in an interactive world. Inability to mass-market and constant change in the market and minds of youthful consumers may weaken branding and loyalty.

- *N-Geners want to try it out.* Peter Zollo says that teenagers, for example, like to "experiment with a brand rather than buy what their parents buy." This historic trend is accelerated by the Net and N-Gen culture, where teens can check out things in ways their TV-generation parents could not.

- *Function and real value count.* Tim Fiala, of the public relations company Burson-Marsteller, explains that in the broadcast and print world "a unique selling proposition" could transform a commodity product into something special and thereby establish a brand. In the digital marketplace this cannot be maintained and can be "co-opted overnight." Consequently, in an interactive world, the real benefit of a product is what comes to the fore. If Tide doesn't actually wash whiter, it will become a commodity, undifferentiated in the market and without sustainable brand loyalty.

It is networked information which is bringing value and real benefits to the fore. Grocery shoppers using the Peapod network can ask for all the products in a certain category, sorted by different criteria such as calorie count or nutritional value. The most frequently used sort criteria are cost followed by fat content. Determining the healthiest peanut butter takes seconds. And the mass marketing of Kraft would have little impact on the purchasing decision. Good brands will correspond more closely to good products. A free market for value is enabled by unmediated access to information. In this environment, products which are undifferentiated in value quickly become commodities.

Even smarter software on the horizon—software agents—will extend this weakening of branding. Rather than trusting the brand, kids may begin to trust their agents. Sometimes called softbots, knowbots, or just "bots," agents are software which gets to know the kids, their preferences, and their sense of style. Kids and everyone in cyberspace are acquiring personal assistants. These tireless

> I think the individual determines what is cool, and it is his or her opinion. What is cool to one person may not be to another. The days of conformity are over.
>
> POOHBEARFAN, 11, f
> FreeZoner

little workers surf the Net for you day and night looking for information you've requested, finding that perfect chocolate chip cookie, evaluating new movies based on your preferences and the opinions of others you trust, organizing your personalized daily newspaper, communicating for you, trying on different types of jeans, and doing other jobs. In many areas, trusting your agent will become synonymous with trusting your own experience.

Conversely, we already have examples of brand development and customer loyalty arising at warp speed on the Net. Conventional wisdom says that a brand can be established if "you have lots of money and lots of time." However, the experience with Netscape turns this thinking on its head. Netscape vice president Kris Younger says, "we had no time and we had no money." Yet Netscape became an instant brand—largely through the molecular, word-of-mouth process of the Net. Netscape's predecessor Mosaic was passed along from person to person on the Net, and when Mosaic became commercial-quality software, the branding was instant. Within 18 months there were 40 million users. According to Netscape cofounder Jim Clarke, "this is not only the fastest growth of a technology product ever, but the fastest growth of any product and the fastest proliferation of a brand in history." Yet the destruction of a brand on the Net can be equally dramatic. Younger says the overnight rise of many software products and companies is evidence of this.

The brand is the catch-22 of N-Gen culture. N-Geners identify and are loyal to brands, but they are building a culture which is antithetical to the mass communications important to brand establishment. The contradiction is formed in the gradual shift from broadcast dictatorship to interactive democracy.

When a teenager buys Gap jeans, the most important aspect of the purchasing decision is not necessarily how this benefits her directly but what others know about what she did. One of the leading thinkers regarding the new media and marketing, Young & Rubicam's Mike Samet, believes such brands as The Gap will survive, but through different means. Samet explains how in this example: brands have a "badge" which displays an instantly apparent "universal meaning." When a teenage boy sees a picture of Michael Jordan wearing Nike sneakers, he believes that others will look at him the way they look at Michael Jordan. "But how do we create the brand badges if we're having all these conversations in a one-to-one world?" Samet says, "If there are 600 million private conversations going on, where are the universal meanings and how do they get established? Television made it very easy to establish universal meanings. The Web makes it very difficult."

"Maybe all these kids will grow up today not needing universal meanings," says Samet. "Maybe they're going to be secure enough in their own world that universal meanings won't be significant to them." He describes his six-year-old son who spends a fair amount of time on a computer and the Net. "He goes where he wants to go and there are no icons there to establish universal meaning. If companies don't have these universal icons, how can companies communicate with these kids?"

The brand appears important for now, as N-Geners still have the need to belong to the familiar and to be cool and there are ways to establish universal meanings for products. Further, cyberspace still lacks the superpowerful smart software agents required to bring value and services to the fore. But the axis of belonging is shifting. In marketing, interactivity equals increased power to the consumer to make informed choices and to buy products which deliver real benefits and value over those which do not.

The N-Gen will cause a change in thinking among marketers, away from focusing on brands and brand equity to thinking about relationships with customers. The Net provides new opportunities to evidence the true value of products and services as well as to create meaningful relationships between providers and customers based on trust. As the power of mass communications declines, to be replaced by the power of the interactive media and therefore the consumer, brand loyalties will make sense for informed and value-conscious purchasers.

Advertising and the N-Gen

The experience with the N-Gen to date also indicates that advertising may be turned on its head. In the print and broadcast world, an advertisement is "there." A kid may chose to beep off the sound of the television or flip the page of a magazine, but the ad *exists* for the child. Nike can broadcast to a mass children's market that Michael Jordan wears Nike shoes. The concept of the commercial break has been established. Kids expect the program to be interrupted because the paradigm is one of no control. What you see is what you get. And teenage girls expect to see and even appreciate ads in their magazines about the latest fashions.

> Off with their heads [re: advertisers on the Web].
>
> GYMNAST, 12
> FreeZoner

In the interactive world, advertisements do not exist in the old sense—they are not "there." With the exception of pushed content—discussed in Chapter 2—the user must seek out an advertisement. As a result, advertising will have to increase in educational or entertainment value and become integrated with digital content to reach this generation.

Not surprisingly, clumsy attempts to integrate advertising with content are being received poorly by N-Geners. Attempts to introduce commercials into chat discussions have been furiously rejected, as have unsolicited e-mail messages. If an ad appears to interfere with the delivery of content or waste time, it is counterproductive. On TV, the broadcaster rules. The kids are viewers. In an interactive environment, the locus of control is shifted to the consumers, who are not viewers but users. They are in control and have a sense of ownership over their environment. They object to having their content invaded by inauthentic corporate messages, just as they would object to a company pitching them in the school yard or in the middle of a book.

"I used to get mad at all the advertising and artwork I had to download. Mostly because I was paying for every minute I was using the service. Now that I have unlimited access, I just chill while I'm waiting for things to load, which doesn't take long at 28,800 bps, and at work it flies through our T1," says Eric Mandela, 14, of New Jersey. "I really don't pay too much attention to the ads unless it's stuff I am *really* interested in. When I am going through a search engine or a site with advertising I am usually on a mission to get in, get what I want, and go on to the next thing. I rarely browse around to just anything they link me to. I go to what I am interested in at that time."

> Advertising on Web pages is not really going to do anything. No one is going to stop surfing to go join AT&T or anything like that.
>
> SONATA, 15, f, FreeZoner
> Naples, Italy

Perhaps the sensitivity toward advertising will change, but there are no signs of that happening just yet. So if it's not feasible to broadcast ads effectively in an interactive world, what's the future of advertising? What's an advertiser to do in a digital environment where your ad doesn't exist unless the child actively seeks it out?

To begin, marketers can reach N-Geners with ads that are rich in informational content or entertainment value, for example on great corporate home pages. N-Geners love sites that are connected to recently released movies and television shows. Publicity photos and stills of scenes from the movie contain the same product placement shots as the film itself.

> [Advertising on Web pages is] a good way to get a message clear to millions of users, but I think too much publicity really is a snore.
>
> AUDREYM, 10, f
> FreeZoner

Second, companies or any organizations can create attractive Net destinations. The 7-Up, Coke, Pepsi, McDonalds, and M&Ms home pages were early examples of sites which engaged the young user in enjoyable activities. On the Avery Dennison kids' site, N-Geners can send virtual stickers to their friends.

Third, the Net enables marketers to target individuals with appropriate messages which they will value. The best people to target with Volvo advertising are people who are looking for a car and who are in the Volvo demographic. Further, the Net enables the communication of much broader messages to these people. As I outlined in *The Digital Economy*, the trend today in the broadcast world is to pinpoint messages and markets. The message—"Volvo is the safety car"—is targeted to pinpointed demographic groups—yuppies with families. The messages are delivered through the mass media to the correct audiences (upscale publications, specific radio and television programs). Alternatively, the message is delivered through direct marketing aimed at selected city boroughs, suburbs, streets, and even individuals. But when the media become based on choice, messages, ironically, can become comprehensive. Volvo can become the "everything car."

For example, the child hears that mom and dad are thinking about buying a new car. She accesses information about Volvos and, sure enough, they have great safety features. She accesses information about acceleration and yes, they do well there. She looks for information about mileage and Volvos do well in that regard as well. Says Dave Carlick of Poppe Tyson advertising, "Instead of having one feature which suits many people, you can have many features which suit one person. Interactivity allows that one person to explore products and services according to their own interests and find out what is important to them." The evidence suggests that the N-Gen is on the cusp of such proactive product exploration. Savvy advertisers will create compelling interactive environments which kids will seek out to do comparative shopping and thereby receive comprehensive and useful marketing messages.

Fourth, ads can be integrated with each other and with transactions in ways not possible in the physical media. Ray Lane, president of Oracle, describes the situation where someone buys a Sony stereo online and is offered a $10 coupon to the electronic Tower Records for any Sony title. The coupon expires in 15 minutes. Lane says, "That's a highly qualified, motivated audience of one."

Fifth, as explained earlier, the N-Geners, with their sensitivity to advertising, are largely skeptical of companies they perceive are wasting their time or exploiting them. Ads which have an authentic reason for being there can be successful. Ads on television are viewed as warranted because the company is paying for the program. The evidence indicates N-Geners will accept unobtrusive advertising if it is clear that the ad pays for the content they value. Inoffensive ads on search engines have become acceptable to most people. The *Growing Up Digital* kids told us that they don't mind unobtrusive ads such as the use of the Digital Equipment company logo on the search engine Alta Vista or the ads for Pepsi, Butterfinger, Mountain Dew, and Crunch along the racing track of the video game Jet Moto. Such integration of ads with content raises some difficult ethical issues.

The Ethics of Advertising to N-Gen

"Broadcasters program to children only when there is no more commercially attractive audience," Nickelodeon creator Vivian Horner has observed. "Since kids don't generally have disposable incomes, TV makes them surrogate salesmen. They want something and pester their parents to buy it.[10]

However, given the growing influence of the N-Gen in adult purchasing, we can expect that advertisers will launch massive campaigns to deliver their messages to N-Geners—on packaging, billboards, print media, television, and, increasingly, the Net.

Guidelines for advertising to children state that content and advertising must be separate. However, lines blur today, even on television. Some of the most popular children's cartoon programs of the past five years, including *Teenage Mutant Ninja Turtles, Mighty Morphin Power Rangers, The Care Bears,* and *My Little Pony,* featured so many product tie-ins that it was difficult for most adults to see these shows as anything more than full-length commercials. Add to this product placement ads in video games and in movies, which, of course, are also played on TV. As the user of an online auto racing game speeds through the virtual desert, empty tequila bottles are only slightly buried in the sand so their labels remain recognizable. People who live only on movie screens also consume; actors in Hollywood productions have to be just as concerned with logo visibility as with maintaining their characters.

As media converge to become multimedia and interactive, this differentiation will be even more difficult to make.

The line between advertising and content is further blurred, not just by ads creeping into content but by content creeping into ads. Advertising must become more information-rich and give potential customers the opportunity to try out their options. In other words, advertising itself has to have content.

Advertisers have new ways to introduce messages into content. A maker of children's cereals was recently criticized for its site, on which children could play with its promotional cartoon characters. This seems harmless enough. A bigger problem, however, arises when such sites promote products which can be harmful to children, such as cigarettes, and mask these products in colorful characters. Breweries and distilleries have come under fire for creating interactive playgrounds populated by beer-drinking cartoon frogs, or coloring-book vodka bottles that can be decorated by the site's visitors.

"The pages attract exactly the visitor we want: male beer drinkers, age 21 to 34. There's nothing on this site that a family will not see on an Anheuser-Busch brewery tour," a consumer awareness spokesperson told *The New York Times*.[11] But it is difficult to know who actually goes there. Only sites that have restricted access to subscribers or other registered users can verify the ages of those users. An open-access site that appeals to the company's demographic target and to children will likely attract both.

This problem of demographic verification is one that has plagued Web site content providers. In order to convince advertisers that the market is an appropriate one, providers have to furnish a profile of the user population which includes a statistical breakdown of demographic and gender groups, general location, and average household income. There are currently no A.C. Neilsen ratings for the World Wide Web, although at time of printing, several companies, including Neilsen, are vying to develop such a service. What this means is that no one knows exactly who is on the Internet or what they do once they are there. More precisely, the only way for a site's sponsors to find out what their user profile is is to ask their users. Where N-Geners are concerned, these practices have raised several privacy and safety issues, discussed in Chap. 11, "N-Gen and the Family."

At this point, it is difficult to gauge just how great a force Web-based advertising is in the lives of N-Geners. Our anecdotal research suggests that their responses to ads online range from complete indifference to annoyance to passing interest. The industry itself seems to reflect that erraticism. The April issue of *Cyberatlas*, an Internet site about the Internet, had two headlines. "Jupiter says Web advertising revenue shrinking," read the first headline. The second read: "IAB says Web advertising revenue growing."[12]

There is a concerted effort on the part of both government and advertising agencies to put some kind of guidelines and regulations in place regarding advertising and children and the Net. Proposals are currently being considered by the U.S. Federal Trade Commission (FTC) that were created by The Center for Media Education, a group that has successfully lobbied the FTC in the past, and by the Children's Advertising Review Unit, an industry watchdog that monitors ads geared toward children on television and all other media.

One of the biggest concerns is the collection of data from children. The Center for Media Education is seeking to end the practice of collecting any personal data about children unless it can be verified that the children have received parental permission. In contrast, the advertising industry itself, the Council of Better Business Bureaus, and the National Advertising Review Council have proposed guidelines that suggest that advertisers simply make reasonable efforts to convince children to ask their parents for permission before they perform any purchase via the Internet or divulge personal information.

At this point, attempts to apply both federal or voluntary regulations on Net advertising are limited by the same practical questions that bedevil every other attempt by government and private citizens to restrict material on the Net: How does one country police an international network? If American children access a German site that violates the regulations, how will those regulations be enforced? And, most importantly, how do we control advertisers and censor unethical behavior without censoring ourselves and our children?

Answers are beginning to appear. Advertisers claim that they can be self-regulated online. The industry does assume that adults and children have different product requirements and that finding an ethical means of addressing those requirements is not only desirable but necessary. One typical case study of self-regulated advertising standards can be found on the Avery Dennison kids' site. One of the largest suppliers of office products in the world, Avery Dennison recently released a line of "printertainment" software. Printertainment is a ridiculous concept, unless you're eight years old and spend a significant amount of free time collecting and trading stickers. With a generation of kids downloading clip art and color printers finding their way into homes, address labels are still address labels, but sticky paper has real creative potential. As we have seen, using the Internet to get kids their sticky paper can have some even stickier issues attached. Avery Dennison took on the challenge of ethical advertising for kids online. The result is a site that conforms to guidelines for self-regulation set out by the Children's Advertising Review Unit.

The site contains commercial and entertainment content that is differentiated visually by the presence of the Ad Bug. The green and purple Ad Bug is an invention of SpectraCom, the Milwaukee company that created the KidsCom online community. Young children are clearly told that if they see the Ad Bug beside content on the site, they are looking at an advertisement rather than entertainment or information content. On the Avery page, the Ad Bug resides beside profiles of the Printertainment products as well as at the top of the list of Avery Kids retailers, and beside the free sample and "contest of the month" offers. There is no Ad Bug visible on the Shockwave puzzles children can play with on the site or on the virtual stickers they can send to a friend, but the red Avery logo is highly visible on each of these activities.

Avery's policies regarding the collection of information about the site's N-Gen users ensure that parental approval is obtained. That is, no information about the children's whereabouts is collected online. Free samples can only be ordered and con- tests can only be entered by mail or fax with a parental signature. The company has also agreed not to sell or share information that it gathers in this manner.

If advertisers like Avery Dennison are prepared to be self-regulated and fol- low industry guidelines to the letter, it does appear that adult concerns about mar- keting to children online can be resolved. "Advertising on the Web is inevitable," 13- year-old Ali told attendees of the 1997 Digital Kids conference San Francisco. "It's going to happen, so you all might as well just stop worrying about it."

The Reinvention of Retail, The Reinvention of Industries

The rise of cyber shopping will change our thinking regarding what it means to be a retail company and what it means to sell.

For example, an N-Gener wants to buy a leather jacket. She may try a few on in a store to choose the brand. She then goes home and lists her criteria to her software agent—style, color, measurements, designer brand, etc. The agent goes onto the Net and finds the best price. As explained in *The Digital Economy,* the digital mar- ket will be a commodity market, because price and availability will be the main fac- tors in sales, just like the commodity market for wheat in Chicago. Further, the price may change dynamically depending on availability on the Net. A seller of jackets might send agents onto the Net to determine today's price or this hour's price or this minute's price. Or the seller may decide that when there are 1000 in inventory, the price is x. When there are 100, the price is y. Or there may be no inventory at all— the seller acts as virtual manufacturer, wholesaler, and retailer for a group of compa- nies who together could manufacture jackets on demand.

In the boomers' economy there were many different industrial "sectors" such as retail, financial services, manufacturing, and education. But these old sectors break down in the new economy with the N-Gen as consumer.

What does it mean to be a retail company in five years when there are a bil- lion people, most young, on the Net? Every company becomes a retail company.

What does it mean to be a financial services company when a 14-year-old purchases a hot new song off the Net, transferring digital cash from her hard drive to that of the recording artist? She and the artist are both the "financial services compa- ny." There is no bank or credit card company involved.

What does it mean to be a manufacturing company in the new economy? A sophisticated aircraft will become, as they say, "a collection of parts flying in forma- tion." Boeing becomes a design, networking, project management, and marketing company working with suppliers and customers to design aircraft in cyberspace. The specifications are shared on the Net with all relevant parties and the plane is con- structed on a network in concert by youthful knowledge workers of a new generation.

What does it mean to be in the educational sector when work and learning become the same activity? Every company will become an "education" company or it will fail. If your company doesn't have plans to establish its own "college," it is probably in trouble.

As Young Adults, What Will They Consume?

N-Gen consumers already have a big impact on marketing because of their substantial purchasing power and influence on adults. As they become young adults, they will drive commerce for decades. We can learn much from their culture regarding how they will change products, services, and markets.

- *Residential real estate.* The market will remain relatively flat for some time as the wave of N-Geners takes a couple of decades to enter the work force and begin to have the purchasing power to buy homes. If you are planning on cashing in big time on your house to buy that condo in the gated golf community soon, think again. There will be no sustained surge in real estate prices. Further, N-Gen will want wired houses, wired apartments, and wired vacation properties.

- *Commercial real estate.* Conventional wisdom would say start creating the office space for a huge demographic wave about to hit the job market. Hold off on building those glass tower office buildings, however. The N-Gen will want flexibility of location, and offices closer to (or in) the home, and N-Geners will not be impressed by mahogany. Expect growth in smart communities which include local commercial offices like "telework centers" connected to smart homes and retail businesses.

- *Real estate redevelopment and restoration services.* The techniques and skills required to install integrated services digital network (ISDN) and fiber optics in the suburban bungalow and country farmhouse to handle the home office needs of former commuters will be in greater demand, but the urban sprawl cannot go on forever. The decline in arable land available for farming also has implications for the future, including higher food prices and shortages of diet staples. Not to mention the fact that suburban and rural life will not suit the tastes of many N-Geners. A growth industry is the conversion of office spaces into living spaces. Roofs will have to withstand gardens and safe play spaces. Converted apartments will also have to have enough square footage to accommodate grandma or granddad who has to move in after a bionic hip transplant.

- *Automobiles.* The biggest generation ever is approaching driving age. They'll want cars, initially inexpensive ones. A generation raised with digital technology will want digital cars. These young people are not looking for great technology but rather great services provided by a car. They'll want the car to be a place for entertainment, learning, and work. Environmental issues will come back with a vengeance as well, as will the fun factor in autos. Sell your minivan soon, as families without children in the house don't need one—and N-Geners will have the same aversion to minivans as the first driving boomers had to station wagons.

- *Clothing.* This is a generation with a strong sense of style. But the cool brands don't necessarily win out. Authenticity is very important to this generation, not only facts are subject to verification. When contemporary fashions take their inspiration from the '60s and '70s, kids run to second-hand stores for the original article. However, even these tastes for the old-fashioned are trend-sensitive and subject to the fickle tastes of the youth market. Just recently, widespread reports reached the United States that early models of Nike sneakers were fetching prices of $100 to $1000 in Japan. Clothing speculators quickly flooded the market and sent Japanese youth in search of another style of footwear from another period.

- *Financial services.* N-Geners will expect to be treated as customers of the financial services enterprise rather than as customers of a specific service. They will be very sensitive to their privacy on the one hand, but will on the other hand expect all their financial activities to be consolidated in one place for their inspection and management. Don't even dream of selling their personal information to a third party. They will expect you to take actions which are in their interests, such as transferring funds to a better interest account if appropriate. They will want to do all their dealings on the Net. In the year 2005 there will be more than 10 million N-Geners over 20 years of age. Two-thirds of them will want to surf to the bank. If you're not a cyberbank, you won't exist for them.

- *Recreation.* N-Geners love to play. They love to communicate and discuss things. Expect to see a growth in Net-based entertainment. They will evaluate which golf or tennis club to join by sending their software agents onto the Net. The spirits business, especially beer, has been suffering because the baby bust reduced the population of the biggest drinkers—that is, youth. Expect a growth in alcohol consumption as the N-Gen wave reaches drinking age, even though the boom is declining in their consumption. N-Geners often have a high interest in body image and also in health. Expect growth in "smart drinks" which are today consumed by teenagers who attend "raves"—huge warehouse and field parties featuring enormous numbers of people dancing to technopop and accompanying laser light shows. "Smart drinks" deliver their hit through amino acids rather than alcohol. They are essentially fruit and vegetable juices fortified with herbs and high dosages of vitamin supplements. Expect mass-market versions of this specialty product.

- *Education.* N-Geners will understand lifelong learning. They'll want help learning everything. They'll expect employers to provide it. They'll want it customized to their needs and they'll expect it to be delivered to them on the Net, whenever and wherever they choose.

- *Travel.* When a child helicopters over the San Diego Zoo on the screen using a program called "The Animals," it doesn't reduce her interest in going to San Diego; it increases it. A search for authenticity will drive much of N-Gen private travel in the future. N-Geners also have a strange view of planet Earth—they think it is infinitesimal. Expect the N-Gener who can afford it to hop on a plane to have dinner with a friend across an ocean. While she's there she may be more likely to stay with her C-friends she's met on the Net, whether on a boat navigating the Hsi River or a villa on the Riviera, than she is to stay at a five-star hotel. When it comes to business travel, there will be a travel substitution effect—where travel is eliminated by networks—in particular for routine business meetings. N-Geners are also not going to be enthusiastic about commuting. Expect them to want to work from multiple locations: home; a local telework office; the company office (laboratory, digital plant); a customer location; a vacation property.

- *Reintermediation services.* Many of the big victims of the digital economy will be the people in the middle: agents, brokers, wholesalers, lawyers, and retailers. They could fall victim to a condition known as "disintermediation." When information shifts from physical to digital form, the old intermediaries can become unnecessary. Suppliers and customers are linked directly to the Net and don't need everyone in between. As commerce becomes electronic, for some this means buying a copy of *What Color Is Your Parachute?* But for others it could mean the biggest new business opportunity of our times. Some of these in-between agents are perfectly positioned to evolve into a role that I call "reintermediation." This is the creation of new value between producers and consumers by exploiting the Internet, and such services will be in big demand by N-Geners in the work force. New services will include evaluating information on everything from news to movies and creating digital shopping experiences for everything from records to cars. Take advertising agencies which conduct focus groups to test product concepts.

This activity will be replaced by reintermediators who conduct such research groups on chat lines and virtual communities. Travel agents will lose their revenue from the suppliers—airlines and hotels can go directly to the market. Having lost their revenue from industry suppliers, the smart agents will create new travel services for consumers, helping with vacation planning and conference organizing.

- *Music.* Get ready for the new music. The music industry has been flat since mid-1975. David Munns of PolyGram records explained to me that this is due in part to the boomers having finally replaced their vinyl records with CDs. True enough. But Discovery Institute Fellow Frank Gregorsky says that the last time music sales collapsed was 1979—a moment of generational change—when disco was dying and MTV was bursting forth. "Just like the arrival of MTV, the impending merger of millennial [N-Gen] teens and digital video will startle almost everyone over 20," he says. "I'd be crazy to predict what it will look or sound like, but a whole new generation of entertainment is virtually guaranteed." The record companies and music stores will also be wiped out unless they transform themselves because N-Geners will acquire their music on the Net. As Alliance president David Ticoll says, "Who needs those racks of tired CDs on the shelf?" September 11, 1996 was an important day. David Bowie was the first artist to release a song on the Net—and not on a conventional CD. Music and rock videos will be available through the digital media and the N-Gen will be the first to line up. Also, get ready for digital radio. The N-Gener can play a song again; ask about the identity of the singer on the last song; request the second cut from a favorite artist's new album; or vote on a daily basis on who he or she thinks is hot.

- *Logistical services.* Invest in FedEx and UPS and maybe even the post office. N-Geners will move less for work. Work will move more for them. Consumption will move to them. They will shop for food staples on services like Peapod or the IGA Cybermarket, not just because such sites are convenient and provide new services like calorie, nutritional value, and price comparisons, but because N-Geners will use their media to consume any commodity. This does not mean that they won't "get out" anymore. They'll get out plenty, but voluntarily—for social, entertainment, tourism, or educational reasons—not because they must.

- *Publications.* N-Geners will still read novels on the beach, magazines in the bathtub, and newspapers on the subway. But increasingly they'll get news, marketing materials, and other information digitally. But publishers who simply "repurpose" their content on the Net will not succeed. Because of the themes of N-Gen culture and consumption, N-Geners will want custom publications. Look to the *Wall Street Journal*'s interactive edition as a good precursor. N-Geners will want publications they can interact with and write for—with real-time letters to the editor. Digital publications will be multimedia and networked—full of hot links. Competition to a newspaper in Charlotte, North Carolina, will not be other newspapers—it will be Charlotte's Web—a community Web site which is bringing the people of Charlotte together in cyberspace to discuss issues, learn about developments in the city, and eventually purchase goods and services. Real estate companies will flock to Charlotte's Web because, unlike the newspaper, it will enable young home buyers to helicopter around the house on the screen to get key contextual information about location—schools, shopping, crime rates, transit.

- *New media.* N-Geners will pay for media services, media content, and media equipment. They'll want it all as part of the air, just like the boomers all wanted a refrigerator and a television when they moved out on their own. N-Geners continue to love movies and favorite TV shows, but prime time is their time. Don't even think about trying to get them to conform to your schedule.

- *Consumer electronics.* It is clear that the digital generation will spend a higher proportion of its disposable income on consumer electronics, which are increasingly digital. According to TRU research, already 5 of the top 10 big-ticket items of today's teens are consumer electronics products. Eight of the top ten provide entertainment.[13]

And where is kids' technology going? Niki Tapscott (now age 14) participated in a kids' panel on "The Consumer of the Future" at a conference held in 1993. She was asked what her ideal computer would be like.[14]

My ideal computer would be about as big as a piece of paper but it would fold up to go in my pocket but you can just press a button and it would blow up into a huge screen. It would be cellular and it would be connected to any other computer in the world. It would also be a television giving me every TV channel and I could watch any movie—but I want to see movies before they come out in the theater. What I would really like is a little credit card on the bottom of the screen and when an ad for something I like comes on I could click on the little card and they would deliver it to my house. It would also be a telephone and you could call your friends on it and see them on the screen and you see what they're wearing that day. It would also be a stereo and give me any CD or music video I requested. But I want really good sound.

I'd also like to have a cyber friend—I'll call her CYBERNIKI. She would look like me, with the same size, and tastes, and if I gain twenty pounds, CYBERNIKI would too and go up a size. She would know all about me and be able to help me. I could send her out onto the Net looking for information to help me with my homework. I could type in "GUESS" and my cyber friend would show up and go into the Guess store. She would walk around on the screen, and if I saw something I liked on myself, I could buy it on screen and it would be charged to my parents' credit card and come in half an hour or so. That's my dream computer.

N-Gen at Work

The N-Gen mind is ideally suited for wealth creation in the new economy. As discussed in Chapters 5 and 6, this generation is exceptionally curious, self-reliant, contrarian, smart, focused, able to adapt, high in self-esteem, and possessed of a global orientation. These attributes, combined with N-Geners' ease with digital tools, spell trouble for the traditional enterprise and the traditional manager. This generation will create huge pressures for radical changes in existing companies. Many N-Geners who meet resistance will decide that the main way to fight the status quo is to abandon it and create their own enterprises.

There is much we can learn from N-Gen culture and also from initial experiences with N-Gen entrepreneurs about how the firm must change to embrace them, their ideas, and their different view of work and working.

Most observers agree that the old model of the firm—the command and control hierarchy—is in deep trouble. This model is described well in the best-selling management book of all time, not one written by Stephen Covey or even Peter Drucker, but by a former telephone company employee named Scott Adams. *The Dilbert Principle* hit a chord. And as for the various management buzzwords and newspeak, from empowerment to reengineering—they were hammered (no pun intended) by Adams as well. The success of *The Dilbert Principle* speaks to the cynicism about traditional approaches to structuring and managing companies as well as to the ineffectiveness of current fads, which are interpreted by Dilbert as ingenuous, manipulative, and injurious both to the employees and the organization.

Dilbert sums up well what many of us have been saying for years: the old model of the enterprise cannot work in an economy driven by innovation, knowledge, immediacy, and internetworking. The old command and control hierarchy divides the world into the governed and the governors. At the top is the supreme governor and at the bottom the permanently governed. In between are those that alternate between governors and governed. These middle managers act as transmitters of the information which comes down from the top. Peter Drucker describes them as "relays—human boosters for the faint, unfocused signals that pass for information in the traditional, pre-information organization."[1] Communication from the bottom up was limited, except through formal labor-management relations. Such communication took the form of meetings, telephone calls, or memos. You were an employee, nested somewhere in the hierarchy of an enterprise owned by someone else. Your goal was to move up the hierarchy and have more people reporting to you. You were motivated by material rewards and fear of punishment. Your work goals were determined by your boss, and his or her goals by his or her boss—all the way up to the top, where decisions were made. You were focused internally rather than on the customer. Innovation, creativity, giving better customer service, or creating products, for example, were typically not part of the picture. Often you found yourself taking credit for the work of those below you in the hierarchy or in seemingly never-ending "turf" battles and organizational politics. You hung in with the company until you retired or were fired. You were the "organization man."

While this picture may seem stereotypical, this was the fundamental model of the enterprise. For some time there has been growing acceptance that this structure stifles creativity, self-motivation, commitment, and responsiveness to market demands, not to mention human needs for fulfilling work. Many business leaders know that fundamental changes—the transformation of the nature of our organizations and how business is undertaken—are required.

But the success of the *Dilbert* book underscores that progress has been slow. Many of the key themes of change—empowerment, teams, virtual organizations, knowledge management, sharing, and cooperation, to name a few, are cynically viewed as management buzzwords rather than achievable approaches to success. It seems that old cultures and old ways of working die hard.

Is it possible that the key to widespread progress lies with a new generation that is used to peer collaboration and working virtually; that is skeptical of authority; that challenges assumptions in everything; and that has grown up with networks and networking?

N-Gen Culture and the New Enterprise—Ten Themes

As the 10 themes of N-Gen culture described in Chap. 4 are extended to the creation of wealth, we can see new directions shaping up for the firm. The relationship between the old culture and the new culture of work is summarized in Fig. 10.1 (below). From my experience working with many firms, these N-Geners have it right. In fact, many of the new ideas regarding how to create innovative, high-performance enterprises may have been slow to take hold in today's firm because these were concepts in search of a generation whose culture suited them.

Figure 10.1
Relationship between N-Gen culture and
the new culture of work.

1. Independence and the molecular enterprise.

N-Geners have high independence and autonomy, growing from their experience as initiators of communication and information handling activity. We can expect that rather than being a cog in the wheel, the N-Gen worker will be comfortable working more like a molecule. As I have previously argued, in a knowledge economy the basic unit of wealth creation shifts from being the corporate hierarchy to the networked individual—like a molecule. Everything that was "mass" becomes "molecular." The word *molecularization* is awkward, but useful. In physics, a molecule is the smallest particle into which a substance can be divided and still have the identity of the original substance. Molecules can be held together by electrical forces—in a sense, networked.

The shift from mass to molecular is helpful in understanding the new environment and the new generation. Mass production changes to production runs of one—from jeans to bread. Mass marketing becomes molecular as every customer is treated like a separate market. The mass media become molecular, from the personal newspaper to a media environment of millions of channels. Mass education can become molecular, with every student treated as an individual learner. Mass transit can become molecular as vehicles become information appliances and roads become smart. It is internetworking that makes all this possible.

Most important, the old corporation of mass society shifts to more fluid molecular structures where media-fluent, young knowledge workers naturally collaborate in ever-changing clusters of teams and networks. A strong sense of independence and self-initiation is required to be a "business unit of one"—perhaps explaining the slowness of the adoption of these ideas in today's workforce. Both characteristics are strong aspects of N-Gen culture and psychology. Expect N-Geners to have less difficulty functioning in these nontraditional fluid structures. Expect old-style managers to have difficulty "supervising" N-Geners.

2. Intellectual openness.

The emotional and intellectual openness of N-Gen culture may lead us to an open enterprise where people focus on sharing ideas rather than suppressing them in order to win turf battles. Openness involves vulnerability, but N-Geners have such high self-esteem that they will be prepared to spill their innermost thoughts—not unlike the '60s model of letting it all hang out. It remains to be seen to what extent the free expression tail will wag the bureaucratic dog. Anticipate some dissonance and conflict here as styles of working clash.

3. Collaboration.

N-Gen culture is inclusive. It reaches out to internetwork new individuals and new ideas. It may be more colorblind and oblivious to gender and other social differences than any culture in history. N-Geners are interested in ideas. They judge people based on their contributions. Expect many traditional barriers to collaboration and teamwork to melt. Expect to see changes in our concept of authority. Today authority in business comes from organizational position as depicted by a job title, similar to the family authority structure. But due to the generation lap, children are an authority on a topic of importance for the first time. In families and in N-Gen culture, people come to respect each other for their expertise or authoritativeness in different areas. This favors peer-oriented relationships rather than hierarchies.

4. Internetworking intellect for organizational consciousness.

N-Gen culture is based on the free expression of strong views—that is, the internetworking of knowledge. It is not simply about the networking of technology but about the networking of humans through technology. Let your mind go regarding the kind of enterprise these N-Gen "molecules" will create. There has been much discussion about creating learning organizations. The concept, first developed by Peter Senge, is a good one. There is no sustainable competitive advantage today other than organizational learning. That is, companies can compete only if they can learn faster than their competitors.

However, progress in creating such organizations has been slow. The problem may be that organizations cannot learn in the same way that people can't learn when they are unconscious. They need to be conscious to learn, and so do organizations. Perhaps internetworking can help organizations achieve consciousness just like the neural networks in the human brain enable a human to achieve consciousness. Will the N-Gen be the first generation to create conscious organizations, and thereby organizations which can learn? Will N-Geners be able to exploit the power of internetworking to create some kind of consciousness in organizations, perhaps the precondition for organizational learning?

In theory, at least, this is possible. The digital age is not just an age of smart machines but of humans who, through networks, can combine their intelligence, knowledge, and creativity for breakthroughs in the creation of wealth and social development. Just as networking distributes and integrates computer processing—the network becomes the computer—so internetworking should be able to distribute and integrate human intelligence to achieve a new form of organizational consciousness. The N-Gen may be the first generation to network intellect for problem-solving and innovation, extending consciousness from individuals to organizations. The network in the N-Gen enterprise may become the basis for the enterprise to become conscious, think, and thereby learn for the first time.

5. A culture of innovation.

Innovation is a hallmark of N-Gen culture. Innovation, rather than traditional factors such as economies of scale, access to raw materials, productivity, and the cost of labor, determines success in the new economy. Twenty-first century enterprises will succeed through the continual process of renewal of their products, their systems, their processes, their factories, their marketing, and their people.

In *The Digital Economy,* I explained how product planners, strategists, engineers, developers, and managers at Microsoft work under the banner of "obsolete your own products." If you've just developed a great product, your goal is to develop a better one which will make it obsolete before your competition does. Compare this view to that of many mainframe aficionados at IBM in the 1980s who fought against IBM shifting resources to the PC, UNIX, and client/server development. The goal of these people was not to obsolete but to preserve and to resist innovation. The results of the two different views rapidly became clear in the marketplace.

The Net Generation will bring a new meaning to the term *innovation*. Their thinking appears utterly unfettered compared to that of the boomers. They have mastered new tools for collaboration. They will ask "why not?" Defenders of the old commercial orders, beware.

6. Preoccupation with maturity.

The preoccupation with maturity is rooted in a desire to be treated like an adult— that is, to be treated with respect and judged based on what you can contribute rather than how old you are. Expect people in the N-Gen enterprise to be judged on contribution. For example, compensation will be based on contribution rather than on position in the hierarchy or old approaches like the "Hay system" where income corresponds to the number of people reporting to you. Expect to carry on a collaboration with someone only to find out that the person is a teenager (as has occurred with me many times).

7. Investigation.

The N-Gen culture of investigating everything and of challenging assumptions will serve N-Geners well in the new economy. Expect N-Geners to want to look under the hood, not necessarily for technical detail but to understand the assumptions behind things. Expect sacred cows to be slain. Just like they hack a video game to eliminate hierarchical levels of play, expect N-Geners to hack the corporate hierarchy and culture. For better or worse, corporate traditions may become irrelevant if they don't withstand scrutiny.

8. Immediacy and the real-time firm.

Another theme of the N-Gen world is immediacy, appropriate for the enterprise of the future which is a *real-time* enterprise—continuously and immediately adjusting to changing customer demands, supplier capabilities, and business conditions. Goods will be received from suppliers and products shipped to customers "just in time"— reducing or eliminating the warehousing function and allowing enterprises to shift from mass production to molecular online production. Customer orders arrive electronically and are instantly processed—with corresponding invoices sent electronically and databases immediately updated.[2] While such an environment may seem frenetic and high-stress for adults, it is the comfortable way things work in the N-Gen world online. With several windows open, doing several activities real-time, involving different people, multiple information sources, and a variety of applications running concurrently, the N-Gen world is a real-time world.

9. Corporate skepticism—N-Gen as capital.

N-Gen unease about big corporations is an obvious problem for big corporations. Companies which seek to attract the new generation must be perceived as ethical, green, and acting in the community interest. Many N-Geners will become entrepreneurs rather than work for "the man." To be effective, advertising must not be seen by N-Geners as "wasting my time" or be inappropriately placed in virtual communities or Web sites. This leads to the bigger issue of N-Gen values, one of which is justice—the view that "I should share in the wealth that I create." Implications of this are discussed in Chap. 12, "The Digital Divide."

> I usually resent being told to do things which I feel are a waste of time.
>
> **DAN ATKINS, 17**
> Malibu, California

Given N-Gen skepticism about corporate interest, how can companies attract and hold the brightest of this generation? The solution is not simply to "be nice to them." The argument that people are human beings and therefore should be treated well by the companies they work for seems to have been ineffective. Many companies treat employees poorly. Work is pretty deadening for many. "Thank God it's Friday" still rings true.

The N-Gen will cause a deeper rethinking of management's attitude toward its people, intensifying the current debate regarding treating people as capital. Some business leaders argue that things like employee knowledge, customer satisfaction, and investments in R&D should be treated as capital. Many, such as the Securities and Exchange Commission's Stephen Wallman, believe that new measures of intellectual capital need to be developed and actually recorded in company balance sheets. Others believe that such measures are impossible and even misleading. Setting aside that debate, it is clear that the N-Gen is the first generation of knowledge workers and, as they say in the workforce, increasingly they are capital. In fact, the N-Gen will become the dominant form of capital.

Treating people as capital? Isn't that a bit Orwellian, you say? Actually, it would be a big improvement over being treated as a variable cost, which is the case for labor today. Alliance associate Riel Miller, who has written a book on human capital,[3] says, "What would you rather be, a cost or an asset?" Miller argues for "turning costs into assets that are treated with the consideration of something which is valuable, rather than a drag on the bottom line" as a new view of people in a knowledge economy. Arguing that people should be given the high status of capital isn't dehumanizing people—it's arguing that increasingly knowledge workers, not money or physical plant, are the key to wealth creation and prosperity.

10. A culture of trustworthiness and trust.

Just as trust is the *sine qua non* of virtual communities, it is the foundation of the Internetworked Enterprise. Management authority Stratford Sherman explains that in the new economy, commercial relationships are evolving from coercive to voluntary. For Sherman, "the qualities for success in commercial relationships are the same as those in personal relationships—promise keeping, sharing, fairness, wisdom"—all resulting in the creation of trust.

One of the key relationships is that between employer and employee. The trend toward molecularization cited above is evidence of this. Increasingly the employee as molecule has high mobility, many options within and outside the corporation. Traditional loyalty to the corporation in gratitude for a career and a job for life are gone—forever killed by the reengineering and downsizing of the early 1990s. Each N-Gener can expect to have multiple careers—to actually change his or her entire knowledge base several times throughout life—not to mention many employers throughout life. The relationships of work will not be those between a boss and an employee, but between a client and contractor; between members of a project team; between a mentor and a student. People will not take action because they are told to, to satisfy their superiors, in fear of punishment or for benefit of reward. New motivators are goals, innovation, and being part of creating something significant or wonderful. All of this demands trusting relationships.

Authenticity is the basis of trust. Throughout their youth, N-Geners hone their authentication skills online. If trust is becoming the glue for the new enterprise, then the N-Gen knowledge worker has what it takes for the new noncoercive business world.

Knowledge Sharing and the N-Gen World of Work

A powerful example regarding how new ways of working may finally be achievable as the N-Gen enters the workforce is *knowledge deployment*.[4] Sometimes called knowledge management, this is the creation, protection, development, and sharing of knowledge assets. The idea is a good one. To succeed in the new economy, firms will need to manage knowledge, not just data or information.

Knowledge deployment is not only necessary but also now possible because knowledge workers can be interconnected through networks. Consider how the capital investment in computers is enhanced considerably by networking them. Imagine if the computers in your company were not connected—that they could only exchange information by physical means—carrying tapes, disks, and cartridges from one to another. When computers are interconnected their value grows. Similarly, humans and their know-how have not been connected. We must use physical ways to share knowledge: meetings, reports, memos, telephone conversations, business travel. By interconnecting people, we not only network human intellect, we network knowledge. As with computers, the value of human capital is enhanced manyfold by interconnecting human knowledge.

Because of this, some companies have moved from having a VP of data processing to a VP of information systems, and from having chief information officers to establishing chief knowledge officers. In a recent survey I conducted of business leaders, 95.7 percent indicated that knowledge management was more important to their success than business process reengineering, the big management fad of the 1990s.[5]

Knowledge sharing is at the heart of this challenge, but it has been slow to get off the ground, stalled in many companies. It seems that professionals and managers in today's firms are uneasy about sharing their knowledge.

When the Alliance for Converging Technologies researched the obstacles to knowledge sharing in today's organization, we observed that a number of perceived objections or barriers existed. We then asked the *Growing Up Digital* kids what they thought about these barriers to sharing knowledge when they entered the workforce.

The kids' reactions were insightful. They found it curious and somewhat strange that adults would have such problems. Says 15-year-old Austin Locke, "Knowledge sharing is something that will enhance culture. If you know more stuff, you can spread this knowledge, and like a multiplier effect, add knowledge to the knowledge base. We are already seeing the collaboration of different schools in different countries over the Internet to work on projects. By doing this, a whole new way of thinking is revealed."

Below are the some of the adult "barriers" and the responses to them by 16-year-old Lauren Verity.

Adults: You can't build a culture of sharing.

Lauren: Kids work together all the time. Not just in computer games, but in projects, homework, or anything like that. We share information all the time when we get something out of it. We work together, probably a lot more than adults do . . . maybe because we don't have enough of society's rules built up on us yet to feel strange about doing this. I don't know. What use is knowledge if you're the only one who knows it?

Adults: You can't work with people you haven't met—face-to-face and hard copy are essential.

Lauren: That's only a barrier if you choose to see it as one. If you can love someone you've never met face-to-face you can certainly learn to work with them. Now people will say that Net relationships are not real. But that's not true. Just because you can't see their face doesn't change anything, you can still talk to them, you can still exchange information, and knowledge, and ideas. You can even use video cameras now to talk to them face-to-face. You make the best of what you've got—it's not a barrier, it's just a new direction.

Adults: People don't know how to work as a virtual team.

Lauren: That's just something that people will have to learn. The Internet is the way of the future. My generation will control the world one day [and] the Internet is not going to go away, and most of us who use it don't want it to either.

Adults: How do you get people out of their comfort zones?

Lauren: Ummmm . . . I guess you have to build trust with people to do that. But I don't see that as a barrier, because of the Net. Comfort zones don't have to exist.

Adults: Knowledge sharing is not part of our culture.

Lauren: Kids are building a new culture and a new way of thinking. A new way of viewing the world. People will always share, but you just have to be careful who you share what you know with. Usually you tell something important to someone you know, someone you can trust. You can build a culture of sharing, but it has to be a selective one. People share information on the Net all the time. That's what Web pages are.

Adults: People don't trust computers and networks.

Lauren: That will depend on what you mean by trust. If you mean as in people who are scared to use computers because they are afraid to do something wrong, then I guess that is true for them. They need to learn that computers don't bite. Kids don't see the Internet as a bad thing. All the adults in the media ever seem to talk about is instructions on how to make a nuclear bomb, pornography, and hackers, etc. They don't see the side we see. They don't understand what the Internet is. We're uniting the world. Race, color, religion—none of this matters on the Internet. It doesn't have to exist, and most of us don't care anyway.

It appears that the N-Gen will be the first generation to be able to network knowledge because they have grown up doing it.

From Lemonade Stand to Web Page Design Shop

A frightening part about being downsized or otherwise unemployed in midlife is the prospect of competing with the recent graduates who hit the job market willing to work long hours of overtime because they don't have families to support, and for less money because they don't yet have mortgage payments to meet. If there is any hope to be gained from learning how N-Geners work, it may come from the advantages of giving your father a job.

"He provides the gray hair in the meetings when you need it," says Phil Smart, 27, of Burlington, Ontario.[6] Phil and his 26-year-old brother, Richard, hired their father when they founded their software company, Visual Applications, which five years later was sold for several million dollars to Symix Systems of Columbus, Ohio. The Smart brothers still manage the company they created, under the terms of an agreement that ensures that both the brothers and their father remain employed until the next innovative idea strikes them.

True, few N-Geners are likely to be giving their parents jobs in the firms they create at the age of 15, hiring themselves out as hypertext markup language (HTML) consultants for $15 an hour, or developing Web sites for $10 per page, but one thing is certain—the era when all kids did to earn money was mow lawns, baby-sit, and flip burgers is over, and N-Geners are learning how to work differently as a result.

N-Geners are more likely to open a Web Page design firm in the rec room than they are to open a lemonade stand in the front yard. Members of N-Gen, some as young as 11, have parlayed their techno-knowledge into part-time jobs and small businesses. One of them is Deanna Perry, 15, from Florida, who is already very busy. "Currently, I am subcontracted with askSam Systems doing work for them," Deanna says. "My friend Ryan and I created Absolute Web Design. We're basically the 'presidents' of the company, so to speak. We use advertising with banners to promote our site. People will then send a request through the order form and we will create a nice home page as closely related to their request as possible."

Deanna, who has been a part-

> I'd also like to tell you that I even make Web pages professionally. Well, not really, I am only 13, but people pay me to make Web pages for them. So far I've made two pages and I have another customer whose page I'm working on. My father is a computer consultant and he gets me jobs from some of his clients.
>
> ALANA JOHNSON, 13
> California

time Web page designer since she was 14, insists that her experience has been nothing but positive. "I am not being exploited at all; the company is very fair with its rates. The work does not stress me out. I find it very rewarding and exciting."

Deanna and N-Geners like her are gaining experiences that change their expectations about not only the role of work but one's role at work. In contrast, the boomer entering the workforce 20 to 30 years ago may have hoped to work for a large prestigious company or organization and rise in the hierarchy. The "organization man" of the '50s had offspring who aspired to similar objectives once they hit the workforce. This was weakened by the youth radicalization of the 1960s and also by changes in the world economy and competitive environment which rendered the organization man and the old hierarchy itself somewhat obsolete.

As the N-Gen enters the workforce in the next decade, the evidence says that the old model of work and the enterprise will be doomed, finally. To begin with, bright, self-confident, and techno-savvy N-Geners will prefer to create new businesses than change old, big ones. By growing their own businesses, they can control their destiny—an N-Gen requirement.

"I've received enough information from the Net to help me improve my life and go out into the world with confidence instead of fear for what's going to happen to me when I turn 18," says Roger Davidson, 17, of Minneapolis, Minnesota. For the past two years Roger has been the Internet's most famous teenage movie critic, providing reviews of both classic and contemporary Hollywood films for his fellow N-Geners. Reviewing is a job he takes seriously—over 1 million people have read his reviews online, and Hollywood has realized it has to take his reviews seriously too.

When he panned *Casper,* its child star Christina Ricci sent him a rebuttal via e-mail. John Singleton, the director of *Boyz in the Hood,* maintains an e-mail correspondence with Roger. "We talk to each other like we're people," says Roger of the relationship. "I like fan mail and all, and John does too, but there is one thing we both agree on—sometimes the fans don't talk to us as if we're real people. We're unreal icons or mythical gods to fans. I like fan mail as much as the next celebrity, but sometimes there are prices to fame." Roger, who has been profiled in *People* magazine and *USA Today,* plans to attend film school at UCLA next year, but thinks the lessons he has learned from having a job based on the Internet will stick with him in whatever career he chooses. "It's affected me in ways that help me discover new things about the world at large," Roger says. "It gives you a new passion to go out and do something meaningful in the world, despite what some anti-Internet folks have been saying."

Andy Putschoegl, the 17-year-old owner of Esquire Pictures, agrees. "It's not like a huge company, it's basically just me," says Andy. "I have a group of people who come to me when they want an anniversary video and I do weddings, I do highlight films." Even though Andy's product has little to with the Internet, all of his film editing and business operations are conducted on his Mac. "I have different letters that I put together for invoicing, or as far as trying to drum up new business with little descriptions about what I've done and also for trying to get funding for my own projects," Andy says. The Internet itself plays a role in expanding Andy's professional development. Like Roger, Andy has an industry veteran to whom he can go for advice. "I've been able to correspond with the guy who produced *Mighty Ducks 2*, Jordan Kerner—he also did *Fried Green Tomatoes* and *Up Close and Personal*. When I worked with him last year (as an extra) I was able to get his e-mail address and it's always really exciting for me to see something from him because he always responds within 24 hours to my messages and it gives me a natural high because he cares enough to respond."

N-Geners who have created vast networks of professional and personal communication require specific tools to support their communications efforts. One N-Gen company has started to take the design of these N-Gen-specific tools especially seriously.

After he finished his summer job on PARC's Workscapes of the Future project, Gautam Vasudevan wasn't about to focus all his energies on high school. Instead, Gautam and friend Phil Scheacter took the final steps toward creating Digital Mirage, a communications software development company. "We have this thing about being very intuitive," says Gautam, 16. "We have to be. No one reads manuals anymore. I don't know anyone who reads manuals—it takes so much time and it's not very productive. You have to make sure things are really human, just like everyone else's stuff."

In designing their major product, a network-based Java application tentatively called Avalon, Gautam and Phil were inspired by the ultimate in N-Gen concerns: preventing a breakdown in communication. "There are a lot of ways we can communicate, but if you aren't an active participant, it defeats the purpose of it all," says Gautam. "We write communications tools in order to make people more productive."

Inherent in the design of Avalon are three major assumptions. The first is that the desired response time for communications is very short and that getting the response is urgent, whatever the medium. N-Geners see delays in communication as a source of annoyance and frustration. Gautam says Avalon is meant to curtail that frustration: "If I wanted to contact someone else to get their opinion on a project and I keep calling and getting their answering machine for three days—I don't know if I'm getting the right number

Right now the Internet department is doing some shuffling and I could easily become a full-time employee. My boss loves me and she knows I am more than capable for the help line, but without some kind of college degree I would not go far in the organization. I hope to return in four years.

JASON MOTYLINSKI, 18
Minnesota

anymore, so I think, okay, I'll send this guy an e-mail, and he doesn't check his e-mail. So I'm writing programs that users can use to say: 'Okay, if I'm communicating with these people, how many ways do I have to do this and how can I use those communications tools efficiently?'"

This N-Gen product design also assumes that there is no barrier in terms of time or space that separate work from other activities. "The technologies are already here, you just have to bring them together," Gautam says. "We have to make a product that lets you sit down in front of the screen, say, 'what are my options?'— and the software gives you options. Then you can try him at work, or at home, or page him and leave him an e-mail; the same message can go to both places. And if it's really urgent, you can call him on his cell phone or on whatever other communications device they have."

Telementoring

The experiences Roger and Andy have had with their e-mail correspondence are more than just professional networking. We have always known that young people benefit from being taken seriously by adults. N-Geners often have access to career advice and expertise through e-mail exchanges that are coordinated by community development agencies out of a desire to introduce students to a variety of professions. This practice is known as telementoring.

One of the best examples of an electronic mentoring program is a pilot project run by the Center for Children and Technology (CCT). The program assigns adult mentors to female high school students interested in the fields of science, engineering, or computing. Often young women stop studying these subjects in school or college because jobs in these areas aren't on the "normal" career track for women. Encouragement and advice from adult women who have successful careers in such fields can persuade these young women to persevere.

Contact takes place entirely via e-mail, so it doesn't matter whether the student and her mentor live 5 blocks or 500 miles apart. The busy mentors like e-mail since they can write their responses during quieter off hours. The students also like the arrangement. "There is definitely something about this medium that invites disclosure," says project leader Dorothy Bennett. "The kids say they are more comfortable discussing issues via e-mail, issues they might find awkward to discuss in person."

CCT's experience shows that the kids communicate regularly with their mentors—usually about once or twice a week. Students and mentors discuss a wide range of topics, including self-confidence, career options, college decisions, project work, content-specific questions, personal relationships, and the work of scientists, engineers, and technologists.

In addition to the one-on-one student-mentor dialogues, the Center arranges discussion groups, called peer lounges, so that all the students in the program can exchange views with each other. Mentors have a similar lounge. The youngsters' subjects include homework projects, personal relationships, and classroom issues. This space assists students in forming stronger bonds with each other and in developing a support system within their classes. The mentor lounge is where mentors can both prepare for establishing one-on-one relationships and gain peer advice for addressing problems or issues that arise in the context of their relationships with students. Former project mentors use their experience as a resource to facilitate discussions.

The Workscape of the Future

Imagine how your work environment would be different if, through a constantly running sound network, you could gain an audio-peripheral awareness of what your colleagues are working on, share expertise, and do multiproject problem solving, whether your colleagues are in the next room or on the next continent. Worried about missing something in the babble? Speech recognition software files on your digital desk keep all the conversations in a searchable database for future reference. Beside your desk is a scanner that, using low-grade radiation, digitizes books you are interested in without having to turn the pages.

Does it sound like your office? It could very well be the N-Gen workscape. All these ideas originated in the final reports of seven 14- and 15-year-olds who spent the summer of 1996 researching the Workscape of the Future in the Xerox Palo Alto Research Center. PARC is the world-class research facility famous for—among other things—inventing the PC, the local area network (LAN), object programming (which didn't really take off until 1996), the graphical user interface (GUI), and the laser printer. The Workscapes of the Future project, cosponsored by PARC and the Fugi-Xerox Palo Alto Laboratories, sought to examine how the world will go to work in the new millennium.

To do this, they chose to look at how young teenagers without previous professional experience would attack research in the world of work. "The theory is that we would get young people who have grown up in this area of technology-saturated media. They would have grown up in homes and schools that employ that technology, and they would be native technology speakers, whereas we feel as adults that we have picked it up as a second language through computers and fax machines," explains Mark Chow, the research scientist who guided the project.

> You will be able to have better communication with people from far away.

JOHN TAYLOR, 17
Researcher,
Workscapes of the Future

There are two types of people: tech heads and everyone else. You look at how people use the stuff—some people love to go in and figure out all the details and then there are others who just want to know what they need to finish a project. I don't think that balance ever really changes. I'm sure when they invented the wheel—the guy who invented it probably knew everything about it. And then, there was a guy who was just using a wheel barrow and he didn't care if it was square or circular.

GAUTAM VASUDEVAN, 16
Workscapes of the Future participant

The Web played a significant role in this stage of the research. "Although we continually dropped hints about maybe using printed material, the first point of reference was always the Web. One of the theories we have is that the Web is the new paradigm for communication," says Chow. "One of the questions you would like to know is what the next generation is going to think about the Web when they have grown up with it there. I think the overall reaction to the Web is that it's not big enough for that generation." They are going to want more interactivity and more control. What that means is that N-Geners like the World Wide Web, but ultimately they want a higher-quality input and output, in terms of an ideal workscape that translates into tools that facilitate a combination of independent work styles and a collaborative decision-making process. In other words, real-time audio and video.

In an earlier experiment, when video conferencing was in its infancy, PARC set up a connection between two groups of researchers—one in Portland, Oregon and one in Palo Alto. People even started using their interoffice hookups. The group did conclude it was possible for two geographically separated groups of people to collaborate on a project in a fluid manner when they had video and audio links between them. "It turned out to be a whole new way of communicating," says Chow. "You could share an office with someone and not have them there—you just leave the connection on all the time."

The N-Geners who made up the Workscapes of the Future research team, even though they initially thought networking two adjacent rooms was "a dumb idea," took to video network hookups like ducks to water. "I thought we could experiment with televisions, microphones, and cameras and see what happened," Chow says. "I brought the equipment down and went up to get the second load and when I came down again it was all hooked up." To master the equipment, the students then held their morning meetings with the project "guides," which included Chow and two graduate students, from different rooms.

Different notions of productivity were a challenge to both adult and student researchers. "These students are smart enough that they never get challenged at school anymore," says Chow of his panic when the student's final presentations were due. "They always leave schoolwork till the last minute and get A's. This was a project that demanded more." The adult researchers were in more of a panic than the student ones especially when, at the last minute, students were still transferring 36-megabyte video files. But the students had given a lot of thought to what kind of work environment would enhance their creativity.

> The ideal workscape would be where you would have a moderation between human and computer interaction.

RYAN BALZER, 17
Researcher,
Workscapes of the Future

One of the things the group realized was that what is technologically possible is often personality-impaired, an issue that often came up when the researchers discussed the possibility of working at home instead of in a workscape. "You can only do so much sitting at your computer," says Gautam. "Unless you have a group working on things and every individual doing their part—which has traditionally shown itself to being productive . . . it's just too hard to do."

"I'm the kind of person that if I worked at home, I would sit in front of my computer, log in and then say, 'OK, that's enough work for this hour,' and go watch TV," says Ryan.

Fellow Workscapes researcher John Taylor, 17, disagreed: "I usually work better independently. I don't think that people who work at home will be completely unproductive. People do realize that in order to get a paycheck, they have to produce results. If they sit in front of the television, they won't get results."

> The ideal workscape would be one where you have electrodes strapped to your brain and all work would be done by pure thought.

GAUTAM VASUDEVAN, 16

All of the Workscapes participants did agree, however, that the ideal corporate culture was not about business suits, but was a culture that would give them the freedom to think and communicate with co-workers and the power to make decisions and explore possibilities.

Imgis—A Taste of N-Gen Entrepreneurship

Many of the brightest and most energetic N-Geners would prefer to create a business than change an old, big one. Because of internetworking, smaller companies can have most of the advantages of larger companies without the main liabilities, in particular a deadening bureaucracy which stifles innovation, immediacy, and collaboration. Besides, by growing your own business, you get to share in the value you create.

That's what Chad and Ryan Steelburg did. They are building a company based on the concept of customized advertising. For example, many national magazines print regional editions that differ only in their advertising content. So northern readers of *Newsweek* or *Time* might see snowmobile ads, whereas their southern counterparts are treated to swimsuits. This way magazines make their ads much more affordable and cost-effective. Some magazines go a step farther and produce different versions of the same magazine depending on the reader's interests. For example, if you have told *PC Magazine* that you are interested in local area networks, they will send you the network edition that contains supplementary articles and ads on this subject.

Consider how powerful this type of targeted advertising will be on the Internet. Fairly soon your television and computer will have similar features, and these information appliances will be capable of delivering to you content and advertising that has been totally customized to your tastes and interests.

You will welcome this arrangement because this means the local video newscast only sends you stories that interest you, and the commercials are only for products and services you might actually buy. If you are a male you wouldn't see ads for pantyhose; if you live in an apartment you wouldn't see ads for lawnmowers; and if you only ride the subway you wouldn't see ads for BMW. On the other hand, you may appreciate the serendipity of receiving information or messages about products and services not on your hot list. It's up to you—customized.

Building and supporting such a customized online existence calls for an extraordinarily sophisticated and expensive information infrastructure. Imgis is a new California company that hopes to provide a large part of the necessary technology. The company was formed in 1994 by brothers Chad and Ryan Steelburg, when they were 24 and 21, respectively.

Chad is a quintessential N-Gener. He was so taken by the potential offered by the Internet that it prompted him to drop out of college in 1992. He has been writing software since grade 4 and was anxious to get in on the Internet action. "Here I was studying mathematics in college, and the Internet is on the horizon, and it is definitely the next revolution in communications. I can always go back to college, since it will always be there. But the birth of the Internet happens just once."

After two years of writing Internet software for an investment company, Chad set out on his own. At the moment the company has less than 30 employees, but if things go according to plan, Chad feels that fairly quickly their company could become "as big as AT&T."

So far, however, the company has operated in a very un-AT&T manner. "From day one we started with the intent of making this a very flat organization. We have a pretty amorphous structure. We assign a task on the fly to whoever is best suited to it, and they go conquer it. It is not the approach of typical top-down organizations. Understanding the importance of employee ownership explained above, every employee is part owner, and the ownership is distributed fairly evenly. The people who are doing the receptionist or support-type roles in our company—when you hire the type of people we do—are making just as valid a contribution as the VP." Everyone at Imgis is of the belief that the Internet is going to change the world, and employees who don't have the religion leave pretty quickly. "So we've boiled down the hiring process to just asking some key questions, such as 'If you had the ability to change the world, would you do it?'

"We have already been offered millions of dollars for the company, which we have declined, not because of the hope of making more money, but in seeing a vision and wanting to take it to completion. Everyone here shares that vision, and would like to see it become a reality, and finally bringing the digital era into the mainstream."

Chad's vision may seem exceedingly ambitious, but he feels this is reflective of his generation. "The depth and breadth of my generation's horizon is different than our parents. We are all a part of earth, and not a part of the United States. We have seen the entire world via the Net. The scope and ambition is greater for us."

Just imagine what kind of world of work these children will create, given their networking orientation and also the pace of technological innovation today.

Adrian Scott is not a typical N-Gener, having acquired his Ph.D. at the tender age of 21, but the company he established in February, 1995, Aereal, is involved in a very N-Gen industry and operates in a very N-Gen manner.

Aereal provides personalized Internet marketing and publishing. The company develops Web sites that will help its clients sell more of their products and services, and current clients include Hewlett-Packard, Symantec, and Charles Schwab. The company also publishes an online magazine on virtual reality modeling language (VRML), with Adrian serving as publisher.

Adrian's clients are big, but his company is not. "We don't have employees in the standard sense. We do various projects and we put together a team for the project, much like the Hollywood model. This way it is easy to scale things up and down, and different projects require different kinds of abilities. This gives us flexibility and mobility, which are useful in business."

A typical project might involve five people, with Adrian acting as director. The team would also include programmers and graphics and sound designers. They live throughout the United States and collaborate over the Internet.

Scott feels that his generation likes to have control over their work circumstances and choose what they want to do. Companies today can be technologically and organizationally flexible, allowing people to work from home if that is important to them, which is what Adrian himself does. "People don't want to feel the boss is looking over their shoulder. Employees might just want to be able to sit on the floor and kick back." In his line of work Adrian feels that many of the easy tasks have been automated. "People don't want to work on the clock. They want to be productive. As an employer, you want your people to think and be creative."

Adrian feels it is a great time to be in business and that if you are a self-starter like he is, there are lots of opportunities and choices. "Even if you don't always make the right choice, you can pick yourself up and get back in gear. The business that we are in changes every six months or so, in terms of the products and the services we provide. The Web continues to change and the market is always changing at high speed. The business must adapt to those realities."

Scott has created an internetworked enterprise which is radically different from the traditional corporation. He has also created a workscape for people which is the antithesis of the Dilbertian model.

The "Executive" of the Future

Assuming that we will still have large corporations for the next period, and that they will have senior managers, what kind of executives will N-Geners make? How might they work differently and what kind of corporate culture will they create in a large organization?

As these are hypothetical questions, I had to identify some current executives who have been using computers for many years and who are also as close to the N-Gen age group as possible. One of the best examples was Michael Dell. Dell started building and selling computers from his university dormitory in 1984. Today his business has grown to be a computer manufacturing and direct-sales juggernaut with 1997 sales of more than $10 billion. Even in the enchanted realm of Silicon Valley sensations, the Dell Computer success story is extraordinary.

The company's mantra is speed, with heavy reliance on electronic communication. "E-mail has been a pervasive part of the company since we started," says Dell. "The first thing it does is break down the hierarchy of the company so that you don't have massive layers. It improves communications."

The company is full of young people, including some of the first wave of N-Geners to hit the workforce. Dell notes that N-Geners feel right at home with a much flatter organization chart and using digital tools to communicate. E-mail is one of the most important—in fact, Dell refers to "the e-mail culture" in the company. "The Net generation you describe is different in that they just assume an immediacy of information that is free-flowing. The e-mail culture—it's like having a conversation with someone—if they take two days to respond, you wonder what's wrong with them. The N-Geners understand the power of this stuff, and to them it is extremely natural. You have folks who are in the middle and upper levels of age who have not had exposure to this and they are not as quick to get it.

"If somebody joins our company, and they're not getting the e-mail thing, we'll tell them very directly that they need to respond in a timely fashion using this medium or else they truly can't function in the company. And people figure it out. Here you have this constant communication that is frank and uninterruptable, pervasive and global. There is an informality that can go on in these conversations because you're talking to people you are familiar with."

An employee who suddenly starts getting less e-mail has cause to worry. "The focus is on results," says Dell. "The challenge a lot of people have with a company like this is that the hierarchy doesn't matter much. You may have a position, but it doesn't really mean much unless you can do the work. The e-mail culture becomes part of a way that people are sized up in an organization—whether they can get on the highway and function. If you don't know what you're doing, people just ignore you. They just go about their business and you become irrelevant. Let's say we make the mistake of hiring someone for our organization and they aren't particularly good at what they do. People will just ignore them. The organization will literally reject people who don't know what they're doing. It's kind of remarkable."

The company has begun an aggressive expansion program to handle its soaring volume of business and Michael Dell understands the need to nurture a corporate culture that is appealing to the N-Geners. Today's young workers are knowledgeable and mobile, have big expectations, and often desire to be entrepreneurs. To harness this energy, Dell creates a flexible environment that he believes is attractive to this generation. "You give them their own challenging goals and turn them loose and let them accomplish whatever they can. Nobody gets bored in a business like ours. If they aren't bored, then they don't have a lot of time to think about going off on their own.

"I also think they get a great sense of accomplishment through involvement, getting to build something of their own within a company without necessarily the risk or uncertainties of having to build a new business from the ground up. We have created a lot of businesses within Dell with bright people who have thought of something and we have said, 'OK, go do it.' It's also important that the people you have doing this stuff are passionate about what it is they are doing. They're a lot better at it if they're passionate." With a personal worth of close to $2 billion, Dell says his own motivation these days is "to build something great and be part of something special."

The road to Dell's current success hasn't always been smooth. In the early '90s the company found itself in serious trouble with uncompetitive products, particularly in the booming market of laptop computers. Dell had fallen far behind in product development and was paying a heavy price: $65 million in inventory writedowns in the first half of 1993 alone.

The sea of red ink caused Dell to intensely reexamine every aspect of its operations. To decide which parts of the manufacturing process Dell should do itself, the company conducted an analysis of the return on capital on each of these. "It turns out you don't have to do all the things that people initially thought you would have to do." Because the input costs for computer companies are constantly dropping, success goes to the company that can keep as few parts as possible in stock and manufacture computers based on actual customer orders. No one does this better than Dell. The company can receive a computer order, manufacture a PC to the customer's specifications, and ship it out the door—all within 48 hours. All this is possible because of networking.

Dell says that suppliers love the certainty of doing business with his company. "They know they put a product in our factory, and within three hours we are shipping it out the door and selling it. They have a much greater confidence in our system because it works." Moreover, there is very little invested capital. The most important capital for Michael Dell is human capital—people.

Just as it has conquered computer sales through toll-free lines, Dell is equally determined to dominate the world of Internet computer marketing. Dell's hip and youthful-looking Web site goes far beyond just touting the company's products. Customers can custom-design their own computer by clicking a mouse, with the price showing a running total. The process is fast and convenient for an N-Generation accustomed to dealing online. It also obviates the need for so many telephone operators, thus driving Dell's prices down further.

This is an example of the second generation of the Web which I described earlier. In the second generation, firms don't simply provide information, they change the way they do business. Rather than "brochureware," annual reports and marketing hype, the second generation of the Net enables companies to actually conduct business on the Net. Rather than saying "we're a great computer company," the Dell Web strategy enables customers to design and, in a sense, manufacture their own computers on the Net.

The Net has extended the Dell direct sales model—where customers purchase directly from the company, thereby disintermediating the middle man. This reduces costs and speeds up everything in the process. "The Internet has become a lightning rod, moving us to a new business model . . . driving improvement and changing the way we interact with customers."

The company's use of the Internet is not limited to sales, manufacturing, distribution, and internal communications. Everybody, including the CEO, uses the Web extensively. Michael Dell says he surfs the Net regularly for information about things such as the industry and his competitors. "Sometimes I have to do a job interview with a candidate and it is pretty typical for me to first of all try to find them on the Internet, say if they were quoted in the press. Probably I would check out the company's Web site that they currently work for to find out a little bit about them, so I can put what they say in perspective.

"This isn't something an assistant can do, because you never, ever get the quality of the experience and the anecdotal findings that you do when you do it your-self. There is no way for an assistant to know which button to click on when you're faced with twenty options. Some of the connections are not at all obvious, and those are some of the most vital ones you could make."

In the N-Gen-led enterprise, leadership as opposed to management, con-sensus, and teamwork are more than buzzwords. Dell works to "set a pace by exam-ple as opposed to telling people what to do." His style is to "ask people questions and let them figure it out on their own," although when consensus is not possible, "you jump in and say, OK, I've heard all the debates and this is where we're going."

This is the model of the N-Gen executive in a large company. He uses the new media personally to support him all day long and to communicate throughout the company and externally. He builds a business on internetworking, creating a real-time company appropriate for an economy which is becoming real-time. The new media enable him to create a flatter, more open company and a "culture" which is dig-ital and responsive. Professionals who create great value can be compensated as well as senior managers. The most important capital is human. People are motivated to achieve team goals, to innovate, to achieve something great, rather than to satisfy superiors. Perhaps a new view of the manager is emerging.

Three New Imperatives

1. Nourish N-Gen capital.

If the N-Gen will become the dominant form of capital, it must be treated not as a variable cost but as both an asset and a resource. This does not necessarily mean that human capital should be recorded on company balance sheets (a complex debate). But it does mean that companies will need to treat N-Gen capital well, as it is pre-cious. N-Geners can't be treated like traditional capital—not just because they're human beings, but also because they are smart, confident, mobile, and connected human beings engaged in knowledge work. To perform effective knowledge work, they must be motivated and collaborate well. Unlike with production machines or blue-collar workers, management cannot simply turn up the speed, as if to say, "Management wants twice as many innovations per month."

Take the trend in the 1990s toward creating temporary jobs—growing 400 percent since 1982.[7] Companies want a flexible work force and they have also found that this is a way to reduce costs by paying workers less and by using people only when necessary. We can anticipate that many N-Geners will actually prefer such arrangements, providing improved work variety and opportunity for skill enhance-ment and lifelong learning. Expect them to look for more flexible arrangements which enable them to manage the challenges of working and family life.

While the work force will become more molecular, the lot of many temporary workers is currently not good. According to the U.S. Department of Labor, over half do not have health insurance; almost half are women with children; few end up in full-time employment; and many report they are treated badly compared to full-time workers. Their lot has received considerable public attention recently. Typical of this is a story in *USA Today* where temp workers describe horror stories such as having a manager whack them on the back of the head with a rolled-up newspaper for making a math error.[8]

Few of the current temporary workers are N-Geners. Companies in the future will not be able to treat N-Gen workers this way. Increasingly, temp jobs will not be the clerical and "industrial overload" variety as most of the workforce becomes knowledge workers. To do effective knowledge work, these young people must be motivated, have trust in their fellow workers and company, and have a real sense of commitment, not just compliance, to achieving team goals. This cannot be achieved with alienated, underpaid, and abused workers.

Many N-Geners will also have additional mobility as they acquire knowledge and the capacity for hyperspeed lifelong learning—critical to innovation and creating wealth. In the aforementioned survey I conducted of business leaders, I asked what their most important assets were. Eighty-seven percent indicated that human, knowledge, or intellectual assets were key, followed distantly by current products, effective business processes, and financial and physical assets.[9]

Further, traditional capital was stuck in a company's bank account or investments. It could not walk away in disgust if it was not being effectively utilized. N-Gen capital has free will. It can walk out the door in ways that traditional capital can not. N-Geners will not accept unfair treatment. They also have a new vehicle to organize themselves—the Net.

There is no reason firms can't create a new kind of contract between employees and themselves. Whether part-time, mobile, teleworking, contingent, contract, or all of the above, relationships can be forged which are based on clear expectations, mutual support and trust, commitment, and community. The ball is in management's court on this one, and if there isn't change there will be trouble.

Expect a rise in Net-based associations of temporary workers and, if conditions do not improve, expect the growth of the first Net-based trade unions. Expect the birth of virtual temp work companies which disintermediate the traditional employment agencies, especially those which do not negotiate good terms and conditions for their stable of workers. As N-Geners acquire political clout, expect pressure on governments for standards. Expect companies which have bad practices to become exposed as young people spread the word on the Net at the speed of light. In extreme cases, expect highly disgruntled N-Geners to damage companies which treat them badly by organizing Net-based boycotts, penetrating "secure" company files, and taking actions which are not yet imaginable. And expect companies which have the old industrial model of workers, temp and otherwise, to atrophy and those which understand human capital to appreciate in value and earning power.

Most importantly, expect companies to require new ways to compensate employees based increasingly on the value they create. This will include a profound democratization of corporate ownership. Even leading opponents of the measurement and recording of intellectual capital on balance sheets believe that the rise of knowledge work requires new approaches to retaining people. For example, merchant banker John Rutledge says, "The real question posed by intellectual capital is not one of measurement of financial reporting, it is how to manage the companies." He argues that the big issue is how to hold people together in an organization long enough to achieve its objectives. Companies can't "own" human assets, they can only rent them, so he says companies will have to ensure that these people "own the income stream created by their own efforts . . . broad and deep employee stock ownership is extremely important."[10]

2. Think digital tools for performance and quality of work life.

The N-Gen brings new dimensions to the debate on the impact of computers on quality of work life. It is true that many jobs involving computer systems have been deadly. In early days, systems were single-function, and job design alternatives were restricted. For example, when word processing came along, many companies took away all the interesting things that secretaries did and made them single-task power keyboarders. Computer systems were implemented to control costs, period. Old, unproductive work processes were automated. But now that technology has embraced multiple media and has become multifunction, it is possible to create whole jobs which are based on technology. Increasingly, the goal of systems is not to automate, but to enable human collaboration, judgment, and the creation of new value.

N-Gen employees will demand fully networked computing environments, which to them are more important than a desk. They will consider poor digital tools as cruel and unusual punishment. In fact, increasingly it will not be possible to create whole jobs without the digital media. There is no joy in unproductive activities—playing telephone tag, waiting for things to happen, looking for information, duplicating work. People receive job fulfillment from productive work—which more and more is enabled by the new technology. Further, the new enterprise and work systems cannot succeed without high employee motivation and identification. In the new world of work, high-performance work systems and quality of work life will tend to go hand in hand.

However, there is nothing inherent in the technology which will ensure quality of work life. Digital connectivity is necessary but insufficient for fulfilling work. It will be incumbent on management to create such humane, enjoyable, and therefore productive workplaces. People design work systems and organizations, not technology.

3. Beware generational displacement.

When the last of the baby boom hit the workforce, all the good jobs had been taken by the older boomers. These Generation Xers, as they are called, had the disadvantage of being the last ones to the table and possessed no particular advantages in terms of their thinking, communications, knowledge, or work skills. Now the first of a wave of 88 million N-Geners are entering the workforce. This is occurring at a time when the corporation needs to reinvent itself through the new technology; when intellectual assets are the most important form of capital; when fresh thinking and innovativeness are the key drivers of success for firms; and when those fluent with the new media and comfortable with nonhierarchical ways of working are critical to success. The writing is on the wall for the technophobic, old-style-thinking boomer. Unless these boomers throw out years of conditioning and old models of work, they will be washed away by a wave of media-savvy, confident, peer-oriented, innovative N-Geners.

Call it generational displacement in the workforce. For traditionalist, die-hard boomers, this is going to bring a whole new meaning to the term "early retirement."

Just like the boomers in Michael Dell's company who are perceived as losers if they aren't media-savvy and new-enterprise-comfortable, boomers in the new economy will be left behind as the N-Gen tsunami rolls into the workforce. The message: boomers, get going and learn from the children.

N-Gen and the Family

PORN

WELCOME to CYBERSPACE

© Don Wright*

Much of what happens in physical reality also occurs in cyberspace. This includes the good—wealth creation, learning, fun, community, friendship—but also the bad—pornography, harassment, criminal activity. Just as parents should do their best to ensure that children enjoy and benefit from their experiences in the physical world, they must take an equally active role to help ensure the cyberworld is safe and positive. This can be tough to do when parents are being stretched increasingly thin.

Goodbye to the Cleavers

Boomer parents simply can't spend the same amount of time with their kids today as their parents spent with them. It's a much harsher economic climate now, and, except for the most affluent families, both parents must work to make ends meet. As a result, women face greater demands on their time today than during the *Leave It To Beaver* era. Most women effectively work two jobs, one in the house and one in the labor force. It would be nice to think that working women exchanged aprons for briefcases, but that's not really what's happened—the apron is still waiting for mom when she gets home at the end of the day, and, increasingly, for dad too.

Those who decry a lack of family values as leading to social problems confuse cause and effect. Economic reality ensures that the traditional arrangement—one parent working and one staying home—is not a viable economic option for the vast majority of families. Sixty-two percent of married mothers with preschoolers are now in the labor force, compared with twenty-three percent in 1965.[1] The solution does not lie in mothers staying at home. Not only is this not economically feasible, it is not fair to women to demand of them what is not demanded of men. Nonetheless, more and more children are at risk as their parents struggle for economic viability and success.

Many more women are also finding themselves heading up a household without a partner. In 1950, one-parent families made up 11 percent of all homes in which children under 18 were present.[2] Today this number has almost tripled. There are two reasons for this. First, many marriages are ending in divorce: the number of currently divorced persons has more than quadrupled since 1970 (from 4 million in 1970 to 17 million in 1994). Second, a lot of fathers are simply choosing not to live with their families—never marrying or even cohabitating. As pointed out by economist Lester Thurow, "Men end up having strong economic incentives to bail out of family relations and responsibilities because they raise their own standards of living when they do so." Economic realities say men should father families without being fathers; divorce without having to pay alimony or child support; in other words, go it on their own to have a better standard of living. The fallout from these economic pressures is borne by everyone; for example, the poorest 20 percent of children are more than twice as likely to repeat a grade and three times more likely to be in remedial learning classes than other children.[3]

The upshot of this is that millions of N-Geners are coming home after school to an empty house. In general, parents spend 40 percent less time with their children than they did 40 years ago.[4]

Despite these constraints, I would argue that there has never been a generation of parents more loving and concerned about doing the right thing for their kids than the boomers. It's not so many years ago that kids were told not to speak unless spoken to; children were to be seen and not heard. This may sound cliché, but it is sadly the truth. For those who could afford it, children were dispatched to boarding schools so as to be out from under the feet of the parents. For the less well-off, children were often viewed as chattel to work endless hours for the family's benefit. The baby boomers were really the first generation of kids to be treated civilly and be seen as having rightful claim to a fair share of the family resources. Today, most boomers devote as many resources as they can afford, and as much time as they can find, to helping their kids grow and develop. Many parents work hard to keep lines of communication open with their children, buy children's books, get computers in the home, pay considerable attention to their children's schooling, and have abandoned corporal punishment. By all accounts, kids acknowledge and respond positively to this attention. Kids look to their parent(s) as the single most important source for guidance, and more than anything they value spending time with their families.[5]

These trends should be of interest to all adults, offspring or no. "Whether or not you have children yourself, you are a parent to the next generation," notes author Charlotte Davis Kasl. "If we can only stop thinking of children as individual property and think of them as the next generation, then we can realize that we all have a role to play."[6]

How can the new media help these kids develop? As an alternative to sitting in front of a television or hanging out at the mall, the new media provide a communications platform to engage in interactive, constructive, social, and learning activities. If we as adults can do this right, the media revolution may enable us to create a new kind of open family. The new media cannot erase all social and societal ills, but they can certainly alleviate some of the disconnectedness of these children and families.

The digital revolution also introduces many new opportunities for parents and children to learn, collaborate, and discover together. It presents an historic innovation to share and in doing so bring families closer together. It also provides a medium for parents to communicate with each other, evidenced by the explosion of parents' chat lines and forums. One of these, Parent Soup, brings together 200,000 parents in a virtual community to exchange experiences and insights and give each other support.

The New Perils of Parenting

Low-income and single parents have special challenges to face to ensure that their children develop good self-esteem, become motivated to learn, and become responsible, productive, and fulfilled adults. It is also more difficult to provide access to the new media without which such children will be seriously disadvantaged. But severe financial hardship need not stand in the way. We met many lower-income parents who understand the importance of access and, because of programs in their community, were lucky enough to find access to the Net even though they could not afford a computer. These parents simply found a way.

Some go with their children to the local library. Others scrimp and save to get a family computer. (See the story of Jimmy Efrain Morales in Chap. 12, "The Digital Divide.") Some work in local organizations to initiate community computing centers like Plugged-In, or launch initiatives in the schools such as the River Oaks School in the lower-middle-class part of Oakville, Ontario. Parents can encourage children to hang out with friends who use the technology or in churches or other nonprofit organizations that have become wired.

At the other extreme are the affluent families. The top 5 percent have seen their incomes grow on average 40 percent since 1985.[7] These children are highly programmed, go to the best schools, play organized sports, and are enriched with dance, music, drama, and art lessons. They come from two-parent families, typically with one parent staying home. Nearly all have access to the Net. By virtue of their social class, these children are virtually guaranteed to develop full digital fluency, to go to college, and to develop productive careers and lives.

All parents, regardless of economic situation, have a responsibility to ensure not only that their children have access, but that their children's experience in cyberspace is a positive one.

We fear for our children. We have great anxiety, and as my colleague Joe Arbucle says, "Anxiety gets in the way of love and of doing the right thing." How can we help and protect children in cyberspace without denying them access to valuable services and trampling on their needs for experimentation, privacy, and autonomy?

Exposure to Inappropriate Material

To begin with, how widespread and serious is the problem? To listen to some of the Web's critics, you would think that distributing porn was the Web's raison d'être. It's not. As it turns out, pornographic images represent less than one half of one percent of images on the Net—far less than on the magazine rack at most newsstands or grocery stores.

Nevertheless, this still means that there are thousands of pornographic images, and no doubt some of them are revolting to many people. And unlike the corner store where they would quickly be shooed away by the proprietor, youngsters could persevere on the home computer for hours until they finally unearthed adult material. Accordingly, pornography is a real issue that needs to be addressed.

Media critic (and parent) Jon Katz suggests that we need to have a calm discussion about talking dirty. "Americans aren't ready to ask the tough questions about this issue: Just how dangerous are dirty pictures? Are our children really damaged by them? How much exposure is a threat? Why are we willing to tolerate so much violence in our

> Many parents have turned away from the Internet because of the bad press it was given at the start of its commercial use in 1995/96 regarding some of the objectionable sites. What a lot of people don't realize is that all that bad stuff is outweighed a thousand times over by the good stuff.
>
> AUSTIN LOCKE, 15
> Ontario

> In terms of government banning, it's not just pornography that would be banned—it's artwork and music. Like Alanis Morrissette has swear words in her music and you might not be able to listen to her CD on the Net just because it had a swear word in one of her songs. Besides, I don't know kids that purposefully go into a pornographic area of the Net. We don't actually want to go into those places.

NIKI TAPSCOTT, 14
during the Kids Panel at the 1996 BOMA Conference

culture but so little sexuality? How can we teach our children to cope with the availability of so much sexual imagery, rather than simply forcing them to pass it around behind our backs?"[8] It is an understatement to say that Katz's thoughtful book, *Virtuous Reality*, is controversial. Katz reports that he is being portrayed as the "Larry Flint of the new media, as the leader of a nation of degenerate Web-porn peddlers."

Some feel that government censorship is the best approach, and many governments favor this notion, including those of China, Singapore, Germany, and the United States. The American version of government censorship was the Communications Decency Act (CDA), passed by the U.S. Congress in 1996 and immediately struck down in the courts for violating the First Amendment. Three federal judges in Philadelphia declared the law unconstitutional soon after its passage and prohibited the Justice Department from enforcing it. The government appealed, but the decision was upheld this summer by the Supreme Court.

Although the Government insisted that its compelling interest in the CDA was to shield minors from access to indecent materials on the Internet, the preliminary court case offered a chilling preview of what could happen to the free exchange of ideas and information in cyberspace if the law is enforced. The CDA decreed that a government body would decide which words and images on the Internet were "indecent" and "patently offensive" in a "contemporary community." If, in its estimation, these unpalatable words and images had no literary, artistic, or educational merit, and could be easily accessed by a person under 18 years of age, then criminal charges would have been filed. As no individual, nonprofit organization, or even large public corporation would risk prosecution for second-guessing the government—miscalculating what it would deem indecent and which community's standards would be used for

> I have never "stumbled" into a site I didn't want to see. Not like on TV where I have occasionally flicked the channel only to "stumble" into some gruesome murder scene.

REANNA ALDER, 15
British Columbia

measurement—communication on the Internet would be limited and guarded. Some providers might have opted for credit card or adult verification, tagging, or blocking devices for protection, but others, such as nonprofit organizations which could not afford such controls, would have to find other outlets for their information. The most important tool for democratizing information since the printing press would have been suffocated at its very source.

Valuable information for youth on relevant topics such as sexually transmitted diseases, rape, incest, abortion, sexual harassment—to name a few—could have been banned based on the way the material is presented. Support groups for those who have suffered any indignity, such as those listed, might also be eliminated. Everything from contemporary films, plays, books, and online newspapers to paintings, sculpture, and photographs—especially the avant-garde—might be banished if the government finds them in part, or in whole, not up to some unknown community's moral standard. The government insisted at the Philadelphia trial that it should be trusted to limit the CDA's application to pornographic materials: serious literary or artistic endeavors would not be prosecuted, but as Judge Sloviter pointed out, "that would take a broad trust indeed from a generation of judges not far removed from the attacks on James Joyce's *Ulysses* as obscene."

> Different parents have different boundaries. There's no real way for governments to control it [pornography].
>
> **JORDAN GARLAND, 13**
> during the Kids Panel
> at the 1996 BOMA Conference

Cybersmart Families

Responsible parents set parameters for their children's activity. As the child gets older the parameters widen, starting with a crib, then a supervised room, the floor of a house, the backyard, the neighborhood, and outside the neighborhood. The child is permitted to watch certain television programs when she is 10 and a wider range at 16. We instruct our kids not to talk to strangers. As children grow, parents face an ongoing balancing act between not knowing what their kids are doing and suffocating them with supervision. We want to respect their privacy but we need to know if they are getting into bad relationships, dangerous situations, or behaviors which could hurt them. We want them to be street-smart but we don't want to frighten them needlessly.

Into this already difficult balancing act enters the Net. Now a child doesn't even need to step out of the house to see the world with all its wonder and pathology. The old boundaries, while still valid, are no longer adequate. The Net adds a whole new dimension, demanding an additional set of decisions and answers from parents.

Smart parents would not—even if they could—accompany their children every time they ventured outside the home, nor would they monitor every telephone call, scan every pamphlet or book, or scrutinize every television or computer screen inside the home. Similarly, cybersmart parents teach their children how best to protect themselves in an imperfect world where strangers may lurk in school yards and disturbing images may appear on the family computer. The government lends a hand through the educational system, community services, and law enforcement agencies, but ultimately the onus for children's safety and quality of life falls on the parents. This has to be the

> Chances are, smaller children will not go to these kinds of sites on purpose. With young children it would be ideal for parents to "surf" with them, but this is very hard to do because of the busyness of parents and children alike. My parents trust me and our family does not use any blocking software, and I do not go to any "adult" sites.
>
> AUSTIN LOCKE, 15

practice in a society where diversity reigns and morals differ from one region to the next. What parents in one community feel is appropriate for their children may not be acceptable to parents in another.

Is Blocking Software the Solution?

Blocking programs such as CyberPatrol, SurfWatch, Net Nanny, and The Internet Filter give some parents a sense of security. These programs will prevent the computer's user from accessing adult Web sites, newsgroups, and similar sources of material. Initially the program makers considered the list of blocked sites as proprietary information which could not be changed by the user. The buyer had to accept on faith that the program's publishers shared the same values and opinions. It was pretty easy for kids, through trial and error, to determine which sites were blocked, and some program manufacturers were deservedly subject to public ridicule when it was disclosed that their list of offensive sites included mainstream public advocacy organizations such as women's support groups.

For families with preteen children, though, it's easy to see why blocking software would be appealing and appropriate. Ten-year-old youngsters surfing the Net may get a little too adventurous for their own good, and if their Net surfing can be digitally chaperoned and kept clean, great.

Increasingly, consumers are choosing newer programs that identify potentially blockable sites but give the parent the option to agree or disagree. This allows the parent to fine-tune the program to more closely reflect the family's values and make allowances for the age of the children. For example, a parent may think a discussion group about homosexuality is inappropriate for a seven year-old but a legitimate subject of interest for a teenager.

A new genre of blocking software has recently been introduced that effectively frightens children into being guardians of their own morals. The software doesn't block access, but keeps a detailed and unchangeable list of the where the user has gone and what material has been downloaded. Once the kids have finished playing with the computer for the evening, Mom or Dad can review the sites visited. Knowing that their behavior can be subject to later scrutiny has a chilling effect on the children, with the goal that they discipline themselves. No doubt it usually works. I personally believe it also gives kids an early introduction to an Orwellian abuse of technology—no different than reading the kids' mail or listening in on their phone calls.

In 1996, I surfed the Net live for a hour on Canadian national television. The program's host, Pamela Wallin, asked me to show an example of something disgusting on the Net, which I dutifully did. We then got into a discussion about how society should handle the issue of blocking software. I explained how these programs work. After the show Ms. Wallin received a number of e-mails from viewers. One of them, age 14, wrote:

Pamela Wallin,

I enjoyed your show last night about the Internet. . . . But in your section about pornography on the Net, let's be rational. There is nothing on the Net that isn't available in the real, physical world. As an eighth grader in Toronto, I know friends who have Internet access, and do go to the Playboy page, or Lisa's House of Steam or whatever, but we could get the same stuff at the local convenience store on Yonge Street. Sure, it would take longer, more of a hassle, but we have access to it.

Also, your guest talked about the various protection programs available to parents (Net Nanny, SurfWatch). As a novice programmer, it is fairly easy to bypass these programs. For example, add a virus to the directory where it is located, run the Virus Scan, the scanner deletes the entire directory, but because it has a virus, the software doesn't disallow it to be deleted. Without the virus, it will now allow a user to delete it without a password. In addition to this, the amount of "bad" material on the Net is about 2 percent of the total material on the Internet. Pick up a NET-GUIDE magazine, and read all the five hundred sites that they recommend EVERY MONTH.

In ending, I liked the show, and myself having "techn-odummies" for parents, it let them see the benefits of the Internet.

Austin S. Locke

The possibility of children accessing material inappropriate to their age is certainly one of the most controversial aspects of the Internet, and understandably so. We don't want young minds corrupted. But the strategy each family adopts for dealing with this issue should be of its own making, not some solution imposed from on high. Some families may think that blocking software is a very appealing option, particularly now that some of the programs can be fine-tuned to closely reflect the parents' values. Blocking is a familiar and accepted concept in our society, from age restrictions at adult movie houses to putting passwords on the pornographic channels of satellite television.

My wife and I have chosen not to install blocking software in our house. Initially we decided that we had a set of family values that didn't really correspond to the values of the blocking software companies. For example, software which describes itself as morally conservative may restrict the online version of your local newspaper because the latter contains personal ads. The software also appeared restrictive—preventing your child from accessing desired information because the blocking programs use algorithms which, for example, block any word ending in uck (*uck). This could be bad news for your child's project on water fowl or large commercial motor vehicles.

As Eric Berlin and Andrew Kantor point out in *The Surfboard,* "When you give someone—or something—the power to pick and choose the good from the bad, you might not always agree with the result." Filtering software not only cuts out materials on sex, violence, and drugs, it may also block political, religious, and environmental issues that depict harsher realities.

As well, there are some things software can't block. For example, someone can send your child an e-mail message with a pornographic picture attached, just like they can send them a physical letter through the mail; make a phone call disguising their voice; or slip an envelope into a mailbox at school. The technical feasibility of installing blocking software in a house with two Net-savvy children is also an issue.

Most important for my family, the issue of inappropriate material raises a wonderful opportunity to be a good parent, to share our values with our children, and to create open relationships. If our kids come across something that is undesirable, we want them to talk to us about it and not feel they have done something bad which needs to be kept secret.

I was recently interviewed by a newspaper journalist who was trying to convince me how useful the new blocking programs were. She told me about a new package which "would prevent your child from taking your credit card and purchasing $2000 worth of games on the Net." I told her that if my child was taking my credit card to steal $2000 from me I'd have a bigger problem—and the solution wouldn't be software!

Your family may be different. As an extreme case, if your child is suicidal or is involved with an extremist militia group, taking dangerous drugs, or participating in criminal activities, it may be quite appropriate to carefully monitor his or her behavior or attempt to restrict access to certain sites which could provide life-threatening information.

Over time, the technology will become more sophisticated, as will the rating systems. I look forward to the day when my family can discuss which rating systems we like, to help every family member decide which material is appropriate for us.

Putting Predators in Perspective

Parents have been alarmed by the sensationalist news coverage before and after the appeal of the Federal Government's Communications Decency Act and many fear that their children will unwittingly come across child predators. The problem has been blown out of proportion. "[T]here is arguably less of a threat to your child online," Mike Godwin writes in *Children, Child Abuse, and Cyberporn: A Primer for Clear Thinkers,* "than there is on the corner across from the school yard. After all, even the most determined child predator can't reach through the screen. . . ."

Children are in real danger of physical harm, but statistically most of the abusers are members of the victims' own families and have no need of the Net to locate victims. "There were some concerns among the urban girls that there were weird people on the Net and around safety issues. If I had a software company and was going to come out with a product, I'd make it one that concentrates on making the girls feel safe, which is very important," says Professor Christine Ward-Gailey, a social anthropologist who has studied girls and computers for the past ten years. "But the message that's not getting out is that kids are more likely to get hurt in their own homes than anywhere else. Most kids have to worry more about their daddies coming home drunk than they do about someone they've met on the Internet."

Every day three children in the United States are murdered or die as a result of injuries inflicted by their parents or caretakers.[9] Of the 3 million reported cases of child abuse annually, 127,100 cases involve child abandonment.[10] From March 1996 to March 1997, the National Center for Missing and Exploited Children recorded 23 cases involving missing children and the Internet. Ten of these twenty-three cases are known to involve the transfer of pornography over the Internet, an adult using the Internet to solicit sexual favors from minors, and sexual contact initiated over the Internet—all of them despicable and intolerable episodes. Of the remaining 13 cases, 2 concerned not children but police officers posing as children. Two other cases involved 15-year-old girls with previous histories of running away; one was under house arrest for criminal charges. Nine of the twenty-three cases involved children over the age of 16 running away from home. Two were known to have run away to be with online acquaintances, while seven of these runaway teens were suspected to have gone to meet someone they met online. Among the unconfirmed reports is the case of a 17-year-old girl who is suspected to have run off to be with an 18-year-old man. Three of these runaways have since returned home on their own.[11]

What these statistics illustrate is that the world is a dangerous place for children where they are 300,000 times more likely to be abused by one of their own relatives than by someone they have met over the Internet. The National Center for Missing and Exploited Children also insists that just because crimes occur online, there is no reason to ban children from using the Internet: "To tell children to stop using these services would be like telling them to forgo attending college because students are sometimes victimized on campus."

Further, whatever dangers exist on the Net do not result only from individual predators. Corporate predators can also do considerable harm. For example, a 1997 study of 300 Web sites conducted by the Center for Media Education over a six-month period found that some tobacco and alcohol companies are targeting consumers between 10 and 20 years old with their online ads. The study's director cited a number of sites "that use lots of color, music, interactive games, and language that appeals to young consumers in order to promote the idea that drinking and smoking are cool." He claimed that "the Internet is a hot new medium whose users tend to be younger, so your target market is there and the fact that it is unregulated gives these companies a loophole."[12]

While the issue of physical danger is exaggerated, there *are* adults who would do children harm and who use the Net as a new medium for contact, added to the drive by automobile encounter, the street meeting, the telephone call, and the mail invitation. But cybersmart kids and families can be protected.

The best protection is knowledgeable children who follow basic safety rules. The *Growing Up Digital* kids were all aware of the issue. "It's fun to have your own page on the Internet. People can look at your site, what things you do, what food you like, what your favorite TV show is and that kind of stuff," says nine-year-old Anna Hinrichs of Houston, Texas. "It also makes me kind of nervous because people, like kidnappers, can look at my Web page and know all about me. All they have to do is find out where I live."

Unlike a car full of boys driving up to a girl walking along the road, on the Net a harasser or threatening person can simply be disconnected. While the old maxim says children are to be seen and not heard, on the Net children can be heard but not seen, and therefore can be protected.

Cyber smarts are like street smarts. Every parent needs to take responsibilities to ensure their kids have both. Some schools are sending a "cyber contract" home so that parents and kids understand their responsibilities.

A good set of rules for cyberspace was developed by the Union City Boys and Girls Club.*

The following "Rules of the Net" should be used by all members when using the Internet at the Club or at home.

I will not give out personal information such as my address, telephone number, the location of my school, or my parents' work address and phone number. I will tell the Boys & Girls Club teacher or my parents if I come across any information that makes me feel uncomfortable.

I will never agree to get together with someone I meet online without first checking with my parents.

I will not respond to any messages that are mean or make me feel uncomfortable in any way. I will tell the Boys & Girls Club teacher or parents if I get a message like that.

I will not copy information created by other people and claim it as my own work. This includes stories, information, pictures, and art.

Harassment, Isolation, Unpleasant Experiences

As for other negative experiences, cyberspace is simply another world where parents need to be available to help their children. The danger here is less severe than in the physical world, where the child can't just turn off a bully or instantly disappear and become someone else. Indeed, the Net simply adds another medium for unpleasantness and harassment. For example, early findings of a study of e-mail use at a large mid-Atlantic university suggest there is, in general, no more harassment by e-mail than by telephone or snail mail.[13]

Children need to develop social skills, the ability to argue, and the courage to stick up for themselves and their values in the school yard and classroom, at the family dinner table, on the street corner, and now on the Net. If parents have close relationships with their children, they can participate in this development. But ultimately, and as time passes, the kids are on their own.

Children Protect Themselves

While it is primarily the responsibility of parents to protect their children, most N-Geners we've met are quite cognizant of the dangers and issues. When Serena received the hateful flame described in Chap. 8, she took the offensive note and posted it on her Web site.

In part because of the exaggerated dangers of cyberspace portrayed by the

---

* Reprinted with permission.

mass media, children have become hyperaware of potential problems. We were unable to find cases where children resisted the adoption of safe surfing guidelines. N-Geners also develop a keen sensitivity to issues of lying, deception, and what is real and trustworthy on the Net. "The best way, I would say, to find out if they're telling the truth is to get to know them. Talk to them, find out more about them. If they have a home page, go to it, learn about them that way too. Trust needs to be earned, not given out. So make sure they earn it from you," says 15-year-old Kelly Richards. "And trust your gut. If you think someone isn't trustworthy, don't trust them. There's a good chance you're right."

"A lot of how I trust people is through intuition," says Andy Putschoegl, 17. "I am wary of those people that I have known for a short time or who e-mail me out of the blue. I have 'friends' on the Internet that I've never met, but have known for two years, I trust them."

Sarah Evans, 15, says: "I don't think that you should trust anyone (except if a friend you already know face-to-face has given his/her e-mail address to you). Never trust people that you meet on mailing lists or any other type of e-mail. Never give out your home address or phone number to anyone. For the first little while that I was on a mailing list, I tried not to give out my age or anything like that. I don't have any desire to ever meet the people I talk to online. There is no way of knowing whether the information you're getting is factual, and that is the danger of meeting up with people you've met over the Internet."

While children are showing remarkable savvy on this issue, ultimately it is the responsibility of parents to ensure our children's safety.

Safeguarding Children's Privacy

Privacy has been an important issue since the first person peeked around the corner of a cave to see what his fellow cave-dwellers had caught for dinner. Since then, various philosophers, writers, politicians, unionists, business people, and concerned citizens have written about and debated the many dimensions of the issue.

However, most people didn't anticipate the digital revolution and its impact on privacy. For example, George Orwell in 1984 got it all wrong when he talked about big brother and surveillance. As it turns out the problem is really "little brother" and "dataveillance." Increasingly, commerce, work, learning, entertainment, social discourse, and even travel will involve interaction with this infrastructure. And every transaction, every love letter, every request for information . . . much of life will use this medium, with obvious implications for privacy.

A trail of digital crumbs is left as we move through life.

Consider your 13-year-old daughter, Vanessa, who is working away on her computer. It wouldn't take a year of such activity for a database profiler to get her "number," it would take a couple of hours—how she works, who she communicates with, what she likes to buy, where she likes to play in cyberspace, among other things—to obtain a real-time animation of her body. There is the potential of an unprecedented and very dangerous destruction of everything that we've come to know as the right to privacy.

Vanessa has what Ann Cavoukian (my coauthor of the book *Who Knows*[14]) calls a "mirror image" of her being constructed in cyberspace. This is an elaborate profile based on her interactions and transactions on the Net and with other related systems from credit cards to school grades. The virtual Vanessa can be very extensive and descriptive—her opinions on things, her behaviors over an extended time, her knowledge, her body. The virtual Vanessa may know more about the real Vanessa than you do or than even Vanessa herself does in many areas. Much of this information is accurate because it comes from Vanessa's actual behavior. But much is inaccurate. Credit bureau information today, for example, has notorious errors in it. The mirror image of Vanessa may have distortions which can be dangerous to the real Vanessa when she becomes a young adult and applies for a car loan, for example. And to whom does she go to find out what the virtual Vanessa looks like and how she might change, control, or even eliminate parts of her mirror image?

Further, the shift to knowledge-based customized products has chilling implications for Vanessa's privacy. It used to be that her shirt, teen magazines, and the family television didn't know much about her. All that is changing. She will not just be a wearer of shirts, she becomes a shirt user as shirts become smart communicating objects. She is not just a reader of her magazine, she becomes a user of a personal version zine. She doesn't just look at her watch, she interacts with it as it interacts with her school diary. She's not simply a viewer of TV, she's becoming a user—and the TV (which is really becoming a computer) learns about her. She doesn't simply push a cart in a supermarket, she may use one of the growing Net-based food shopping programs, and when she orders something from the pharmacy another piece of data is added to her profile. Increasingly we interact with our world rather than viewing or hearing it.

This is not science fiction. Today, when your child is using one of many Net services, this trail of crumbs is collected (knowingly or unknowingly) into something called a "cookie" on her hard drive. The next time she visits that service, she brings the cookie. In fairness to many Internet service companies, she will often be given a choice regarding whether she wants to have her crumbs collected into a cookie. But how informed is her choice?

This choice is just the tip of the iceberg. She will soon be confronted with other choices such as: "The movie you have requested is $3.50. However, if you fill out the following form providing us with information about yourself which we can use for marketing and other purposes, the cost will be $1.50. Which do you prefer?" There have already been cases of marketers soliciting information about adults by asking their children: "Fill in the form about your mom, dad, house, and car to win a prize."

There will be considerable debate on this topic among businesses, lawmakers, and advocacy groups. At the time of writing, various groups had developed voluntary guidelines on responsible marketing to children over the Internet and had submitted them to the Federal Trade Commission. One difference between the proposed guidelines is the positions they take on how children might be asked to furnish personal information about themselves or their families. Industry guidelines ask advertisers to make "reasonable efforts" to persuade children to get parental permission before supplying such information; the guidelines from the advocacy groups take a harder line, and specify that no personal information should be solicited from children unless parental permission has been verified—even if verification is difficult to obtain.[15]

The best protection of children's privacy is an informed family, where every member is his or her own privacy watchdog.

Creating an Open Family

In the world of technology, the direction is "open systems": software that works on computers regardless of brand or size and computers that not only interconnect but can really talk to each other. Previously, islands of computing dotted a company's organizational chart, but such "proprietary" systems couldn't communicate with each other, let alone with systems outside the firm. This was changed by the Internet, which is based on standard protocols accepted by everyone.

In previous books I have introduced the idea of the "open enterprise," where the walls between traditional departments break down and the firm reaches out through networks to its customers, suppliers, and others for new kinds of relationships and wealth creation. This is very different from the old hierarchy with its bureaucratic communications channels, turf battles, and Dilbertian behavior. Open enterprises can be extended into politics. We need open governments which break down walls between departments and between government and citizens.

To break down the walls between generations, perhaps it's time to work toward "open families." Perhaps the new media provide a platform for openness and also an issue around which to forge open relationships based on listening, frank exchange, and trust. Growing kids need to differentiate themselves from their parents; they become their own person, they have secrets. It is the challenge of parents to understand this and encourage open lines of communication by earning the trust of their children. From personal experience with my family, this is not easy—we're a long way from being there. In some ways this doesn't matter, as forging new relationships is a journey, not a destination.

Openness should not be confused with permissiveness. Parents do not abdicate their role of authority prematurely, but rather manage, time, and phase such "abdication" effectively.

In the open family, members share the experience of the digital media. In the past, good parents may have watched *The Simpsons,* a news report, or an adult-theme movie together with their children and taken the opportunity for dialogue, even if it's quite informal. Is this TV show trying to tell us something? What about the context? Do we/you agree with what is being said about the mid-east conflict? What do you think about Homer Simpson's attitude toward Marge?

Similarly, it now makes sense to share experiences with the digital media together. If you are a neophyte, embrace the generation lap and tag along the next time your child is about to blow by you on the technology track. Ask your children to show you their favorite Web sites. Show them amazing sites you have found. Exchange browser bookmarks. Create a climate where your child will want to discuss that racist statement someone made in a chat group or tell you that they have received something which has made them uncomfortable. I remember that one of the first times my daughter was in a chat group, a boy her age started chatting with her about football. She called my wife, Ana, over to get her advice on what might be an appropriate thing to say because after all she didn't "know anything about football."

Harry Loyle lives in Linwood, New Jersey. His son Benjamin, 13, spends a lot of time surfing the Net. He's a pretty typical kid. He plays a lot of computer games, surfs the Net, and uses a computer to do his homework. He rarely goes to the school or public library—most of the resources he needs are on the Net. His dad says it's only been on a couple of occasions that he's walked into the room and Ben has quickly cleared the screen. "We've taken the approach to not censor our children's activity but rather have discussions about responsible behavior." The situation is not perfect, but placing trust in their child creates the conditions for an open and mutually trusting relationship.

The starting point for an open family is for the parent(s) to understand the potential of the new media and to accept kids' culture. Listen to Beckie Househ of Illinois, who spends a lot of time with her eight-year-old son Christopher:

> I think the Internet, if supervised and used moderately and in a constructive way, is very beneficial to children. Children who have access to the Internet all have the same resources in their reach. Because the Internet is becoming increasingly more available to people everywhere, children who use it learn that we all have a connection to one another. They are more open-minded and accepting overall. I think it's very valuable for children to feel they are a part of the world and the Internet helps them to feel like they belong.

Open families are based on curiosity, on the wonder of childhood being shared with parents. For a parent this can be hard. There aren't enough hours in the day to be curious about kids' culture, this new technology, or what your children are doing with it. It may seem hard enough to get your business wired, let alone your family. As for a sense of wonder—the Net is so frustratingly slow, and for every gem found you have to wade through a pile of garbage.

> Hey Dad.
> Check this out:
> http://www2.southwind.net~
> wknapp/miracle/sono.html
> Niki :-)

One of many e-mails from
NIKI TAPSCOTT, 14
to her father in 1997

Notwithstanding, I'm convinced that curiosity is one of the best predictors of successful families, successful people, successful businesses, and even successful national cultures. Your children are full of curiosity. Let them infect you with it. Try to set aside your cynicism, demands for immediate payback, and unease with something new, and see the new media through the eyes of the child.

Open families adopt the interactive model—bringing new meaning to the verb "to listen." In the old command and control corporation, communication was one way—top-down. The old model of computing was hierarchical and centralized, as were the broadcast media—one way. Just as the new media are interactive, communication in the open family can go both ways as well. The traditional authoritarian model is changing due to the generation lap in that, for the first time, children know more than their parents about something really important—they are authorities. This does not mean that parental authority is ending, but it does tend to open us up to considering what parenting techniques will be best in these new circumstances. While many times parents must lay down the rules, especially at earlier ages, it may make sense to spend more time listening, explaining, building common views, and negotiating.

> My teacher only has one computer and he teaches all of us at one time. My mom watches me but she lets me look for things by myself. She asks me to find things and she helps me if I need it.

CHRISTOPHER HOUSEH, 8
when asked "How is
using the Internet with
your Mom different
from using it at school
or alone?"

Listening is the precondition for this. If we listen to our children, we can learn from them. This is not the listening of the "uh huh, uh huh, riiight" variety. Rather, it is listening as if you were talking to a mentor—someone for whom you hold respect and from whom you can learn. By working hard to draw out and understand a child's point of view, we will change our own. Such opportunities for listening and open communication are less likely to occur during a "man-to-man" chat or a walk in the park with your daughter than serendipitously—selecting a radio station in the car, discussing a film, or showing an interesting Web site.

The open family discusses the issue of inappropriate material and develops a mutually acceptable approach to dealing with it. Children cannot be encased in some protective shield. Regardless of what Congress, the courts, blocking software companies, online service providers, or you do, your child will be exposed to inappropriate material. Denying children access to the Net, refusing them television, curtailing their reading material, or anything else you do will not change this fact. As psychologist David Elkind writes: "Because we cannot control all that our children see, hear, and play, it is tempting to throw up our hands and do nothing. Although we cannot do everything, we can do something, and this is talk with our children and teenagers about unexpected encounters with inappropriate violence, sexuality, and profanity."[16] The fact of pornography on the Net provides an opportunity to discuss and share values more than an opportunity to exercise parental authority.

Members of an open family are media critics. They all feel it is important to "look under the hood," to authenticate information and understand underlying assumptions. "I've tried to show my daughter basic bullshit-detecting techniques," says Susan Douglas of Ann Arbor, Michigan. For example, she and her daughter discuss the content of television and commercials. ". . . the simple act of intervening—of talking to your child about what's on and why it's on there—is one of the most important factors in helping children understand and distance themselves from some of the box's more repugnant imagery."[17]

The open family is internetworked. Parents communicate with their children at college using e-mail. Within a few years, home local area networks will be requirements for many moderate-income and affluent families. Family members will share common computing resources—sending messages to the television from the home office or leaving messages for a student at school on her e-mail account. My family uses e-mail extensively, not just because of our hectic schedules but because we are always forwarding material to each other that we have found interesting. Sometimes I find myself in a Net-based discussion group which is attended by someone in my family. I find the Net brings us together and facilitates dialogue and family cohesion. None of this replaces family dinners, handwritten thank-you notes after a birthday, or barbecues by the lake. It's just another dimension of family life, just like Sunday evening phone calls to family members.

The new media hold the promise of strengthening the family by moving many family activities dispersed by industrial society back into the home. These include working, learning, shopping, entertainment, health care, caring for the elderly, and even participation in democracy.

It is a curious paradox that children of Net-savvy parents aren't necessarily the first ones to use the Net. This is especially true if their parents are very active users or very strong believers in the new media. Kids resent the time their parents spend on the computer if they don't understand it. Like all children, they also resist embracing something their parents love out of a desire for independence and differentiation. There seems to be a reaction against what some N-Geners perceive as their parents' computer habits. If parents are not enthusiastic about computer use, the kids are. If parents are enthusiastic, the kids may not be. I have found this with both of my children. Hyping computers and encouraging them to get involved was met with some resistance, especially given that they initially resented the time I spent online.

Steve Snow is the director of Charlotte's Web, a fabulous site which won the 1996 NII award for best community site. His son was so incensed about the amount of time he spent working online that he put a note on the door to the family computer room that read: "No Dads Allowed In This Room." He hated computers, hated the Net, and vowed never to have anything to do with it because he was angry about his dad's absence.

One day he sat down at the computer by himself and, using dad's bookmarks, discovered the *Gargoyles* home page. (*Gargoyles* is a TV animation show.) He kept on surfing, requesting information about other TV shows he knew. Suddenly captivated, he went on to learn how to create Web sites on the Net. He now has two very large sites and does IRC with friends several nights a week for one hour. He is so active that Dad has had to limit his time online!

Steve thinks his son's initial resistance was evidence of the "children of wired parents syndrome" which I have described. To break the syndrome, Steve believes that children need to, in their own time, "find personal value in what is online, *then* they will find a use for the medium. Not before."

In the open family, members respect each other's cultural choices. Just as the Beatles are not labeled as "old fogy music," alternative rock is not called "noise." Members of the open family understand that there are alternative views on most topics.

In the open family, children have responsibilities and also rights, as John Katz explains in *Virtuous Reality*, which can be agreed upon in a new form of social contract. For example, children have responsibilities to work hard in school, to carry their weight at home, to be socially responsible, and not to harm other people. These "responsible children" have the right to be respected; to have access to their culture and new technology; to form like-minded communities through the Net; to have new media tools in their schools; to have open access to information of their choice; and to freedom of speech. Such a contract, by definition, must be agreed to rather than imposed.[18]

Parents need to take the lead in defining rights and responsibilities. While children can tell when their rights are violated and they can sense that they have responsibilities, they often have difficulty articulating what exactly those rights and responsibilities are.

In the open family, both parents and children accept responsibility for safety on the Net and off. The open family keeps this issue in perspective, understanding that auto accidents, drugs, smoking, alcohol abuse (especially as it pertains to automobiles), and gangs (in some neighborhoods) are the truly serious threats to physical safety, not unknown abductors or Net prowlers.

The open family can learn as a family. Just as businesses need to create learning organizations[19]—a firm's only sustainable advantage is its ability to learn as an organization—so we can create families which can learn together. The new media, a new youth culture, and the experience of a new generation provide a unique opportunity for parents and children to grow together. There are so many new issues to discuss. The pace of change is so much faster than for previous generations of families. Just as businesses must be constantly innovating, so must families. Family learning as a concept is very different from the traditional view that learning is something done to children by parents.

This learning family evolves, adjusting itself to changing conditions. The family designs itself, consciously. For example, parents and children have awareness about and shape the family. Despite its unhealthy impact on people, television at least brought families together around an electronic hearth. But in my family today, it's not unusual for the four of us to be clicking away on our keyboards in separate rooms. As a result, we have designed activities into family life—one of them being the family supper (perhaps a radical concept today). Every day we sit down to dinner together and have a conversation. No one leaves till the conversation is over. We all work to make it a pleasant and interesting experience.

Although open family members have common interests, members understand that goals or desires might be different. Parents must sometimes make decisions which the kids don't agree with or understand. But these should be the exception. Blind obedience is increasingly not viable for a generation which holds unprecedented power to communicate outside the family, to sift through information, and to learn.

Open families live long. We raise our children so that they will leave us. Families based on trust, mutual respect, negotiated agreements, and loving two-way communication can grow more effortlessly into open, loving relationships between adults. Such relationships can also be perpetuated in further generations.

What will your children remember about you? How will they remember your treatment of them, their culture, their media? Will they remember you as someone with curiosity who encouraged them in everything important and who shared your power with them and in doing so increased their personal power, self-esteem, self-reliance, and ability to make appropriate life choices? Faced with pervasive hostility and ignorance by a host of technophobes, antiyouth academics, old-media propagandists, government ideologues, corporate manipulators, and paralyzed educators, will your children have found a place of refuge, two-way communication, and trust in your open family? Are you prepared to step up to this challenge and opportunity?

The Digital Divide

Is it my turn yet?

© Owen Baggott*

Have-nots, Know-nots, and Do-nots

This is a time of promise and of peril. What kind of world do we want our children to inherit?

The most widely feared prediction surrounding the digital revolution is that it will splinter society into a race of information haves and have-nots, knowers and know-nots, doers and do-nots—a digital divide. This revolution holds the promise of improving the lives of citizens but also the threat of further dividing us. As philanthropist Mario Marino says: "The technology of interactive communications will change the status quo with or without your involvement. The question is how and to what extent we will use it—to help people empower themselves and give those at every social and economic level a voice and an option, or to trigger a division among us that may never be healed."

The issue is not just access to the new media, but rather whether differences in availability of services, technology fluency, motivation, and opportunities to learn may lead to a two-tiered world of knowers and know-nots, doers and do-nots.

It is the responsibility of adults to tackle this problem for the new generation. However, there is a dialogue of the deaf on this issue with two extreme perspectives. In one corner are the *stateists,* who argue that the Net, like the highways, is an essential service and a key infrastructure for any economy. As such it is best planned, controlled, and (in some countries) even owned by government.

In *The Digital Economy,* I argued against this view, explaining that, "because public coffers are empty and leading-edge innovation is desirable, the private sector needs to take the front-line role in financing, building, and operating the information highway." The highway analogy is a limited one. It is not feasible to plan the digital infrastructure like a highway for many reasons, including the fact that no one knows for sure what technologies are best. Through an open, competitive market these issues will get sorted out. An open market also enables and promotes the kind of innovation that the five-year master plan cannot. The development of the digital media will be molecular. It will grow in chaotic and unpredictable ways. If its direction (technological, services, information) is left alone, it will behave like an ecosystem or organism, constantly changing, evolving, and mutating as the myriad forces within it and upon it change. An open competitive market is essential for the new media to evolve rapidly and to fulfill their potential. Countries which are bound by old monopolistic structures are falling behind in technological innovation, penetration, and use.

The stateist view has weak support in North America. However, there are numerous suggestions for increased government control to end the "anarchy" of the Internet. The most popular theme is censorship and control of the Net through laws and other techniques. Such efforts are undesirable, unnecessary, and unfeasible—as explained in the previous chapter on parenting.

In the other corner are the market determinists. The need for an open market has caused many to conclude that market forces should be the sole determinant of technology growth and use. In fact, it has become fashionable to ridicule government, corporate, or community efforts for universality. The Net, it is said, is an organic ecosystem (true), unlike a highway (true), and therefore cannot be planned (true) and should not be controlled by any force (true). From this, the market determinists conclude that there is no role for social policy and that efforts to achieve universal access are basically silly and even dangerous.

Typical of this view is an article in the Libertarian publication *Reason Magazine.* ". . . the call for universal service is a red herring. It masks a fundamental mistrust of a process that will deeply reshape society and yet is almost entirely beyond government control. A process that is chaotic and self-organizing, utterly without a central plan. In other words, a market." The author ridicules vice president Al Gore's objective of universal access. "Imagine that in 1895, some 13 years before the Model T, Al Gore's great-grandfather had correctly identified the potential importance of the new 'horseless carriage' to future employment and led the government push to ensure that we did not become a nation of 'motorized transportation haves and have-nots.'"[1]

The author continues: "A television, today's prime source of information and entertainment, can be found in upwards of 99 percent of American homes, higher even than the 93 percent of homes with a phone. Without a hint of government subsidy—let alone a domestic producer—TV reaches more homes than telephones, despite six decades of sweeping universal telephone service policy courtesy of the Communications Act of 1934."

"The best thing government can do is get out of the way," said Michael Bloomberg at the aforementioned panel discussion in Davos, Switzerland. He argued that governments are basically an obstacle to progress.

The digital media cannot be compared to the television, as the market determinists would have us believe. TV is basically a passive form of entertainment. The new media require the active, informed, literate participation of a user. The pattern of TV growth will not be replicated, because purchase and use of the new media are skewed toward those who are literate and motivated for active participation. It is precisely those children who are disadvantaged in education, family income, and personal empowerment who will be least able and least motivated to embrace the new media. While access is critical for universality, it is also inadequate. Have-nots lead to do-nots. It's not simply having access, but what you do with it that counts. As Joan Chiaramonte of Roper Starch says: "It's really important what demands people make on the technology. One group will have greater knowledge, motivation, and vision, creating [greater] possibilities." The term have-nots should not be used to mean lacking access only; rather, a growing underclass does not have fluency, motivation, and integration of digital tools with various aspects of their lives. Having, knowing, and doing go hand in hand.

By the time—if ever—the "free market" catches up to the nots, they will no longer be children. Denied the opportunity to assimilate the new media in their youth, they will, instead, have to adapt to it. They will be on the wrong end of the generation lap—lapped by those of their own generation. Moreover, their employment prospects in a knowledge economy, their potential income levels, their prospects for stable families, and their potential for a fulfilling life will all be greatly diminished. This is a downward spiral. Poverty causes digital impoverishment, which in turn contributes to continued povertization.

"Leave everything to the market," or "It'll all come out in the wash." Such statements reflect a growing belief in Social Darwinism. The economic view that competitive markets are required for economic growth and success is extended to an ideology regarding society and governance. In this ideology there is no such thing as the public interest. It is said that governments should get out of the business of social policy and helping disadvantaged people or groups and instead be defenders of individual rights. Darwin's views on the evolution of the species were extended in an earlier period—the late nineteenth century—to a social view about nations. It was argued at the time that within the human species, nations are locked in a struggle for survival in which civilized nations were supplanting barbarous nations. Advanced civilization, obviously, has inherited valuable traits from its ancestors. Underdeveloped cultures will soon die off. Therefore, natural order obligates powerful, civilized nations to appropriate the limited resources of the weak.[2]

A century later the new god is not a superior species but the market. In my debates on haves and have-nots I have heard the statement "the poor will always be with us." I have heard people say the issue is really "information haves and have-laters." I have heard people say, "don't concern yourself with these things. It'll all be fine." Many leading technology and business thinkers, who should know better, have become champions of this cause. The view is extended to the digital economy as a whole. It is argued that governments today are a legacy of the old industrial economy and need to be eliminated. It is not always clear what should replace them.

What is driving this view? Some critics have argued it is greed—the ideological rationalization for unfettered capitalism and a gold rush in cyberspace.[3] Others see it as ironic that those who favor an end to government involvement in the Net are precisely those who benefitted from initial government subsidization.[4] A kinder view is that many well-meaning thinkers are just naive—smart on technology and business issues and lacking experience on social issues.

The wealthy in America are information-rich. The poor are information-poor. Whites are generally haves. Blacks are have-nots—two-thirds less likely to have a PC in the home. The solution to this problem is not the market. The problem has been created, in part, by the market—or more precisely by the lack thereof among the dispossessed. Just as there is no market for food in areas where people are starving—because food cannot be profitably sold—so there is no market for the digital media in the inner city, the reservation, or parts of the rural south.

This situation is not improving. It is being exacerbated with every passing day as the gap grows. As Fig. 12.1 indicates, the rate of penetration for the haves is rapid, while for the have-nots it lingers. Each day that the haves get not only better access but more services, improved technology, and, most important, improved fluency and motivation, the gap grows.

As Brad Fay, who led the seminal work for Roper Starch on *The Two Americas,* says, "The logical implications of this is that we are moving into two dis-

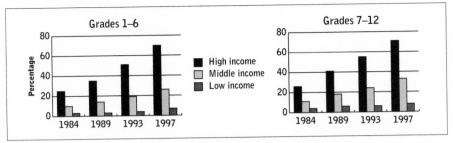

Figure 12.1
Used a computer at home—grades 1–6; grades 7–12.
Data: U.S. Census Bureau.

tinct societies where people have very different life experiences, lifestyles, and attitudes. Part of it is economically driven—what people can and cannot afford." According to their research, 24 percent of people without high school diplomas and 37 percent of low-income people are interested in using the computer to obtain product information. This compares to 64 percent of college graduates and 69 percent of those earning more than $50,000 per year. Hardly any lower-income households have a computer (7 percent), in comparison to those making between $30,000 and $50,000 (32 percent). Of those making over $50,000, usage increases to 53 percent. Households earning more than $75,000 are 10 times more likely to be surfing the Net than those making less than $30,000 per year. Most Americans know what this will lead to: 59 percent say divisions between those who understand the new technology and those who do not will be a serious problem in 25 to 50 years.[5]

Poverty begets information poverty begets poverty. Racial divides beget a racial gap in media access begets racial divides. Opposition to efforts for universality, regardless of the intentions or lofty ideologies of the perpetrators, result in actions which uphold and amplify social differences.

What Are the Facts on Universality?

The first problem with the market determinist view is one of fact. If you look at the data, there is a growing information apartheid already in the United States. Parallel to this, there is a growing polarization in the distribution of wealth. Unless a new social contract is achieved, these two gaps will continue to interact, strengthening trends toward the consolidation of a large, permanent underclass.

The problem is not limited to America, and becomes much clearer when one considers the rest of the world, particularly the developing countries.

"Picture this scenario: somewhere in South Africa a person spends two whole days manually sending out a bulletin to about two dozen subscribers by fax," writes South African journalist Gumisai Mutume. "Often the line breaks down and the process starts again. Eventually all the pages go through and then the phone calls start pouring in. 'The fax is blurred, we did not get page three of the document. Could you please resend the whole thing?' At the end of it all, a phone bill of some $150 U.S. dollars is the tab for the effort. This is the stark reality of communications between African countries."

The information gap between have and have-not countries is growing. According to Jupiter Communications, of the 23.4 million households connected to the Net in 1996, 66 percent were in North America, 16 percent in Europe, and 14 percent in the Asian Pacific.[6] The gap is not just one of developed countries versus underdeveloped countries. Amazingly, Western Europe (excluding Scandinavia) and Japan—countries which currently have some of the highest GNP per capita—are falling behind badly in terms of access and use. Sales of PCs in Europe slipped below those in Asia for the first time in 1996. "Tiger" economies in Asia are leapfrogging both Japan and Europe in their use of the new media. In Malaysia, the government has launched an "information superhighway corridor" project which will deliver high-capacity networking through core elements of the country. Asian/Pacific Rim markets will grow from 3.6 million online households from year-end 1996 to 10 million by 2000.[7]

The Myth of Universal Access at School

Additionally, market determinists argue that government and corporate programs to get technology into the schools are unnecessary. They argue that universality will be and is being achieved in the schools through market forces. They draw comfort from data that indicates that computers and Net access are flooding into the schools. For example, calculations based on a 1995 survey conducted by Grunwald Associates showed that the parents of 19 million American children believe that their kids have access to the Internet either at home or at school. According to those parents, 6 million children had Internet access at home. Of the 13 million children whose parents believe they are accessing the Internet from either the library or school, 5 million did not have computers at home. Here the phrase "believe they are accessing the Internet" becomes problematic. Access to the Internet from school, like Internet access from home, is both enabled and limited by one factor: family income.

By 1996, 65 percent of United States public schools had access to the Internet, but schools with richer student populations were still 25 percent more likely to be connected than schools with poorer student populations. According to the National Center for Education Statistics, 58 percent of schools where more than one-third of students are eligible for free or reduced-priced lunches were connected to the Internet, while 78 percent of schools where only 1 in 10 students is eligible for the same lunch discount had access.[8] President Clinton has said that the legacy of his administration will be that every K-12 public school in the United States will be hooked up to the Internet—a promise he has backed up with a pledge of $500 million dollars. There are 84,000 public schools in the United States, which means the government will pay just under 12 percent of the $50,000 cost of wiring each school. Furthermore, fewer than 15 percent of instructional classrooms have Internet connections, which means that in many schools Internet access is limited to the library or to the staff room (see Fig. 12.2). Teachers can download instructional materials but their students cannot participate in the search for those materials or learn the process of that search.

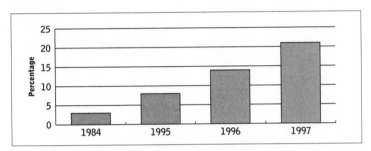

Figure 12.2
Percent of instructional rooms* with Internet access.
Data: National Center for Education Statistics.

*The percent of instructional rooms across the country is based on the total number of instructional rooms (e.g., classrooms, computer labs, library/media centers) in all regular public and secondary schools.

According to the Alliance for Converging Technologies, the average ratio of students to computers in United States public schools is expected to reach 9:1 by the beginning of the 1998 school year. The ratio of students to multimedia computers (with capability to access the Net), however, will only be 33:1. So charts like Fig. 12.3 below are misleading because the number of computers in the classrooms which are actually usable for the reinvention of education is tiny.

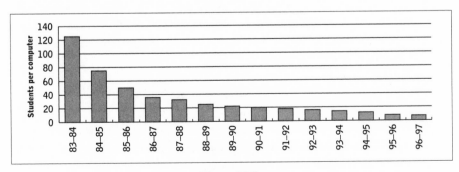

Figure 12.3
Students per computer, U.S. public schools (per school year).
Data: QED—Quality Education Data, Alliance for Converging Technologies.

Access Is Not Enough in the Schools Either

Wiring the schools and populating them with computers is necessary but insufficient to ensure equal opportunity to share in the digital revolution. Children need access to computers and the Net, but they also need appropriate software and services. They need motivation to learn. They need a redesigned education system and teachers who have been retrained and reoriented. Innovative technologies cannot make up for educational professionals who lack innovative methods and merely replicate learning models that don't work.

In fact, programs to get technology into schools don't even ensure that students will have access, let alone relatively equal access and all the other requirements for participation. At present, more than 74 percent of schools have computers, but only 10 percent of students say they have used a computer at school in the past week. Many students who responded to our forum said that they had never seen the single computers in their classrooms used by either teacher or student. Meanwhile, many teachers do not allow their students to compose homework on computers because it would give them an unfair advantage over those students who do not have computers at home. Some teachers also mistrust words which have been typed with a computer. We discovered more than one N-Gener who purposely put spelling and formatting errors into projects so that the teacher wouldn't think their parents had done the work or that text had been cut and pasted from another source.

Two of the factors contributing to the present underutilization of the technology are the fact that only one-half of all teachers have any kind of computer training, and the widespread belief that work done on outdated computer hardware and software is useless. Is it really likely that knowledge of WordPerfect, for example, is a hindrance to learning Microsoft Word later? One certainly wouldn't say that the knowledge of French is a hindrance to learning Spanish.

"Kids here don't have the fastest processors and they don't have the most up-to-date software," says cyber arts teacher Kathy Yamashita of her school in North York, Ontario. "They have enough of the basics to allow them to fly once they get there. So I don't believe that public education should have state-of-the-art everything." Yamashita, like most teachers, is not a computer science specialist but an English literature major.

Even though not all school environments are hostile to the use of technology, there are other factors hindering schools from providing the experience with the new media their students need. Many schools are not a part of their students' neighborhoods or communities. Almost 60 percent of American students are sent to school by bus, and the vast majority of those students come from lower-income neighborhoods.[9] (The percent of instructional rooms across the country is based on the total number of instructional rooms—classrooms, computer labs, library/media centers—

in all regular public and secondary schools.) It's a story Michael Bouyer, a Palo Alto, California, consultant with The Arts Resources & Talents Association (ARTA) who works with children and youth, knows well. "They take a bus across town to go to school (the bus leaves at 3:15, they get out at 3:05) and make their way back, glad to escape an environment that's not very friendly to them," Bouyer explains. "In the meantime the school has 20 computers, but those aren't really available to the students who have to take the buses."

Even when schools are wired, they are not welcoming places for many students, discouraging them from using the technology after school. In 1993, 44 percent of high school students reported that they had had something stolen from them at school and 42 percent reported that they had been threatened.[10] While the number of students who have actually been injured with weapons at school fell by almost 4 percent between 1980 and 1992, suggesting that schools are becoming physically safer, they are still not places where most kids want to be in their free time. Student participation in extracurricular activities is down. Participation in athletics, including cheerleading and drill team, has fallen from 67 percent of all seniors in 1980 to 50 percent in 1992. Remarkably, the number of students involved in academic clubs and the newspaper or yearbook dropped by only 0.5 percent and 1.1 percent during the same period.[11] One possible reason these activities have managed to retain their participants is that desktop publishing programs and computer clubs may have begun to play greater roles in school yearbook and newspaper production.

None of this means that schools do not belong online, it means that wiring schools alone is not enough to compensate for other factors that are failing to ensure that all students have free and equal access to both information technology and digitized information. That will come out of endeavors that seek to ensure that computers and connections are available after classes have been dismissed and that the model of education as a whole is changed. This requires retraining of teachers, rethinking of curricula, redesign of pedagogical models, and overall significant investment.

For those who believe in open markets and market forces, I would propose that we take precise steps to open the school market. The schools are currently a terrible "market" for the new media. They are impoverished when it comes to budgets for technology. Old cultures of teaching inhibit proliferation of the digital media. And teachers and educators have little comprehension of how to transform the schools from broadcast to interactive learning, and may lack the motivation to do so anyway. Rather than pretending that somehow schools with no technology budgets and massive cultural legacies will become magically wired, replete with glistening multimedia computers that will magically transform to interactive learning, we would do better to take radical steps to address this problem. Governments and corporations need to provide leadership to address the funding obstacle preventing the transformation of education. And the private sector needs to get beyond lip service to see that children from all walks of life have access to the Net.

Access is a critical first step. In the 1995 study on home computing conducted by Carnegie Mellon University, cited in Chapter 3, researchers concluded that "Once financial barriers [to access] are lowered, lower-income and less well-educated people are as likely to become [Internet] enthusiasts."[12] Race and gender, however, predicted lower usage in the study. The reasons? Culturally the Net may be seen as more foreign to women and minority races. Some blacks, for example, view the Net as a thing for white kids. And Net content is still largely oriented toward white males.

Reinforcing the myth that universal access at school is well under way are media events that suggest daily miracles in communications are happening through technology even in the worst of circumstances.

Burrville Elementary School in Washington, DC is one of the poorest schools in Washington's inner city, but for a few brief moments it showed the world all the promise of what the digital media can do for education. In April of 1997, Canadian prime minister Jean Chrétien and his wife Aline paid a state visit to the United States president and first lady. Mrs. Clinton and Mrs. Chrétien, accompanied by dozens of reporters, visited Burrville Elementary while its students participated in an Internet exchange with students at St. Elizabeth's School in Canada's capital, Ottawa. Unbeknownst to the first lady and Mrs. Chrétien, as they, their entourage, and the journalists left Burrville, the computers the students had used during the visit were packed into boxes and taken away.

In this case only one journalist, Paul Koring of *The Globe and Mail,* covered the striking of the stage. Before and after the official visit and press event, Burrville Elementary School owned only one computer that was connected to the Internet. "That's what happens when you talk to the kids instead of just hanging around," Koring said in an interview. "The kids knew the stuff was leaving and so did the teachers, but it certainly wasn't in the press release."

Following the incident, which embarrassed both the Clinton Administration and the Canadian Embassy in Washington, Northern Telecom rescued both governments from further press scrutiny on the episode, and, more importantly, saved the students from becoming part of the Not-Generation by donating 10 computers to Burrville Elementary School. Unfortunately, we don't know how many similar events held in the past have been constructed and then disassembled once the dignitaries and journalists left the classroom.

The New Responsibilities of Business

This is not some utopian call for everyone to somehow be "equal." Of course, social differences will exist for the foreseeable future based on variables like intelligence, effort, and choices in lifestyle. However, it is dangerous to polarize society further—in terms of opportunity to participate in the revolution of our times and to have a chance at a rewarding and fulfilling life.

How can we achieve universal access and take the other steps necessary to narrow the digital divide? If leaving it to the market is not a strategy, whose responsibility is it? The new media, the new economy, and the new generation are causing every institution to rethink itself and every person to reevaluate his or her values and behavior. Every institution and every person will need to get involved.

Governments can make a significant contribution. Most importantly, governments need to be one of the partners in the shift to a networked society. This means many things: for starters, taking the lead in funding the reinvention of education. Governments need to create the regulatory conditions whereby prices are fair. The best way to do this is to ensure that there is open competition—which, as a rule, drives prices down. Governments can also be model users of the digital media themselves, reinventing government to improve services and lower governmental costs. Governments can participate in projects that catalyze the kinds of partnerships which will be required to avoid the digital divide.

There is also a role for each of us as volunteers, as popularized by U.S. General (ret.) Colin Powell in the Alliance for Youth program. The program is calling on corporate America and citizens to provide their time in revitalizing the country. Another example of an important volunteer initiative is 2B1, whose goal is to break down the barriers to access, ownership, and development caused by economics, geography, gender, and culture.

The digital divide raises new imperatives for business leaders as well. Increasingly, it will be difficult and inappropriate for business people to say, "these issues are someone else's problem," or "my only responsibility is to my shareholders."

The business community needs to rethink its role in the new economy and its responsibilities to the new generation. Business should provide leadership for the broader changes to come, not only through altruism but also through self-interest. The success of businesses will depend on the rapidity and smoothness of the societal changes which are being unleashed by the N-Gen. Business in any nation state can only succeed if it has a "new-economy" workforce—one that is educated, motivated, stable, and healthy. The federal deficit is a tame problem compared to the potential social deficit lurking in the wings of a poorly managed transition to the new economy.

Is it unthinkable that business could lead in addressing the digital divide and the far-reaching issues it raises? Can the business leaders of a new generation understand their common self-interest in achieving social justice and a smooth societal transformation?

Community Computing

What concretely can be done?

One way of tackling the digital divide is by creating community computing networks—nonprofit Internet service providers (ISPs). These can use community-based computer networks or FreeNets that provide Internet access free of charge to those who cannot afford to pay for computers or connections. FreeNets, the most common of these, offer two services. They provide computers in public spaces such as libraries or laundromats from which users can access the Internet. But they also provide dial-up access to the Internet for people who already have access to a computer, say through a friend or school, but don't have an ISP.

Homeless people online at the local library can log on to the community information bulletin board to find beds in a shelter, a hot shower, or even medical and counseling services. Children can find information about services available to them. As fashionable as the Social Darwinist stance against social services may be, arguing against the dissemination of information that prevents homeless people from freezing to death on city streets and deaths by child neglect or abuse is anything but trendy.

Those who espouse an Internet law of the jungle have another ideological predator. These predators number in the thousands of individuals who run the hundreds of community computing centers in North America. In a poll of young people living in San Francisco, "positive alternatives for youth" ranked number one as the way to reduce juvenile crime. When asked what equipment they considered most important for a youth center; the teens gave the highest priority to computers—ahead of swimming pools, pool tables, and even video games.[13]

According to Community Technology Centers' Network (CTCNet), there are over 150 nonprofit community computing centers operating in the United States. The vast majority of those that serve the needs of children are open about four hours a day, with a half-dozen computers in neighborhood community centers and Boys' and Girls' Clubs. Others are independent organizations with enough space and staff to provide access to dozens of computers for 10 to 12 hours each day. Whatever the size of the operation, the experiences of community computing centers show the potential that would be wasted if kids in low-income communities were denied access to communications technology. Such centers are also places of hope for youth where, as described by Mario Marino, "children are treated not as problems to be handled, but as resources to be encouraged."

A New Activity in the Mall

The Lakeforest Library Connection (LLC) is a computer community-access center open seven days a week in a large Rockville, Maryland, shopping mall. The access center has 17 computer terminals offering Internet connections and educational software. It attracts more than 1000 users per week.

The project is a joint effort of the area's libraries and schools in combination with more than a dozen private-sector sponsors and supporters. Barbara Harr runs the center and says its purpose is to provide "free and equal access to electronic resources to the community at large and particularly for those in the community who do not own a computer or may have a computer but no modem.

"There is this world of information out there, and it should be freely and easily accessible to everyone in all its formats. This is the heart of the public library system. The nation is founded on this. It is at the heart of our ethics. We feel strongly about intellectual freedom and the right of access for all citizens."

The mall setting is a deliberately nontraditional library site, designed to be inviting in a way that a typical library might not be. Harr notes that many segments of the community liken libraries to fortresses, but the mall setting helps break down this perception. The LLC is open seven days a week, and is often open when regular libraries and school libraries are closed. Since opening in May 1996, the site has been tremendously popular, with the LLC relying mainly on word of mouth for promotion. There are often lines of people waiting to use a computer.

The center has received inquiries from groups around the country that would like to replicate its success. The center is appealing to all age groups, from toddlers to senior citizens. Children under 13 must be accompanied by a parent. "You will often see the parent and a four- or five-year-old working on the computer together," says Harr. "The kids are all whizzes and put us to shame. It is not unusual to see a group of kids just laughing and exploring. The older generation seems a little bit more reluctant. You can tell by the language they use.

"Middle-age users could be using the center for job hunting or looking for information to help their businesses. This is very new to them. That is where the staff come in, and they are needed to provide assistance. But the kids don't need them. In fact, the kids are thrilled with this site, and you will often see teenagers just hovering, and if they see a mature person that looks like they need help, the kids will offer their assistance." In fact, a community organization is working with Lakeforest to develop a program that will bring senior citizens to the center for courses in computer literacy that will be taught by high school students! Rather than fighting the generation lap, they will be rolling with it.

Kidzonline

Kidzonline claims it's "the coolest place for kids to hang out in a secure environment." It's also a great example of one family taking the initiative to make the cyberworld freely accessible to kids that otherwise would be shut out.

The Intranet-style site boasts 24 incoming phone lines for children who have access to a computer at home or through the Boys' and Girls' Clubs that Kidzonline works with in Washington. Kidzonline also has a 15-PC LAN available in a training center set up in donated space in the basement of a local bank.

The project began much more modestly in 1994 when Wesley Cruver, then 11 years old, thought it would be neat to set up a bulletin board system for his friends. "He is not a child genius, he is just a regular guy. But man, is he good with computers and software," says his dad, Phil.

When Sharon, Wesley's mom, saw the fun her son and his friends were having with the bulletin board, she realized that many kids would be denied this source of entertainment and learning simply because they didn't have access to computers.

Sharon asked local businesses to donate the equipment and enlisted the area's Boys' and Girls' Clubs to help make the technology available to inner city kids. The goal was to "introduce kids from all economic levels to the networking technologies that will play a major role in their futures."

Today the site is a roaring success, with teenager Wesley making sure the technology functions properly and his mom orchestrating the creation of more than 800 pages of content. The site offers file libraries, educational resources, local after-school activities, and fun things like comics, reviews, stories, e-mail buddies, and more.

Kids can post software, movie and book reviews, among other things. Commenting on the *Bailey School Kids* book series, Robyn "Tweety Bird" Andrews, age 10, says, "some of the stories are funny, some are sad, but they're cool. If you read one, you'll want to read another."

In the Girlz Only section, boys are asked what turns them off when dating. Matt, 16, writes: "The worst thing is going to a girl's house and being put through half an hour of talking to her parents because she's still getting ready." Tobin, 14, says that, "heavy makeup and smelly perfume are major turnoffs."

"A lot of the material is educational, but the curriculum isn't math or science. They are learning computer skills, how to upload, download, unzip files," says Phil Cruver. "Once those kids get that mouse in their hand, they pick it up really fast. But you've got to give them the exposure."

Plugged-In: A Model for the Future

Imagine, if you can, a miracle in which street kids give up their weapons and gang affiliations to spend time playing, learning, and doing their homework in a community computing center. Sounds like a stretch, but this is actually happening in the low-income neighborhoods of East Palo Alto, California.

Muki Izora gives kids exposure to the digital media every day, an experience that gives him the ability to speak with all the confidence of a person who really knows what he can do. "I can get kids interested enough to come in here off the street, I can teach them how to use a computer to tell a story, I can teach them how to type as quickly as they can talk, I can give them a safe place to be with their friends, and then I can give them a part-time job."

Izora, 26, is the project director for Plugged-In, a community computing center located in East Palo Alto, that is successfully working to address the issue of the technology-poor on several levels. Plugged-In has become "the community center that never was in East Palo Alto," says Izora, who has worked with the organization since 1992 when it was "six donated computers in the back room of the Boys' and Girls' Club in Menlo Park." Plugged-In now occupies three storefront offices where the organization offers classes to children, teens, and adults; gives free Internet access to members of the community; and hosts an innovative program known as "Plugged-In Enterprises" where teens apply the programming and design skills they have learned to a business in which they build and maintain Web pages.

Encircled by the cities and companies that make up Silicon Valley, East Palo Alto itself has not benefited economically from the computer industry's growth or profits. Located inside a confusing triangle created by the construction of Freeway 101, bad urban planning contributed to cutting the population off from its neighbors and many of the technological innovations that had shaped the surrounding cities. That is, until the arrival and growth of Plugged-In. According to the teens who use Plugged-In, the center has changed the city of East Palo Alto itself.

"This city is the only one that's been left out, maybe because of the violence—that's changed in the past few years though," says Dominic Bannister, 15, of East Palo Alto. "I think they should have a place like Plugged-In in every community, especially in troubled neighborhoods. Here, this has helped the community a lot and it's a great place to be at. Everybody treats you like you're family. There are no fights over here, no conflicts like that, nothing like that."

"I think it's a new way of seeing technology, especially in East Palo Alto," says Thomas Gomez, 14, of River City. "You don't see that much technology around here. It's the only place you might see a computer and access the World Wide Web, which most people around here don't know about."

Even more impressive than the changes to East Palo Alto are the changes to the kids themselves. N-Geners at Plugged-In seem almost surprised to find themselves enjoying a safe environment that encourages learning.

"When I first came here, I was sort of afraid because everybody was looking at me because I was new," says 15-year-old J. R. Organez who is relieved that Plugged-In is so different from school. "Every hour there's always fights at school, you know. . . . They judge the way you dress, the way you look." That doesn't happen at Plugged-In, says J. R. "When I came here I was like 13 years old and, like a month later, everybody knew my name and that felt good."

"I like being here because I can do my homework. Here is a bit quieter than school. They give you more access to computers and when you need help somebody comes to help you. At school, people don't do that very much," Dominic says.

"They're always on your back about your grades. I should know that," says Thomas, who has raised his GPA from 1.7 to 2.5 since he started going to Plugged-In. "I was getting a low grade in biology because I changed classes—I was taking computer science. Then they moved my whole schedule around and I didn't make up my work and stuff. Then when they found out about it, they made sure I didn't play no games. When I came in I just did my homework and stuff. That's what they made me do, they took away my privileges and stuff."

The "they" who got on Thomas' back about his homework are the dedicated staff and volunteers at Plugged-In. The people who prove that support for role models is as important as technical support for community computing centers are staff like Julian Lacey, a 25-year-old skills instructor at Plugged-In. Lacey hassles Plugged-In's students about their homework and is treated with the highest degree of respect in return. "Julian is the man," says Dominic. "He's like a psychic. He knows everything, practically. He knows when there's something wrong with me. He studies all of us. He knows when something is bothering you, he talks to you about it."

"When Julian sees me and I have homework to do," Thomas adds, "and he sees me playing a game, he's going to turn it off and make me do my homework. Or else, if I'm not doing that, he says, 'you could be learning something new,' and he makes me look up stuff on the Internet."

Lacey, who works for a courier company from 4 to 11 a.m. before he begins teaching at the center, knows he has an effect on the kids at Plugged-In and has made it his priority to help people out. "There are a lot of people in Silicon Valley who have a lot of money who want to come here and help because they feel like there's something missing from their lives," Lacey explains. "I don't feel that way because I know I'm giving something back."

That sense of responsibility for the community has created a cycle of role modeling among the N-Geners at Plugged-In that challenges the belief that computers and the Net prevent kids from developing social skills. Older N-Geners help younger ones, a process that enhances their self-esteem.

Juliana Maciel, a 15-year-old East Palo Alto girl, is a student and part-time worker at Plugged-In, where she answers the phone and technical questions from the center's clientele, who range in age from 3 to 75. Juliana's favorite part of the job is helping little kids. "It's nice when little kids call you over and say, 'help me with this, show me that,' and you get to have a real friendship with them and they start liking you a lot," Juliana says. "It makes me feel important. It makes me feel wanted. It is important to have that kind of support because [without it] I probably wouldn't even be here—I would probably be somewhere else doing something bad."

At Plugged-In, Juliana says she learned more than how to program HTML to build Web pages. She says she also learned how to give speeches. "I'm a lot more talkative. I used to be shy, now I'm not." This skill, acquired through participation in the Plugged-In Enterprises program, led to Juliana's participation in Youth Community Service, where, Juliana says, "We clean out graffiti in the community, and we are filming a project about homeless people learning how to use Macintosh computers. I'm also working on another project where I talk to eighth-graders about gangs and the problems they can cause."

It is her own experience with neighborhood gangs that makes Juliana credit her parents, her friends, and the staff at Plugged-In for giving her a stronger sense of self.

"There's this gang that hangs out near where I live, and they saw me with my friends and they came up and asked me if I was claiming 'blue,'" Juliana explains, referring to the colors local gangs use to mark their allegiances and identify rivals. "Every day I used to have to confront them, most days I had to run away from them, but I put up with it. One day they were asking me to fight with them and I was like— 'If you want to fight me, let's fight right here now. One by one.' They weren't used to what I said, so they stopped fighting me."

> PART 1: I'm here because my dad wants me to learn about computers, because he came from another Island, Tonga, where there were no computers. And so, he came here with his wife and he had kids and he found this place and he told us about it and he told us he wants us to learn how to type and he said he'll come here and learn how to type too.

The staff at Plugged-In don't take all the credit for their students' rising levels of self-esteem. While pure skills like touch typing are taught to even very young children at Plugged-In, embedded into the center's curriculum is an emphasis on storytelling. The process begins with teenage N-Geners reading stories to the neighborhood preschoolers, who quickly become the youngest Plugged-In students, learning basic computer skills as they make slide shows about their community using storyboard software.

> PART 2: I had a report to make and I typed it on the computer and so I printed it out and it came out good. Martin Luther King, I learned about how he had a brother named Daniel and another brother, Alfred, and he had only one sister, and her name was Christine. And Martin Luther King was born in January.

"Storytelling is a collaborative act that is focused around building communication and life skills," explains Muki Izora. "That's our heart and that's really what it's all about: teaching kids how to work together, tapping into their creativity and their potential to use a variety of disciplines to find solutions to problems."

> THE END: I can't talk right now. I have to get my report done.
>
> *Theresa Tenisi, 9-year-old typist and storyteller*
> *Plugged-In, East Palo Alto, California.*

While these N-Geners are learning the skills to help them navigate their generation's medium, they're also learning how to access their creativity, take on leadership roles in their communities, and survive in a business environment. In short, N-Geners at Plugged-In have access to more than just computers and the Internet. They have access to a safe environment that supports friendship and learning, and the support of staff who are both caring and knowledgeable. As a result of this access, the N-Geners of East Palo Alto have said that gang participation is down and GPAs are up. These indicators may not be related to the value of computers, but to the value of knowledge itself. Plugged-In's students use a specific compliment when someone has done something new, original, and enviable at the computer terminal: "You are Ph.D. . . . Stanford Ph.D."

What Isn't Working

East Palo Alto is a great success story, but every community computing center is not like Plugged-In. The more typical model resembles Plugged-In's origins in the back room of the Boys' and Girls' Club, but it is difficult to see how many centers will grow to replicate the good influence Plugged-In has had on its community. As with wired schools, at community computing centers access itself is crucial, but not all access is equal.

The solution to this dilemma would seem to be corporate sponsorship, but a few free computers, despite what the computer industry would have us believe, are not enough to create another Plugged-In. Microsoft's KidReach program is one body that funds community computing centers in lower-income neighborhoods. This is a positive approach, and when it comes to working to close the digital divide, Microsoft is one of the better companies. One of Microsoft's initiatives resulted in this mention in a press release: "The leading charity in the field of product philanthropy, Gifts In Kind International and Microsoft Canada, have recently opened the Technology Learning Center at the Dovercourt Boys' and Girls' Club in Toronto, giving access to technology to over 700 children in that community."

The Technology Learning Center at the club is by no means as big as its name suggests. It is five computers, donated by Compaq, running Microsoft software in an office-sized room. "When those computers came, it was like Christmas around here," says executive director Tony Puopolo. "The kids kept asking 'when are we going to get to use them?' for weeks while we got the room ready."

> I have a "previously owned" system at home and the internal modem is really slow. Someone recently stole one of the Pentiums at school. . . . So I really like to use the computers here.
>
> FRANK, 12
> Dovercourt Boys' and Girls'
> Club Member

Three groups of 10 to 12 students use the five computers for 30 minutes each during the center's after-school program. Due to funding limitations, only one of the computers has an Internet connection, on a telephone line shared with the center's fax machine. Puopolo does not yet know where the money to pay for Internet access will come from once Microsoft's one-year funding commitment for the ISP runs out. Ensuring that there is also adequate staff is also a concern. "Supervision is really important," says Puopolo. "If I don't have a supervisor for the room, then I have to close the room. You can't just turn kids loose on equipment like that."

This limited exposure is probably adequate to teach these budding N-Geners to play an online game and do a little chatting, but not enough to build a Web page or to research and type a history report. The club members also have no access to e-mail, so they cannot build up global networks through longer-term communication.

Club members do get some other exposure to computers. The club has retained its collection of 15 Commodore 64s and 286s with equally ancient software that it acquired through donations from local businesses that upgraded their systems. They would not have had to keep these machines had the corporation involved followed its original plan to give the club 15 computers and the technical assistance of "a National network of Microsoft employee volunteers" which Microsoft told the club it had in place.

> Kids have to learn how to use the Internet so that they can do whatever they want and learn whatever they want.
>
> KELLON, 10
> Dovercourt Boys' and Girls'
> Club Member

Computer industry professionals do play a significant role as volunteers in the wiring of both schools and community computing centers. NetDay serves as the best-known example of such altruism. Since 1995, NetDay has mobilized tens of thousands of computer industry and telecommunications professionals who have donated their time and expertise toward wiring U.S. schools in what has often been called "a modern-day barn raising." One organization, San Francisco-based Compumentor, provides technical assistance to schools and community computing centers that serve low-income populations. Compumentor looks at the organization's mission, resources, and technical issues and then, says Compumentor's mission statement, "we develop solutions that are appropriate in terms of affordability, sustainability, and level of technology." The organization can help beginning community computing centers, like the Dovercourt Boys' and Girls' Club, define their mandates and construct their plans for growth.

While Compumentor and other organizations like it can assist organizations, the problem of funding, not a lack of ambition, is at the root of many community computing centers' woes. Puopolo emphasizes that both he and the club are extremely grateful to have the five computers but he doesn't have the funding for telephone lines, ISP fees, another staff member, or the equipment to take the Technology Learning Center to the next level, which Puopolo believes would be sharing its resources with the larger community. To address the shortfalls in staffing, technological support, and the communication infrastructure, corporations have to move toward a more meaningful model of funding community computing ventures.

Creating a Meaningful Model for Corporate Involvement

Often corporate donations are given to schools or community groups without the needs of the recipient being the uppermost consideration. Frequently the guiding factors are the potential tax credits stemming from the donation, or good publicity, or the thought of future sales. For example, used equipment which would otherwise be written off when discarded anyway, often doesn't have multimedia capabilities and therefore cannot use CDs or access the Net fully. Often appropriate software, which is no longer on the market, has to be found. As often happens with machines injected with shared disks, computer viruses proliferate. The machines also break down often.

Even when new equipment is donated to community computing centers, it is rarely accompanied by technical support or commitments to offer infrastructure support. One-time gifts do generate positive publicity for the corporate donor, attracting attention to the community computing center itself, which finds its service in greater demand without a greater pool of resources with which to serve the community.

"These are our future consumers," one telecommunications corporation representative said of her company's school initiatives. "So certainly we're looking to present these offers in the home, through the schools, to our future and current consumers." While this approach to corporate donations is certainly of more benefit to the community than any ad campaign, it is a disempowering one for the members of that community. It considers what products or packages the corporation wants to give, rather than what is needed by that community or the knowledge of the instructor who facilitates use of the tool by that community.

There are a number of steps corporations could take that would make a positive and meaningful contribution:

1. Wire your employees, wire a family.

The easiest way for all corporations to ensure universal access is to provide all of their employees computers to take home. This proposal is not naïve. It makes good business sense to increase fluency of human capital in the knowledge economy. Computers in the home will be instantly embraced by children, who will train their parents, thereby reducing training costs and time taken away from work for training. N-Geners, the children of corporate employees, are the answer to boomer fluency. I have made this proposal to many senior management audiences over the last year and while the idea has been received well, the actions have been piecemeal and low profile. Imagine the impact of a number of leading companies jointly announcing their decision to ensure that every family of their employees would get wired! One such initiative could have a rippling effect across the economy and strike an historic blow for access, fluency, and fairness.

2. Give your employees time, give a community time.

Professionals in the computer industry are famous for the long hours that they work in an extremely competitive industry. While these professionals are putting in hours of overtime, their expertise is needed elsewhere as well. Give your employees time to volunteer in their communities as well as in under-privileged communities. In community computing centers, these employees are needed to train the instructors who, while they may be expert users, are often confronted with donated software they haven't necessarily come across before. In addition, children who have no understanding of corporate culture or professionalism desperately need mentors.

3. Fund the connector to make the connection.

A community computing center needs more than just computers and Internet access. It also needs to be able to pay for staffing, telephones, and telephone lines. But even covering these expenses isn't enough to ensure that the venture is a true success. Corporations have to recognize that community computing centers provide more than just access to computers.

"Our problem is that we have to reach into the community of people who know nothing at all about—not just computers—but planning their lives," says consultant Michael Bouyer, who sits on the board of directors at Plugged-In. "Corporate sponsors need to understand that we're dealing with a huge lack of life skills. We try to put programs together for people who want to come on a regular basis. We give them the kind of jobs where they have to be finished on time and they must be consistent. We need corporations to help with the resources to get the training to the second level all the way to a job in corporate America." In other words, to get return on investments in a community, corporations must be willing to invest in teaching real skills and to stand by their own investments by hiring people from the communities they train.

"We ask corporations to deliver skills that they are going to benefit from in the end," says Bouyer. "Even if the kids don't all become computer programmers or data processors at some corporation, at least they have the dignity and self-esteem to not be out on the street, banging you on the head while you're at the ATM. If they have a job, they are doing something meaningful. They won't be so underskilled and desperate that they'll be on the street."

This means creating partnerships the right way, rather than the easy way or the way that is expedient from a short-term corporate perspective. Firms should think cooperation and partnership for closing the digital divide, rather than simply seeding fertile young minds with their products. A Kodak program is a good example of the right approach. "All of our really meaningful partnerships are cooperative," says cyber arts teacher Kathy Yamashita, whose school has made several successful partnerships with corporate sponsors. The school is not bound to purchase Kodak products because of its relationship, nor does it take what it does not need.

Yamashita notes:

> My Kodak partner's mandate does not require us to use her product. They give me stuff, for example: paper, film, the time of a chemist. If I have a project going, she will make me a CD. They also gave us a trainer who is an expert educator. She teaches the students and finds out activities that would be profitable. For example, at the Metro Convention Centre, the kids had a booth sponsored by Kodak at the multimedia 1996-1997 event. In exchange we provide her with things she needs. We do conferences for her, but she always pays us, so the kids get something back again. Those are the kinds of partnerships that we like to form that generate really dynamic collaboration.
>
> She runs courses for teachers and, in return, I provide her with students as TAs and so she has a ready labor force of experienced students that can go out. They have presentation leadership skills in technology and they can go out as TAs when she does her workshops. And she pays the students, so it just breeds upon itself.

Bring the Community Together: The Tech Corps and CyberEd

Some of the most successful corporate initiatives have recognized that a good program is one that brings together the energies of community-minded organizations. The corporation serves as a facilitator and can achieve far more impact with the group effort than if it just acted by itself.

When President Clinton challenged corporate America to help bring information and education technology to every classroom in the United States, communications giant MCI responded by building and equipping a state-of-the-art multimedia classroom that was completely plugged in to the Internet. What made this classroom unique is that it was built inside an 18-wheel big-rig truck. From April to September of 1996 the truck, dubbed CyberEd, traveled more than 25,000 miles, visiting 15 federal empowerment zones from New York City to Oakland, California. The tour was orchestrated by Tech Corps, a national nonprofit organization that helps K-12 schools with their technology initiatives.

The purpose of the truck was not to roll into a community, dazzle everyone with gee-whiz technology, and then depart. By itself, that would accomplish little. "We felt the truck could be most effectively used as a catalyst for schools and communities to move their educational technology agenda forward," explained Karen Smith, the executive director of Tech Corps.

At least a month before the truck would arrive in each community, Tech Corps would arrange for a meeting with the mayor's office, the superintendent's office, and the director of the empowerment zone. Tech Corps would outline the strategy it felt could make best use of the truck. Its first recommendation was to ask the schools to send the teachers who knew the least about technology, not the most. Says Smith: "We didn't want to be preaching to the choir." Tech Corps also recommended bringing in other community stakeholders who are crucial to getting technology into the schools, such as Boards of Education, City Council, and the Chamber of Commerce. The Tech Corps view was that "to be successful, these groups will also need to know why you should have the Internet in your classrooms here."

The truck would spend a week in each community and on the last day of the visit a roundtable discussion would bring all of the stakeholders together in a setting that was open to the public. Representatives of the companies that helped sponsor CyberEd would outline what they would leave behind, such as equipment, software, or Internet accounts. Other groups who were already involved with helping implement technology in the community's schools would outline what services they were currently providing. Within this framework, recalls Smith, "someone, usually the mayor's office, would say, 'Here is our vision of what we want to do, and here is what is currently being provided. What pieces of the puzzle are we missing?'

By doing this we left behind a group of people who were committed to continue working together to advocate for educational technology in the schools."

Getting Wired in the Developing World: Jimmy Efrain Morales

Even in the most difficult, poverty-plagued environments, N-Gen is rising to the challenge of the new media. This became clear to me recently when I gave the opening address to the Latin American Bankers Association conference in Bogotá, Columbia. My graphic material was organized into a fairly sophisticated multimedia presentation using a complex program called "Macromedia Director." Each time I use this presentation in such a large setting it is important to have a perfect technical setup, preferably with an on-site expert.

As I walked onto the stage for a technical rehearsal I was assured that the situation was well under control because the "chief systems engineer" was very knowledgeable and experienced. Beside the stage was a complex computer configuration with dozens of wires connecting various peripherals and, in turn, connecting to a huge video projection system. And sitting at the console was the chief systems engineer—a boy who looked about 13 years old! He was introduced to me as Jimmy Efrain Morales. Sure enough, he was the computer expert I needed and my software ran like a top.

Jimmy's story is an amazing one. Born in Bogotá, he is the eldest of four children. His father was a watchman at the local college (University Distrital) and is now on a modest pension. By American standards, the family is poor. They had no phone in the house until Jimmy was 12 years old. His mother knits to supplement the family income. Jimmy has a growth hormone deficiency which gives him the appearance of a boy half a decade younger than his actual age. Such problems are simply treated in richer countries. Jimmy never liked school, as the teachers used rulers to beat kids who didn't perform or who misbehaved. He failed grade 9.

During high school he saw his first computer on television and became curious about the technology. When Jimmy was 16, his local library converted to a computer card index system and the boy was thrilled. He was going to get to use a computer. He entered the library, sat down in front of the terminal, and "looked up books" for the next four hours. He was exhilarated to see that it was so easy and also useful. "Kids my age don't go to libraries because it is too hard and too intimidating to find a book. Now it is easy." Every day he went back to the library to "look up books," just to be able to use the computer. He began to take friends to the library to show them this amazing new thing.

Jimmy's time in the library led to a new motivation to learn and do better in school. He managed to graduate from high school in 1993 and because his dad had worked at the college, he was able to attend college tuition-free.

To his delight, Jimmy discovered that at college there was a room where students could go to use computers. Better still, these computers did a lot more things than looking up books. There were all kinds of applications, and Jimmy learned "anything I could get my hands on." He says, "I was pretty driven to see what computers could do." There were no instruction manuals for any of these applications. As Jimmy says, "If you went into the computer room you were supposed to know what you were doing," so he had to quietly "learn for myself."

During one of his sessions Jimmy met a friend who showed him many new tools like e-mail, simulators, and computer-aided design. One day his new friend, who came from a wealthy family, announced that he was going to buy a computer and asked Jimmy to come along. The two boys stayed up all night, they were so excited to have their own machine to configure and experiment with.

Another new-found friend was asked to make a presentation about the future of education to a government committee. Jimmy decided to help him out by learning Director, a multimedia resource handler requiring strong technical skills in a number of areas. When the local production company which set up the equipment for the presentation found out that Jimmy knew Director, they were delighted to learn about this new resource. Jimmy had himself a part-time job.

Then his father took out a loan for $3500 to buy a computer for all the children. Jimmy says, "My parents felt it was the best investment they could make in their children after they saw what an impact computers had had on me."

An N-Gener in Bogotá. For Jimmy, "Computers changed my life. They are the most important tool for man ever. Computers don't replace man. Man replaces himself."

Give them access to good technology and they will find a way—not just to assimilate it but to change their life circumstances.

13

Leaders
of the Future

© Mike Keefe*

As the N-Gen comes of age, what kind of world will they create? They are the best-informed and most active generation ever. These young people will dominate most of the twenty-first century. As they take, transform, or smash the reins of power, culture, and social development, what can we expect? What values will they hold? How will they shape the world?

Few if any technologies could be described as values-free. The technology innovation introduced to the baby boom—TV—had strong values. It assumed that communications should be controlled centrally, by broadcasters. These broadcasters understood your needs and desires for entertainment, news, information. They programmed, creating a schedule which they estimated corresponded to the largest mass. The value of consumption is inherent in the media, funded primarily by advertising rather than use. The medium values passivity and downplays the importance of reading, writing, and the written word.

Such values were enshrined by governments, which regulate TV, and the advertisers who dominate the medium. There is careful licensing of broadcasters to ensure that ideologies which challenge tenets of the social order do not have a loud or sustained voice. For example, trade unions, civil rights groups, social activists—or, for that matter, children—are not permitted to be broadcasters because they may challenge existing social norms.

The interactive media cherish a different set of values. These media embrace the two-way, interactive model of the telephone and extend it a thousand fold. To Bell's invention the new media add information banks that can be created by anyone. Multiple media—text, data, image, video, and soon kinesthetic, olfactory, and other forms—are added to offer the full texture of human communications. These media also add rich, multiperson collaborative environments controlled by the participants, not some central licensed authority.

The Ideology of N-Gen

If the new media are creating a new youth culture, are they also leading to an N-Gen ideology? Out of the chat-room clatter, the flurry of e-mails, the bursting Web sites, can we begin to discern the contours of a new world view, a new perspective? What values are N-Geners embracing? How will the Net Generation change the body politic and society?

If you listen to the traditional media, you hear a sad tale. Today's youth are described in ways that make the "me" generation look like a generation of philanthropists and social activists. They are said to be self-centered and obsessed with short-term gratification.

One of the reasons offered for the moral decay of youth is "soft" parenting. In the past two years, there have been no fewer than six well-read books on the issue. One analyst writes: "These experts contend that many baby boomer parents are so concerned with building youngsters' self-esteem, protecting them from stress, and making them partners in the family that they are raising a generation of selfish, ill-mannered, troubled children."[1] Seminars like *Spoiled Rotten: Today's Children and How to Change Them,* by former telecommunications salesman Fred Grosman, advise parents to impose stricter codes of discipline.

The influence of the "spare the rod, spoil the child" school of thought is so widespread at present that materialism and impulsiveness enter into expert analysis of youth crime. Charles Ewing, a juvenile-crime expert at the University of Buffalo in New York, says: "Juveniles have little impulse control, and a gun is an impulsive weapon."[2] Judy Sheindlin, a judge on the juvenile bench in New York City for 24 years, says: "You're dealing with a population of kids who have been deprived of their childhood. They don't think of themselves as growing old. They are out for immediate gratification."[3] While some might argue that the fear of youth crime has created the market for disciplinarian advocacy, our focus on materialism, selfishness, and impulsiveness is distracting us from addressing the issues of poverty, racism, and the antiyouth sentiments that surround youth crime.

A commonly held view is that our children are greedy, self-centered, and concerned only about their own possessions and financial success. After spending the better part of a year talking to hundreds of N-Geners, our team has come to a different set of conclusions.

Our evidence suggests that conventional wisdom is dead wrong. There appears to be a new sense of direction which is very positive. There are also storm warnings that this perspective may clash with those of older generations and lead to a period of great turmoil. The ideology which is arising is not being created by some visionary and sold down to a generation. There is no big issue like Vietnam, although the volatile geopolitical situation may well precipitate such an issue. There is no full articulation—no Declaration of Independence, Communist Manifesto, *Mein Kampf,* or *The Fountainhead.* This perspective is percolating up through the intensive interaction of millions of youth in their C-world.

Conventional wisdom took a beating in the spring of 1996 when Harvard students effectively challenged their administration's million-dollar contract with PepsiCo which would have given the soft drink manufacturer exclusive beverage rights on campus. The challenge came about as a direct result of a 1993 notice placed on the Internet by university students in Canada. The notice examined PepsiCo's holdings in Burma, now known as Myanmar, a country ruled by the Social Law and Order Restoration Council—a military government that refused to hand over power to the democratically elected National Party led by Nobel Peace Prize laureate Aung San Suu Kyi. When students at schools facing similar deals between administrators and Pepsi e-mailed the site for more information, calls for a boycott of all Pepsi products were renewed on university and college campuses all over the continent. In January 1997, PepsiCo announced its full disengagement from Burma.

This generation contains many differing classes, races, religions, and social perspectives. It spans a 20-year age group, and, being composed of young people, it hasn't yet developed a strong world view. There is no unified set of values. Their ideology defies description. However, there are some themes emerging from our work with the more fortunate of those who have access to the new media. As you can see from the stories in this book, these children are not just rich white kids, but children from many backgrounds, and from ages 4 to 20.

Most pundits have noted their interest in material things. The N-Gen teenager is the "material girl." Says journalist Ian Haysom about teenagers: "They want stuff.

283

Lots of stuff. Lots of brand new stuff. In the '60s teenagers rebelled against materialism. Today their kids are embracing it."[4] The N-Geners have been called the designer generation. They are said to be more interested in $100 Nike Air shoes, Calvin Klein Jeans, and DKNY tops than in solving the world's problems. As the alternative rock band The Presidents of United States sings: "I've got myself a brand new tube amplifier and it smells just like a dream . . . I've got myself a brand new Big Bertha driver. It's large and lovely to behold." Sounds a little different from "Give peace a chance!" you might say.

> Occasionally, I think that this earth will be a bloody, violent world due to all the gory movies and video games out there. Sometimes I feel as if it's going to be a world that will be very smart as the sharing of information on the Internet becomes more popular.
>
> **RUFO SANCHEZ, 11**
> Rochester, New York

It is true that the N-Gen wants material things—not too surprising for the progeny of the baby boom who traded in their picket signs for picket fences some time ago. But according to Teenage Research Unlimited (TRU), of Illinois, teens of the '90s are less materialistic than their '80s predecessors. As the children of the boomers, most of the N-Geners have become accustomed, or aspire to, certain material standards. They want their own computers and top-of-the-line roller blades. "Today's kids don't want luxuries," says Brad Fay of the research company Roper Starch. "They just have a longer list of necessities." He says this is not the materialism of ostentatiousness, but rather that "they want the tools that they feel are a necessary part of life." Joan Chiaramonte, who is responsible for the Roper Starch Youth report, notes a very high degree of frustrated expectations across all demographic groups: "The gap between what they have and what they want has never been greater."

It appears that the more affluent, better-educated youth are more optimistic about the future. As Alliance for Converging Technologies president David Ticoll says, "The top end of this generation is the most prosperous in history by far." But overall, and even for the top end, there is a widening gap between their desires for a good life and fulfillment.

While N-Geners today are a savvy, confident generation, they are confronted with very different prospects than their boomer parents. An uncertain future tops a frightening list of problems which includes AIDS, violence, drugs, lack of parental involvement, urban crime, broken families, pollution, seething racial tension, unemployment or underemployment, lack of downtime, teenage suicide, and a dangerous, volatile planet. Prized possessions become a material fortress against economic insecurity. They validate one's difficult life and become an antidote for uncertainty. They are a refuge. Retreat to your mountain bike. Enshroud yourself with The Gap. Celebrate with your new Sony stereo.

In the 1960s, economic prosperity and the need for youth in the workforce created a sense of security among youth. When they marched down the street, their careers were the last thing on their minds. It didn't even occur to them that when it became time to get serious about a job and raise a family there might be a problem.

Compare this to the vast unknowns faced by today's students. Yes, as a generation, they are smart and confident in their abilities, but the economy is a source of unease for many. In many places including Canada, Western Europe, and countries in the developing world, unemployment is chronic and high, even for those with university degrees. In the United States, unemployment is currently low and many have hypothesized that we are entering a period of sustained boom.[5] Needless to say, a "long boom" of 25 years would, over time, bring greater optimism and confidence to this generation. However, regardless of the outcome, early N-Geners have seen the impact of unemployment on their parents during the recessions of the mid-'80s and the early '90s. Unemployment in late 1982 was almost 11 percent, and in 1992 it was 8 percent. Many N-Geners have seen their parents lose jobs through reengineering, downsizing, rightsizing, smartsizing (as business strategist Gary Hamel says, "smart" and "right" always seem to be down). Yes, they are encouraged by good economic times and a booming stock market, but these are offset by speculation of a coming market crash and international social turmoil. If the kids' families are not in the upper 20 percent income bracket, they have seen the standard of living of their parents remain pretty flat or erode dating back to before 1977 (the year the first N-Geners were born). The N-Geners understand the promise of technology to create and innovate and collaborate. Yet they see much technology in business and governments being used simply to cut costs.

They've concluded that it's not sensible for them to experiment for important parts of their lives. For better or for worse, they can't drop out to pursue their idealistic dreams like the flower children of the '60s. They need to work hard to develop a competency to get out into the work force.

Boomer writers are wrong to be cynical and characterize the pragmatism of youth today as greed or a "me" orientation—not just because they have become a rather pragmatic generation themselves, nor just because the desire of

> I believe that the Internet will greatly affect our lives. The future will be a more technological world—but when we hit 2000, the world isn't going to suddenly be all futuristic. We won't have floating cars like some might imagine. It'll just be another year just like [1997] was. In fact, 2000 will most likely be a setback for computers knowing that we've got to fix them all with the CMOS fixes, etc.
>
> GREG KUBARYK, 14
> Ohio

young people for material things is completely legitimate and understandable, but because N-Geners are taking a very different route than their parents, questioning fundamental tenets of the social order. Their idealism is coming, paradoxically, from pragmatism and from their own personal experience. The practical reality of the N-Geners' immediate future and their prospects for a decent income and life are different than those of their parents decades earlier. They also have very different tools for the collective formulation of ideology, for learning as a generation, and for organizing.

N-Geners have no fear of technology, but they have fear. This was made quite clear to me early in our research, when I wrote an article for the magazine *Advertising Age* introducing the concept of the Net Generation. In the article I explained the idea of the generation lap and also explained that the N-Gen has no fear of technology. The editors inserted a subheadline which referred to the N-Gen as having "no fear." I received many comments about the article. (According to editor David Klein, e-mails were still coming in two months later.) One of these was from 22-year-old Chaim Lodish, who wrote:

> I enjoyed reading Don Tapscott's article about the N-Generation . . .
> It is true that we work and learn differently from our parents . . .
> but in contrast to Don's statement that we have no fears, on the
> contrary we have more fears than our parents. No fear—what kind
> of statement is this? Especially today with AIDS, over-population,
> homelessness, militant militias, guns in the schools, heroin—this is
> not all video games and Web surfing. We are in a position to be
> worse off than our parents, a first in American history.
>
> Also he states that it is difficult to convince [N-Geners]
> that they must have anything except a computer, high-speed
> Internet access, storage space, faster this and faster that. Of course
> they must have that . . . all kids need the Internet. But it is only a
> privileged few that are getting access. What about those unfortu-
> nate people who do not have money for heat and food?
>
> Without sounding too hard on Don's article, I really did
> like the way he described those using the Net "crystallizing around
> a new communications medium," and that censorship will have no
> place with the N-Geners who are used to accessing all of the world.
> Who would have figured out that a communication system created
> by the defense department is becoming the biggest tool of anarchy?

N-Gen Values

To understand where this might be headed, let's take a snapshot of the evolving values of the Net Generation. Yes, they value material things—the good life. The evidence is strong that they are no less idealistic, socially conscious, or connected with others than their boomer parents. In fact, the opposite to conventional wisdom seems to be true.

The N-Geners are the young navigators. They have sent their ship out onto the Net and it returned home safely, carrying riches. They know that their future cannot be trusted to someone else—no corporation or government will ensure them of a full life. One of the collaborators of the Alliance for Converging Technologies, Barry Clavir, coined the term "young navigators" several years ago.[6] The Brain Waves Group, which conducted a survey on young Americans, called them "the self-navigators."[7] Youth must chart their own course and captain their own ship. According to Chip Walker and Elisa Moses of American Demographics, they know that "it's up to me to create my own well being." It's called YO-YO—You're On Your Own.

This should not surprise us. The N-Geners' future is uncertain. While they have great self-confidence and high self-esteem—having been empowered by the digital media—they are nevertheless worried about their future. It's not their own abilities that they are insecure about—it's the external adult world and how it may lack opportunity. They also mistrust governments and elites, a surprising finding given that youth are typically less jaded about such than older people. The N-Geners main priority in life is to get a good education, and their core value is personal competence. And when it comes to actual goals, their focus is not on making money. In 1988, when asked by TRU to define success, 54 percent responded in the category "making money." In 1996, the percentage had fallen to 37 percent.[8]

This generation also strongly values individual rights: the right to be left alone, the right to privacy, the right to have and express their own views. As the N-Geners enter adolescence, and later, they tend to oppose censorship by governments and by parents. They also want to be treated fairly; there is a strong ethos, for example, that "I should share in the wealth I create."

Self-navigation does not mean a rise in individualism, self-absorption, or an ethos of individuality, as pundits of the left sometimes bemoan and pundits of the right and libertarian persuasion sometimes celebrate.

Self-absorption was a theme of the last few years of the boom (Gen-X) and the bust generation, not today's youth. According to Roper Starch, the age group that measures highest on self-absorption is 34-year-olds. N-Geners rely strongly on close personal networks of friends and family. As mentioned earlier, unlike previous generations, they view their parents as the most important source for guidance and emotional support. They also have a great desire to be connected with others—especially with family and close friends, in schools, neighborhoods, interest groups, and online in the virtual communities described in this book.

Our experience indicates that they also have a very strong sense of the common good and of collective social and civic responsibility. They are more knowledgeable than any previous generation and they feel more strongly than adults about social issues. Seventy-five percent of teens believe children are not getting a good education, compared to sixty-two percent of adults. Seventy percent are worried about the economy getting so bad that there will be a major depression, compared to fifty-eight percent of adults. Seventy-four percent are worried that someone in their family will get AIDS, compared to sixty-one percent of adults.[9]

> I think the world will be mostly factories and industry. There's gonna be ,a lot of pollution.
>
> ADAM PERETZ, 11
> California

A whopping 78 percent of teens are concerned that "the environment is so polluted that it will affect our health."[10] However, many researchers have noted a small decline in teen concern on this issue. This should not be interpreted as a turn away from social concerns, as some have argued. Joan Chiaramonte explains this decline as a feeling by youth that environmental protection is an area where they can change things. The child says, "I'm the family recycler," and we're making progress.

Roper Starch measured the issues for which teens (13 to 17) are "very concerned" and found that the top issues were the spread of AIDS (61 percent), kidnapping of children and teenagers (46 percent), use of illegal drugs (44 percent), homelessness (44 percent), crime in your neighborhood (40 percent), discrimination against minorities (42 percent), and pollution of air and water (35 percent).

TRU's 1996 teen survey asked them what values they believe are fundamentally important. The statement tied for the highest level of support was, "It's very important for me to get involved in things that help others and help to make the world better—even if it's not that important to others my age."[11] N-Geners care about others. Bad news for the theorists of Social Darwinism.

N-Geners not only care, they are doing more to try to change things. According to the Higher Education Research Institute at the University of California at Los Angeles, in 1996 a record 72 percent of freshmen reported having performed volunteer work "frequently" or "occasionally" during the past year. This was up 10 percent in the last 8 years. Thirty-eight percent reported spending one or more hours per week volunteering—up from a low of twenty-seven percent when the question was first asked in 1987. Forty-nine percent reported tutoring other students "frequently" or "occasionally" during the past year. This was up from 42 percent in 1986. Thirty-two percent of freshmen considered that "becoming a community leader" is "very important" or an "essential" life goal, versus only thirteen percent in 1971.[12]

N-Geners are big on equal rights. According to Roper Starch, discrimination against minorities is in the top five issues about which youth are "very concerned."[13] Many youths seem to have trouble comprehending racial and gender discrimination which they view with terms like "weird" or "stupid" or "really unfair." Unlike their boomer parents, they are growing up in an increasingly multicultural world. In their virtual worlds the issue of race doesn't come up that much and girls dominate discussion groups and online forums through adolescence. The older discussion groups are still dominated by men, although that will change as the N-Gen gets older. N-Geners have a keener sense of social justice and a greater awareness of privilege than older people. But they also believe that they are the caretakers of the planet and they are as likely to blame themselves as to blame big polluters or companies exploiting child labor for messing up their planet.

Self-reliance is not an ideology but rather is seen practically as something which is necessary. There is no evidence, at least for young people, that self-reliance is extending itself into political terms—that the social safety net should be reduced or eliminated. The N-Geners are alienated from government and the political process but not from the idea of collectively taking social responsibility. Conversely, values of equality and social justice do not translate into support for government or other large institutions. N-Geners are even more mistrustful than their parents of institutions and elites. And as I learned many times working with these young people, authority is not something decreed or announced, but something which must be earned.

N-Geners value their culture with a ferocity which should make boomers proud. They love their music, movies, magazines, some TV shows, video games, computers, software, and the Net.

N-Geners value their body image. Against a backdrop of adults who are overweight and out of shape, boys are pumping up and the girls want to be skinny. Clearly, in the case of girls this is a problem. Over the last few years, the fashion and advertising industries, in association with the print and broadcast industries, have defined a size 2 as the attractive body type. Models used to average size 10. My daughter's teen magazines are full of skeletal child models and articles like "Killer Legs for Summer," "Are Your Thighs Ugly?" and "Stop. How Much Fat is in that Snack?" Will the growing discussions among teenage girls on the Net about the obsession with body image start to turn the tide or perpetuate the myths?

> One major concern I have, which I envision happening in the next few years, is the legalization of marijuana. I firmly believe that this is detrimental to our entire society in much the same ways as smoking is. Yet 75 percent of Americans between 13 and 19 have smoked marijuana before they graduate. The legalization of marijuana will be, and currently is, one of the first things they will ask for.

MATTHEW MACDONALD, 18

A Force for Transformation in All Institutions

As N-Gen culture is extended into society, every institution will have to change. In technology there is a fundamental shift occurring from relationships based on force to relationships based on mutual acceptance. Prior to open systems, computer companies "locked in" their customers with software which would only work on their brand of machine. Computer systems were also hierarchical, centered on mainframe "hosts." Today networks based on open standards have replaced the old paradigm.

The N-Gen will transform business along the same lines. In the old hierarchical firm, employees worked for bosses who told them what to do. If they satisfied their superiors they could advance. People were held within the walls of a given department—in management jargon, "organizational stove pipes." The N-Gen wants networks—internetworked enterprises—not hierarchies and bureaucracies.

As this openness infuses the marketplace, power and authority will shift toward the consumer because of the ease and thoroughness with which savvy buyers can comparison shop. Customers will have the knowledge to be more demanding and will expect products and services tailored to their requirements. We will see the power of openness extending well beyond commerce into other institutions and society as a whole.

Families are becoming more open—not in the sense that they are more permissive, but rather in that authority is shared more than in the past because children are an authority on an important issue. This does not mean that parents abandon their role as parents, but rather that there is a trend toward more discussion, consensus, and family learning.

The very concept of education is also changing as we move from the paradigm of teacher as transmitter of information to students learning through discovery and through new media. The teacher's role is still critical, but changing—to structure the learning experience, motivate, provide context, and integrate disciplines. N-Geners who are used to interactive learning will be increasingly unsatisfied with the old model. As they enter the workforce as teachers and policy makers, they will bring the new paradigm of interactive learning with them.

Governments will also have to become more open as the old hierarchical bureaucracies are becoming irrelevant to the new generation. The N-Gen expects interactivity, responsiveness, and access. Government as broadcaster is in its final days.

None of this means that hierarchies will vanish completely. Society still needs authority and control in areas ranging from child rearing and executive decisions to law and order. But as the N-Gen grows in influence, the trend will be toward networks, not hierarchies, toward open collaboration rather than command, toward consensus rather than arbitrary rule. As students, children, and consumers, N-Geners are causing upward pressure to change the schools, families, and markets. As knowledge workers, educators, government leaders, entrepreneurs and customers, N-Geners will be an unstoppable force for transformation. In the past, many of the so-called post-modern concepts were ideas whose time had not come. They were awaiting a new generation which could embrace and implement them.

From Technology Revolution to Kid Revolution

Our experience with these N-Gen children flies in the face of conventional wisdom on this matter. Their collective experience with the new media and the new youth culture is leading to a rethinking of many tenets of contemporary society. This is not simply a phenomenon of all youth. The bust generation which preceded the N-Gen was markedly staid and conservative in orientation. But today there is a stronger rejection of many aspects of the status quo. A good example is that N-Geners are completely alienated from the two-party political system in the United States.

But this is not all negative, and far from nihilistic. There is much discussion of new ways of thinking, new values, a new "digital nation," and new life goals. Media critic and *Wired* magazine columnist Jon Katz wrote in early 1997: "Although many would balk at defining themselves this way, the digital young are revolutionaries. Unlike the clucking boomers, they are not talking about revolution: they're making one. This is a culture best judged by what it does, not what it says."[14]

True enough. However, the latest news is that N-Geners are starting to articulate, define, and talk about their revolution too. Listen to some of the *Growing Up Digital* kids who, unsolicited, raised the idea of a new revolution.

- "Kids of today are really rebelling against the baby boomer generation. We see the faults in how they want us to grow up," says 18-year-old Courtney Angerer of Oakdale, Minnesota. "I think that has been going on for a long time, but it keeps getting worse and worse and kids are starting to say 'Hey! That's not right, we shouldn't have to live with this.' Maybe kids of today are growing up a lot faster than our parents are letting us, and this is what has resulted from the battle between generations."

- "Although it might be called a technological revolution, or even a child's revolution, I believe it to be a worldwide revolution," says Kelly Richards, 13, of Calgary, Alberta. "One which every person on this planet can gain something from, a revolution of the human spirit in general."

- "I believe that a kid revolution is the technical revolution. I feel that my age group [14 to 18] has missed this revolution," says Jason Motylinski, 18, of Oakdale, Minnesota. "The kids who will really lead a 'kid revolution' are those who are getting experience at home when they are 5 to 10 years old. Those are the kids who will reap the most profit from this Internet growth."

- "I think the Net is probably changing the nature of childhood because it opens the world to you," says 16-year-old Lauren Verity of Victoria, Australia. "You can get information on anything, whereas before I don't think kids cared that much. Now I think we are starting to want to care."

- "The information revolution is revolutionizing culture and spurring a revolution [in society]. The upcoming revolution will not be violent but rather a revolution in consciousness. The globalization of ideas is spawning a global communication, not just among the elite. It is creating a new global awareness and consciousness, which we need, because things are not the way they should be," says Chaim Lodish, 22.

One attribute common to boomers when they were teens and today's teenagers is disaffection. This has been described as an eternal feeling among groups of young people. But this capacity to feel disaffected, isolated, alienated, and even oppressed changes from generation to generation. This is not to say that adolescents are paranoid. Yet they are often treated as political nonentities even though they have begun to develop political identities. They are considered by many social institutions, including government and the media, to be more of a menace which must be regulated with curfews and school metal detectors, than as an asset with the secured funding of, say, community programs during the preschool or after-school years, having access to life- and job-skills training and peer-mediated conflict resolution training.

Historically, youth have had a culture dictated from within that excludes the participation of other age groups. This has always affected parents, educators, and marketers who have found the mystique of adolescence an intriguing subject for study if only because this mystique was impossible to decode. Simply taking into account the typical cultural by-products such as fashion, popular music, and hairstyles, which stand as benchmarks for measuring the attitudes of particular groups of youth, everything seems to suggest that feelings of alienation, disenfranchisement, and disaffection are a stronger force among the present crop of young people than among previous groups. Remarkably, fashion, popular music, and hairstyles are less of a factor in binding N-Geners together as a group. In fact, this group prefers to defy grouping.

"I think kids being able to express themselves more openly comes from the realization that it is OK not to be a popular airhead, sports-oriented, conforming-to-what-everyone-believes type person," says 18-year-old Courtney Angerer. "To tell you the truth, in my school it's become 'cool' to be weird and not part of the popular crowd."

Courtney wasn't the only N-Gener who noticed that teenagers, increasingly, seem to have the ability to turn alienation, disaffection, and disenfranchisement into independence, individuality, and activism. With this shift in attitude has come a demand that the perception of youth change, and young people are using technology to express this shift in attitude. They are, in fact, taking back and taking over the media.

"It's time for people to erase this view that older people have of teens and youth today. You know, that we're all just these drug-crazed kids, or whatever, who are never going to understand what responsibility really is," says 14-year-old e-zine writer Neasa Coll. "I think this is a chance to get rid of that and show them what we can really do."

The critical, questioning aspect of the N-Gen psyche, noted earlier, is naturally leading to a questioning of the way things are. According to 18-year-old Matthew MacDonald: "If you are good at giving the teacher what he or she wants, you will do well and be considered 'responsible.' But have you really accomplished anything?" He concludes: "Questioning things won't get you anywhere in today's world, but in the future, it will be the people who questioned and were ridiculed—the people who did not 'understand'—who will inherit the earth."

Boom and Echo: Four Scenarios for the Future

What kind of relationship can we expect between the Boom and its Echo? Many factors will determine what happens, but two intersect significantly. First is the degree to which the baby boom and the boomer attitudes toward youth, their culture, and their use of the new media are hostile or positive (unknown at this point). Second is the degree to which N-Geners embrace the new media, both in terms of what proportion of the N-Generation becomes digitally active and to what extent the new media create a forum for the discussion, learning, and action of the new generation (likely). The four possible outcomes are depicted in Fig. 13.1.

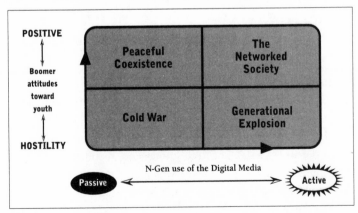

Figure 13.1
Four scenarios for the future.

1. Peaceful coexistence.

The boomer media and other institutions come to accept youth. They understand that youth culture is not something bad but the natural expression of a generation of their own lifestyle, media, and autonomy. They realize that the threat of youth crime is a myth; not only is it on the decline, but if you separate out the drug-related crimes of a tiny proportion of the population, crimes which are restricted to small parts of some cities and some schools, then there really never was an upsurge in violent youth crime. At the same time, for reasons unpredictable, the N-Gen's participation in the digital media is passive. As digital television enters the digital world, N-Geners revert back to watching TV programs rather than interacting with information sources, chat rooms, games, discussion groups, MUDs, and the other technologies described in this book. Computers and the Net end up having little impact in their lives; the schools do not change; young people stay a relatively passive force. The two generations get along, and society muddles along as it has done for the last few decades.

2. Cold war.

The unease and hostility of the boomer media and other institutions about youth increases to a level of full metal nastiness. They are on kids' cases even more. They are successful in censoring the Net, curtailing youth activities, and reducing the Net to a rigid, tepid, and sterile environment—not unlike television. Boomers resist ceding leadership in business and society to the N-Gen. Young people, lacking the new media as a tool for learning and organizing, remain relatively powerless and become cynical. Opportunities in the work force are limited because the economy is not expanding and the boomers continue to hold the good jobs. The relationship between generations is tense but a standoff.

3. Generational explosion.

Boomer society and institutions intensify negative attitudes toward youth and youth culture but cannot or chose not to control the new media and its evolution. Parents permit their children to use the Net at home and at school. The Net grows in ubiquity, function, reliability, and speed. A generation of close to 90 million young people in the United States and Canada alone uses the most powerful communications medium to learn as a generation. A new youth radicalization emerges as youth take their media to debate, advocate, acquire knowledge, mobilize, and fight for their rights. New contending ideologies emerge which are counterposed to the growing conservatism of older generations. New youth leaders come to the fore to challenge the status quo. Major social dissonance and conflict occurs. The environment is volatile and explosive.

4. The networked society.

Boomer institutions lighten up on youth. Governments and businesses start tackling the social origins of drug use and crime rather than building jails for young people. The education system is reinvented, embracing the new models of learning. Businesses learn from N-Gen companies—shifting to become "internetworked enterprises," thereby becoming more effective and growing the economy. N-Gen entrepreneurs have an opportunity to flourish and N-Gen-style businesses proliferate. Social development, tackling racial imbalances and improving the lot of the growing underclass are all possible because of improved levels of wealth creation in a new economy. The digital divide has been addressed and an entire new generation shares in the largesse of a new communications medium. Parents and children share the experience of this revolution together, creating open families. The generation lap is reduced because adults are learning about the new media from children. New models of governance emerge and governments are reinvented. Truer forms of democracy emerge, in which citizens have more control over their own destiny.

The Coming Generational Explosion?

Unfortunately, given current trends, the most likely scenario is number three. There is no sign of *glasnost* in the attitudes toward kids and their media. And the kids seem quite determined to push forward with their media and culture.

As the first of the N-Gen come of age, there are some serious contradictions between generations emerging. These foreshadow dissonance, conflict, or worse. While there are many exceptions, the dialectics are clear.

Contradiction 1: *The N-Gen is best equipped to create wealth.* Older generations are hoarding power and wealth. They are stashing massive fortunes in mutual funds and other investments. Mutual fund companies now have more than $3 trillion in assets. Last year more than $223 billion was added to equity funds. This is $28 billion more than all the money in equity funds only nine years ago, i.e., total equity fund holdings were $195 billion in 1988. The wealthier of these older people are locking themselves in their gated communities, afraid of "youth crime." When it comes to cutting, they have an affection for the things that seem to hurt children most—child care, youth programs, education, support to single moms. Older people want more spending in health care. Youth want the problems causing crime to be addressed. Older people want tougher sentences, more prisons, and more police. They voted for governments which created huge deficits through not just social but military spending. They have come up with a potpourri of plans to relieve themselves of taxes, from cutting capital gains to a flat tax. If these efforts are successful, it appears one of their legacies to the N-Generation could be crushing debt or a decimated social safety net.

Contradiction 2: *The echo is a generation which seeks to control its destiny.* Boomers have control. This is unlike the natural process of one generation taking over from another who is retiring. It appears that the N-Gen will be ready to take over or transform the reins of power while the boomers are still in their prime. There is much irony in this situation. Children today seek more democratic families and environments. They want greater influence in the schools. They are concerned about war, poverty, and the environment and want do to something about these problems. They want to enjoy their pop culture. They are a threat to boomers for seeking the same things that their parents wanted a generation earlier. The difference is the TV generation was poorly equipped to follow through, compared to the generation of the digital media.

Contradiction 3: *Adults own and control the new media, but it is children who are most fluent.* Media Lab director Nicholas Negroponte argues that middle-aged people are "too busy to hassle with hard-to-use computers, sluggish services, and the noisiness of the Internet." He describes such people as the digital homeless and then notes that they "also happen to run our schools, our neighborhoods, our companies, and our country." This is creating a misalignment between those who control and those who understand. Of course, there are millions of boomers who understand the new media. Most Net users are adults. But increasingly the proportion of N-Geners fluent with the new media will grow relative to the proportion of boomers who are fluent. By the year 2017, when the last N-Gener turns 20, the vast majority of the largest generation ever will have fully embraced the digital revolution. This will not be true for the boomers.

Contradiction 4: *The great promise of the N-Geners' technology and their generation is dissonant with the perceived and possibly real opportunities before them.* The N-Gen culture and the new media seem ripe with possibilities, but N-Geners' future integrating into boomer-controlled organizations is often pretty bleak. Will they get jobs? Will they be forced to work in disciplines outside those they love? Will they be stuck in a company of people who don't "get it?" This problem is present in America and severe in many other countries of the world.

Contradiction 5: *There is a conflict between the adult world of accepting black-and-white absolutes and the N-Gen world of complexity.* On television and for the

TV generation, things are black and white. Many things are posed in terms of good guys and bad guys. For example, citizens don't debate differing perspectives in elections, we have campaigns based on TV advertising and the 40-second clip on the evening news. Candidates are respectively proposing to destroy the country or save the country—no middle ground.

But this is not the N-Gen world. Here is a generation of youth who are constantly being reminded that everything they see and hear may not be true. What is real on the Net and what is not? What should I say in response to that comment from Mooselips? What contextual anchors can I evoke to make what's happening here make sense? This half-tone, complex world of information, pointers, judgment, and interpersonal interaction is the antithesis of the good guys/bad guys world of adults. The growing wisdom of the new youth stands in stark contrast to the utter dumbness of much of the adult world.

Contradiction 6: *There is a gap between what adults say and what they do.* As Cityspace cocreator Coco Conn says: "Corporate America is everywhere with billboards and advertising. The message is consume, consume, consume—from alcohol to cigarettes. But we keep telling our kids to 'say no to drugs,' no to this and that, but they wonder why we can't 'say no' to war, or pollution, or poverty." Perhaps it has always been like this. Clearly, such contradictions of government and business leaders who spoke of peace and made war in the '60s fueled radicalization of the boomers as well. However, given the interactive and many-to-many nature of the new media, such contradictions surfaced more readily.

Contradiction 7: *There is a gap between what adults say and what they really say.* It is not just words and actions in conflict but the words themselves—serving to drive further wedges between generations. Some examples:

- The most vociferous opponents of the new technology are, curiously, some of the loudest critics of the danger of a digital divide. In literally dozens of discussions where I have attempted to explain that the Net is not wrecking the lives of our youth, someone always seems to raise the issue of unequal access—as if that were another criticism of why technology is so bad for society. But it seems contradictory to be concerned about media "have-nots" when the media are defined as a bad thing.

- Critics like Theodore Roszak oppose the use of technology in the schools for reasons which include, "By the time a school decides to buy anything it will be out of date."[15] That is, we shouldn't use technology because it keeps improving.

- Many of the most vocal authorities on the dangers of the new technology for children have never actually used this technology themselves, and therefore make statements which appear contradictory and foolish to children.

- The loudest supporters of government censorship of children's access to the new media purport to be acting out of concern for children's rights—rights they would trample.

Surely the boom is becoming a generation stricken with cognitive dissonance.

Contradiction 8: *There is a conflict between today's youth and a generation of boomers that clings to youth beyond its time.* The baby boom was followed by the baby bust. Generation X (the last six years of the boom) and the baby bust children are the displaced ones. They've had trouble getting into the job market, trouble getting the good jobs (which were already taken), and difficulties purchasing homes, and they have been shut out of much economic and social activity. They lack the confidence of the boomers, and have, except for those who became interested in computing before their time, no special qualities which would threaten boomer hegemony. The middle- and upper-class boomers have had a pretty easy ride. They also tend to romanticize their youth as, after all, it was a good time to be young.

Francois Ricard in *The Lyric Generation,* describes a generation that will not, need not, grow old. "When there is no one to follow, when the young, as they become older, no longer have to step aside, when they are no longer displaced or dislodged by the younger behind them, why should they become old? Why should they not continue, even as the wrinkles deepen on their faces, to consider themselves as the natural custodians of youth?"[16] A generation whose creed was *don't trust anyone over 30,* has settled into the groove of running things. And surely our birth certificates lie, as we are forever young—that's why we are doing such a good job in power. The only problem with the narrative is the N-Generation—this rather huge wave of people whose birth certificates say they *are* young. In a brilliant article on youth crime, Katrina Onstad discusses this: "The result is that their relationship with the younger generation is tenuous at least, hostile at best." The boomers have concluded that the kids "are doing it all wrong."[17] Or, as the saying now goes, "Don't trust anyone *under* 30!"

Kids' culture—their attitudes, their weird obsession with technology, and of course their violence—are all evidence that they have it wrong and the boomers have the true youth franchise. After all, can you really compare the greats like Roy Orbison, Led Zeppelin, Credence Clearwater Revival, and Janis Joplin with today's "alternative music"? Rap doesn't even have a melody, and it's causing all this violence, right? And what's with MTV and those chat groups?

But the N-Gen is not the baby bust. This new generation is not the puny 90-pound weakling its predecessor was. It has the demographic muscle to take on the baby boom. The boom's echo is bigger than it is. Plus, the N-Gen has all the advantages in terms of the historically critical capabilities described throughout this book.

Further, N-Geners rather love their media and culture. As a result, many middle-aged people attempt unnecessarily, inappropriately, and often unsuccessfully to censor, stop, curtail, or otherwise control it. The old song "You won't take away my music" rings with some irony.

This is setting us up for the battle of the generational titans. Unless the boomers have a change of heart, the two biggest generations in history are on a collision course. Given their knowledge of and access to powerful new communications tools, their revolt will make the '60s protests look like kid stuff.

What might be the big issues in such a conflict? Clearly, this is difficult if not impossible to predict. However, in a context of generational tensions domestically, and volatility on the world scene, many fault lines can open. The list could include differences regarding the allocation of social and governmental resources; the distribution of wealth if it polarizes either along generational lines or along class lines—with a huge proportion of the N-Gen feeling disenfranchised; differences regarding values as the massive baby boom grows defensive and possibly cantankerous with a siege mentality; the nature of governance, with the N-Gen favoring new models; a global versus isolationist or protectionist perspective; and conflicts within corporations, the educational system, governments, churches, and other institutions regarding differing perspectives which flow from N-Geners' and boomers' very different cultures and views of things. Add to this list differences regarding methods of responding to the international crises which undoubtedly will arise as the world reorders itself. Within each nation there are also unique issues, and already there are storm warnings in many countries that youth are experiencing a gap between their expectations and reality.

Interactivity and Youth Radicalization

The '60s antiwar and related movements were primarily phenomena of youth who broke from the values and ideology of their parents, government, business, and other major social institutions. Sociologists refer to this as *youth radicalization*. Television played a role. How might the interactive media affect the formation of values and world view of the N-Gen? Could it provide an historically unprecedented platform for social organization and struggle?

The shift is one from the mass to the molecular media, as explained earlier. Similarly, children are like free molecules which, with the right change in conditions or catalyst, can turn from a silent solid to a boiling fluid to an explosive gas. Think pressure cooker and the transformation of water to steam.

The boomer watched a village in Vietnam being napalmed and saw the aftermath, almost real-time, as a naked, burned child ran screaming down a country road. Like today's N-Gen child, the boomers had time to question authority, relative freedom from responsibility, and access to information (albeit limited compared to that of the N-Gen). But what could you do to learn more about an issue or to meet like-minded youth who were also uneasy about the way of the world? Perhaps you saw a poster for an antiwar demonstration. You might come across an article. If you were a university student, perhaps the student council organized a teach-in or a campus debate to discuss the issues. Basically, your vehicles for knowledge and collaboration were pretty similar to those of previous generations. But unlike previous generations, you saw the war and some of its effects on a daily basis, and occasionally a more in-depth analysis documented by Walter Cronkite, through the medium of TV.

The youth radicalization of the 1960s was primarily a function of two factors—a massive demographic wave of young people combined with the effects of a new communications medium. These created a generation which could question the status quo, such as segregation or wars, and which could feel its power through television.

Multiply those effects tenfold and we can begin to anticipate what an N-Gen radicalization would be like. Today's young people who question some aspect of government policy, business practice, or anything else can instantly find others who share their concerns. They can present their views, listen to others, and more. They have a powerful, global medium to organize. At the speed of light.

We can already see this in nascent social movements around the world, from the media guerrillas organizing to expose unethical corporations that are pushing smoking or anorexia or exploiting child labor, to the surging students in Serbia working to topple a bankrupt and authoritarian regime. The Net is their vehicle for revolution—their tract, megaphone, teach-in, bookstore, fundraising event, demonstration, makeshift stage, and war room all in one.

I recently discussed this issue with a group of business leaders. Lawrence White, who is an executive with a very large American engineering company, made an insightful comment. As a father of three, he speaks with some personal experience (his 15-year-old daughter asked for a high-speed ISDN Internet connection for Christmas). White agreed that a generational explosion is likely, but added that youth have the upper hand because of their alacrity with Net. "The kids will win. They'll out-organize us," he said. "They also trust each other more than we trust each other. I wouldn't worry about them. I'd worry about us."

Furthermore, in the '60s the boom youth radicalization had a finite number of competing paradigms regarding how youth could fulfill its aspirations and make a better world. There was the liberal capitalist perspective; communism (various flavors); the third-world revolutionary view as expressed by Che Guevara; black power; radical feminism; anarchists; and socialism or the social democracy stream (primarily outside the United States). There were also tiny right-wing and libertarian sects. Any mass demonstration from the '60s was divided not only by Vietnam veterans' group, school, or city but into contingents representing these contending ideologies. Problems in the society posed the question of ideology—how do we move forward?—and the number of alternative views was limited. Today, most of these have vanished, to be replaced by a myriad of competing molecules ranging from every conceivable political perspective to every imaginable religious group or unimaginable bizarre sect. This creates a much more volatile and unpredictable situation. It has promise as fresh contending ideas have an opportunity to debate and fight it out for clarity. It is also full of peril for children and for everyone because when molecules are put into motion, their direction is quite unknown.

From Broadcast to Interactive Democracy

The biggest storm warning is the N-Gen attitude that young people need to control their own destiny. We can expect that this will evolve to embrace *political* control. This is a generation which will not be happy just watching politicians from the vast selection of 2 parties doing 30-second ads in election campaigns and then watching them doing 20-second clips on the evening news for the next 4 years.

Just as the new media and the N-Gen spell trouble for broadcast learning and the schools, they also spell trouble for broadcast democracy and current forms of governance. Tectonic demographic, technological, and economic shifts typically bring far-reaching changes in the political infrastructure. Democracy as TV show is in deep trouble.

Largely through the initiative of vice president Al Gore, much work has been done to understand the implications of the new infrastructure for the "reinvention of government"—a euphemism for fundamental changes to the business of government and the delivery of government programs enabled by the new technology. However, as the N-Gen comes into voting age, it may be time to think about the Net and its implications on the democratic process itself.[18–27]

In *The Digital Economy,* I referred to works by Harold Innis and his student, Marshall McLuhan, who previously explained how new media have precipitated political changes throughout history. As Innis wrote in 1953: "Monopolies or oligopolies of knowledge have been built up . . . [to support] forces chiefly on the defensive, but improved technology has strengthened the position of forces on the offensive and compelled realignments favoring the vernacular." Or, as interpreted by Alliance president David Ticoll: "Libraries based on clay documents enabled the priest-based monopoly of knowledge in ancient Babylon. The invention of papyrus scrolls and the alphabet was a key to the limited democracy of Greek city states and the rule of law in ancient Rome. The improved portability, ease of use and durability of parchment-based, bound books created by the papacy and monastic orders were critical to the speed of conversion to Christianity. Paper and the printing press reproduced religious text in the vernacular and led to the Reformation, the end of feudalism, and the emergence of parliamentary democracy in tandem with the industrial revolution."

In ancient civilizations, slaves had no access to knowledge and consequently no economic or political power. In the agricultural age, knowledge began to disperse, first to the feudal nobility, and to some extent to the serfs who acquired access to land and its fruits for their efforts. In the 19th century, access to machinery created the industrial revolution. In the industrial age, the silk-hatted tycoons dominated, but the worker was more than a cog in the machine. Work became social, rather than done in isolation; literacy and knowledge rose in the population. Workers could organize to acquire formal strength—through trade or labor unions—to defend their interests. The silk-hatted tycoons acquired wealth, but the standard of living of others rose as well—as did their economic power. Unions took political action in the 19th century through the creation of political parties—which continue today as the social democratic parties of most developed countries.

In the 21st century, wealth will flow from knowledge—an asset more widely and freely available than ever before. As information flow becomes democratized, the distribution of real power, if not formal power, is changing. The Age of Networked Intelligence could bring new power and freedom, particularly for that two-thirds of the workforce who are knowledge workers.

In the 1992 election, many people cringed when Ross Perot proposed the electronic town hall, conjuring the image of the electronic mob. To many observers, voting "yes" or "no" from your home or place of work could be dangerous. In addition to possible manipulation, such daily referenda could actually undermine a true democratic process which is based on participation. Motions put to a vote are usually well-refined dis-

> There are so many young people voicing their own conflicting opinions that our future world will contain hundreds of political parties and groups, and no one will be able to decide on anything. It will be the first time our world hasn't had to deal with voter apathy.
>
> NEASA COLL, 14

> Well, that Craig Kielburger has a whole worldly campaign going on, I think he calls it "Free the Children." He went to India the same time our Prime Minister went to make a trade deal with them and upstaged him so that we couldn't possibly make the trade thing until they would stop child slavery and he's only in gr. 8!
>
> He's raised hundred of thousands of dollars from speeches that he makes to organizations. My teacher says that if our schools get involved and get petitions out, it could really stop it. We saw in this movie that this 7-year-old girl was made to take apart syringes and she was stepping on all the needles and had no protection at all!

FREERAIN, 13 tells MOOSELIPS
in the FreeZone Election Chat

tillations of large and complex issues. They result from a long process involving conflicts, contradictions, and compromises. To understand a motion and to vote responsibly, citizens need to participate in some form of a refining process. The notion of an "instant referendum" conducted electronically has been widely viewed with skepticism by most analysts.[28] The Perot campaign did, however, serve to raise the issue of electronic democracy in a high-profile manner.

While there has been much discussion about electronic democracy, few governments show any seriousness about the issue and virtually none are doing anything about it. The main impediment is said to be the digital divide—that is, how can we contemplate changing the democratic process when universal access does not exist. But this is an excuse for inaction. The divide can be addressed, as described in this book. Besides, with digital TV and digital radio just around the corner, and with computers in libraries, community computing centers, and workplaces everywhere, access should not be an issue. I'm convinced the real issues are cultural. Older generations of lawmakers and citizens can't even think about changing the paradigm of democracy. But the Net Generation can and will.

The N-Gen will want to use their media to shape the body politic. Allison Ellis described MOOSELIPS' campaign for United States President on FreeZone. "But the kids were campaigning and making their own home pages and debating over their issues and promises about what they would do for FreeZone—MOOSELIPS had his own campaign staff—they had weekly meetings and wrote press releases—it was all funny stuff, but there were some good debates about where the economy should go and that politicians should be more fun and lighten up."

The FreeZone children participating in this election were 10 to 14 years old. They are not talking about some new concept of democracy—they're doing it.

They are accustomed to empowerment, open discussion, and immediacy—all anti-thetical to the disempowerment, myopic discussion, and bureaucratic governance processes of today. They want to interact and get to the bottom of things, to sift information and decide. They care deeply about social problems and cannot com-prehend why governments seem so ineffectual. Their orientation is their neighbor-hood and their global virtual communities, not the nation-state. They are used to being actors, not spectators.

When the N-Gen comes of age, the world will be smaller and infinitely more complex. We have no idea what problems will be presented to these young people, what new dreams they will dream, what bold new solutions they will forge. One thing is for sure: democracy as we know it will be finished. Perhaps we should get serious today about rethinking our notion of governance and what it means to be free.

A Medium-in-Waiting

Until recently, the Net has been a place primarily for outsiders, geeks, radicals, or visionaries to engage in marginalized debates, esoteric discussions, and vanguard contemplation. As one of these people, dating back to the '70s, I was struck by how someday this milieu might come into the mainstream and be a force for change. But the impediments for two decades were not simply technological; nor were they caused by any lack of hosts on the Net. Rather, this was a *medium-in-waiting*. It was a technological revolution not in search of a problem, but in search of a new gen-eration which, unencumbered by old paradigms, could embrace and exploit it to its full potential. Through the N-Gen, the Net is becoming a medium for social awakening.

The N-Gen is transforming the new media from a cult enclave to a cacoph-onous cauldron of millions. Through their massive demographic muscle and uncon-strained minds, N-Geners are creating a new world. The N-Gen is constructing a place where, unlike the tepid, sterilized one-way conduit of the mass media, any idea, no matter how threatening to the contemporary order, can have a voice. For better or for worse, the biggest generation in American history is beginning to take its medium for discovery, for debate, for clarity, and for action.

The second half of the century was dominated by a generation. During that period, strong models of mass media, the enterprise, work, commerce, family, play, and social life were established. The new media and the new generation are beginning to shatter those old ways—and our evidence points to a better world, if we will it. This massive wave of youth has rights, growing aspirations, truly awesome capabili-ties, and nascent demands which are far-reaching.

These young people will bring and implement radical views regarding how business should be conducted and on the process of democratic governance. They will be a generation which can learn, as a generation, unlike any other. They will seek to protect the planet, and I believe they will find racism, sexism, and other vile remnants of bygone days both weird and unacceptable. They will seek to share in the wealth they create. They will want power in every domain of economic and political life. The big remaining question for older generations is whether we will share that power with gratitude or will the N-Gen be forced to take it from us? Will we have the wisdom and courage to accept the N-Geners, their culture, and their media, and grant them the opportunity to fulfill their destiny?

Listen to the children.

Appendix

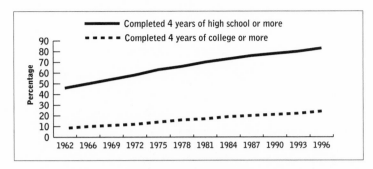

Figure A.1, Chapter 7

Percentage of population completing 4 years of high school or more vs. percentage of population completing 4 years of college or more.

Data: U.S. Census Bureau: Education and Social Stratification Branch, Alliance for Converging Technologies.

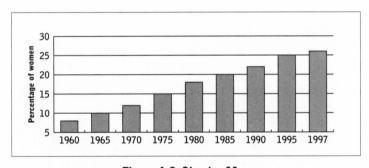

Figure A.2, Chapter 11

Percent of women in the labor force who have children.

Data: U.S. Bureau of Labor Statistics.

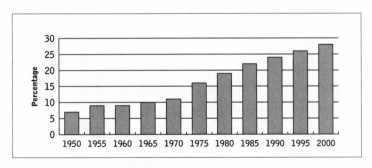

Figure A.3, Chapter 11

One parent families as a percentage of total families with children under 18.

Data: U.S. Census Bureau, Alliance for Converging Technologies.

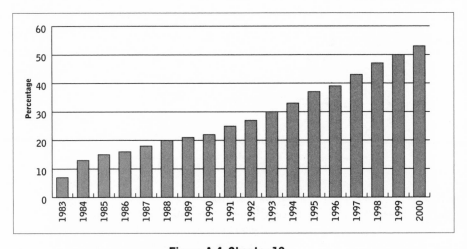

Figure A.4, Chapter 12
U.S. computer ownership
(% of households owning a personal computer).

Data: Electronic Industries Association, Jupiter Communications.

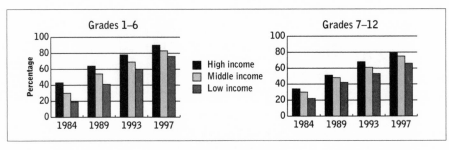

Figure A.5, Chapter 12
Used a computer at school.

Data: U.S. Census Bureau.

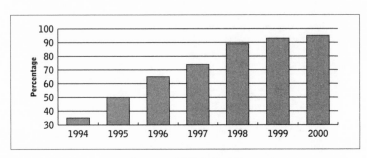

Figure A.6, Chapter 12
Internet access in public school.

Data: National Center for Education Statistics.

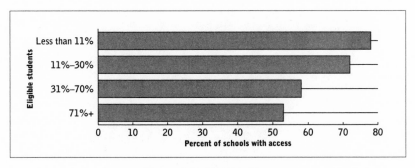

Figure A.7, Chapter 12

Schools with Internet access by percentage of students eligible
for free or reduced price lunch, 1996.

Data: National Center for Education Statistics.

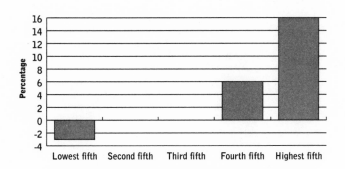

Figure A.8, Chapter 12

Percentage change in mean inflation-adjusted income
since 1973.

Data: A Roper Starch Worldwide Analysis of U.S. Census Data.

Notes

Chapter 1

1. "Roper Youth Report," 1996 Roper Starch Worldwide Inc. Sixty-seven percent report to having used a personal computer at home, at school, or someplace else, in the last 30 days. Survey taken in 1996.
2. Teenage Research Unlimited press release, January 1996, and "Teenage Marketing & Lifestyle Update," Spring 1997.
3. Jenkins, Henry. "Putting 'Boy Culture' Back in the Home: Gender Genre and Virtual Play Spaces," from Barbie to Mortal Kombat: A Conference on Gender and Computer Games, MIT, 5 April 1997.
4. The Electronic Industries Association.
5. "Teenage Marketing & Lifestyle Update, Spring 1997/Wave 29," Teenage Research Unlimited, Inc.
6. Kay, Alan. From a speech given to the Superhighway Summit at the University of California at Los Angeles, 1994. As cited in *Wired*, May 1994, p. 76.
7. Lasch, Christopher. "Revolt of the Elites: Have They Canceled Their Allegiance to America?" *Harpers Magazine*, November 1994.
8. Data from a presentation by Rick Little, president of the International Youth Foundation, cited at the World Economic Forum, Davos, Switzerland, 1997.
9. As cited in a column entitled "2B1" by Nicolas Negroponte in *Wired*, June 1997, p. 184.

Chapter 2

*"Charlie" reprinted with permission: The Toronto Star Syndicate.

1. Foot, David. *Boom, Bust and Echo*. Toronto: Macfarlane, Walter and Ross, 1996, p. 19.
2. U.S. Department of Commerce, *The Statistical Abstract of the United States*. Bureau of the Census, Washington (various years).
3. Edmondson, Brad. "The Next Baby Boom," *American Demographics*, September 1995.
4. U.S. Census Bureau, *Families by Presence of Own Children Under 18: 1950 to Present*. U.S. Census Bureau Web site, www.census.gov/
5. Foot, David. Ibid., p. 21.
6. U.S. Census Bureau, Ibid.
7. Stoler, Peter. *The Computer Generation*. Facts on File, New York, 1984, p. 8.
8. Ungar, Harley Guttman. "Computoys Dawn on Computer Horizons," *Digital Kids Report*, August 1996.
9. According to a *Wall Street Journal* study reported 14 April 1997.
10. Jupiter Communications, "Demographics," *Digital Kids Report*, August 1996.
11. As cited on *CyberAtlas* site, http://www.cyberatlas.com, May 1997.
12. "Teenage Marketing & Lifestyle Update, Spring 1997/Wave 29," Teenage Research Unlimited, Inc.
13. I must confess culpability in the phrase "Paradigm Shift" becoming a buzzword. (I heard someone recently talking about how they were going to have a paradigm shift in the decoration of their living room.) However, as one of the people who first used the term as applied to technology, business, and society, I hope you will indulge me. Besides, I think the term, properly used, is a good one.
14. Bank, David. "Selling Pants on PointCast," *Wall Street Journal*, 13 December 1996, p. A1.
15. *BusinessWeek*, 24 February 1997, pp. 95–104.
16. AOL Press Release
17. Jupiter Communications
18. Odyssey Research
19. The Promise and Perils of Emerging Information Technologies.
20. *CyberAtlas* Web site, www.cyberatlas.com, 19 March 1997.
21. From comments at dinner at the World Economic Forum, Davos, Switzerland, February 1997.

Chapter 3

*"Adam" reprinted with permission: Universal Press Syndicate.

1. "HomeNet: A Study of Electronic Communication by Families and the Transformation of Home Computing." Human Computer Interaction Institute, Carnegie Mellon University, Pittsburgh, 1995, (http://homenet.andrew.cmu.edu).
2. Papert, Seymour. *The Connected Family.* Atlanta: Longstreet Press, 1996, p. 30.
3. For example, the groundbreaking work by Turkle, Sherry. *The Second Self.* New York: Simon & Schuster, 1984.
4. "Nerve Wracking Demo News from U.S. State Department," *Washington Post,* 20 February 1997.
5. For a good collection see Carroll, Jim. *Surviving the Information Age.* Prentice Hall Canada, 1997.
6. McLuhan, Marshall. *Understanding Media: The Extensions of Man.* Toronto: The New American Library of Canada, 1966, p. 45.
7. Kraut, Scherlis, Mukhopadhyay, Manning, Kiesler, et al. "HomeNet: A Study of Electronic Communication by Families and the Transformation of Home Computing." Human Computer Interaction Institute, Carnegie Mellon University, 1996. (Downloaded from the World Wide Web, 29 July 1996.)
8. Mitchell, Susan. "The Next Baby Boom," *American Demographics,* October 1995, http://www.marketingtools.com/publications/AD/95_AD/9510_AD/AD813.htm
9. Hulbert, Ann. "Politicians, Like, Really on Teens Case," *USA Today,* 21 November 1997.
10. Roszak, Theodore. "Internet as Teacher Makes Students Stupid," *New Internationalist,* 1997.
11. Reimer, Susan. "The Internet, Nude Women and Your Son," *The Baltimore Sun,* 26 January 1997.
12. Kapica, Jack. "Heaven's Gate Thrown Open to the World," *Globe and Mail,* 4 April 1997.
13. Bly, Robert. *The Sibling Society.* New York: Addison Wesley, 1996, p. 169.
14. Drotner, Kirsten. "Modernity and Media Panic," *Media Cultures: Reappraising Transnational Media,* p. 43.
15. "Video games are good for you," *The Next Generation,* May 1997, p. 9.
16. Ibid., p. 162.
17. Drotner, Kristen. Ibid., p. 57.
18. Thorsby, Mary. "Making the Grade: Apple in Education," Apple Education World Wide Web site, 28 May 1996.

Chapter 4

*"Hi and Lois" reprinted with permission: The Toronto Star Syndicate.

1. Mostly this definition is from the ArtLex Web site—www.aristotle.com/skystorage/Art/ArtLex.html
2. Reingold, Howard. *Virtual Communities: Homesteading on the Electronic Frontier.* New York: Harper Perennial, 1993, p. 5.
3. *CyberAtlas,* www.cyberatlas.com, 12 March 1997.
4. Postman, Neil. *Amusing Ourselves to Death: Public Disclosure in the Age of Show Business.* New York: Penguin Books, 1985, p. 8.
5. Postman, Neil. Ibid., p. 12.
6. Tapscott, Don. *Office Automation: A User-Driven Method.* New York: Plenum Publishing, 1981.
7. Stephensen, Neal. *Snow Crash.* New York: Bantam Books, 1992.
8. Eco, Umberto. "Afterward from The Future of the Book," *Harper's,* October 1996, p. 30.
9. WGBH Research. *The Coach Potato Chronicle.* December 1994, www.wgbh.org.
10. The New Museum of Contemporary Art, "alt.youth.media" exhibit held 6 September to 5 November 1996.

Chapter 5

*"For Better or Worse" reprinted with permission: Universal Press Syndicate.

1. Barr, James, and Barr, Theodore. "The Pentium Bug War Ends PR as We Know It," © Omegacom Inc., 1994. See Omegacom's home page for a discussion of the topic.
2. Mead, G. H. *Mind, Self and Society.* University of Chicago Press, 1934.

3. Piaget, Jean. *The Construction of Reality in the Child.* New York: Free Press, 1954.
4. Erickson, E. H. *Childhood and Society,* New York: Norton, 1950.
5. Berk, Laura E. *Child Development.* Boston: Allyn and Bacon, 1997. A balanced and comprehensive discussion of the self and identity along with the other major issues in child development.
6. Turkle, Sherry. *Life on the Screen.* New York: Simon & Shuster, 1995, p. 14. The contemporary tour de force on computers and the self.
7. "Intelligence: Knowns and Unknowns: Report of a Task Force established by the Board of Scientific Affairs of the American Psychological Association," 7 August 1995.
8. Sternberg, R. J., and Detterman, Dr. D.K. (eds.). *What Is Intelligence? Contemporary Viewpoints on Its Nature and Definition.* Norwood, NJ: Abler.
9. Gardner, H. *Frames of Mind: The Theory of Multiple Intelligences.* New York: Basic Books, 1983.
10. Piaget, Jean. *The Psychology of Intelligence.* Totowa. NJ: Littlefield Adams, 1972.
11. "Kid Currents," *Smart Kid Magazine,* July 1996, p. 12.
12. Berk, Laura E. Ibid., pp. 603–4.
13. Valkenburg, Patti, and van der Voort, Tom H. A. "Influence of TV on Daydreaming and Creative Imagination: A Review of Research," *Psychological Bulletin,* 1994, p. 335.
14. Negroponte, Nicholas. *being digital.* New York: Random House, 1995.
15. Atkinson, R. C., and Griffin, R. M. "Human Memory: A Proposed System and Its Control Processes." In Spence, K. W., and Spence, J. T. (eds.). *Advances in the Psychology of Learning and Motivation.* New York: Academic Press, 1968. (Vol. 2, pp. 190–195).
16. Berk, Laura E. Ibid., p. 260.
17. Englebart, Douglas. *Augmenting Human Intellect: A Conceptual Framework.* Stanford Research Institute, 1962.

Chapter 6

*"Sally Forth" reprinted with permission: The Toronto Star Syndicate.
1. "Expect a Mess, and a Smile," *St. Louis Post Dispatch,* 5 August 1996.
2. Miller, Eric. "In the Shadow of the Baby Boom." Miller's thoughtful report discusses the Baby Bust and is full of good demographic data.
3. Dewey, John. *Experience and Education.* The Kappa Delta Pi Lectures. London: Collier Books, p. 48.
4. Scholnick, E. K. "Knowing and Constructing Plans," *SRCD Newsletter,* Fall 1995, pp. l–2, 17.
5. Berk, Laura E. Ibid., pp. 264–269.
6. Tarullo, Louisa B. "Windows on Social Worlds: Differences in Children's Play Narratives." *Children at Play.* Oxford University Press, 1994, p. 170.
7. Fried, SuEllen. "Kindness Is Contagious, Catch It!" *Spreading Kindness Interactive Magazine,* Fall 1995, www.kindness.org/issuel/main.html
8. Elkind, David. *Ties That Stress,* Boston: Harvard University Press, 1994, Chapter 6.

Chapter 7

*"Fisher" reprinted with permission: Philip Street, 1997.
l. U.S. Census Bureau, Education and Social Stratification Branch.
2. "Investing in America's Future, A Statement by U.S. Secretary of Education, Richard W. Riley," from "A Back to School Special Report: The Baby Boom Echo," August 1996, National Center for Education Statistics.
3. U.S. Bureau of Labor Statistics.
4. Postman, Neil. *The End of Education: Redefining the Value of School.* New York: Vintage Books, 1995.
5. As quoted in *Investor's Business Daily,* 30 April 1997.
6. Roszak, Theodore. "Internet as Teacher Makes Students Stupid," *New Internationalist,* 1997.
7. Malveaux, Julianne. "Make Basics a Higher Priority than Intemet," *USA Today.*
8. Becker, H. J. "How Computers Are Used in United States Schools," Basic data from the 1989 I.E.A. Computers in Education Survey, *Journal of Education Research,* pp. 407–420.

9. Senge, Peter. *The Fifth Discipline.* New York: Doubleday, 1990.

10. Market Data Retrieval cited in *USA Today,* 11 March 1997.

11. A study of 1,001 teachers conducted by Jostens Learning Corp. and the American Association of School Administrators found that while 94 percent of teachers and school superintendents believe computers have improved teaching and learning, they are most frequently used for "teaching computer skills, classroom instruction, and record keeping."

12. *Chronicle of Higher Education,* 17 January 1997, p. A24.

13. Owston's course can be found at www.edu.yorku.ca/~rowston/found.html

14. The term "culture of learning" is used by many but related well to the new media by educator Seymour Papert in his lucid book, *the connected family: bridging the digital generation gap.* Marietta, GA: Longstreet Press, 1996.

15. Schutte, J. G. "Virtual Teaching in Higher Education," http://www.csun.edu/sociology/virtexp.htm

16. Papert, Seymour. Ibid., p. 68.

17. Papert, Seymour. Ibid., p. 47.

18. Papert, Seymour. Ibid.

19. *Christian Science Monitor,* 21 April 1997.

20. Postman, Neil. *Amusing Ourselves to Death: Public Discourse in the Age of Show Business.* New York: Penguin Books, p. 144.

21. Davis, Stan, and Botkin, Jim. *The Monster Under the Bed: How Business Is Mastering the Opportunity of Knowledge for Profit,* New York: Simon & Schuster, 1994, p. 23.

22. Davis, Stan, and Botkin, Jim. Ibid., p. 88.

23. Drucker, Peter. *Forbes,* 10 March 1997, pp. 126–7.

24. Speer, Tibbett. "A Nation of Students," *American Demographics,* August 1996.

Chapter 8

*Reprinted with permission: The New Yorker Magazine, Inc.

1. Quinn, Joanne M., and Rubin, Kenneth H. "The Play of Handicapped Children," *Child's Play: Developmental and Applied.* Yawkey, Thomas D., and Pellegrini, Anthony (eds.). Hillsdale, NJ: Lawrence Erlbaum Associates, Publishers, 1984, p. 63.

2. Athey, Irene. "Contributions of Play to Development," *Child's Play: Developmental and Applied.* Yawkey, Thomas D., and Pellegrini, Anthony (eds.). Hillsdale, NJ: Lawrence Erlbaum Associates, Publishers, 1984, p. 22.

3. Greenfield, Patricia. *Mind and Media: The Effects of Television, Video Games and Computers.* Cambridge: Harvard University Press, 1994, p. 102.

4. Kinder, Marsha. *Playing with Power in Movies, Television and Video Games.* University of California Press, 1991, p. 112.

5. Tarullo, Louisa B. "Windows on Social Worlds: Gender Differences in Children's Play Narratives." *Children at Play.* Oxford University Press, 1994, p. 172.

6. Tarullo, Louisa B. Ibid., p. 184.

7. Tarullo, Louisa B. Ibid., p. 172.

8. Tarullo, Louisa B. Ibid., p. 172.

9. *FZ Times* (the electronic newspaper on FreeZone), Issue #7.

10. Athey, Irene. Ibid., p. 24.

11. Turkle, Sherry. *Life on the Screen.* New York: Simon & Schuster, 1995.

12. Turkle, Sherry. Ibid., p. 227.

13. Howard Rheingold. *The Virtual Community.* New York: Addison-Wesley Publishing Company, 1993, p. 153.

14. Bruckman, Amy, and Resnick, Mitchel. *The MediaMoo Project: Constructionism and Professional Community.* http://www.souri.edu/~wlerio/Bruckman-MediaMoo.html

Chapter 9

*Reprinted with permission: The New Yorker Magazine, Inc.

1. According to *American Demographics,* in 1994 teens spent $63 billion of their own money and $36 billion of family money (e.g., money given to them to buy such things as groceries, etc.). This $99 billion does not include their influence on their parents' spending. Zollo, Peter. "Talking to Teens," *American Demographics,* November 1995.

2. According to Jupiter Communications, preteens spend $17 billion given to them by their parents and influence the spending of another $150 billion. Jupiter Communications. *The 1997 Online Kids Report.*

3. Thompson, Emily. *The Kid Revolution.* http://www2.bitstream.net/~astrokid/kidrev.html

4. Yahoo/Reuters. "Disney Online Launches Subscriber Service," 31 March 1997.

5. *The Economist,* 8 March 1997.

6. Calderbank, Allison. "Online Sales Open Up Huge VAR Opportunities," *Computer Reseller News,* 6 January 1997.

7. Cooper, Lane F. "Webbing for Dollars," *Communications Week,* 13 January 1997, Issue 645.

8. Calderbank, Allison, op. cit.

9. Meringer, Maney, Chatham and Wallace. "Sizing the Internet Economy," *Money,* September/October 1996.

10. Dennis, Everette E., and Pease, Edward C. (eds.). "Symposium I," *Children and the Media.* New Brunswick, USA: Transaction Publishers, p. 5.

11. Schiesel, Seth. *The New York Times,* "Kids 'Liquored' on the Web Playground," *The Denver Post,* 8 March 1997.

12. "Highlights From Around the Web," *CyberAtlas,* April 1997, http://www.cyberatlas.com/

13. Zollo, Peter. *Wise Up to Teens. Insights into Marketing and Advertising to Teenagers.* New York: New Strategist Publications Inc., 1995, p. 51.

14. Edited by Niki Tapscott, compiling her comments from transcripts at two conferences—Spirit (Consumer of the Future panel), 27 September 1993, and the Building Owners and Management Conference, June 1995.

Chapter 10

*Reprinted with permission: David Sipress, 1996.

1. Drucker, Peter. *The New Realities in Government and Politics/in Economics and Business/in Society and World View.* New York: Harper & Row, 1991.

2. Davis, Stan, and Davidson, Bill. *2020 Vision: Transform Your Business Today to Succeed in Tomorrow's Economy.* New York: Simon & Schuster, 1991. According to Davis and Davidson, the "real-time organization" does not yet exist. For a good popularization of the concept refer to the above.

3. Miller, Riel. "Measuring What People Know: Human Capital Accounting for the Knowledge Economy," Paris: OECD Publications, 1996.

4. "Knowledge deployment" is a term first explained by the Alliance for Converging Technologies.

5. Conducted through interactive key pads at the *BusinessWeek* conference on the New Technology in Business, December 1996, San Francisco.

6. Brethour, Patrick. "Smart Brothers Strike It Rich," *The Globe and Mail,* 22 January 1997, p. B15.

7. U.S. Department of Labor, Labor Bureau of Statistics.

8. Neuborne, Ellen. "Temporary Workers Getting Short Shrift," *USA Today,* 11 April 1997.

9. Results of an interactive survey of business leaders at the December *BusinessWeek* conference held in San Francisco, December 1996.

10. Rutledge, John. "You're a Fool If You Buy Into This," *Forbes* ASAP, 7 April 1997, p. 44.

Chapter 11

*Reprinted with permission: Don Wright, *The Palm Beach Post.*

1. Higher Education Research Institute, UCLA. "The American Freshman: National Norms for Fall 1997."
2. U.S. Census Bureau
3. Statistics Canada investigation into education and class. Center for Educational Statistics, 16 April 1997.
4. Thurow, Lester C. "Changes in Capitalism Render One-earner Families Extinct," *USA Today,* 28 January 1997, p. 7A.
5. "Teenage Marketing & Lifestyle Update Spring 1997/Wave 29," Teenage Research Unlimited, Inc. TRU asked teens to evaluate themselves on two key dimensions: What they think about themselves (self-perception) and what values they believe are fundamentally important (fundamental values). "I like to spend time with my family" tied for first place on fundamental values.
6. Davis Kasl, Charlotte. *Finding Joy: 101 Ways to Free Your Spirit.* New York: HarperCollins, 1994, p. 136.
7. Kacapry, Elia. "Are You Middle Class?" *American Demographics,* October 1996.
8. Katz, Jon. *Virtuous Reality,* New York: Random House, 1996, p. 72.
9. Beck, Joan. "Taking Children Out of Harm's Way," *The Chicago Tribune,* 18 April 1996, p. 27.
10. National Center for Missing and Exploited Children. http://www.missingkids.org
11. Ibid.
12. *Miami Herald,* 7 March 1997.
13. *New York Times,* 16 February 1997.
14. Cavoukian, Ann, and Tapscott, Don. *Who Knows: Safeguarding Your Privacy in a Networked World.* New York: McGraw-Hill, 1996.
15. Mifflin, Lawrie. "New Guidelines on Net Ads for Children," *New York Times,* 21 April 1997, p. 5.
16. Elkind, David. *Ties That Stress.* Cambridge, MA: Harvard University Press, 1994, Chapter 4, p. 83.
17. Cited in *The Utne Reader,* January 1997.
18. Katz, Jon. *Virtuous Reality,* New York: Random House, 1996, pp. 188–89. The discussion of a social contract is excellent. Every parent should read this.
19. Senge, Peter. *The Fifth Discipline,* New York: Doubleday, 1990.

Chapter 12

*Printed with permission: Owen Baggott, 1997.

1. Gibson, Steve. "Universal Disservice," *Reason Magazine,* April 1995.
2. "Social Darwinism: Reason or Rationalization?" http://www.smplanet.com/imperialism/activity.html
3. Bennahum, David S. "Mr. Gingrich's Cyber-Revolution," *The New York Times,* 17 January 1995.
4. Borsook, Paulina. "Cyberselfish," *Mother Jones,* July/August 1996.
5. "The Two Americas: Tools for Succeeding in a Polarized Marketplace," Roper Starch, 1996.
6. Jupiter Communications, *World On-line Markets Report,* 1996.
7. Ibid.
8. National Center for Education Statistics. *Advanced Telecommunications in US Public Elementary Schools,* 1995. www.ed.gov./NCES/
9. National Center for Education Statistics. *Digest of Education Statistics,* 1995, table 50.
10. National Center for Education Statistics. *The Condition of Education,* 1995, Indicator 47.
11. National Center for Education Statistics. *The Digest for Education Statistics,* 1996.
12. HomeNet: "A Study of Electronic Communication by Families and the Transformation of Home Computing." Human Computer Interaction Institute, Carnegie Mellon University, Pittsburgh, 1995. http://homenet.andrew.cmu.edu.
13. Survey conducted by Coleman Advocates for Children and Youth, San Francisco, 1996.

Chapter 13

*Reprinted with permission: DePixon Studios, Inc.

1. Salmon, Jacqueline L. "Firm Support for Stricter Upbringing: Disciplinarians' Advice Finds Parental Favor," *The Washington Post,* 24 November 1996, p. B1.

2. Kwiatkowski, Jane. "Armed Teens Hold Death in Their Sights," *Buffalo News,* 4 June 1996.

3. Ibid.

4. Haysom, Ian. "Today's Teens Want It All," *Toronto Star,* 22 April 1997, p. D1.

5. Schwartz, Peter, and Leyden, Peter. "The Long Boom," *Wired,* July 1997. A provocative and thoughtful article. The authors' idea is that this view is a plausible scenario, not a prediction.

6. Clavir has conducted an annual "young navigators" panel at the annual CIO Summit. In 1996 he established a not-for-profit foundation called the "Young Navigators." It presents awards annually to those young entrepreneurs who have shown leadership in the digital media.

7. The Brain Waves Group study is explained in *American Demographics,* September 1996. Downloaded off the World Wide Web.

8. "Teenage Marketing & Lifestyle Update Spring 1996/Wave 28," Teenage Research Unlimited, Inc.

9. "The Family-Surviving Tough Times in the '90s, American Board of Family Practice," from *In The Shadow of the Baby Boom,* 1994, EPM Communications, Inc.

10. Ibid.

11. "Teenage Marketing & Lifestyle Update Spring 1996/Wave 28," Teenage Research Unlimited, Inc.

12. "The American Freshman: National Norms for Fall 1996," Higher Education Research Institute, UCLA.

13. "The Roper Starch Youth Report," Roper Starch Worldwide Inc., New York, 1996.

14. Katz, Jon. "Birth of a Digital Nation," *Wired,* April 1997.

15. Roszak, Theodore.

16. Onstad, Katrina. "What Are We Afraid Of? The Myth of Youth Crime," *Saturday Magazine,* March 1997, p. 58.

17. Katrina Onstad. Ibid., p. 58.

18. Braman, Sandra. "The Autopoetic State: Communication and Democratic Potential in the Net," *Journal of the American Society for Information Science,* July 1994.

19. Dervin, Brenda. "Information—Democracy: An Examination of Underlying Assumptions," *Journal of the American Society for Information Science,* July 1994.

20. Anthes, Gary H. "Digital Democracy," *Computerworld,* 12 April 1993.

21. Yarn, Richard J. "Electronic Democracy: Jeffersonian Boom or Teraflop?" *Spectrum: The Journal of State Government,* Spring 1993.

22. Miller, Steven E. "From System Design to Democracy," *Communications of the ACM,* June 1993.

23. Bloomfield, Shirley. "Bringing Democracy Home," *Rural Telecommunications,* July/August 1993.

24. Mantovani, Giuseppe. "Is Computer-Mediated Communication Intrinsically Apt to Enhance Democracy in Organizations?" *Human Relations,* January 1994.

25. Millichap, Nancy. "The People's Right to Know: Media, Democracy, and the Information Highway," *Online,* July 1994.

26. Martinez, Michael E. "Access to Information Technologies Among School-Age Children: Implications for a Democratic Society," *Journal of the American Society for Information Science,* July 1994.

27. Sun, Su-Lien, and Barnett, George A. "The International Telephone Network and Democratization," *Journal of the American Society for Information Science,* July 1994.

28. Frey, Bruno S. "Direct Democracy: Politico-Economic Lesson from the Swiss Experience," *AEA Papers and Proceedings,* May 1994, Vol. 82, No. 2, p. 439.

References

The main reference source for this book was the Web. For further information see **www.growingupdigital.com**. The following is a listing of the books referenced.

Bazalgette, Carol, and Buckingham, David. *In Front of the Children: Screen Entertainment and Young Audiences.* London, England: The British Film Institute, 1995.

Berk, Laura E. *Child Development.* Boston, Massachusetts: Allyn and Bacon, 1997.

Bly, Robert. *The Sibling Society.* New York: Addison-Wesley, 1996.

Cavoukian, Ann, and Tapscott, Don. *Who Knows: Safeguarding Your Privacy in a Networked World.* New York: McGraw-Hill, 1996.

Chadwick, Bruce A., and Heaton, Tim B. (eds.). *Statistical Handbook on Adolescents in America.* Phoenix, Arizona: Oryx Press, 1996.

Chomsky, Noam. *Keeping the Rabble in Line.* Munroe, Maine: Common Courage Press, 1994.

Coles, Robert. *The Moral Intelligence of Children.* New York: Random House, 1997.

Davis, Stan, and Botkin, Jim. *The Monster Under the Bed: How Business Is Mastering the Opportunity of Knowledge for Profit.* New York: Simon & Schuster, 1994.

Davis, Stan, and Davidson, Bill. *2020 Vision: Transform Your Business Today to Succeed in Tomorrow's Economy.* New York: Simon & Schuster, 1991.

Davis Kasl, Charlotte. *Finding Joy: 101 Ways to Free Your Spirit.* New York: Harper Collins, 1994.

De Kerckove, Derrick. *The Skin of Culture.* Toronto, Ontario: Somerville House Publishing, 1995.

Dennis, Everette E., and Pease, Edward C. (eds). *Children and the Media.* New Brunswick, U.S.A.: Transaction Publishers, 1996.

Dertouzos, Michael L. *What Will Be: How the New World of Information Will Change Our Lives.* New York: HarperEdge, 1997.

Drucker, Peter. *The New Realities in Government and Politics/ in Economics and Business/ in Society and World View.* New York: Harper and Row, 1989.

Dunn, William. *The Baby Bust: A Generation Comes of Age.* Ithaca, New York: American Demographics Books, 1993.

Elkind, David. *The Hurried Child: Growing Up Too Fast Too Soon.* Reading, Massachusetts: Addison-Wesley Publishing, 1988.

Elkind, David. *Ties That Stress.* Cambridge, Massachusetts: Harvard University Press, 1994.

Englebart, Douglas. *Augmenting Human Intellect: A Conceptual Framework.* Stanford Research Institute, 1962.

Erickson, E. H. *Childhood and Society.* New York: W. W. Norton & Company, 1950.

Foot, David. *Boom, Bust and Echo: How to Profit from the Coming Demographic Shift.* Toronto, Ontario: Macfarlane, Walter and Ross, 1996.

Gardner, H. *Frames of Mind: The Theory of Multiple Intelligences.* New York: Basic Books, 1983.

Gilder, George. *Life After Television (Revised Edition).* New York: W. W. Norton & Company, 1994.

Goffman, Erving. *The Presentation of Self in Everyday Life.* Garden City, New York: Doubleday, 1959.

Greenfield, Patricia. *Mind and Media: The Effects of Television, Video Games and Computers.* Cambridge, Massachusetts: Harvard University Press, 1994.

Hamel, Gary, and Pralahad, C. K. *Competing for the Future: Breakthrough Strategies for Seizing Control of Your Industry and Creating Markets of Tomorrow.* Boston: Harvard Business School Press, 1994.

Harel, Idit. *Children Designers: Interdisciplinary Constructions for Learning and Knowing Mathematics in a Computer-Rich School.* The Media Laboratory: Massachusetts Institute of Technology. Norwood, New Jersey: Ablex Publishing Corporation, 1991.

Hayward, Philip, and Wollen, Tana (eds). *Future Visions: New Technologies of the Screen.* London, England: BFI Publishing, 1993.

Healy, Jane. *Endangered Minds: Why Our Children Don't Think.* Toronto, Ontario: Simon & Schuster, 1990.

Innis, Harold. *The Bias of Communication.* Toronto, Ontario: University of Toronto Press, 1951.

Jones, Glen R. *Cyberschools: An Education Renaissance.* Englewood, Colorado: Jones Digital Century, 1996.

Jupiter Communications. *The 1997 Online Kids Report.*

Katz, Jon. *Virtuous Reality.* New York: Random House, 1996.

Kinder, Marsha. *Playing with Power in Movies, Television and Video Games.* University of California Press, 1991.

Kraut, Scherlis, Mukhopadhyay, Manning, Kiesler, et al. *HomeNet: A Study of Electronic Communication by Families and the Transformation of Home Computing.* Human Computer Interaction Institute, Carnegie Mellon University, 1996.

Loftus, Geoffrey, and Loftus, Elizabeth. *Mind at Play.* New York: Basic Books, 1983.

Martin, Chuck. *The Digital Estate: Strategies for Competing, Surviving, and Thriving in an Internetworked World.* New York: McGraw-Hill, 1996.

McLuhan, Marshall. *Understanding Media: The Extensions of Man.* Toronto, Ontario: The New American Library of Canada, 1966.

Mead, G. H. *Mind, Self and Society.* Chicago, Illinois: University of Chicago Press, 1934.

Miller, Eric. *In the Shadow of the Baby Boom.* New York: EPM Communications Inc., 1994.

Miller, Riel. *Measuring What People Know: Human Capital Accounting for the Knowledge Economy.* Paris, France: OECD Publications, 1996.

Moore, James F. *The Death of Competition: Leadership and Strategy in the Age of Business Ecosystems.* New York: Harper Business, 1996.

National Center for Education Statistics. *A Back to School Special Report: The Baby Boom Echo.* August 1996.

Negroponte, Nicholas. *being digital.* New York: Random House, 1995.

Papert, Seymour. *The Children's Machine.* New York: BasicBooks, 1993.

Papert, Seymour. *the connected family: bridging the generation gap.* Atlanta, Georgia: Longstreet Press, 1996.

Perelman, Lewis J. *School's Out.* New York: Avon Books, 1992.

Piaget, Jean. *The Construction of Reality in the Child.* New York: Free Press, 1954.

Piaget, Jean. *The Language and Thought of the Child.* New York: Harcourt, Brace & World, 1959.

Piaget, Jean. *The Psychology of Intelligence.* Totowa, New Jersey: Littlefield Adams, 1972.

Postman, Neil. *Amusing Ourselves to Death: Public Discourse in the Age of Show Business.* New York: Penguin Books, 1985.

Postman, Neil. *Conscientious Objections: Stirring Up Trouble About Language, Technology and Education.* New York: Vintage Books, 1988.

Postman, Neil. *Technopoly: The Surrender of Culture to Technology.* New York: Vintage Books, 1993.

Postman, Neil. *The End of Education: Redefining the Value of School.* New York: Vintage Books, 1995.

Provenzo, Eugene F., Jr. *Video Kids: Making Sense of Nintendo.* Cambridge, Massachusetts: Harvard University Press, 1991.

Reingold, Howard. *Virtual Communities: Homesteading on the Electronic Frontier.* New York: Harper Perennial, 1993.

Roper Starch Worldwide Inc. *Roper Youth Report,* 1996.

Roper Starch Worldwide Inc. *Roper Youth Report,* 1997.

Rushkoff, Douglas. *Playing the Future: How Kids' Culture Can Teach Us to Thrive in an Age of Chaos.* New York: HarperCollins Publishers, 1996.

Schwier, Richard A., and Misanchuk, Earl R. *Interactive Media Instruction.* Englewood Cliffs, New Jersey: Educational Technology Publications, 1993.

Senge, Peter. *The Fifth Discipline.* New York: Doubleday, 1990.

Shenk, David. *Data Smog: Surviving the Information Glut.* New York: Harper Edge, 1997.

Skovmand, Michael, and Schroder, Kim Christian. *Media Cultures: Reappraising the Transnational Media.* London, England: Routledge, 1992.

Stephensen, Neal. *Snow Crash.* New York: Bantam Books, 1992.

Sternberg, R. J., and Detterman, D. K. (eds.). *What Is Intelligence? Contemporary Viewpoints on Its Nature and Definition.* Norwood, New Jersey: Abler, 1986.

Stoler, Peter. *The Computer Generation.* New York: Facts on File, 1984.

Tapscott, Don. *Office Automation: A User-Driven Method.* New York: Plenum Publishing, 1981.

Tapscott, Don. *The Digital Economy: Promise and Peril in the Age of Networked Intelligence.* New York: McGraw-Hill, 1996.

Tapscott, Don, and Caston, Art. *Paradigm Shift: The New Promise of Information Technology.* New York: McGraw-Hill, 1993.

Tapscott, Henderson, and Greenberg. *Planning for Integrated Office Systems.* Toronto, Ontario: Holt, Rinehart & Winston of Canada, 1985.

Toffler, Alvin, and Toffler, Heidi. *Creating a New Civilization.* Atlanta, Georgia: Turner Publishing, Inc., 1994.

Turkle, Sherry. *Life on the Screen.* New York: Simon & Schuster, Inc, 1995.

Turkle, Sherry. *The Second Self.* New York: Simon & Schuster, Inc, 1984.

Wave 29 Teenage Research Unlimited, Inc. *Teenage Marketing & Lifestyle Update* Spring 1997.

Wahlroos, Sven. *Family Communication: The Essential Rules for Improving Communication and Making Your Relationships More Loving, Supportive, and Enriching.* Chicago, Illinois: Contemporary Books, 1995.

Zollo, Peter. *Wise Up to Teens: Insights Into Marketing and Advertising to Teenagers.* New York: New Strategist Publications, Inc., 1995.

Index

Ability On-Line, 90, 91
Acceptance of diversity, as characteristic of N-Generation personality, 86
Accommodation, as more difficult learning process than assimilation, 40–41, 98
Adams, Scott, originator of *The Dilbert Principle,* 210, 228
Advertising, effect of cyber commerce on, 196–199
Advertising Age, 286
"Age of Television" (Postman), 62–63
"Age of Typography" (Postman), 62
Albright, Madeleine, 40
Alliance for Converging Technologies, 5, 261
  estimate of Net users, 23
Alliance for Youth, 265
American Cancer Society, 75
American Demographics, 43
American Psychological Association, 97
America Online (AOL), 30, 57
Amusing Ourselves to Death (Postman), 62
ASCII:
  limitations of, and N-Generation cyberspace communication, 64
  and N-Generational additions of nonverbal elements to written communication, 135
Assertiveness, and self-reliance, as characteristic of N-Generation personality, 87–88
Assimilation, versus accommodation, as key to children's faster mastery of technology, 40–42, 98
Asynchronous discussions, in Internet chat rooms, 56
Athey, Irene, on play as essential element of healthy human development, 161
Authentication and trust, as themes of N-Generation culture, 75–77
Authority, children as, concerning knowledge/use of digital media, 36–38
Avatars, design of, 71

Baby boom echo (1977 to 1997), 20–21
  coincident with digital revolution/computer sales, 22–23
  labeled as Net Generation (N-Generation or N-Geners), 22
Baby boom generation (1946 to 1964):
  and generational displacement in workforce, 10
  impact of television on, 2
  magnitude of, eclipsed by baby boom echo (N-Generation), 15
  relationship to N-Generation, introduction of possible scenarios in, 12–13
  shaping/perpetuating of worldview/ideology of, 9
  as TV generation, 17–19
  view of computer revolution through "couch potato" mentality, 31
Baby bust (1965 to 1976):
  as demographic label, 19–20
  as so-called Generation X, 19–20
Babysitter's Club, The, online serial storybook, 71
Back to School Special Report: The Baby Boom Echo, A (U.S. Dept. of Education), 130
Baggott, Kate, on self-reliance of N-Generation, 87
Baltimore Sun, 45
Barbie Interactive, 167
Batch, versus real time, movement of informaton, 73–74
Baywatch, 17, 95
Behaviorism, influence of, on education, 129
Bell Curve, The (Herrnstein and Murray), 97
Berk, Laura E.:
  on intellectually numbing effect of television viewing, 99
  on N-Generation information-processing model, 102
Berlin, Eric, and Andrew Kantor, on implications of filtering (blocking) software, 243

Berners-Lee, Tim, inventor of World Wide Web, on information about information as "new enlightenment," 33

Biondi, Frank, on passive nature of television, 26–27

Blocking software, 241–244

Bloomberg, Michael, 24, 25, 136, 257

Bly, Robert:
on impaired N-Generation thinking, 85
on youth/technology/decline of adult authority as roots of societal woes, 46–47, 49

Bonanza, 19

Boomer parents, new challenges facing, 235–254

Boomers (*see* Baby boom generation)

Bot, 32, 86

"Bozo-filtered," 74

Brand name recognition, effect of cyber commerce on, 193–196

Broadcast teaching model, and implications of student growth, 131

Broadcast technology, hierarchical (vs. interactive) nature of, 79

Broadcast view of learning:
inadequacy of, 129–131
versus interactive learning, 139–149

Brown, John Seely:
on changing role of child at home, 36
on changing roles of authority/learning, 37
on learning as experiential, 143

Bulletin boards, 63, 134
N-Generation use of, 71

Bulletin board service (BBS), 90–91

BusinessWeek, 27, 50

Carnegie Mellon University, 264
Human Computer Interaction Institute at, 42–43
study conducted by, on teenagers as catalyst for home Internet use, 36

CD-ROMs, 1, 45

Center for Children and Technology, 222–223

Center for Media Education, The, 200–201, 245

Cerf, Vinton, Internet pioneer, on gauging authenticity on Web, 77

Changing roles, example of, Finnish students as teacher trainers on use of computers, 37

Channel Zero, 82–83

Charged-coupled device, 25

Chat groups, 5

Chat rooms, 6, 30
N-Generation use of, 71, 94, 134
as real-time system, 74
synchronous and asynchronous discussions in, 56

Child development:
in interactive world, 7–8
linked with productive play time on digital media, 8
self-esteem in:
academic, 91
physical, 91
social, 91

Children, Child Abuse, and Cyberporn: A Primer for Clear Thinkers (Godwin), 244

Children's Advertising Review Unit, 200

Cityspace, as N-Generation community, 39, 57

Clarke, Jim, 23

Clarke, Jorian, president of KidsCom, 57

Clinton, Bill, pledge of, for Internet access for all American public school children, 260–261

Closed communities, 62

CNN, 17

Coca-Cola, 194

Cold War generation (*see* Baby boom generation)

Collaboration:
as hallmark of corporate "internetworked enterprise structures," 16
as N-Generation mindset, 10

Collateral learning, and attention span, 109

Kodak, creation of cooperative partnerships by, 276

LA Law, 17
Landers, Ann, 173
Leaders, future N-Generation:
  evolving values of, 286–289
  as force for pan-institutional transformation, 290–291
  ideology of, 280–286
  of new "digital nation," 291–293
  and possible baby boom/baby boom echo scenarios, 293 (figure)
    cold war, 294
    generational explosion, 294
    networked society, 295
    peaceful coexistence, 294
  and youth radicalization, 299–301
LEAP Computer Learning Center, 149–150
Learning, for children, as discovery—not accommodation, 40–41
LeFevre, Arlette ("Dr. Froggy"), 90
Lyric Generation, The (Ricard), 298

MacWorld magazine, 4
Malveaux, Julianne, on computer literacy, 136
MaMaMedia, 109, 147
  new learning products developed at, 150–151
Martin, Chuck, on children's unstudied, intuitive use of computers, 40
McLuhan, Marshall, 134, 170
  on classification of media, 42
  "medium is the message" aphorism of, 63
Mead, G. H., on characteristics of "the self," 91
Media coverage, negative, on Internet/World Wide Web, 44
Media panic, concerning new media at heart of youth culture, 48–49
Mental strategies, computer simulations of, and N-Generation thinking, 102–104

Mickey Mouse Club, 19
Microsoft:
  KidReach program of, 272
  and Slate, 74
  Technology Learning Center (Toronto) established by, 272–274
Miller, Eric, on kids' attention span, 109
Multiple selves, as N-Generation character trait, 95–97
Multitasking, effects of, on attention span, 108–110
Multiuser domain (MUD), 95, 141
Multiuser dungeons (or dimensions), 169, 174–176
Murray, Charles, and Richard J. Herrnstein, on nature of intelligence, 97

National Advertising Review Council, 201
National Center for Education Statistics, 260
National Center for Missing and Exploited Children, 244–245
National Coalition on Television Violence, 164
Net (see Internet)
Net addiction:
  Caleb Murphy's Net Abstinence Diary as example of, 117–123
  differing views on, 115–117, 124
Net-aholic (see Net addiction)
"Net appliance," automobile as, 25
Net-based games, emergence of, 107
NetDay, 273
Net Generation (N-Generation; N-Gen):
  as antithesis of television generation, 26
  as baby boom echo, 1, 20–22
  brief glossary of abbreviations, 66
  character traits of:
    acceptance of diversity, 86
    contrarian, 88–90
    curiosity, 86–87
    intelligence, 97–101
    multiple selves, 95–97
    self-esteem, 90–95

333

About the Author

Don Tapscott is the best-selling author of six books, including *The Digital Economy,* and the coauthor of *Paradigm Shift.* He is chairman of the Alliance for Converging Technologies, a research think tank funded by many of the world's leading technology, manufacturing, retail, financial, and government organizations. He is also the president of New Paradigm Learning Corporation.